# Reform of Retirement Income Policy

## International and Canadian Perspectives

# Reform of Retirement Income Policy

## International and Canadian Perspectives

*Edited by*
Keith G. Banting & Robin Boadway

School of Policy Studies
Queen's University, Kingston, Ontario

**Canadian Cataloguing in Publication Data**

Main entry under title:

Reform of retirement income policy : international and Canadian perspectives

Proceedings of a conference entitled Reform of the retirement income system,
held at Queen's University, Kingston, Ont., Feb. 1-2, 1996.
Includes bibliographical references.
ISBN 0-88911-739-X

1. Old age pensions – Congresses. 2. Old age pensions – Canada –
Congresses. 3. Retirement income – Congresses. 4. Retirement income –
Canada – Congresses. I. Banting, Keith G., 1947-   . II. Boadway, Robin W.,
1943-   . III. Queen's University (Kingston, Ont.). School of Policy Studies.

HD7105.3.R43 1996      331.25'22    C96-932027-2

# Contents

# List of Tables and Figures

## TABLES

## FIGURES

# Acknowledgements

This book grew from a conviction that independent research has a contribution to make to policy reform. During the great Canadian pensions debate of the early 1980s, a substantial body of research was conducted by task forces, royal commissions, advisory councils, and independent institutes. The resulting studies and reports filled more than one library shelf, and enriched public discussions about the issues and alternatives confronting the country. By contrast, our contemporary debate about reform of the retirement income system has drifted forward with a much more limited contribution from the research community. One looks in vain for the substantial studies and reports that normally constitute the intellectual substructure of public debate. The contrast is striking, especially since the policy changes emerging from this cycle of pension politics are likely to be far more substantial than those that flowed from the debates of the early 1980s. This book represents one attempt to fill the research gap.

The broad focus of the book reflects the fact that the issues confronting Canadians find parallels in other countries, and that an international perspective has much to offer. Globalization is more than an economic phenomenon. Ideas, evidence and experience flow across political boundaries with ever greater ease, creating an international discourse on policy issues that draws on and also informs the debates of individual nations. By its inclusion of a variety of comparative perspectives, this book seeks to contribute to that wider distribution of policy intelligence.

From the outset, this project has been a collaborative effort, and we wish to record our appreciation of the generous support of many individuals and institutions. The papers were first presented at a conference held at the School of Policy Studies of Queen's University. In designing the conference, we were guided by the counsel of a number of people, including Gordon Betcherman, Tom Courchene, Lisa Powell, Mark Rosenberg, and Art Stewart. We also wish to acknowledge with gratitude the financial support of two departments of the federal government, Human Resources Development and the Department of Finance. Their contribution was essential to this entire project. In addition, the administrative complexities of the conference were managed with consummate ease by Sharon Alton and Art Stewart.

Finally, thanks are due to the School of Policy Studies Publications Unit: Mark Howes, Valerie Jarus, and Marilyn Banting. Once again, we have depended heavily on their professionalism and their patience.

*Keith G. Banting*
*Robin Boadway*
*Kingston Ontario*

# CHAPTER ONE

# Reforming Retirement Income Policy: The Issues

*Keith G. Banting and Robin Boadway*

## INTRODUCTION

During the postwar decades, Canadians constructed a complex retirement income system, composed of a variety of public and private programs, each with distinctive purposes and parameters. Collectively, these programs represent massive financial flows, and their reverberations are felt throughout many dimensions of Canadian life. Socially, the system carries the heavy burden of protecting the incomes of older people, and contributing to a wider sense of fairness and security in society as a whole. Economically, the impact is also enormous. The design of retirement income programs has important implications for the overall level of savings, investment and productivity growth; and occupational pensions represent large pools of capital which control substantial portions of private industry in Canada and most other Western nations, prompting commentators to reflect on the consequences of "pension fund capitalism" (Drucker 1993). Politically, the beneficiaries of pensions represent one of the most powerful political constituencies, and politicians approach questions of reform with considerable delicacy.

The retirement income system that developed in the years after the Second World War has served Canadians well, significantly reducing the levels of poverty among elderly Canadians. However, the existing programs are under tremendous pressure, and policymakers are now fully engaged in a process of reform. The federal government has already announced its intentions in some areas, and federal and provincial governments are actively debating changes in other elements of the system. This process of restructuring retirement income programs is one that Canada shares with almost every other Western nation.

This book examines the reform of retirement income policy. Given the pervasiveness of the issues, the book draws heavily on international comparisons as well as Canadian experience. In Part One, Estelle James introduces the reform agenda that is engaging governments around the world, and outlines the policy approach favoured by the World Bank in its recent report, *Averting the Old Age Crisis* (World Bank 1994). Andrew Dilnot then provides a conceptual discussion of the roles of the public and private sectors in the provision of retirement income. Part Two focuses on Canada. Michael Wolfson and Brian Murphy analyze the implications of demographic and other changes for the future of the public pension system; Newman Lam and his colleagues explore the issues confronting contributory pension programs; Ken Battle examines the reform of transfer programs for the elderly; and Jack Mintz and Tom Wilson analyze the tax treatment of private pensions and retirement savings. Part Three expands the discussion again to the comparative dimension to investigate the politics of reform. Paul Pierson develops a general interpretation of the features that make pension reform a distinctive political process in democracies; and John Myles and Jill Quadagno undertake a comparative analysis of pension reform across OECD countries, highlighting the distinctive responses of different countries to the common policy agenda confronting policymakers almost everywhere. Finally, Part Four provides two broader perspectives, as Tom Courchene and Monica Townson chart the way ahead.

This introduction provides an overview of retirement income policy. The purpose is to introduce the broad issues, and no attempt is made to summarize the rich content of all of the papers that follow. The first section describes the major components of the Canadian retirement income system. The second section examines the rationale for a public role in retirement income, and the critical design issues implicit in the public role. It then takes up these design issues in the context of the current debates in Canada; and the final section explores the political factors that constrain the policy debate and give shape to the changes that will reshape the retirement income system of the future.

## THE CANADIAN RETIREMENT INCOME SYSTEM

As in many other OECD countries, the Canadian retirement income system is often described as consisting of three pillars. However, the construction of the pillars in Canada differs in important details from that in many other countries and from the model advanced by the World Bank, which is outlined in Estelle James' contribution to this volume. The Canadian pillars are illustrated graphically in Figure 1.

FIGURE 1: Canadian Retirement Income System

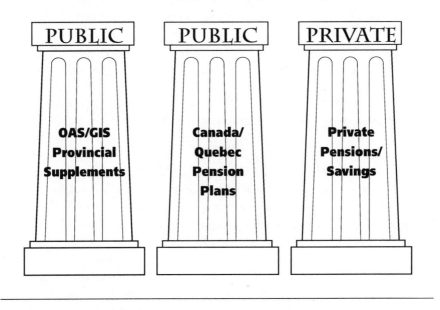

Source: Authors' compilation.

The first pillar consists of public programs that are funded fully from general government revenues: Old Age Security (OAS), the Guaranteed Income Supplement (GIS), and a number of smaller supplements offered by provincial governments. The OAS was introduced in 1951 as a universal, flat-rate benefit given to all individuals at retirement age; and for the next few decades, it was the principal source of retirement income for most elderly Canadians. In effect, the OAS represents an intergenerational transfer from working-age Canadians to retired Canadians. However, as the other pillars of the retirement income system have matured, the first pillar has evolved towards a more limited function, the provision of supplementary income support to low-income retired people only. This evolution has been lengthy. It began in 1965 with the introduction of the GIS, an income-tested benefit, and a number of provincial supplements which appeared shortly thereafter. In the decades that followed, the balance between the OAS and the GIS gradually shifted, as the GIS was repeatedly enriched in real terms, usually just before or after an election, whereas the OAS remained constant in real terms. The next decisive step came in 1989 with the phasing-in of an income test for OAS, as benefits were clawed back from upper-income recipients through the tax system. The final step, announced in the 1996 federal budget, will see the replacement of OAS, GIS and two income-tax credits currently available to the elderly by a single income-tested Seniors' Benefit (Canada 1996b). To give people some time to adjust their retirement planning, this change will take effect in the year 2001. Thus, at the outset of the new millennium, the first pillar will have completed its historical transition from the primary retirement income vehicle for most Canadians to a redistributive instrument designed to support the low-income elderly.

The second pillar is composed of the Canada and Quebec Pension Plans (C/QPP), which were introduced in 1966. The Canada Pension Plan (CPP) operates generally in all provinces except Quebec, which from the outset established the Quebec Pension Plan (QPP). The two plans operate in parallel, with a broadly similar design: benefits differ only marginally, and contribution rates are identical. The basic function of this pillar is income replacement. The C/QPP are contributory programs that are financed through contributions: in 1996 the contribution rate, shared equally between employers and employees, was 5.6 percent of earnings between the basic exemption of $3,500 and the maximum pensionable earnings of $35,400. Benefits are earnings-related. The pension replaces up to 25 percent of average earnings, yielding a maximum monthly pension in 1996 of $727.08. The Canada and Quebec Pension Plans are essentially pay-as-you-go programs. With the exception of a small fund for each plan, equal to about two years of benefits, current benefits are funded by current contributions. In effect, today's pensioners are supported by today's workers.

The third pillar of the system consists of tax-sheltered private savings, in the form of occupational pensions and personal savings. From their origins, public pensions in Canada left considerable room for the private sector. Because maximum C/QPP benefits are limited to 25 percent of average earnings, and the first pillar is increasingly focused on income support for the poor elderly, middle- and upper-income Canadians tend to seek additional income replacement through occupational pensions or private savings. Governments have encouraged the expansion of these forms of savings through tax assistance. Taxpayers may deduct from their taxable income contributions to Registered Pension Plans (RPPs) and Registered Retirement Savings Plans (RRSPs); and income earned by these plans is also free from tax. In 1996, the limit for tax-free contributions to RPPs and/or RRSPs was $13,500. However, these savings do become taxable when they are withdrawn from the plans, normally during retirement years, and the provisions are best thought of as instruments of tax deferral. Between 1991 and 1993, almost 60 percent of tax filers aged 25 to 64 saved for their retirement, either through a RPP, a RRSP or a deferred profit sharing plan (Statistics Canada 1995, p. 123).

In combination, these three pillars of the retirement income system represent a massive financial system. One indicator of its size is given by Table 1, which

TABLE 1: Accumulated Assets in Selected Retirement Income Programs

| Type of Program | 1984 $M | 1984 % | 1986 $M | 1986 % | 1988 $M | 1988 % | 1990 $M | 1990 % | 1992 $M | 1992 % | 1994 $M | 1994 % |
|---|---|---|---|---|---|---|---|---|---|---|---|---|
| Public Plans (C/QPP) | 39,269 | 16.3 | 45,963 | 14.4 | 50,754 | 12.6 | 54,997 | 11.2 | 56,916 | 9.7 | 54,354 | 7.9 |
| RPPs | 163,825 | 67.9 | 215,659 | 67.4 | 270,779 | 67.3 | 324,192 | 66.3 | 384,318 | 65.3 | 453,032 | 65.7 |
| RRSPs | 38,319 | 15.9 | 58,424 | 18.2 | 80,531 | 20.0 | 110,057 | 22.5 | 147,256 | 25.0 | 182,176 | 26.4 |
| Total | 241,413 | 100.0 | 320,046 | 100.0 | 402,064 | 100.0 | 489,246 | 100.0 | 588,490 | 100.0 | 689,562 | 100.0 |

Source: Statistics Canada (1996a, Table A).

reports the accumulated assets of the selected programs. Different Canadians depend on different components of this system. Table 2 highlights this reality by identifying the sources of income for elderly by income quintile. Public pension programs provide an overwhelming 84 percent of the income of the poorest quintile; this proportion drops to 42 percent for the middle quintile and only 18 percent for the richest quintile. Figure 2 speaks to the same pattern, demonstrating the extent to which the two public pillars provide much higher levels of income replacement for individuals and couples with low and average levels of pre-retirement income.

The expansion of the retirement income system over the last decades has provided Canadian social policy with one of its greatest successes. While many social problems seem intractable, the poverty rate among elderly Canadians has declined dramatically. In the postwar years, poverty was much more prevalent among older Canadians than among younger people. As Figure 3 demonstrates, the poverty rate for elderly families has dropped significantly below that for young families. Figure 4 reveals that the pattern is less marked for single individuals, although once again the position of elderly single people has improved more than that of their younger counterparts. The expansion of the retirement income system, in combination with the introduction of universal Medicare, ushered in a major improvement in the well-being of elderly Canadians during the last generation. Retired Canadians are the biggest winners from the introduction of the welfare state.

TABLE 2: Sources of Income of the Current Elderly

| Source | Q1 | Q2 | Q3 | Q4 | Q5 | Total |
|---|---|---|---|---|---|---|
| | *Percentage of Income by Source and Quintile Group, 1992 (Lone Persons and Couples Combined)* | | | | | |
| OAS/GIS | 67 | 41 | 22 | 16 | 9 | 30 |
| C/QPP | 17 | 23 | 20 | 15 | 9 | 18 |
| Pensions | 3 | 14 | 26 | 30 | 24 | 20 |
| Employment Income | 0 | 3 | 7 | 13 | 18 | 8 |
| Investment Income | 5 | 2 | 18 | 21 | 36 | 18 |
| Other Income | 8 | 7 | 7 | 5 | 5 | 6 |

Source: Data from Statistics Canada, *Survey of Consumer Finances.*

FIGURE 2: After-Tax Replacement Rates: Public Programs

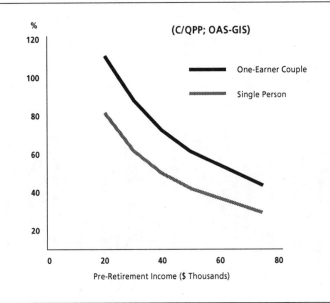

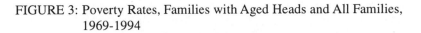

Source: Calculations supplied by Human Resources Development Canada.

FIGURE 3: Poverty Rates, Families with Aged Heads and All Families,
1969-1994

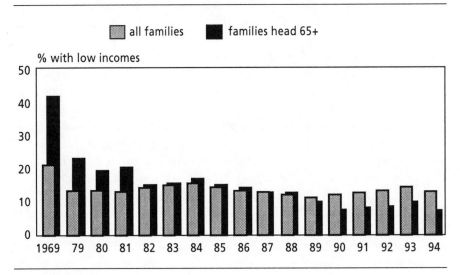

Source: Statistics Canada.

FIGURE 4: Poverty Rates, Aged Unattached Individuals and
All Unattached Individuals, 1969-1994

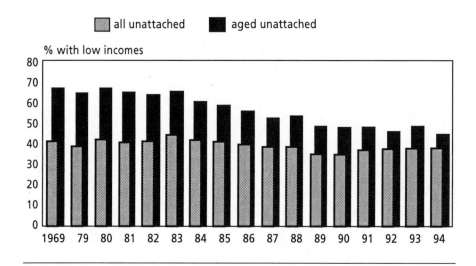

Source: Statistics Canada.

Despite these obvious successes, the retirement income system is under pressure. Demographically, Canadian society is aging. Canadians are living longer and enjoying longer retirements; and after the year 2010, the large postwar "baby-boom" generation will begin to retire. This transition has powerful implications for social policy generally, and especially retirement income policy. Pay-as-you-go financing makes the public pillars of the retirement income system especially sensitive to the changing balance between beneficiaries and contributors. During the 1990s, there are five people of working age for each person aged 65 and over. By the year 2030, there will be only three. As Tom Courchene emphasizes in his paper, such ratios overstate the intergenerational burden, since the elderly themselves will represent an increasing component of the taxpaying public, and will pay for a larger portion of some of their own benefits. Nevertheless, demographic change represents a major challenge to the retirement income system.

Demographic pressures are accentuated by the weak performance of the economy. The public pillars of the retirement income system were constructed in a period of strong economic growth, and increases in real wages and salaries automatically enhanced the flow of contributions into the government treasury. During the last 20 years, however, productivity growth has slowed sharply and wages and salaries have stagnated in real terms, necessitating larger than expected increases in contribution rates to support benefit commitments undertaken in an earlier era (Canada 1996*a*).

Finally, the pressures on the retirement income system are compounded by fiscal crisis of Canadian governments. A long string of deficits and the resulting accumulated debt have wrought a revolution in the country's public finances. By the mid-1990s, debt-servicing was consuming approximately 35 percent of federal tax revenues, placing tremendous pressure on all other spending commitments. Although public pensions have been less affected by the politics of fiscal restraint than some other programs, they have not escaped completely unscathed. More generally, the fiscal weakness of governments and the sense of taxpayer resistance to further tax increases sets the context within which policymakers consider how to manage the mountain of unfunded liabilities implicit in a pay-as-you-go system and an aging population.

These demographic and economic pressures have eroded public confidence in the retirement income system. Canadians have been subjected to a blizzard of stories claiming that the C/QPP will soon be broke. They have also witnessed their governments retreating from a number of social commitments established during the postwar decades. When combined with the uncertainties generated by rapid technological change, stubbornly high levels of unemployment, polarization in the labour market and diminished economic prospects for young people, the result is a pervasive sense of insecurity about many aspects of Canadian life, including the retirement income system. As Figure 5 demonstrates, the erosion of confidence in public pensions is particularly evident among younger people. Strikingly small percentages of those under 50 years of age are confident that they will receive OAS and C/QPP benefits.

Not surprisingly, the result has been active debate about reform of the retirement income system. In approaching this debate, it is important to avoid scenarios of doom. As Michael Wolfson and Brian Murphy demonstrate in their contribution to this volume, demographic change is not the only important factor that will shape the future. Over long periods of time, even modest improvements in the rate of economic growth or in unit costs in important public programs such as health care can make a large diference. Policy choices will also be critical. For example, if the federal government continues to provide only partial indexation of both pension benefits and income tax thresholds, even modest levels of economic growth and inflation would significantly improve public finances, eliminating any crisis over the affordability of existing programs. Pension benefits would decline in real terms, to the point that poverty among the elderly would re-emerge as a serious problem; and tax revenues would rise dramatically. Obviously, planning on the basis of such assumptions is unrealistic. Political pressures would undoubtedly emerge to improve pension benefits on one side, and to stop

FIGURE 5: Public Attitudes Towards Public Pension Plans

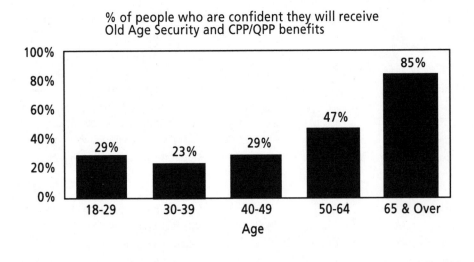

% of people who are confident they will receive
Old Age Security and CPP/QPP benefits

Source: Gallup Poll, October 1994.

the steady escalation of taxes on the other. As Betcherman points out in his commentary on the Wolfson-Murphy paper, even if conventional crisis scenarios prove wrong, we still confront the problem of designing a retirement income system that is fiscally sustainable and provides adequate retirement income. Nevertheless, Wolfson and Murphy do underscore the diversity of factors shaping the future, and the scope for choice that we do have.

Before turning to the details of the contemporary debate about our choices, it is important to develop a more general conception of the role of the public sector in the retirement income system.

THE PUBLIC ROLE IN RETIREMENT INCOME

Providing for one's retirement, unlike many other economic decisions that households take, seems inherently to be a matter for public policy. The public sector is involved in virtually every major form of saving for retirement, from public pensions to company pensions to personal savings. This section outlines the rationale for public sector involvement in pensions, the forms that the intervention can take, and the major design issues that emerge for each form of intervention.

## The Purpose of Public Involvement

As with most economic policies, the rationale for public involvement in pensions can be traced to either equity (redistributive) or efficiency (market failure) arguments. Pensions can serve two sorts of redistributive roles — intragenerational and intergenerational. The former involves transfers from the better off to the less well-off of a given age cohort, while the latter involves transfers from one age cohort to another. Intragenerational transfers naturally arise as part of the general system of taxes and transfers that governments engage in, and are based on income or other measures of need. Intergenerational transfers are specific to the pension system.

The need for intergenerational transfers arises because different cohorts have systematically different levels of well-being; some are unlucky relative to others. Cohorts that face adverse shocks such as wars, famines, natural disasters or major depressions are worse off than those that do not. In addition, cohorts that are larger than average tend to be worse off. Their large numbers mean that they fare less well in the labour market, when their wages and employment opportunities are depressed, and when they retire capital is more abundant so the return on their saving for retirement will be less. Intergenerational transfers can thus play an intergenerational insurance or risk-sharing role. Such a role involves public pensions that are temporarily unfunded, while unlucky cohorts are in retirement, but over a long period of time the funds are replenished by subsequent generations.

The case for permanently unfunded public pensions, that is permanent intergenerational transfers from young to old, is much weaker. It may well be that younger cohorts are systematically better off than their parents; technical progress accounts for that. But, permanently unfunded public pensions will typically make all cohorts worse off in the long run except for those that are part way through their working lives when the pension is introduced. As is well-known in the economics literature, this will be true as long as the rate of interest exceeds that rate of growth of the economy.[1]

Market failure arguments for public pensions rely on alleged imperfections of capital markets, especially the market for annuities, which is what pensions most closely resemble. One form of the argument is what economists refer to as adverse selection. It is argued that insurance companies are not well enough informed to be able to classify different persons according to their riskiness (of disability or longevity). In these circumstances, bad risks dominate the purchase of annuities and the market offerings become very inefficient. At the same time, capital markets seem not to be very good at insuring against inflation by offering indexed annuities. This may be because inflation is not a very "insurable" risk, since it is largely under the control of monetary authorities rather than being a purely statistical phenomenon.

It is not at all obvious that market-failure arguments provide much justification for the sorts of public intervention one actually sees. For one thing, the arguments are not altogether convincing. For example, it is difficult to see why adverse selection should be a major problem in the annuity market; it seems not to be an issue in the market for life insurance, which insures against the same kind of contingencies. Even if adverse selection were a problem, it is not obvious that public intervention could improve matters, since the public sector is not likely to be better informed than the private sector. Moreover, if market failure were the source of the difficulty, the kinds of interventions that we actually observe are hardly the appropriate ones. For example, unfunded pensions would not be an appropriate policy response.

Still, it is hard not to suspect that some form of market failure is at work. A substantial proportion of the population does not save adequately for their own retirement by any reasonable reckoning. Faced with this, governments naturally come to their assistance with transfers funded out of current revenues (i.e., unfunded pensions). Why do most people save too little for their retirement and end up relying on the public sector? One possibility is that they are simply myopic and are not able or willing to foresee far enough into the future to plan for their own retirement. The other, which tends to appeal to economists who have faith in individual rationality, is that far from being myopic, individuals are superrational. They anticipate correctly that, no matter what the government might say, it cannot avoid coming to their aid in the event that they do not set aside enough retirement savings.

Whether it is based on myopia or superrationality, the fact that a substantial proportion of the population, if left to their own devices, saves too little for their own retirement, and that government inevitably comes to their assistance, has an important policy implication. It provides a rationale for governments taking measures to induce more saving for retirement so that the need for *ex post* transfers based on current revenues is avoided. The case for inducing more saving for retirement is buttressed by the argument that a higher national saving rate carries benefits of its own in the form of higher rates of growth and productivity.

## Forms of Public Involvement

Government intervention in the provision of retirement income can take a number of forms. The following threefold classification seems to capture most of the alternatives that are typically used.

*Public Provision.* The public sector may provide retirement incomes in two major ways. First are transfers to the elderly made out of general revenues. Transfers represent a very flexible mechanism, and can take a variety of designs. They may simply be contingent on age, and be pure intergenerational transfers; or they may also be contingent on income and incorporate intragenerational transfers. More generally, the redistributive tax-transfer system may implicitly favour the elderly because their incomes are typically lower than average. Transfers to the elderly, especially the elderly poor, may also be in kind as well as in cash. Thus, the retired benefit disproportionately from health expenditures, social housing, transportation services, and social services.

The government might also operate contributory public pensions of various forms, where one's pension depends upon one's previous contributions. Public pensions are typically compulsory, though that is not a necessary feature of them. The extent of participation may be limited by earnings or employment. And, the system may be funded or unfunded, or its extent of funding may be allowed to vary across time as demographics and external shocks vary. That is, the system may involve no intergenerational redistribution, it may involve permanent intergenerational redistribution from young to old, or it may involve periods of temporary intergenerational redistribution.

*Incentives for Private Provision.* Industrialized countries commonly offer incentives for providing for one's retirement income, typically through preferential tax treatment for retirement savings. A common method is to allow tax sheltering whereby eligible savings are deducted from taxable income, accumulate tax free and become taxable when they are drawn down in retirement. Alternatively, instead of allowing an up-front deduction, part of the capital income earned on saving for retirement may simply be exempt from tax as it is earned. Indeed, one of the most common forms of implicit savings for retirement, the acquisition of equity in housing, is effectively treated in this way. If imputed rent is exempt from tax, the purchase of equity in owner-occupied housing is tax-sheltered. Retirement savings eligible for tax sheltering may include individual savings as well as company pension plans. The amount of such saving eligible for sheltering may be limited, and the form of assets that may be held may also be restricted (e.g., domestic versus foreign assets). Moreover, the tax treatment may vary according to whether the plan is of the defined benefit form or the defined contribution form.

More generally, tax-sheltered private pensions are often subject to a variety of regulations. Auditing and reporting provisions may be in place to ensure actuarial fairness. Rules may govern vesting and portability. The asset structure may be restricted to control exposure to risk. Antidiscrimination rules may constrain variations in the benefits available to certain identifiable groups, in order to protect the contributor or enforce social norms.

*Mandating Private Provision.* Rather than the carrot of incentives, one can always use the stick of mandating private provision. That is, persons may be forced to contribute to a private pension scheme, or companies may be required by law to provide pensions for their employees. As with all policies, mandating has advantages as well as disadvantages. It may impose high administrative costs on individuals and firms, and may be difficult to enforce. It may also induce inefficiency in the behaviour of private markets. For example, firms may be more reluctant to take on full-time employees, they may be induced to change their hiring and layoff behaviour, or they may change the form of their compensation package offered to employees. At the same time, mandated private pensions avoid some of the disadvantages of public pensions or of providing tax inducement to private savings. Mandating avoids any direct cost to the government, including the cost of tax incentives. It also avoids the problem of governments not being far-sighted enough to be able to maintain fully-funded pensions.

## Issues in Policy Design

Many countries, including Canada, combine various aspects of these forms of public intervention in providing for retirement incomes. In choosing the most appropriate forms of intervention, many issues are involved. This section summarizes some of the more prominent ones in the three areas: public provision, incentives for private provision, and mandating private provision.

*Public Provision of Retirement Income.* The two major variants of public provision — transfers to the elderly financed from general revenues and contributory public pension schemes — raise distinctive issues.

The most obvious issue in the design of transfers to the elderly is the extent to which they should be universal as opposed to being targeted to those most in need. The response to this issue depends upon the importance of intergenerational relative to intragenerational transfers as the redistributive objective. Transfers based on intergenerational risk-sharing concerns call for a more universal benefit during periods when relatively unlucky cohorts are in retirement. However, if transfers to the elderly are viewed as a backstop device for ensuring that the less well-off have adequate incomes, a more targeted approach is appropriate. Targeting of pensions to those in need requires much less tax revenue and for that reason is a more efficient way of achieving a given amount of redistribution. In addition, intergenerational transfers through the public pension system are not the only way to redress inequities suffered by unlucky cohorts. The use of public debt is arguably a much simpler way to do so. To the extent that debt is used for this purpose, transfers to the elderly could concentrate on targeting the elderly most in need.

The other type of public pension program is the contributory or contractual form, and it raises much different issues. A contributory pension plan is a system of forced savings. We have seen that people might systematically save too little for their own retirement either because of myopia or because of the rational expectation that governments will provide for them in retirement. In either case, forced savings is a reasonable response, and a contributory public pension is one way to force people to save more for their own retirement. Alternatively, people may not participate in organized pensions because they are not employed steadily or because they are employed by small firms for whom the administrative costs of providing pensions for employees are prohibitively expensive.

Given that contributory public pensions are ultimately a method of forced savings, it makes little sense to think of them as being suitable devices for redistribution, either intergenerational or intragenerational. On the contrary, being contributory and based on earnings, they do little for those with low incomes or no incomes at all (e.g., non-working spouses). An implication of this is that they ought to be fully funded. It is hard to justify making transfers out of current revenues to the retired based on their earnings history (regardless of the expectation they might have based on their past contributions).

The issue of funding of public pensions is of more general importance than just being a depository of forced savings. The extent of funding of payments to the elderly, or conversely the extent to which public pensions reflect intergenerational transfers, has a potential bearing on the aggregate savings rate on the economy, which in turn is related to the amount of investment. There is a large literature on the effect of unfunded public pensions on savings rates. Though the consensus of that literature is far from complete, the presumption is that unfunded public pensions, like public debt, crowd out at least some saving, and that in turn investment falls. This tends to reduce the rate of growth of productivity and employment in the economy and make it less competitive. Much of the economic argument against both budget deficits and unfunded public pensions relies on their effect on savings, investment, and growth.

The fact that contributory public pensions should be funded poses a serious dilemma for policymakers. Governments have not had exemplary records maintaining the funding of public pension plans, and it is easy to be pessimistic about their having greater foresight and discipline in the future. The existence of a fund is very tempting for governments whose life in office is only temporary. For this reason, one might be led to considering other alternatives for forcing an increase in saving for retirement. One such policy is mandating private provision to which we return shortly.

*Tax Treatment of Retirement Savings.* Preferential tax treatment for retirement savings is contentious because the form of the preferential treatment is often seen as favouring those who are best able to save for retirement, that is, higher income persons. In assessing this concern, it is therefore important to have a clear idea as to the rationale for the preferential treatment. There seem to be two main justifications for providing tax incentives for retirement saving, and they may have different implications for the design of the tax system. On the one hand, the tax sheltering of savings may simply be seen as a means of turning the personal tax system from one based on income to one based on consumption. Consumption tax advocates argue that taxing consumption rather than income is both more efficient and fairer than taxing income. It is more efficient because it removes from the tax system discrimination that would otherwise exist against future consumption in favour of present consumption — discrimination that is reflected in too little savings. It is fairer because it taxes persons according to what they take out of the social pot (consume) rather than what they put in (earn). Moreover, vertical equity need not be sacrificed by taxing persons on their consumption rather than their income because any desired degree of progressivity can be achieved by adjusting the rate structure.

On the other hand, if the purpose of tax incentives for saving is not to achieve the appropriate base, but to counteract the tendency for people to undersave, quite a different form of tax preference might be appropriate. By this view, tax incentives that induce higher savings for retirement reduce the need for future transfers to the elderly. In this case, the tax incentives may be more effectively applied by providing higher subsidy rates to those with the greatest tendency to undersave. This may well be the lower income persons. Since tax deductions provide a higher implicit subsidy to savings by higher income persons, they would not be ideal from the point of view of inducing less dependency on future transfers. A system of credits perhaps declining with income would provide more incentive to lower income persons. Unfortunately, as we shall see in more detail below, administering such a system of credits can be complicated compared with the deduction system if the pension savings are sheltered as they accumulate.

There are some other economic issues involved with the granting of tax preferences for retirement savings. As with the funding of public pensions, allowing tax preferences for retirement savings should increase the level of aggregate savings and investment in the economy. Economists also point out that sheltering pension savings essentially puts them on a par with some other major types of assets, especially housing and human capital investment. In fact, it is probably the case that more investment is undertaken in assets that are sheltered from tax than in those that are taxable. Allowing savings for retirement to be tax-sheltered may reduce the extent of inter-asset distortions in the economy.

*Mandating Private Pensions.* Requiring persons to participate in a mandatory private pension scheme is an alternative way to address the issue of undersaving for retirement. Its attractiveness lies in the perceived inadequacies of publicly operated contributory pension schemes of which two main ones stand out. The first, discussed above, is the seeming inability of governments to keep the required funding of pensions intact. The second is the fact that funds that are maintained may be better managed by the private sector than by the public sector. In recent years, many analysts, including those at the World Bank, have argued in favour of private management of pension funds on these sorts of grounds.

The mandating of compulsory pension contributions requires a number of policy issues to be addressed. The scope of coverage must be defined. Should the covered group include part-time workers and the self-employed? Should workers be able to opt out and obtain their own coverage, and even manage their own funds? Should employers be responsible for obtaining coverage for their workers, or should individuals deal with outside agencies? Should there be free entry of financial institutions into the provision of pensions? What sorts of regulations should govern the pension funds? Should there be restrictions on the type of assets (and their nationality)? Should the schemes be defined-benefit or defined-contribution, or both, given that the two types of schemes have different risk-sharing characteristics? Should there be rules governing non-discrimination by, say, health status, age, gender, disability, etc.? What should be the responsibility of the state in the event of financial difficulty? Obviously, there is considerable scope for public sector intervention into the operation of such schemes. The more public intervention there is, the more likely that the potential benefits from private management are undermined.

What seems clear is that if the private sector is given the responsibility for operating mandatory pension schemes, it cannot be expected to fulfil the redistributive objectives of pensions. These would have to be addressed by complementary public programs as necessary.

CURRENT POLICY ISSUES IN CANADA

Our discussion of the issues involved in retirement income policy has been at a very general level. We now turn to a consideration of how they apply to the Canadian case. We can be brief since these issues are treated in more detail in the papers that follow.

## Transfers to the Elderly

We have suggested earlier that intergenerational transfers such as the OAS are justified mainly as forms of intergenerational risk-sharing. In such a role, they would be temporarily in place for unlucky cohorts rather than being permanent.

Whether or not the current elderly and their immediate successors ought to be regarded as unlucky cohorts is a matter for generational accounting. Evidence seems to suggest that the cohort that is due to retire soon is far from unlucky, and that therefore the case for a universal transfer to the elderly is not as strong as it was for, say, those who grew up during the Depression and the Second World War.

The federal government apparently agrees with this line of argument. The decision to replace the current combination of OAS and GIS transfers with the Seniors Benefit will essentially complete the removal of a primarily intergenerational transfer from public pensions in favour of a system tested by family income. This is not to say that the Seniors Benefit will not have an intergenerational transfer element to it. Given that it is financed out of general revenues, it obviously will. However, its objective will not be to address inequalities arising across generations per se. In the future, governments will have to pursue intergenerational equity objectives through other instruments, such as the use of debt policy.

The need for some form of transfer to the less well-off elderly will presumably always exist. The exact form of that transfer is a matter of debate and depends upon such things as the weight one puts on redistributive equity, the extent to which one thinks that adverse incentives for saving will be affected by the generosity of public pensions, the presence of complementary programs of assistance to the poor elderly, such as transfers in kind, and the success of the other two pillars in inducing sufficient saving for one's own retirement. As well, the design of the transfer will depend upon how one measures need. Does it depend upon individual or family income? Should asset ownership be considered, especially ownership of homes, cottages, and the like? What about health or disability status? Should men and women be treated differently? Some of these issues are taken up in Ken Battle's paper.

## Tax Treatment of Retirement Savings

As the paper by Jack Mintz and Tom Wilson notes, the debate about treatment of retirement savings outlined earlier remains a vigourous one in Canada. Critics argue that allowing RPP and RRSP contributions to be fully deducted from taxable income discriminates in favour of higher income persons because they are in a higher marginal tax bracket and are able to take advantage of retirement savings plans to a greater extent than lower income persons. The solution proposed by critics is to reduce or eliminate altogether the differential tax treatment of retirement savings, or to move to a system that does not favour high-income people, such as a tax-credit system.

Mintz and Wilson reply with the view discussed earlier that deductibility of savings for retirement is essentially a means of turning the tax system into one that taxes consumption as opposed to taxing retirement. They also argue that the emphasis on the tax benefits of the deduction system for vertical equity is misplaced for a couple of reasons. One is that any degree of vertical equity can be achieved by revising the rate structure. The other is that the extent of the unequal treatment afforded by the deduction system is much less over the lifetime than it is over any given year. In other words, inequality based on lifetime income is much less than that based on annual income.

Critics might well respond in turn that consumption is not an acceptable basis for redistributive taxation. Moreover, the current tax system explicitly accepts income as being the appropriate base. As noted earlier, they might argue that the purpose of tax assistance for retirement savings is really to provide an incentive to those who otherwise might not save enough for their own retirement, and that targeting of tax incentives for retirement savings to lower income persons is warranted. They also suggest that there is no strong evidence that tax-sheltering increases savings much for higher income persons. For the latter, it simply serves as a windfall tax gain.

Whichever side one comes down on in this debate, certain administrative problems arise in restricting the extent of tax preferences given to retirement savings. Moving from a deduction to a credit system might seem to resolve the issue of unfair treatment of higher versus lower income persons as far as the value of the deduction is concerned. However, changing from a deduction to a credit when funds are put into the pension requires for consistency that the system of allowing capital income to accumulate tax-free and taxing the fund fully on withdrawal must also be changed. A fair system can become administratively very complicated. One alternative might be to replace the sheltering of pension savings completely with a system of tax crediting up front. This, however, could be very cumbersome since it requires that income accumulating in pension funds be taxed at the personal rates of the individual owners.

An alternative approach which might avoid some of these complicated administrative issues while at the same time limiting the tax benefits accruing to higher income persons would be to retain the deduction system, but condition the limits on a person's income. The concept of income used might be a longer term one, perhaps even lifetime income. This approach would make most sense if one both rejected the consumption tax argument and supposed that the stimulation to saving was most needed at the lower end of the income distribution.

## Canada/Quebec Pension Plans

Perhaps the most controversial aspect of public pensions from a policy perspective is the public contributory pension system. The controversy results mainly from the fact that, whatever the initial intentions, the system is largely an unfunded one. For example, the unfunded liability of the CPP was estimated by the Chief Actuary to be $556 billion at the end of 1995, comparable in order of magnitude to the national debt (Canada 1996a). Moreover, given the shifting demographics, the continuation of the promised level of benefits for future retirees will mean higher contribution rates for working generations in the near future, an intergenerational transfer that is hard to countenance on the grounds of intergenerational equity.

In assessing the reform options of the C/QPP system, it is worth bearing in mind the earlier discussion of the rationale for public intervention. A compulsory occupational pension like the C/QPP which is related to earnings is essentially a system of forced saving operated through the public sector. Its rationale is presumably based on the idea that persons will not save enough for their own retirement, possibly because they are not far-sighted enough, or because not all employers are well-placed to offer pension plans for their employees, especially employees that change frequently. Viewed from that perspective, it makes little sense for the system not to be funded. It serves no legitimate intergenerational transfer objective; indeed, it would be hard to justify intergenerational transfers that are based on one's earnings. As a result, many reform proposals start from the premise that the funding of the system should be strengthened in some way. A fully funded C/QPP system would make sense not only from the point of view of the rationale for the system as a form of forced savings. It would also make the system less of a hostage to demographic shifts of the sort that we are now witnessing.

The issue then becomes how to build up the fund, and how rapidly. Various options are available, ranging from increasing the contribution rates to decreasing the benefits to some combination of the two. Which option is chosen depends upon the weight one places on the implicit contract given to past contributors, as well as on the outcome of generational accounting. Various scenarios for reforming the C/QPP are debated in this volume, especially in the paper by Newman Lam and his colleagues, and in the commentaries by Robert Baldwin, Tom Courchene, Monica Townson, and William Robson. Not surprisingly, there is considerable diversity in their views.

Of particular relevance for the current policy debate is an option contained in the information paper released by the federal, provincial, and territorial governments (Canada 1996a). The document notes that, under the current system, the contribution rate will have to rise from the current level of 5.6 percent to 14.2 percent by the year 2030 to maintain the current benefit structure for future retirees. To avoid such a high tax burden on the post-baby-boom generation, the paper considers the building up of a fund over the near future. Specifically, it suggests a gradual increase in the contribution rate to 12.2 percent over a six- to eight-year period. Although the resulting fund would not fully cover future liabilities, it would be sufficient if invested at market rates to stabilize the contribution rate at 12.2 percent into the foreseeable future. In addition to partially funding the CPP, which is of value in itself, this would spread the burden of maintaining the existing level of benefits across several generations, including those who are due to retire in the near term. This particular option is predicated on the assumption that the existing level of benefits should be maintained. Other possibilities involve some reductions in benefits. For example, if benefits were cut by 10 percent, the contribution rate would only have to rise to 10.9 percent.

The partial funding option developed in the information paper is also contingent upon the fund being invested at market rates of return (3.5 to 4 percent real over the long term), something that the current CPP is not likely to be able to achieve. Reaching this goal probably requires both that the funds not be earmarked for provincial government use and that sound financial management of the funds be in place. This may require that the funds be managed privately, a practice that would depart sharply from existing ones.

This raises the fundamental issue concerning the role of the public sector in operating compulsory saving schemes like the CPP. As discussed by Estelle James and Andrew Dilnot, mandatory retirement savings systems could, in principle, be operated by the private sector. There are two main arguments in favour of private as opposed to public provision. The first is that the public sector seems to lack the foresight or the political will to maintain the required fund intact. There is plenty of evidence from around the world to support the contention that governments often surrender to the temptation to run down assets like pension funds or their equivalent. Private sector management would remove from the public sector the temptation to use the funds for current needs as opposed to setting it aside for productive investments. The second is that even if the public sector could maintain a fund, it is unlikely to manage it as efficiently as would the private sector. Among other things, there is no reason to believe that the public sector has the financial management expertise equivalent to that of the private sector.

Against this, many would argue that public provision for mandatory savings through programs like the C/QPP allows for wider social objectives, objectives that are not incompatible with the plans being funded. Examples include spousal and survivor benefits, provisions for those temporarily out for work for childbearing and childrearing, and disability benefits. Each of these incorporates some element of redistribution, or social insurance. In addition, the floor on earnings before contributions are calculated in the C/QPP incorporates an element of redistribution. Given the broad political support for these supplementary benefits, the question becomes how they should be financed. Three options seem to exist.

The first is to follow the current practice and to finance them from the fund created by the general system on employer and employee contributions. This is not incompatible with the C/QPP system as a whole being fully funded, but it does imply that the system is not being run on purely actuarial principles; that is, there is cross-subsidization from ineligible workers to those who will be receiving one or more of these supplementary benefits. If one wished to avoid this, the supplementary benefits could be financed out of general revenue, leaving the purely earnings-related portion to be financed from contributions. As a third alternative, these redistributive or social insurance elements could be removed from the C/QPP system and dealt with as part of the Seniors Benefit program, which is an explicitly redistributive instrument. If so, it would have to be decided whether they should be income-tested as with other elements of the Seniors Benefit.

## THE POLITICS OF REFORM

The politics of pension reform are intense in all democratic countries. Cuts in pension benefits are sensitive politically for reasons developed in the paper by Paul Pierson. Older voters tend to be electorally active, certainly more so than young people. The elderly tend to be seen as deserving beneficiaries, and concerns about work incentives which constrain the design of benefits for working-age unemployed are much less relevant. Moreover, the burden of cuts to pensions are highly concentrated on the elderly but the benefits to taxpayers are generally more diffuse. In this context, it is not surprising that politicians tend to seek as broad a consensus as possible before implementing significant changes, and that they tend to prefer lowering the visibility of change through adjustments to the formulas governing the indexing of benefits or increases in contribution rates, rather than making direct and explicit reductions in benefits.

The other distinctive feature of pension politics, in Canada as elsewhere, is the temporal dimension of pensions. In comparison with most other policy areas, the relevant planning horizons are immensely long, creating an interdependence between generations. Pierson argues that this temporal dimension also inclines policymakers to rely on incremental change in mature systems for several reasons. Relatively small changes in benefits, indexation or eligibility rules can generate very substantial savings over time. Most of the successful efforts to trim public sector pensions have taken the form of revisions that phase in gradually, often in ways that affect only future retirees. The slow transformation of the function of the first pillar of the Canadian system from an intergeneration transfer to income support for low-income elderly over the period from 1965 to 2001 is a classic example.

Second, the long time horizons of pension systems also tend to embed particular program approaches, creating a form of path dependency in pension politics. The historic choices that countries made during the building of the welfare state, which are embedded in the existing pension programs and the decision-making processes that govern them, constrain the choices now open to policymakers. For example, a mature pay-as-you-go system may accommodate incremental changes in existing parameters, but is more resistant to radical reform. As noted earlier, proposals for a sudden shift to full funding, including proposals to privatize the C/QPP, confront a double-payment problem: a shift to full funding requires current workers to continue to finance the previous generation's retirement while simultaneously saving for their own. To what extent this logic will constrain the proposal for partial funding of the plan remains to be seen.

One factor with the potential to disrupt the natural political preference for incrementalism in pension politics is intergenerational conflict. Tom Courchene's contribution to this volume lays considerable emphasis on the danger that the excesses of the soon-to-be-retired age cohort are piling an immense burden on young people — in his words, putting "generation X against generation XS." The underlying fear that haunts a pay-as-you-go system is that the young generation will rebel, and refuse to pay for the benefits of the elderly, especially if they feel that the intergenerational bargain is stacked against them. Despite numerous prophesies, however, Pierson argues that there is remarkably little evidence of intergenerational conflict in Western democracies. In part, this is because the young tend to be much less politically active than older generations. In addition, today's elderly are the parents of this generation of workers; and this generation of workers wants to receive pensions in due course. The commentary on the Pierson paper by Harvey Lazar suggests that it might be possible to mobilize young workers in Canada against pension burdens. But clearly the balance of interests at work are not as simple as the rhetoric of intergenerational warfare suggests.

The paper by John Myles and Jill Quadagno extends the emphasis on incrementalism and path dependency through a comparative analysis of pension reform across OECD countries. They argue that contemporary political battles over pension reform are constrained by the distinctive developmental paths along which different countries have travelled over the last century. One group of countries, the "Beveridge" countries, opted initially for universal flat-rate pensions for all citizens meeting age and residency requirements. A second group, the "Bismarck" countries, adopted an earnings-related social insurance model, with benefits related more or less closely to contributions. More recently, a number of the Beveridge nations have added a second tier of earnings-related pensions to their systems, leading to a "Beveridge plus Bismarck" model. Canada fits comfortably into this group.

These historic pathways continue to shape the contemporary politics of pension reform, more decisively even than the predominance of governments of the political left or right. In "Beveridge" countries, the debate often centres on the role of universality in the system, and a number of these countries have moved away from the universal basic pension by reducing or eliminating benefits for high-income seniors, producing a needs-based pension. The essence of this model is the redistributive tax-transfer system often characterized as a negative income tax (NIT), which parallels the World Bank's recommendations for the first pillar of the pension system. However, countries in the Bismarckian tradition face enormous difficulties in moving in this direction because of the double-payment problem. Instead, the trend of reform in these countries is to reinforce the employment-based approach by tightening the link between contributions and benefits. As Myles and Quadagno note, nowhere in the OECD have employment-based systems been rationalized along the lines recommended by the World Bank.

Although Myles and Quadagno do not discuss the trend among the "Beveridge plus Bismarck" group separately, such countries clearly have the potential to combine both reform dynamics. Certainly, Canadian governments seem to be proceeding cautiously down both paths. First, the new Seniors Benefit will complete the transformation of the first pillar into an income-tested model, albeit in a manner carefully crafted to minimize political fallout. As noted earlier, the new benefit will not take effect until 2001, and both current beneficiaries and those who retire before then will not be affected adversely by it. Moreover, the program has been designed to ensure that the vast majority of seniors — 75 percent — will be as well or better off. Second, the most likely outcome in the reform of the C/QPP is a set of adjustments to the parameters of the existing system that will tighten the relationship between benefits and contributions. A consensus appears to be emerging among federal and provincial governments in favour of an acceleration of contribution rate increases to create a partially funded plan, perhaps augmented with minor reductions in benefit provisions.[2] More radical changes along the lines discussed by Estelle James and William Robson in this volume and by others elsewhere are not on the table for active debate, at least in this round of pension reform. Indeed, the idea of privatization was not included in the discussion of the reform options in the information document published by the federal, provincial, and territorial governments (Canada 1996a).

CONCLUSIONS

The retirement income system constructed during the postwar decades is under pressure, and Canadian governments are in the middle of making critical changes in core components of it. Pension reform is complex, and this book is dedicated to illuminating the issues, the conflicts and the choices before the country. The papers that follow in this book provide different perspectives on the issues and options for retirement income policy, and no single way forward emerges from its pages. Nevertheless, several broad conclusions do stand out.

First, although the pressures on the system are intense, solutions are available, and the pessimism that pervades much public debate is overstated. The analysts in this book differ on the appropriate balance between public and private sectors, and on the specific adjustments needed in public plans. But the survival of a multipillared system to provide for the retirement income of future generations of Canadians is not in doubt.

Second, the future of the first pillar of the system seems clear. The introduction of the Seniors Benefit in the year 2001 will complete the historic evolution of this pillar from a universal program to a redistributive transfer to the low-income elderly. The Seniors Benefit represents the logical culmination of a longstanding policy trend, and the protection of existing pensioners and the advance notice for future retirees has reduced the political costs of the change. Although articulate proponents of universal benefits remain, future policy debates are likely to revolve around the modalities rather than the principle of a targeted benefit.

Much the same can be said about the third pillar. Controversy continues to rage over the redistributive implications of the current tax treatment of private pensions and RRSPs. Nevertheless, the basic principle of tax sheltering seems deeply entrenched, and the political fallout from radical change would be significant. Although the relative merits of tax deductions versus tax credits will undoubtedly be debated, the core of this pillar of the system seems secure.

The real uncertainties about the future of the retirement income system centre on the Canada and Quebec Pension Plans. The range of options here is large, ranging from maintenance of the current program to its complete privatization. Moreover, the current round of policy debate is unlikely to be the last. The process of adjusting to demographic change will extend over the next three decades, and will be sensitive to the shifting economic and political currents over that time. The parameters of the contemporary debate in official circles tend to be reasonably narrow, much narrower than the range of options debated in the papers that follow. In the short term, this seems consistent with the proposition that path dependency and inertia shape the continued evolution of contributory public pension programs. Yet the transformation of the first pillar serves as a reminder of the extent of change possible over extended time periods. Canadians will undoubtedly debate the future of the second pillar of their retirement income system for decades to come, and it is our hope that this volume will contribute to the debate.

NOTES

1.  The reason for this is that unfunded public pensions substitute for private savings. Whereas funds put into private savings yield a return equal to the rate of interest, funds that are used to pay for the pensions of the currently retired, with the expectation that one's pension will be paid by the next generation of workers, will have an implicit rate of return equal to the rate of growth of the economy.
2.  Quebec has announced its intention to accelerate the increase in contribution rates for the Quebec Pension Plan; and the federal and provincial governments appear to be coalescing around a similar strategy for the Canada Pension Plan (*The Globe and Mail*, 14 and 19 June 1996).

REFERENCES

Canada (1996*a*), *An Information Paper for Consultations on the Canada Pension Plan: Released by the Federal, Provincial and Territorial Governments,* Ottawa: Department of Finance.

_____ (1996*b*), *The Seniors Benefit: Securing the Future,* Ottawa: Department of Finance.

Drucker, P. (1993), *Post-Capitalist Society,* New York: Harper Collins.

Statistics Canada (1995), *Retirement Savings Through RPPs and RRSPs: 1991 to 1993,* Ottawa: Minister of Industry.

_____ (1996*a*), *Trusted Pension Funds: Financial Statistics, 1994,* Ottawa: Minister of Industry.

_____ (1996*b*), *Canada's Retirement Income Programs: A Statistical Overview,* Ottawa: Minister of Industry.

World Bank (1994), *Averting the Old Age Crisis: Policies to Protect the Old and Promote Growth,* Washington, DC: World Bank and Oxford University Press.

# PART ONE

## PUBLIC AND PRIVATE ROLES

# CHAPTER TWO

# Canada's Old Age Crisis in International Perspective

*Estelle James*

## INTRODUCTION

Over the next 35 years, the proportion of the world's population that is over 60 will nearly double, from 9 to 16 percent. Because of medical improvements and rapid fertility decline, populations are aging much faster in developing countries than they did in the industrial countries. As young working-age people near retirement — around the year 2030 — 80 percent of the world's old people will live in what today are developing countries. More than half will live in Asia and more than a quarter in China alone (see Figures 1 and 2). These countries need to develop their old age systems quickly and make them resilient to rapid demographic change. The World Bank report, *Averting the Old Age Crisis: Policies to Protect the Old and Promote Growth*, was prepared with this need in mind. However, the study also has relevance for industrialized countries, such as Canada, that are now reevaluating their existing systems of old age support.

Population aging is welcome because it indicates that many people have an opportunity to live longer and healthier lives. But it also creates problems because the working-age population must now support a growing number of people who are no longer actively generating economic output. Cross-sectional analysis shows that public spending on pensions increases exponentially as populations age and now exceeds 15 percent of GNP in some countries (Figure 3). Canada is still at a low point on this trajectory compared with other OECD countries, but its expenditures will rise rapidly in the years ahead. *Averting the Old Age Crisis* argues that how this money is generated and spent affects the entire economy by influencing productivity and the size of the GNP pie. Increasing productivity is

FIGURE 1: Percentage of the Population over 60 Years Old, by Region, 1990 and 2030

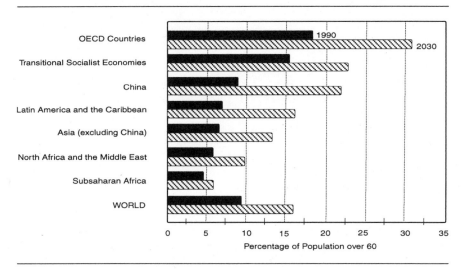

Note: Japan is included with the OECD Countries, not with Asia.
Source: World Bank (1994, p. 26).

FIGURE 2: Number of Years Required to Double the Share of the Population over 60 from 9 to 18 Percent, in Selected Countries

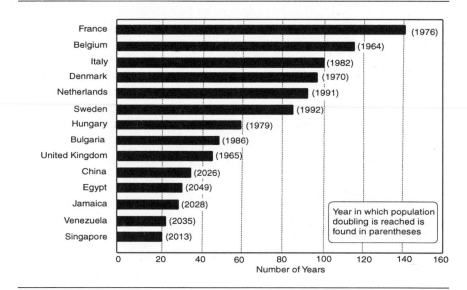

Source: World Bank (1994, p. 34).

FIGURE 3: Relationship between Percentage of the Population over
60 Years Old and Public Pension Spending

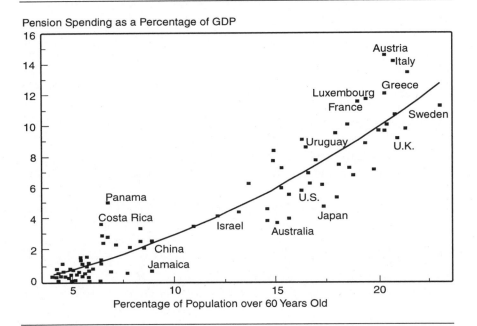

Source: World Bank (1994, p. 41).

especially important as populations age, and a relatively smaller number of workers must support a growing number of retirees. Therefore, countries should use
two overarching criteria for old age programs: they should protect the old (in an
equitable way) and they should promote (or at least not hinder) economic growth
— which is important both for the old and the young.

Growth effects are always hard to prove, so careful judgements about both
theory and evidence are necessary and are presented in the report. If you do not
buy the premise that old age systems affect efficiency and growth, you will not
buy our recommendations. But countries that do accept this basic premise will be
forced to reexamine their existing programs. We believe this reexamination will
push them inexorably in the direction of partial funding, private management of
the funds and increased use of defined contribution programs.

In this paper I describe the most common problems found with dominant systems today, emphasizing their negative impact on growth and the inequities they
perpetuate; I will present the recommended framework for a reformed system,
including responses to the most common objections and make some comments
on the applicability to Canada.[1]

## PROBLEMS WITH CURRENT SYSTEMS

Most formal systems of old age security are publicly managed, pay pensions that are positively related to the worker's earnings, and are financed by payroll taxes on a pay-as-you-go (PAYG) basis — meaning that today's workers are taxed to pay the pensions of those who have already retired. As we studied these systems around the world, the same problems appeared over and over again, both in industrialized and developing countries. This led us to believe that these problems are not accidental design flaws; rather they are inherent in the politics and economics of pay-as-you-go systems, which makes it easy for politicians to promise present benefits at the expense of large future costs or to misuse the reserves that sometimes accumulate in the early years of a plan. (See Appendix.) A new system is needed that is more immune to these dangers. The problems are:

*High payroll tax rates.* In pay-as-you-go systems, when populations are young, small contributions from the large number of workers make possible generous benefits to the few pensioners. However, as populations age and systems mature, these systems must charge very high payroll taxes to keep these benefit promises. Even some countries with young populations have surprisingly high payroll taxes, because of the way their systems have been abused. Thus, payroll taxes for pensions are already over 25 percent in Egypt, Hungary, Russia, Kyrgyzstan, Brazil, and Italy. As populations age, contribution rates in almost all countries — including Canada — will have to rise dramatically over the next 30 years. This will mean lower take-home pay if borne by workers or more unemployment if borne by employers, particularly as markets become globalized and countries with younger populations and lower tax rates compete with older ones. If present systems are retained, payroll taxes (for pensions, medical care, and other age-related elements of social insurance) are likely to use up much of the productivity increase accruing over the next 30 to 40 years, leaving little for augmenting the standard of living of the average worker.

*Evasion.* High payroll tax rates that are not linked to benefits lead to evasion and labour market distortions. In many Latin American countries over 40 percent of the labour force works in the informal sector, partly in order to avoid payroll taxes, and the informal sector is growing rapidly in Eastern Europe. The underground economy and underreporting of income, particularly among the self-employed, is also common among OECD countries. Evasion undermines the system's ability to pay pensions, makes it necessary to raise payroll taxes still further, and hurts the economy, since people who work in the informal sector are often less productive.

*Early retirement.* One of the most common forms of generous benefits is the provision for early retirement with little or no reduction in pension amount. In Hungary, more than a quarter of the population are pensioners and the average retirement age is 54. In Turkey many people retire below the age of 50 or even 40. In all OECD countries, including Canada, the labour force participation rate of men over the age of 55 has fallen substantially over the last couple of decades, even as longevity has been increasing. Early retirees stop making contributions and they begin drawing benefits, thus doubly hurting the scheme financially — while also depriving the economy of their effort and experience. Raising the retirement age may seem difficult in a context of unemployment, but actually early retirement only hides unemployment in the short run and adds to it in the long run by raising labour costs. So once again, this has not been good for the old age system and it has not been good for the economy.

*Misallocation of public resources.* In 1990, Austria, Italy, and Uruguay spent more than one-third of their public budgets on pensions. Since the government's ability to tax is limited by economic and political considerations, high public pension spending can squeeze out government spending on growth-promoting public investments such as infrastructure, education, and health services, and it can lead to inflation if the government tries to maintain this spending through deficit finance.

*Lost opportunity to increase savings.* Many countries believe they have inadequate national saving that hampers growth. One reason why people might save is to support themselves in old age, but current systems have not been used to induce people to save more and some economists believe that in fact they have induced people to save less. The impact of PAYG systems on saving is highly contentious, and in *Averting the Old Age Crisis* we spell out the arguments pro and con. But whether or not you think that PAYG schemes have decreased saving, it is clear that they have not increased saving. Funded systems that require people to save at a rate in excess of what they are doing voluntarily could be used as a tool to increase national saving, and this has not been done in most countries.

*Failure to redistribute to low-income groups.* Publicly-managed tax-financed systems are sometimes justified on grounds that they help the poor. But, despite seemingly progressive benefit formulas, studies of public plans in the Netherlands, Sweden, the United Kingdom, and the United States have found little if any redistribution from lifetime rich to lifetime poor. This is partly due to design features — the failure to cover low-income groups in the early years of the plan, the taxation of labour income but not income from capital, the low ceiling on taxable earnings and the tendency to base pensions on wages during the last few years of employment, which benefits those with steeper age-earnings profiles. In addition, there are important hidden reasons for the lack of lifetime redistribution, including the fact that high-income people enter the labour force later and so contribute for fewer years and live longer, thereby receiving benefits for more years.

*Positive transfers to early cohorts, and losses to their children.* Generally covered workers who retire in the first 20-30 years of a scheme get back much more than they contributed, but their children and grandchildren get back less than they paid in and lower rates of return than they could have earned elsewhere. I believe that this has been shown for Canada, as well as for other countries that have instituted PAYG schemes. Sometimes we may want to redistribute across generations, perhaps favouring cohorts who have lived through a depression or war. However, redistribution through PAYG takes place without a full discussion, or even without a full public understanding, of what is going to happen once the system is instituted. In many cases, the people who are being redistributed away from were not old enough to participate in the discussion; only the gainers participated. Often the people in the older generations who have collected the most are high-income groups, while today's young people, many of whom are earning low wages, are paying substantial payroll taxes to finance these benefits. Many of us would agree that this is not an equitable procedure or outcome.

*As a result of all these forces, old age systems are in serious financial trouble and are not sustainable in their present form.* The situation has been most acute in Latin America and Eastern Europe, whose systems have been close to bankruptcy. In the past, the most common way these countries have escaped from these unrealistic promises is to allow inflation to take place without indexing benefits. In Venezuela, the real value of benefits plummeted 60 percent during the 1980s due to inflation without indexation (see Figure 4).

Fortunately, OECD countries are not likely to use this solution, but we also face serious problems in the years ahead. Figure 5 shows the implicit public pension debt — the present value of the amounts that have been promised to current retirees and workers — in several OECD countries, including Canada. The implicit public pension debt is much larger than the explicit conventional debt, it exceeds 100 percent of GNP in almost every case and sometimes exceeds 200 percent. Current payroll tax rates are much less than needed to pay off this debt and most countries will have a hard time raising them enough to close the gap. Pension benefits or other public goods will have to be reduced in the future.

Thus public pension plans have not always protected the old, they especially have not protected the old who are poor or people who will be old in the future,

FIGURE 4: Real Pension Levels in Venezuela, 1974-1992

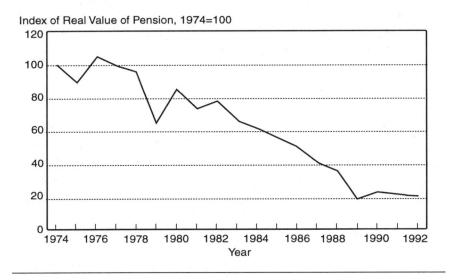

Source: World Bank (1994, p. 154).

FIGURE 5: Explicit Debt versus Implicit Public Pension Debt in Seven OECD
Countries, 1990

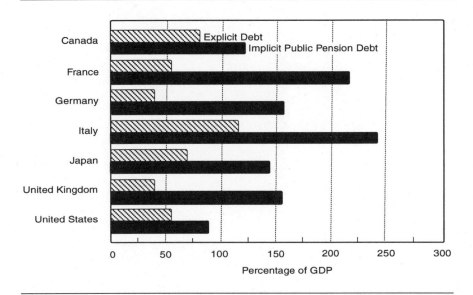

Source: World Bank (1994, p. 139).

they often have not distributed their benefits in an equitable way, and they have hindered economic growth. In addition, the systems are not sustainable in their present form. They are all going to have to change, one way or another. As industrialized countries make their piecemeal design changes, they should consider carefully whether structural reform is also desirable.

## A FRAMEWORK FOR REFORM

This brings me to the second point — a framework for reform. We recommend a multipillar system that puts greater emphasis on saving, that has separate financing and managerial mechanisms for redistribution and saving and that shares responsibility between the public and private sectors (Figure 6).

*The first pillar* would resemble existing public pension plans in that it would be publicly managed, defined benefit, and tax-financed. However, unlike most current systems, the reformed public pillar would focus on redistribution — providing a social safety net for the old, particularly the old whose lifetime income was low. The benefit formula could be flat, as in Argentina and the Netherlands

FIGURE 6: The Pillars of Old Age Income Security

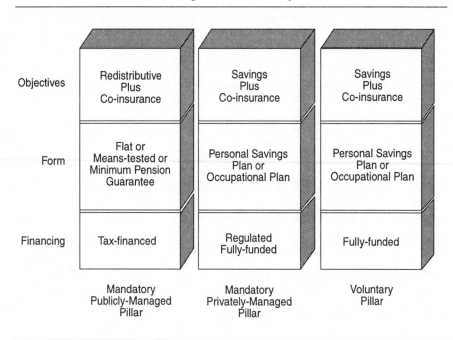

| Objectives | Redistributive Plus Co-insurance | Savings Plus Co-insurance | Savings Plus Co-insurance |
|---|---|---|---|
| Form | Flat or Means-tested or Minimum Pension Guarantee | Personal Savings Plan or Occupational Plan | Personal Savings Plan or Occupational Plan |
| Financing | Tax-financed | Regulated Fully-funded | Fully-funded |
| | Mandatory Publicly-Managed Pillar | Mandatory Privately-Managed Pillar | Voluntary Pillar |

Source: World Bank (1994, p. 15).

(uniform for everyone or related to years of covered employment), means- and asset-tested (as in Australia), or could provide a minimum pension guarantee (as in Chile). Financing could be out of general revenues or a payroll tax with a floor and a high ceiling on taxable wages (in some respects similar to Canada's OAS and GIS). Because of its limited scope and broad tax base, tax rates to support this pillar would be much lower than the public system requires in most countries today.

Such redistributive programs are sometimes attacked on grounds that they will lose political support from high-income groups so that ultimately low-income groups will not be protected. Recall, however, that current defined benefit plans (that are positively related to earnings) have, in fact, produced little if any protection in the form of net transfers from the rich to the long-term poor. The important political economy assumption underlying this recommendation is that upper-income people will be no less (and possibly more) willing to redistribute through a smaller but more targeted benefit program.

*The second mandatory pillar* would differ dramatically from most existing systems. It would be fully funded, would link benefits actuarially to costs, and would be privately and competitively managed through personal saving plans or occupational pension plans. Essentially, people would be required to save for their old age, and this pillar would handle their savings. Its form would differ sharply from Canada's earnings-related pillar, the CPP (Canada Pension Plan), which is defined benefit, pay-as-you-go, and publicly managed. Let me explain the reasoning behind these differences, and why we believe the funded private pillar should be mandatory rather than voluntary, as in Canada.

*Why mandatory?* Because it will require people to save for old age, which some are too shortsighted to do, and because this is a more efficient arrangement than PAYG as a way to provide the earnings-related part of the mandatory pension.

*Why link benefits to contributions?* To discourage evasion and other labour market distortions, since people are less likely to regard their contribution as a tax. In particular, defined contribution plans, in which the capital accumulation is turned into an annuity or gradual withdrawal upon retirement, give people an incentive to take into account the costs of early retirement before choosing it.

*Why fully funded?* To make costs clear and payable up-front, so countries will not make promises now that they will be unable to keep later; to avoid large tax increases as populations age; to prevent large intergenerational transfers, because each generation is, essentially, paying its own way; to help build national saving, especially saving committed for the long term, which increases future productivity and wages; and to help finance future pensions out of·the return to this saving.

The positive impact on saving will be particularly large if the mandatory contribution rate exceeds the amount that people were previously saving voluntarily, if the opportunities for consumer borrowing against these savings are limited, and if fiscal constraint is observed so governments do not dissave an equivalent amount.

Two objections are often made to this strategy: first, some analysts have argued that full funding will cause a capital glut. In reply, it is necessary to remember that only part of the over-all system is funded, the build-up of funds will be very gradual, it will not occur in all countries at the same time, some of it will be used to finance the transition to a new pension system, and some should be invested abroad in countries that have low capital-labour ratios. Thus a capital glut is not likely to be a problem in the foreseeable future.

Second, it is sometimes argued that past savings are irrelevant because the consumption of today's retirees can only be supported by the output of today's workers. However, this common belief, like many in this field, is overly simplistic: past savings can enhance the productivity and therefore the output of today's workers, they can be imbedded in consumer durables that continue to provide a stream of services, and they can be invested abroad, then redeemed to finance an in-flow of consumer goods. Thus, saving can be an important ingredient of a long-run strategy for providing additional domestic consumption when the dependency rate increases.

*Why privately managed?* To produce the best allocation of capital based on economic rather than political objectives, to earn the best return on savings, and to help countries develop their financial markets (the latter especially important for middle-income countries). Figure 7 provides some of the evidence that led us in this direction. It displays data on the rates of return to publicly and privately managed pension reserves during the 1980s — data that is not generally available, for reasons that will become apparent. Most publicly managed pension reserves fared poorly and in many cases lost money throughout the 1980s, because they were required to be invested in government securities or loans to failing state enterprises — at low nominal interest rates that became negative during inflationary periods. Even in the case of the United States, Singapore, and Malaysia, where the returns were not negative, they were not nearly as high as the positive returns that were earned on average by privately managed funds. Clearly this poses a problem for the pension funds. It also poses a problem for the economy as a whole if the exclusive access to these funds makes it easier for governments to run large deficits or to spend more wastefully than they could if they had to rely on more transparent and accountable sources of funds. Even if the current government is fiscally responsible future governments may not be, and the accessibility of publicly managed pension reserves enables them to spend without taxing

FIGURE 7: Gross Average Annual Investment Returns for Selected Pension
Funds, 1980s

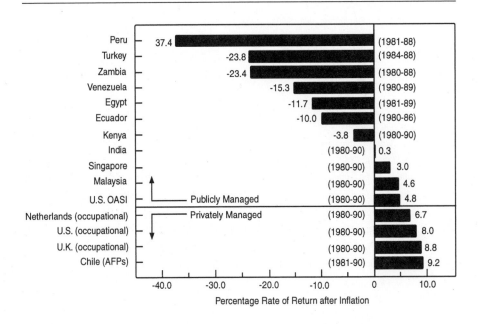

Note: Simple averages for countries with at least five years of data during the 1980s.
Malaysia, Singapore, Kenya, India, and Zambia are publicly managed provident funds.
Rates reported are returns credited to worker accounts. Peru, Turkey, Venezuela, Egypt,
Ecuador, and the US are publicly managed reserves of partially funded pension plans.
Amounts reported are gross returns to the funds. In many cases data on administrative
costs are not available. The Netherlands, US, and UK are privately managed occupational plans; estimated average net returns have been reported by subtracting one
percentage point from simulated average gross returns. Actual average net returns, after
all administrative expenses, are reported for the Chilean AFTs; average gross returns
were 12.3 percent. For the occupational plans and AFPs actual returns and expenses
varied by fund.
Source: World Bank (1994, p. 95).

or borrowing through the market. For example, the build-up of the US debt during the 1980s dovetailed with the build-up of the social security trust fund, and
work by some economists suggests that there might be a causal relationship.

Competitively managed funded pension plans, in contrast, are more likely to
be invested in a mixture of public and corporate bonds, equities and real estate,
thereby earning a higher rate of return. They can enjoy the benefits of investment
diversification — offering opportunities to increase the yield, including yields

from countries where labour is abundant and capital relatively scarce, and decrease the risk, especially the risk of country-specific shocks. These private pension funds could take the form of personal saving plans where the worker chooses the investment manager, as in Chile and Argentina, or of occupational plans where the employer and/or union chooses, as in Australia, Switzerland, Denmark, and the Netherlands. In either case, defined contribution is more likely than defined benefit to prevail, and to provide the right incentives.

*Caveats.* But two caveats are essential here: first, countries must have at least rudimentary capital markets (such as a secondary market in government bonds) at the beginning — and these markets will develop further together (disclosure requirements, credit rating institutions, stock exchanges) as the pension funds grow. And second, considerable government regulation is essential to require diversification and to avoid investments that are overly risky or managers who are fraudulent.

Of course, it is possible that the regulation will become excessive and, in effect, direct the investments, almost as much as in publicly managed pension funds. However, a countervailing force has been set up as private pension funds grow — the funds themselves, their clients, and the private sector enterprises that gradually come to depend on them as a financing source. Thus, an important political economy assumption underlying this recommendation is that mandatory privately managed pension funds are more likely than publicly managed funds to be insulated from political pressures in choosing their investment strategies.

Finally, a *third pillar* would offer additional protection, through *voluntary* occupational pension or personal saving plans, for people who want more in their old age. An important public policy issue here: Should governments offer tax incentives for voluntary saving and annuities? The answer depends on whether such incentives are consistent with the country's over-all tax policy towards consumption versus saving, since special incentives for retirement accounts could otherwise lead to a shift of assets, with no net increase in voluntary saving for the individual or for the economy as a whole.

The *insurance* function would be provided jointly by all three pillars, since broad diversification is the best way to insure in a very uncertain world. Remember the old adage that modern finance has rediscovered — don't put all your eggs in one basket. In the system just described, each mandatory basket would carry between one-third and two-thirds of the total mandatory eggs for covered workers as a group, while the voluntary basket would carry varying amounts depending on personal references. Insurance against specific risks such as longevity, disability, and dependent survivors would be provided by each pillar and, moreover, the three pillars together would co-insure against unknown risks by diversifying across types of management (public versus private), sources of funding (income from labour versus capital), and investment strategies (equities versus bonds, domestic versus international). Whatever unpredictable disasters occur in the future — as they surely will — this diversified system is most likely to continue to provide protection for the old.

*How to make the transition.* At least two methods are available for making the transition — abrupt and gradual. Under the *abrupt transition* the clock would be stopped on the old system, giving people credit for their service under the old system (as by the "recognition bonds" that were issued in Chile or the compensatory pensions in Argentina) and putting all entering workers or all workers under a specified age into the new system. (Workers above the specified age may be given a choice.) In effect, the implicit pension debt is converted into an explicit debt. While this may place such countries on an improved long-term path, it may also involve upheaval and uncertainty in the short run. For example, we do not know for sure how the financial market will react to the conversion of implicit into explicit debt. On the one hand, it may not react at all if full information was incorporated into previous decisions; on the other hand, it may react negatively if the transition suddenly makes people aware of how large the implicit debt is or hardens the obligations; or on the third hand it may react positively if this signals that the future debt and fiscal burden will contract instead of continuing to expand. In the Latin American countries where the public system was virtually bankrupt the financial markets reacted well to the switch, but in most industrialized countries the uncertainty involved may inhibit the willingness to make an abrupt transition.

Under the *gradual transition*, the clock does not stop on the old system. Instead, a plan is developed for reducing the implicit debt by gradually downsizing and flattening out benefits and raising the retirement age in the old system, so it becomes the smaller public pillar in the recommended multipillar system. If wages are growing, this can be accomplished by setting a real cap on benefits so that, over time, public pension expenditures fall relative to the wage bill. At the same time, a second funded pillar is started immediately out of incremental contributions and is gradually augmented out of resources saved in the public pillar. Benefits from the private pillar increase as benefits from the compressed public pillar decrease. Hopefully the incremental contributions that start this off will be less distortionary, more politically acceptable and in the long run smaller if allocated to a funded defined contribution pillar rather than to a PAYG-defined benefit pillar. This strategy is most easily applied in countries (such as Canada and the United States) that currently have a relatively low contribution and benefit rates. But for all countries, the sooner they start building the second pillar, the more gradual the transition can be.

Nevertheless, a *financing gap* is still likely to exist, albeit smaller in the gradual than in the abrupt transition. This financing gap can be covered through taxes, proceeds from the sale of public enterprises and/or (as in Chile) by a pre-existing budgetary surplus. In most cases, some degree of debt finance will be involved, so that a heavy double burden is not imposed on the transition generation of workers. Some of this debt will undoubtedly be purchased by the new pension funds. A strategy needs to be developed to repay this debt — over what time period will the repayment be made and by what form of tax? Spreading repayment out over many generations may be more equitable and politically palatable, but by perpetuating a larger government deficit it also fails to increase national saving and thereby defeats part of the purpose of the reform — so important trade-offs are involved.

*Reforming countries.* For the reasons discussed above, variations on the recommended multipillar scheme have recently been adopted in Chile, Argentina, and other Latin American countries, which used an abrupt transition towards mandatory saving plans in their second pillar; and Australia and Switzerland, which are gradually building mandatory occupational plans. In the Netherlands and Denmark collective bargaining has made funded occupational plans quasi-mandatory. In Japan employers are now permitted to opt out of the earnings-related part of the public program into their own decentrally controlled funded plans, while in the UK employers can opt out of the state program, workers can opt out of their employer's plan into their own personal retirement plans and the state earnings-related plan is disappearing as a result.

SOME QUESTIONS FOR CANADA

Following are some comments and questions that arise out of this analysis for Canada.

Canada already has the "redistributive public pillar" of the World Bank's multipillar system — the Old Age Security and Guaranteed Income Supplement (OAS and GIS). Means- and asset-tested programs are sometimes opposed on grounds that they are costly to administer and discourage voluntary saving. Tying such programs to the income tax system, as in Canada, is a simple way to administer them and accompanying them by a mandatory saving plan, as in Australia, would help solve the moral hazard problem.

The clawback mechanism currently in place for OAS essentially makes it means-tested, but at a relatively high income level. What are the criteria for setting the threshold for the clawback? Should the permissible income level be lowered and/or the degree of clawback raised? This would leave Canada with two different means-tested public pillars that apply over different income ranges. Should these two pillars (OAS and GIS) be merged, to simplify the system? Should an asset test be added to the GIS? This would make it much like Australia's means- and asset-tested public benefit, which is received, in whole or part, by about two-thirds of the population?

Canada's second or earnings-related pillar is the Canada Pension Plan (CPP), which is quite different from the second pillar recommended in *Averting the Old Age Crisis*. It is defined benefit, largely PAYG, and publicly managed, while *Averting* recommends a second pillar that is defined contribution, fully funded, and privately managed. Should the CPP be retained, but with moderate benefit cuts? A rise in the retirement age is one of the first cuts to come to mind. The important questions here are — how far and how fast? Should the retirement age be indexed to longevity, to remove it from the political arena over long periods? Or should a shift be made to a notional defined contribution plan (as in Sweden and Lativa), that automatically adjust the retirement age upward or index benefits downward for increased longevity?

Should pre-funding be added to the CPP, to avoid a major upswing in required contributions when the baby-boomers retire? If this is done, who will manage the funds? Is it feasible to have management by an "autonomous" government agency and what incentives will it face? Should the funds be invested in private as well as public sector securities and what effect will this have on corporate governance; will it lead to back-door nationalization of industry? How can political interference, low rates of return and excessive deficit finance be avoided? Will the resulting concentration of power imply centralized control over capital allocation in Canada?

Alternatively, should the CPP be eliminated or greatly downsized in order to create space for a mandatory fully-funded privately managed pillar, which would probably be defined contribution? If so, who will choose the investment managers — individual households, employers, and/or unions? How will the new mandatory funds be regulated, how will annuities be provided and what will be the impact on administrative costs?

Major arguments for continuing the CPP, albeit with funding, are that this will be least disruptive and people prefer the security of defined benefit plans. Major arguments for shifting responsibility to a new privately managed funded pillar are the poor experience of numerous countries with public pension reserves, the general observation that a country's capital stock is best allocated by the private rather than the public sector, as well as the political judgement that people are more likely to accept a higher contribution rate and its effect will be less distortionary if it goes into their own retirement savings accounts.

If a shift is made to a privatized second pillar, should the transition be abrupt or gradual? In either case, how will it be financed? That is, how will the government continue paying the promised benefits to current retirees and older workers, while part of the contribution of younger workers is diverted to the private pillar? To what extent will benefit promises be reduced, how much debt finance should be used and how will the debt be repaid?

Should Canada begin to keep track on a regular basis of its social security and other unfunded liabilities and of the probable intergenerational tax and transfer burdens implied by alternative systems, in order to remove the current bias in favour of implicit over explicit debt?

Canada also has a tax-advantaged voluntary pillar consisting of RRSPs. Should these tax advantages be extended to encourage more voluntary saving, or cut back, to reduce the taxes lost? If they encourage additional saving and thereby reduce the demand for public pension spending, tax deductions or credits may be a cheap way for society to buy old age security and increased capital formation, but if they merely encourage a substitution of tax-advantaged for non-tax-advantaged forms of saving, the tax subsidy constitutes a redistribution to upper- and middle-income groups without any net efficiency impact.

FINAL THOUGHTS

The major message of this report for developing countries is: the system that seemed best for industrialized countries 50 years ago is not the best system for you today; you can learn from their mistakes and do better. Once a PAYG system has been adopted and coverage is widespread, it is very difficult to change. So think carefully before you start or expand your systems in this direction.

The major message for industrialized countries is: the world has changed dramatically over the past 50 years, closing some opportunities but opening others. Real wage growth has slowed down and population growth has come to a halt in OECD countries, so that tax rates will have to go up sharply if the pay-as-you-go system is retained. It has become increasingly important to minimize work disincentives and to increase labour productivity through capital accumulation, which the public pillar alone is not well suited to do. Financial markets are better developed than they were before and are global in nature, allowing funded plans to benefit from international diversification. Under these changed conditions, the PAYG payroll-tax-financed system that seemed right to many in the past is not necessarily right for the future.

In addition, in the past poverty among the old was reduced without much lifetime redistribution from rich to poor, largely because the entire retired generation benefited from a positive income transfer through the old age security system. But that positive transfer has now come to an end and is about to turn negative. Unless both the benefit and contribution structure become more targeted, as in the recommended design of the public pillar, old age systems will contribute to the growing polarization of income among workers and will fail to avoid poverty among the old.

When today's retirees entered the labour force 50 or 60 years ago, the economy was very depressed, but it got better over their lifetimes and now they are one of the wealthiest groups in the population, enjoying a comfortable old age. Will today's young workers fare similarly well? Are they worried about the availability of jobs? Are they optimistic about wage growth? How will they feel if their net disposable income and therefore their standard of living increases little over their working lives, as contribution rates demanded by PAYG pension, health and social insurance systems rise? Relatedly, how will they feel when they realize that they are getting back a low, perhaps even a negative, return on their lifetime contributions? Are the baby-boomers saving enough voluntarily to provide a cushion if the post-baby-boomers refuse to pay these high contribution rates and benefits are cut unexpectedly?

*Averting the Old Age Crisis* argues that old age security systems that contain a large funded component, have decentralized competitive management of these funds, give workers ownership rights over the funds, and also include a social safety net, are most likely to address these concerns — by promoting growth, protecting low-wage earners and diversifying, thereby reducing risk. While every country may not choose this path, every country should give these arguments careful thought.

# APPENDIX

## Myths and Realities About Old Age Security

Myths abound in discussions of old age security. Consider the following:

*Myth 1.* Old people are poor, so government programs to alleviate poverty should be directed to the old.

*Fact.* The old are better off than the young, when comparisons are based on (expected) lifetime income rather than current income. Why? Because people with higher incomes are more likely to live long enough to become old, whereas people with low incomes are more likely to have many children and die young. Targeting young families with children, or reducing payroll taxes of these groups, is a better measure for alleviating poverty than targeting the old.

*Myth 2.* Public social security programs are progressive, redistributing income to the old who are poor.

*Fact.* Empirical studies in countries such as Sweden, the Netherlands, the United Kingdom and the United States show little or no redistribution from the lifetime rich to the lifetime poor. Even in countries where benefit formulas look progressive, four factors neutralize most of this effect: the first people covered by new plans are invariably middle- and upper-income groups, and they typically receive large transfers. Ceilings on taxable earnings keep the lid on tax differences between rich and poor. When benefit formulas are based on earnings near retirement upper-income groups benefit even more. And finally, the rich tend to have a longer life expectancy, hence collect these benefits for more years.

*Myth 3.* Social security programs insure pensioners against risk by defining benefits in advance.

*Fact.* Benefit formulas have been redefined frequently, so substantial political risk remains.

*Myth 4.* Only governments can insure pensioners against group risks, such as inflation, and most do so.

*Fact.* Most developing countries do not index pensions for inflation in their publicly managed programs, and some privately managed plans do index benefits.

*Myth 5.* Individuals are myopic but governments take the long view.

*Fact.* Governments have repeatedly made decisions about old age programs based on short-run exigencies rather than long-run effects. Pay-as-you-go programs, overly-generous benefits and early retirement provisions are prime examples.

*Myth 6.* Government action is needed to protect the interests of unborn generations.

*Fact.* Most public pay-as-you-go pension schemes provide the largest net benefits to workers who are 30 to 50 years old when the schemes were introduced. The unborn children and grandchildren of these workers are likely to receive negative transfers as the system matures and the demographic transition proceeds.

*Myth 7.* The consumption of today's retirees can only be supported by the domestic output of today's workers, so past saving is irrelevant.

*Fact:* Past saving can enhance capital accumulation, hence make today's workers more productive, some past saving can be embedded in consumer durables that continue to provide a stream of services for many years, and some can be invested abroad; when these are redeemed they finance an inflow of consumer goods produced by foreign workers. For all these reasons, past saving enhances current domestic consumption capacities, which is especially important as the dependency rate rises.

NOTE

1.  This paper draws heavily on *Averting the Old Age Crisis: Policies to Protect the Old and Promote Growth*, of which Estelle James was the principal author. All facts and figures are drawn from that book.

REFERENCE

World Bank (1994), *Averting the Old Age Crisis: Policies to Protect the Old and Promote Growth*, Washington, DC: World Bank and Oxford University Press.

# CHAPTER THREE

# Public and Private Roles in the Provision of Retirement Income

*Andrew Dilnot*

## INTRODUCTION

Pension provision has come a long way since Bismarck's desire to avoid revolution by tying German workers into the future of the state in the early 1880s, or the first UK provision of state pensions in 1908 to the "very old, very poor, and very good."[1] Most countries now have highly developed state and private regimes. But there is great turmoil in pension provision. There is a widespread concern about the future tax implications of continuing with state provision on the current scale as populations age, but also concern about relying on private sector provision.

In this brief paper, the second section outlines a range of possible roles for government in pension provision. In the third section we consider the development of state pension provision in Europe, and especially the United Kingdom, how that is now changing, and what the future may hold. In the fourth section we move on to discuss a number of issues that relate to the role of government with respect to a larger private sector share in pension provision. The conclusions follow.

## WHAT ROLES FOR GOVERNMENT?

### Redistribution

At least three types of redistribution exist within most pension schemes provided by the public sector: redistribution within generations; redistribution between generations; and redistribution across individual lifecycles.[2] All three of these may have as their primary goal the alleviation of poverty, or some more complex distributional objective. The redistribution within generations comes partly from explicitly higher returns on contributions for some individuals, such as those with low lifetime earnings, or who have performed caring duties, and partly from systematic differences in mortality, such as that between men and women, and that between the typically longer lived affluent and the shorter lived poor. There may also be provisions for, for example, earlier entitlement to pensions for women in general, or even, as in France, especially early entitlement for those who have borne many children.

Redistribution from one generation to another can be particularly dramatic when pension schemes begin, as in much of Western Europe in the postwar period, and when they decline, as in much of Western Europe now. When state pension schemes are set up, it is often the case that those already retired or close to retirement are treated more favourably than would be implied by their complete or substantial lack of contributions in the past. Conversely, when state systems unwind, the working population must still pay contributions to fund the typically pay-as-you-go (PAYG) pension of the retired, while needing to make contributions to provide themselves with a funded pension.

State involvement in individuals smoothing their lifetime income and consumption paths is common, and can appeal to the imperfection of capital markets, but in the case of pension provision seems more closely related to pure paternalism.

## Paternalism/Coercion

A minimalist view of the role of government might condone a closely targeted poverty alleviation benefit for the elderly poor, but would be unlikely to support the type of comprehensive and compulsory state provision seen in much of the developed world. Three sets of arguments can be put forward for such paternalistic and coercive action.

The first is information failure. Here the suggestion is that individuals simply do not have the range of information they need to make sensible decisions in this area, or cannot understand it. Individuals may make poor estimates of their likely longevity, of when they will retire, of what other resources they will have to rely on, of how private pensions will perform, or of how much they need to save to provide a given post-retirement standard of living. In principle all these questions could be answered, but the most effective response may simply be for government to step in and make compulsory public or private provision so as to "save people" from their own ignorance. And if this seems too bold, the provision of information both directly and through compulsory information provision from providers of private products seems clearly desirable.

The second is preference failure, and in particular inconsistency in preferences at different ages. At 20 years of age, 30 may seem a venerable age, and retirement hopelessly distant and so boring as not to be worth making any current sacrifices for. At age 70, the exuberance of youth may seem like excess with hindsight, and worrying about whether there is enough money to pay the heating bill may not be compensated for by hazy recollections of misspent pension contributions. It may be perfectly sensible for government to seek to avoid individuals finding themselves in such a situation, by education at least, but perhaps also through state provision or compulsory private provision.

The third is free-riding. Where a country provides an income and/or asset-tested benefit for the retired, there is clearly a potential problem of discouraging saving for those who cannot accumulate enough private savings to gain much from the act of private saving. For those whose private income in retirement would have the effect of reducing state benefits but giving little net gain, the temptation to make no provision, and simply rely on state benefits paid for by the taxes of others is strong. If this is believed to be a problem the obvious response of government is to make private pension contributions, whether from employee or employer, compulsory.

## Market Failure

A third general set of arguments for state involvement is that there may be inherent market failures in a private market for pensions. Market failures in general arise for two main sets of reasons: market power wielded by buyers or sellers and asymmetries of information between buyers and sellers. Both of these forms of market failure potentially affect pension provision, and public provision has been suggested as a response to this. We should be clear though that unless all asymmetries of information or sources of market power are removed, scope for problems is likely to persist.

The most serious form of market failure here seems likely to be adverse selection in the market for annuities. Individuals are likely to know more about their life expectancy than a pension provider. If firms sell annuities at a price that reflects average longevity, those expecting long lives will buy heavily, and eventually push up the price, making annuities bad value for those of average longevity or below. Compulsory scheme membership, either of a government scheme or of a private scheme removes this problem, except in so far as there is self-selection of individuals into particular firms in the case of privately provided plans.[3]

## Regulation

The three general arguments for government involvement in pensions that we describe above — redistribution, paternalism, and market failure — are typically thought of primarily in terms of direct provision by government. But there is also a substantial role for government in regulation of any private sector provision that does exist, and the regulatory role crosses all of the other types of state activity. Although many problems arise where governments attempt to enforce redistribution within private sector contracts, as we discuss at greater length later, such attempts are often made. Differing compulsory retirement ages according to gender, compulsory equal annuity rates for men and women despite clear and systematic mortality differences, are two examples of relatively common features of regulation of private pensions. Where, as in Australia for example, employer contributions to private pensions are compulsory, we see a clear regulatory intervention into private contracts. And insurance market failures can be tackled within private schemes if governments allow scheme membership to be a compulsory part of the employment contract. In the United Kingdom the 1988 reforms made it illegal to compel workers to join employer-based pension schemes. Close to 20 percent of those eligible now do not join (Dilnot *et al.* 1994).

Regulatory activity also clearly has scope to reduce information and preference failure through imposition of rules about what must and may be said when selling pension products. The UK experience has been one of fairly substantial requirements made of providers, but as yet there is little evidence as to whether the information provided is improving understanding or making matters worse.

Beyond the regulation of information there is widespread acceptance of the need for high standards to be maintained in the monitoring and regulation of investment behaviour. The extreme libertarian might be content to leave these issues to the market, but especially in a world where there is increasing reliance on private provision, such a route seems hard to defend. This though, is not to deny the possibility of self-regulation, essentially through club-like mechanisms (see Pension Law Review Committee 1993).

### DEVELOPMENT OF STATE PENSIONS IN EUROPE

The beginnings of modern state pension provision in Europe were in the early 1880s in Bismarck's Germany. There, one of the declared intentions was to preempt revolutionary sentiments by giving a wider group of the population something to lose. With sentiments ranging from this to much more egalitarian and redistributive ones, many Western European countries had reasonably extensive, although nowhere comprehensive, schemes in place at some time before the World War II.

These varied in character, with some claiming to be funded insurance schemes, some pay-as-you-go social insurance schemes, and some means-tested schemes funded from general taxation. The disasters of the First World War, hyper-inflation, and the Great Depression destroyed some of these schemes completely, and left most in tatters. So the scene was clear in most countries for fairly bold reform after the Second World War, and in many cases bold reform was delivered.

Much has been written about the extent to which the UK Beveridge Report of 1942 drove the reform process beyond the United Kingdom. It is clear that many countries built "social insurance" schemes, but it is also striking that the UK scheme was rather untypical in that it began as a flat-rate scheme — all were to make the same lump-sum contribution, and all to receive the same lump-sum benefit on retirement. Most continental European schemes were explicitly earnings-related, with earnings-related contributions and earnings-related benefits. The funding method was almost exclusively pay-as-you-go.

During the postwar period the number of elderly people grew throughout Europe, and particularly rapidly in the UK. At the same time, benefit levels generally kept in line with average living standards at least. These two forces led to a need for substantial increases in revenue, which led in 1961 in the UK to the introduction of partially earnings-related contributions and in 1975 of fully earnings-related contribution. Although some element of earnings relation was introduced into a top-up benefit, the shift from lump-sum tax to a combined 20 percent tax on earnings through employee and employer contributions was arguably the single largest change in the tax system for the bulk of the population in postwar Britain (Dilnot and Kay 1990).

Throughout Europe, the last decade has seen many changes made to state pension provision to reduce its generosity in response to the growth of spending, and the very substantial further growth in prospect because of the shift in demographic structures towards a larger elderly population (HMSO 1993). In the UK, the big change come in 1980 when we moved from a policy of (generally) uprating the flat-rate state pension in line with earnings inflation to one of price uprating. The state pension was 20 percent of average earnings in 1977, is now less than 15 percent, and could well be only 6 percent or 7 percent by the year 2040. The corollary of this and/or that which has allowed it to happen, has been an increase in the generosity of means-tested benefits, and a growth in the general level of pensioners incomes from non-state sources, both in coverage and level of private pension receipt and in investment income.

In the United Kingdom, the flat-rate state pension is now effectively condemned to a slow death. In the 1983, 1987, and 1992 general elections the Labour opposition was committed to a return to earnings indexation. Their position now accepts that earnings indexation from the current position would simply maintain a benefit that is not enough to live on. Returning the pension even to its 1977 position would mean tax increases equivalent to 5 percentage points on the rate of income tax, which it seems they will not contemplate. So from here we seem likely to see, at best, price indexation of the main benefit, more rapid increases in the benefits for the least well-off, and perhaps some attempt to improve the workings of the income- and assets-tested benefits to reduce problems of non-take-up. Alongside this "poverty alleviation" strategy will be some state role in providing earnings-related pensions of some type and possibly in making private provision compulsory.

All this is a long way from the postwar consensus of universal comprehensive social insurance. Why have we come so far in the UK, and are we to be followed down a similar path by much of Europe? At least four developments seem important. First, the growth in the tax cost of increasing numbers of elderly was not clearly analyzed, nor its scale realized. In some countries, such as the UK, this was because it was assumed that it would be acceptable to see benefits increased only in line with prices while economic growth provided extra tax revenue. But in others, it was simply expected to be sustainable.

For a wide range of reasons, politicians now seem to believe that tax increases are out of the question, at least during election campaigns, and despite tax shares in Europe ranging from 36 percent of GDP in the UK to 58 percent in Denmark, there is a popular orthodoxy that globalization makes tax increases impossible (see OECD 1995).

Second, as the underlying distribution of pensioner incomes has become much more like that of those of working age, the efficiency of comprehensive state provision as a means of alleviating low incomes has fallen. In the immediate postwar period the correlation between old age and poverty was high, and simply paying benefits to all retired people quite efficient. Now there is a growing sense that many elderly people do not need to be supported by tax-funded benefits.

Third, as the underlying distribution of earnings has widened, and with it the distribution of contributions, the implicit rate of return for those on above average incomes has fallen.

And fourth, clearly endogenous, there is a growing realization among those of working age that any pension they receive from the state will be small, and may not exist at all, which further reduces the constituency for higher taxes for higher benefits now, which are increasingly seen as unsustainable.

The UK response to this has been a growing political consensus that we must concentrate direct state provision on those with low incomes, while also thinking about ways of enabling, encouraging or compelling the provision of top-up pensions, both private and possibly public. If the attitude to taxation of the last 20 years persists, which seems at least plausible, we seem likely to see this kind of model spread further across Europe (see e.g., Social Justice Commission 1994; and Retirement Income Inquiry 1995).

This new structure of state activity, with poverty alleviation or prevention achieved primarily through income- and/or assets-tested provision which does not really claim to be "social insurance," alongside state exhortation or compulsion or both to make additional provision is a very long way from the systems envisaged by the postwar settlement. And it is worth repeating that simply privatizing the provision of a large section of retirement income will not change the sum of individuals' net payments of taxes, social security contributions, and private pension contributions in steady state *unless* the underlying redistributive intent of government is changed at the same time. This, of course, is what has happened in the UK and elsewhere; what has been accepted is that while those at the bottom of the income distribution for the elderly should still be substantial net recipients, those slightly higher up must rely more heavily on shifting their own lifetime incomes across their own lifecycles.

The reason that this shift has been accepted is, at least in part, that the underlying distribution of pensioner incomes has changed dramatically, even over the last 30 years, so that the state pension which used to be closely targeted on those at the very bottom of the overall income distribution now spreads much further up, making a general benefit for all pensioners, set at a level adequate for a decent life, seem much harder to defend. The trend towards higher non-state incomes among the elderly thus perpetuates and supports itself.[4]

These changes seem reasonable enough as choices for politicians to offer and for electorates to accept, but the reality has been that such changes are rarely discussed fully and openly. In the UK since 1980 the level of the basic state pension, which the retired believed they had paid for through their contributions to a "social insurance" scheme, has fallen by 40 percent relative to earnings. This shift happened without those who were retired, or close to retirement, having any chance to alter their accumulation of private pensions so as to adjust for reduced expectations from the state, and many have suffered hardship. If such changes are to be made fairly, it would be much better to have them phased in slowly, ideally affecting the accumulation of state pension rights by those of working age rather than the pensions in payment of the already retired. Such a route would require rare openness from politicians.

## Are Payments from the State Really Pensions?

All this leads to a fundamental question about how we should think of state "pensions." The pervasive name for European state pensions has been "social insurance," but this has covered so wide a range of schemes, from funded schemes with little redistributive intent to unfunded schemes with very substantial redistributive intent, that the term is now almost empty of any coherent meaning.

Alongside the enormous cross-section variation in types of regime with a single name, are the dramatic changes in individual schemes over time. It takes 70 years for a pension scheme to reach maturity. I am not aware of any state "pensions" scheme that has come even close to reaching its seventieth birthday in a form that leaves it close in form and function to that which it had at birth. The "contract" between citizen and government is typically simply insufficiently clearly defined to make controlling change feasible.

With hindsight it seems that in Europe at least, and especially in the United Kingdom, we should have thought of social security contributions as a loosely hypothecated tax, and certainly not as anything resembling a contribution to a savings scheme.

This is one of the arguments used by those who favour shifting public pension provision from the almost universal PAYG format now seen, to a funded basis. The suggestion is that by moving to funded public pensions, governments' ability to renege on pension promises will somehow be reduced. It probably is fair to argue that this is true in part, but in practice the experience of funded state pensions has been rather similar to that of unfunded pensions and funds have been mismanaged, or not replenished, or simply inadequate.

Other defences for moving to funded provision exist, the most commonly advanced of which is that such a move would increase aggregate savings.[5] The evidence on this claim is unclear, and while higher savings would normally lead to higher investment in a closed economy, in open economies with a relatively free international capital market such a link seems unlikely.

THE PROSPECTS FOR PRIVATE PROVISION

Even without the types of change to public sector provision outlined above, the scale and coverage of private pension provision seems certain to grow in the next few decades. Pensions are classically superior goods, the paid labour market participation of women has grown and will continue to grow, and general prosperity is increasing alongside a widening of the underlying earnings and income distribution. But if the trends we have seen in the United Kingdom, and to a lesser extent in the rest of Europe, continue, further questions will arise about private provision and the role of government.[6]

Perhaps the largest issue facing governments with respect to private provision is compulsion. We have already described the potential free-riding problem caused by generous, or even not terribly generous, income- and/or assets-tested state provision for the elderly. Compulsory contributions to private pension schemes are an obvious response to such concerns, and have now risen to quite high levels in, for example, Australia. Even where free-riding is not a concern, paternalistic arguments can be put forward for compulsion.

Compulsion raises many difficult questions, but perhaps one of the most central is: When is a compulsory contribution not a tax? The least unsatisfactory answer to this seems to be that compulsory contributions to a pension scheme where there is a genuine choice over the form and provider, and where no intentional and systematic redistribution occurs, might not be called a tax or thought of as such.

Further avenues for state intervention in private provision are many. One of the central features of state provision has traditionally been portability, while one of the motivations for private provision from the employers' point of view has been centred over labour market turnover for certain staff. The general trend has been towards encouraging portability, which raises particular difficulties with defined benefit schemes, but seems likely to remain an issue.

The taxation of private pensions is an increasingly contentious issue, as governments seek to find ways of raising revenue through widening tax bases to be cut. The almost universal tax regime is one where contributions to pensions are tax relieved, fund income and capital gains are untaxed, and receipt of pensions is taxed (see Dilnot 1994). This regime effectively treats pensions as deferred earnings, and confers an expenditure-tax-type tax treatment. This seems the most appropriate system, but has the fault that it can be suggested, for example, that taxing fund income and capital gains would raise substantial revenues.

Two responses are necessary to such suggestions. First, finding a way of taxing the income of financial institutions holding assets on behalf of individuals with varying marginal income tax rates, and where the income is unadjusted for inflation, is extremely difficult, and in practice impossible to do fairly, as argued in Dilnot (1994). Second, if such an attempt is made, as in New Zealand, where both contributions and fund income are taxed, the resulting system imposes a tax penalty on pension saving, which in the New Zealand experience has reduced substantially the scale and coverage of private pensions, and driven savings into other less penally taxed assets. The result has been lower pension saving and rather little tax revenue.

Perhaps the most contentious issue in this general area, and one that has already generated much heat in Europe is gender-neutral annuity rates. Equality is a grand word, and perhaps all the economist should aim for professionally is to be clear about what types of equality are being discussed. In the case of gender-neutral annuity rates much confusion exists between those advocating equality of outcome (that women should receive the same annual payments as men for a given payment, although they live longer) and those advocating equality of treatment (that a given payment should buy a flow of income of the same present value whatever the gender of the purchaser). Attempts to enforce equality of outcome are deliberately redistributive, and need to be seen as such if they are to be effective.

More generally the future for private provision seems likely to see a continued shift from defined benefit to defined contribution schemes. This shift raises many issues, but most importantly that of dealing with capital market uncertainty. The traditional defined benefit final salary scheme has many attractive features, but perhaps the most important was the intergenerational pooling of capital market risk. This was no doubt done perfectly, but nonetheless was done, and was one of the features that allowed relatively high returns to be earned through heavy reliance on equity investment rather than interest-bearing assets.

Capital market solutions to the problem of risk-pooling within and between generations for populations with individual-based defined contribution schemes do exist, but are at an early stage of development. Unless such solutions can be made effective, there is a substantial risk of a shift towards generally lower earning assets so as to reduce risk. Such a shift would be extremely unwelcome.

This discussion of risk points to the reality that whereas in public debate the tendency is to assume that certain types of pension are far riskier or less risky than others, in fact all types of pension are risky, they simply face different types of risk. At least six types of risk exist:

1. *capital market risk*, reflecting fluctuating rates of return;

2. *earnings risk*, reflecting fluctuating earnings;

3. *labour market risk*, reflecting fluctuating unemployment rates;

4. *political risk*, reflecting the uncertainty of state provision;

5. *job tenure*, reflecting unknown duration; and

6. *inflation*, reflecting uncertain future prices.

Public pensions, for example, are at little risk from capital market fluctuations, but are subject to political risk, inflation shocks, and labour market risks, and in some cases to earnings risks. Defined benefit, final salary private schemes are relatively free from capital market risk for individuals, but highly sensitive to earnings and job tenure risk. Defined contribution plans, on the other hand, are less vulnerable to job tenure or earnings risk, but can be highly subject to capital market risk. The reality is that all pension saving is risky, and we must identify and manage the risk associated with whatever form of pension we have.

Finally, it is perhaps worth making two more speculative points. First, while for many individuals the development of adequate private pension saving will be hard to achieve, for a small but growing minority pension provision at an adequate level may well be secure. For this group, typically at the top end of the income distribution, forms of saving which are subject to fewer controls are likely to become more attractive. As traditional models of lifecycle income and consumption patterns become less and less representative of typical experience, the need and demand for non-pension wealth will grow. In the United Kingdom since 1987 we have seen Personal Equity Plans (PEPs) and Tax Exempt Special Savings Accounts (TESSAs), schemes that give tax relief on the return to saving in equities and interest-bearing assets respectively, grow to aggregate levels of £50 billion, relative to total private pension assets of £600 billion, and GDP around £700 billion. These trends seem likely to continue.

Second, there is growing awareness that a flat profile of income in retirement, even flat in real terms, is inadequate. Over a 30-year period of retirement, not unusual for a woman, price indexation of a pension could imply as much as a halving in the relative living standard. And perhaps more important still, costs may well rise in the later stages of life, to deal with care and disability, implying the need for some additional insurance element within pension schemes. Over the next few decades, pension plans will need to respond to major changes in demands and expectations. We are not even close to a quiet, stable retirement for either pension providers or interested economists.

CONCLUSION

The high point of the share of state provision in the overall level of pension provision has almost certainly been reached. For the future, it is vital that governments and electorates face that reality openly, since the last two decades have seen a number of cases of governments effectively breaking implied or at least believed contracts. Provided there is openness there is no necessary disaster in a shift to greater reliance on targeted benefit spending by government.

But a more narrowly defined role for government in provision will still leave much regulation and control of the private sector to be done. And the private sector faces a great need to innovate and develop if it is to meet the demands of a growing and increasingly affluent retired generation.

NOTES

1.  See Kohler and Zacher (1982) for discussion of early development of social insurance.
2.  See Diamond (1977) for the classic discussion of the functions of social security.
3.  See Brugiavini (1993) for an interesting insight into the timing of annuity purchase.
4.  See Goodman and Webb (1994) for evidence on changing UK income distribution.
5.  See Aaron (1966); Feldstein (1974) for early contributions to this debate; and Dilnot (1994, ch. 3) for a summary of the current position.
6.  See OECD (1995) for a discussion of the growth and role of private provision.

REFERENCES

Aaron, H. (1966), "The Social Insurance Paradox," *Canadian Journal of Economics*, 32: 371-74.

Brugiavini, A. (1993), "Uncertainty Resolution and the Timing of Annuity Purchases," *Journal of Public Economics*, 50:31-62.

Diamond, P. (1977), "A Framework for Social Security Analysis," *Journal of Public Economics*, 8:275-98.

Dilnot, A. (1994), "Taxation and Private Pensions," in *Private Pensions and Public Policy*, Paris: OECD.

Dilnot, A. and J. Kay (1990), "Tax Reform in the UK: The Recent Experience" in *World Tax Reform*, ed. M. Boskin and C.E. McLure, San Francisco, CA: ICS Press.

Feldstein, M. (1974), "Social Security, Induced Retirement, and Aggregate Capital Accumulation," *Journal of Political Economy*, 82:905-26.

Goodman, A. and S. Webb (1994), *For Richer, For Poorer*, London: The Institute for Fiscal Studies.

HMSO (1993), *Containing the Cost of Social Security – The International Context*, London: Her Majesty's Stationery Office.

Kohler, P. H. and H.F. Zacher, eds. (1982), *The Evolution of Social Insurance*, London: Frances Pinter.

Organisation for Economic Cooperation and Development (1995), *OECD Economic Outlook*, Paris: OECD.

Pension Law Review Committee (1993), *Pension Law Reform*, London: HMSO

Retirement Income Inquiry (1995), *Pensions 2000 and Beyond.*

Social Justice Commission (1994), *Social Justice,* London: Vintage.

# Comments

## Robin Boadway

### INTRODUCTION

In my comments, I want to address some of the principles of public finance that might guide our thinking about the role of the public sector in the provision of pensions. My comments will be complementary to those of both Andrew Dilnot and Estelle James.

Andrew stresses three sorts of reasons for public intervention in the provision of retirement income, and I am in broad agreement with him. The first of these is a redistributive motive, interpreted to include redistribution across generations, redistribution across households within a given generation, and redistribution across each household's lifecycle. The second is a paternalistic motive said to arise because of what he refers to as information failure and preference failure, as well as free-riding on the system. The final one is conventional market failure arising from monopoly power and adverse selection in insurance markets. Let me begin with some observations about each of these from a slightly different perspective.

*Observation One.* It is a fact that a surprisingly large proportion of the population does not save enough for their own retirement based on any sensible reckoning about intertemporal preferences and rational decision making. This seems to be one of the main reasons why governments lend a hand. This deficiency in own retirement savings is especially startling given the need not only to save for normal expected consumption during retirement, but also to self-insure against two main forms of risk that exist in retirement (uncertainty about the length of life and uncertainty about the need for extraordinarily high expenditures) and to satisfy normal bequest motives. Moreover, the form in which households save for retirement, to the extent that they do, is typically quite bizarre. Apart from the highest income groups, wealth is held disproportionately in the form of equity in housing and other durables. These are not particularly suitable instruments for self-insurance. They may be suitable as forms of bequest, but even those who have no heirs often hold wealth in this form at death.

The question is: Why is saving for one's own retirement so low and in such forms? Economists do not have well-documented answers for that, but it seems to me there are two possible answers: one is based on irrationality and the other on super-rationality. Irrationality covers what Dilnot refers to as preference failure or what some refer to simply as myopia. Public intervention is called for in this case for paternalistic reasons. Economists are naturally not very content with either the notion of irrationality as an explanation for behaviour or paternalism as a rationale for public sector intervention.

Could there be an alternative explanation for the fact that people systematically save too little? Economists now argue that maybe people are extremely smart and know that if they do not take care of their own retirement savings, society will do it for them. To use economic jargon, there is a classic Samaritan's Dilemma problem, with savers exploiting the time inconsistency of government policy. We can call this super-rationality, because people are essentially correct in predicting what will be the consequence of their behaviour. Governments universally do, in fact, come to the rescue of those who do not provide for themselves. This explanation has a certain appeal to it both because it fits the facts, because it does not depend upon irrationality of individuals or of the government, and it lends itself to a reasonable justification for public intervention, and one that the literature is increasingly coming to recognize as perhaps the single most important reason for public intervention in the provision of pensions.

Responding to the shortage of saving for retirement by simply redistributing *ex post* towards the retired has adverse consequences. It essentially validates and perpetuates the inefficiencies of the low level of savings. Thus, economists call for policies with longer planning horizons that offset the tendency to rely on the public sector to provide for one's retirement, and that requires policies that one way or another induce much greater savings for retirement by households themselves. Public intervention could, in principle, take many forms. It could be forced saving into funded plans (either in the public sector of the private sector). Or, it could be subsidizing saving for retirement, such as through tax-sheltered company and/or personal retirement saving plans. Or, it could be some combination of those.

Relying on increased saving for retirement by households themselves does not constitute a complete pension policy. Some persons will not have adequate lifetime resources to support themselves throughout their lives. Thus, some supplementation of private savings on purely redistributive grounds is inevitable.

*Observation Two.* The second observation I make is that public pensions are essentially annuities, so it is natural for economists to look, as Dilnot has done, to market failure in annuity markets as a rationale for public provision. I am suspicious of that argument for a couple of reasons. The first is that the types of market failures that are alleged to exist on annuity markets are hard to accept. As he mentions, this commonly takes the form of assuming that individuals have better enough information compared to insurance companies about their life expectancies to cause serious adverse selection problems. I somehow doubt it; informational problems of this sort do not deter the same companies from offering reasonably actuarially fair life insurance policies, assisted by medical records. This is not to say that annuity markets are perfect. They are probably far from it. But I suspect that asymmetric information is not the culprit.

The second reason to be suspicious is that, if annuity markets were so poor, individuals would make up for it by self-insurance (except those who are able to do it through company pensions). This would imply holding significant amounts of precautionary wealth, something that, as we have observed above, is counterfactual. Thus, we return to the first problem, which is that people do not save enough for their own retirement. In my view, market failure is not the culprit.

*Observation Three.* The third observation, or set of observations, concerns public pensions as intergenerational transfers, something that Dilnot mentions but is worth developing further. I think most public finance economists who study the rationale for public pensions would focus on their role as intergenerational redistribution devices. In so doing, they would recognize two main forms that a system of intergenerational transfers can take.

First, they can be permanent (ongoing) transfers from the young to the old, as in the case of Old Age Security/Guaranteed Income Supplement (OAS/GIS) in Canada, social security in the United States or public pensions in Europe. It is extremely difficult to make an economic case for permanent transfers from the young to the old. They make older cohorts better off during their phase-in, but, by reducing aggregate savings, they reduce long-run welfare significantly. On the contrary, if any ongoing intergenerational transfers are called for, it is in the other direction (from old to young).

Alternatively, intergenerational transfers that are temporary can provide a form of social insurance to unlucky cohorts, that is, intergenerational risk-sharing. Some cohorts are simply unluckier than others, such as those subject to adverse shocks like wars, natural disasters, or abrupt fluctuations in demographic make-up. Intergenerational risk-sharing involves transfers from lucky to unlucky ones. They are, by their very nature, of a temporary or transitory nature. Whether pensions are the best instruments for intergenerational risk-sharing purposes is an open question. Other forms of intergenerational transfers, such as debt, could also be used. Notice that implementing such policies requires both farsightedness and discipline on the part of governments.

It is the intergenerational transfer rationale that is important for determining the extent of funding of public pensions. The call for more funding is essentially equivalent to a call for reducing intergenerational transfers. It involves a judgement both about the adverse consequences of savings rates being too low, and about the desire to redistribute income across generations. Changing the extent of funding of public pensions inevitably involves a value judgement because it cannot be done without making some cohort worse off.

In making judgements about the funding of public pensions, it should be borne in mind that here are lots of other intergenerational transfers in the system besides unfunded pensions. For example, there is public debt, the current size of which is surprisingly of the same order of magnitude as the unfunded liability of the Canada Pension Plan (CPP) system, and probably even lower. There is also the provision of public services that are used especially intensively by the retired, including health and social services. These are also implicitly transfers from the young to the old, and serve to exacerbate the adverse savings effect of pensions (unless one believes in Ricardian equivalence, which in my view is very hard to accept). We could also include among intergenerational transfers from future generations to current generations the running down of public property, such as the environment, public infrastructure, and natural resources as an indirect form of intergenerational transfer.

The fact that intergenerational transfers typically run from younger to older cohorts means that saving for retirement is likely to be depressed. There is some uncertainty about the magnitude of this adverse effect on savings, and some of the literature on this is recounted in the World Bank document, *Averting the Old Age Crisis*. However, there is enough evidence, direct and indirect, to satisfy me that saving is adversely affected to a significant degree by existing policies, and that this may well entail domestic investment being reduced. Policies that respond *ex post* to shortages of saving for retirement are perfectly reasonable policies in the circumstance; but they are inevitably unfunded and so depress savings. Again, this points directly to the need for long-term planning on the part of governments.

To me, these observations together suggest that, in principle, government intervention in the provision of retirement income ought to be of three main sorts:

- It needs to make up for the observed shortage of private saving for retirement by at least part of the population. This intervention could be of various forms: it could involve forced saving, either into private pension schemes or public pension schemes (the coercive or "stick" solution); or, it could involve incentives for private saving for retirement, such as tax preferences for such savings. To be successful at raising savings rates, these schemes must be "funded" and the funds must go to their most productive uses. To repeat, this requires farsightedness by governments.

- The use of explicit intergenerational transfers, at least those that run from young to old, ought to be directed to intergenerational risk-sharing. This is of a transient nature and can involve various forms of intergenerational transfers, such as public pensions or debt, with debt perhaps being the more flexible.

- There inevitably needs to be a back-up system of redistributive transfers to the currently retired who simply do not have the resources to support themselves. By its nature, this should be a targeted program to those who need it most. Given that this would be financed from general revenues, some intergenerational transfer is inevitably involved, as is true for most government programs. But the intergenerational transfer is incidental and not a major purpose of the program.

But all of this presumes governments that are both benevolent and have very long time horizons. On the spectrum of views of economists (which probably does not overlap much with the spectrum of views of most other people), I would say I am near the end that thinks of government as being reasonably benevolent and well-meaning. That is, I think we can count on governments on average to redistribute reasonably well when needed. However, more than benevolence is needed when it comes to pension policy; governments also need to be far-sighted. Different people have different views about this, but I find it hard to accept that governments have anywhere near the length of time horizons required to implement ideal pension schemes involving full funding accompanied by transient intergenerational transfers for unlucky cohorts. Thus, we have to look at next-best policies.

In the context of Canada, I am driven to the following conclusions, which are quite compatible with those of Estelle James, though for slightly different reasons:

- We need to increase the use of reliance on incentives to private savings, such as tax assistance for private savings or mandated savings into private schemes.

- We need to give up on the idea of a fully-funded public pension, even one whose funds are managed privately, because we cannot be sure that full funding will be maintained.

- We probably need to phase out CPP as it now exists and design our pensions as a component of government redistributive policy to target those in need. It is hard to support an unfunded occupational pension plan like the CPP. There is simply no good argument for a pay-as-you-go pension whose payouts are based on past earnings.

# PART TWO

## CANADIAN EXPERIENCE

# CHAPTER FOUR

# Aging and Canada's Public Sector: Retrospect and Prospect

*Michael Wolfson and Brian Murphy*

## INTRODUCTION

Concerns about Canada's public pension system have risen significantly in the past year or so, following over a decade hiatus. The differences between the current debate and the "great pension reform debate" of the late 1970s and early 1980s, however, are considerable. A central question in the debate 15 years ago was whether Canada and Quebec Pension Plan (C/QPP) benefits should be doubled for everyone, or augmented by a homemaker pension (Canada. Task Force on Retirement and Income Policy 1980; Canada. Department of National Health and Welfare 1982; Canada. House of Commons 1983). Today, the proposals are virtually all in the opposite direction. Robson (1996) explicitly proposes abolishing the CPP, while 12 of 14 options presented in a recent government discussion paper involve cutbacks in benefits; the remaining two being increases in CPP payroll taxes (Canada. Minister of Finance 1996, p. 41). After more than a decade of stagnant real family incomes, and steadily rising cost projections for the CPP by its chief actuary, concerns about the costs and sustainability of Canada's public pension system have come to dominate concerns about the expected adequacy of future retirement incomes.

The objective of this paper is to provide a fairly detailed set of projections of the costs of Canada's public pension system under a range of scenarios. The scenarios themselves have been chosen mainly to clarify which factors are quantitatively most important. In addition, these cost projections have been set within a more comprehensive framework that includes cost and revenue projections for related government activities such as health-care expenditures and personal income tax revenues. Moreover, the analysis will consider not only aggregate figures such as costs, but also estimates of impacts of the various projection scenarios on the distribution of income among families generally, and the elderly in particular. This analysis is substantially an update and extension of Murphy and Wolfson (1991), which in turn built on Fellegi (1988).

We start with a brief review of historical trends in the aggregate costs of public pensions and public health care, the two major public sector activites disproportionately benefiting the elderly, and trends in the incomes of Canada's elderly. The main part of the analysis is then a series of computer simulations giving projections of the costs and distributional impacts of these programs under a range of scenarios, including anticipated demographic aging, changing labour force participation, maturation of the Canada and Quebec Pension Plans (C/QPP), alternative real economic growth scenarios, and legislated indexing provisions for income taxes and cash transfers.

Many of the results are similar to those of our earlier (Murphy and Wolfson 1991) paper. The results, as before, are also contrary to some of the conventional wisdom in today's pension debate. The main area where conventional wisdom continues to go astray is in its failure to appreciate the longer run implications of current tax/transfer indexing provisions. As a result, the public generally is overestimating the likely costs of the public pension system when the baby-boom cohorts attain age 65, and correspondingly underestimating future income tax revenues.

As was pointed out in our previous paper, however, these implications were understood by the technical *cognoscenti* in a 1986 International Monetary Fund analysis (Heller *et al.* 1986). A decade later, very similar conclusions were reached in a 1995 OECD analysis (Leibfritz *et al.*. 1995). Both studies project Canada as having one of the lowest economic burdens for public pensions among G7 countries at the time when the baby-boom cohort is having its most adverse impact on old age dependency ratios. For example, the OECD study, which examined not only C/QPP benefits and payroll taxes but also OAS/GIS, health care, and personal income taxes, concluded "Canada, with relatively favourable demographics, and pension schemes that run in surplus until 2020, also experiences a fall in net debt, despite health care expenditures rising more quickly than elsewhere [among the G7 countries]" (Leibfritz *et al.* 1995, p. 6).

The simulation scenarios to be presented below should help the reader understand these apparently sanguine views of the expected affordability of Canada's public pension system, emanating from two major international institutions, each with biases towards fiscal prudence.

On the other hand, both the 1986 International Monetary Fund (IMF) and 1995 OECD analyses, as well as the standard analyses available to the Canadian public such as those of the chief actuary (Canada. Office of the Superintendent of Financial

Institutions 1995), fail to point out the corollary implications of their projections in terms of income adequacy and the incidence of low income for the future elderly. The other side of the coin of the IMF's and OECD's projected public sector pension costs, costs they project as *not* unduly burdensome to the economy, is a substantial increase in the incidence of low income amongst the elderly. This analysis therefore points again to the horns of a dilemma — a substantial deterioration in the economic position of the elderly (the currently legislated scenario) or, if such deterioration is to be avoided, larger public sector costs for an aging population.

RETROSPECT

To begin, it is helpful to place the current costs of Canada's public pension system into an historical context. Since one of the factors underlying concerns about the future affordability of these programs is the anticipated aging of the population, it is also important to include other large government programs whose costs are sensitive to changes in the age structure of the population. Key among these is publicly funded health care. Figure 1 shows these program costs over the past 40 years, expressed as percentages of GDP.

FIGURE 1: Public Pension and Public Health-Care Expenditures as a Percentage of GDP

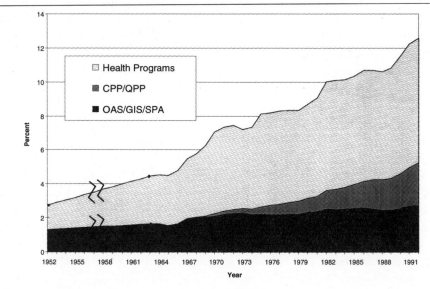

Source: Canada. Human Resources Development (1994).

As the figure shows, since the introduction of the income-tested Guaranteed Income Supplement with its companion Spouses Allowance program (GIS/SPA) in 1966, the major general revenue-financed portion of Canada's public pension system (i.e., OAS and GIS/SPA) has been growing steadily but slowly as a share of GDP since 1952 when the OAS first became a universal program, rising to about 2.8 percent in 1992. However, the C/QPP, which are payroll tax financed, have grown since their introduction in 1966 to almost the same share of GDP, 2.5 percent by 1992. Benefits from both parts of Canada's public pension system accrue almost entirely to the elderly (about 85 percent to those age 65 or over in 1994).

It is also worth noting that, in the context of increasing discussion of intergenerational equity, it is difficult to see in these trends any very dramatic "windfall" to the elderly in the late 1960s and early 1970s. The largest increases in these public pension programs, aside from the introduction and gradual maturation of the C/QPP, were increases in the basic level of the GIS. These increases, the last of which was in the early 1980s, were structured to benefit particularly the single elderly with the lowest incomes.

Concerns abut the impact of an aging population are directed not only to the public pension system, but also to the costs of publicly financed health care (e.g., Canadian Institute of Actuaries 1996). Public spending in this area has grown even faster, almost tripling since the mid-1960s. Of course, not all health care is directed to the elderly, about 26 percent in 1994. Moreover, almost *none* of the growth in health-care costs shown in Figure 1 is associated with aging of the population (Barer *et al.* 1989). Most of the increase in total health-care spending over this period is due to greater costs per person-year of population within any given age/sex grouping. In particular, overall spending has been rising mainly as a result of more intensive health-care servicing for individuals of all ages, in turn due to a combination of rising relative prices of health-care services, and more frequent and intensive interventions.

A similar situation with regard to costs applies to the major public in-kind benefit provided to the other end of the age spectrum, namely education. The school age population has fallen by about one-third as a proportion of the total population over the past two decades, while public sector education expenditures have fallen slightly from 5.6 percent in 1971 to 5 percent of GDP in 1991 (Gendron 1994). The reason these aggregate costs have not fallen in line with the drop in the student-age share of the population is that costs per pupil have risen about 0.7 percent per year faster than GDP and 3 percent faster than average wages over the past two decades.

Another important part of the retrospective is the evolving level and composition of the incomes of the elderly. While it is generally appreciated that government transfers (principally public pensions) make up a large portion of the incomes of the elderly, the usual statistics understate their importance. This is illustrated in Figure 2 giving data for 1993. The left-most column of the figure shows the usual data — the shares of public transfers, private investment income (interest, dividends, annuities), and labour income for the entire elderly population. From this viewpoint, over half of elderly incomes come from government sources, but almost 40 percent come from private investments.

However, private investment income is highly concentrated among the more well-off elderly. If we exclude the tenth of the elderly population with the highest total incomes, the resulting stacked bar graph is shown in the second column of Figure 2. When we consider this group of the remaining 90 percent of the elderly population, the overall share of private investment income falls to about 30 percent, while the share of government transfer income rises to about two-thirds. This is an instance of the general adage, "beware of the mean." The impression one gets from examining overall aggregates may not be representative of the typical situation for individual elderly families.

FIGURE 2: Income by Source as a Proportion of Total Income for All Elderly Individuals and for the Bottom 90 Percent of Elderly Individuals, Canada, 1993

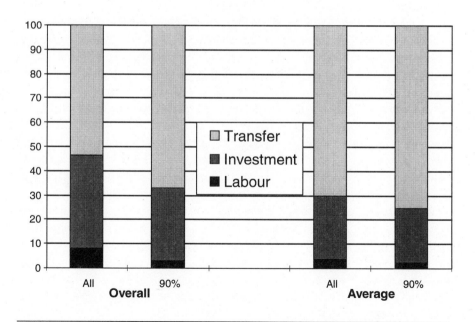

Source: Statistics Canada, 1993 *Survey of Consumer Finance*, Special Tabulations.

The right-most two columns in Figure 2 also address this statistical concern by showing incomes by source calculated differently. In these cases, we first compute the proportions for each income source at the micro level, that is, for each elderly person in the underlying sample database, and then average these proportions over all elderly individuals.[1] Generally, this indicator shows that the average proportion of income an elderly individual receives from public sources is about 70 percent, with investment income accounting for a bit over one-quarter (the third column). Finally, combining both steps by excluding the top 10 percent of the elderly population as well as averaging proportions (the last column), we see that government transfers average 75 percent of total income, while investment income averages 22.5 percent. In other words, for a large majority of the elderly, public pensions are a very important source of income.

Figure 3 uses these "average of proportions" indicators to trace the historical importance of different income sources. The left panel is for the non-elderly. Not surprisingly, labour income provides the major share of total income, though the share of transfers has more than tripled, moving from 5.5 percent to 18.5 percent over the period from the late 1960s to the early 1990s.

The right panel gives the corresponding data for the 65+ population. As a share of income, government transfers have been relatively stable, particularly for the last 20 years. The main trend has been a fall in income from working, with a corresponding increase in the average proportion of income from private investment.

A major question is the prospect in the future for a much more substantial growth in the importance of private investment income. The main reason for this widespread expectation is the dramatic increase in the volume of accumulated savings in registered saving arrangements (i.e., RRSPs and Registered Pension Plans or RPPs). These assets have more than doubled, as a percentage of GDP between 1981 and 1991(Statistics Canada 1992) and in 1991 had reached 71 percent of GDP, about $481 billion. However, if this growth in tax-assisted savings among the current working age population is skewed towards the upper end of the income spectrum in a way similar to recent patterns of private investment income among the current elderly, then the pattern shown above for the bottom 90 percent is unlikely to change significantly in future.

Unfortunately, data on the distribution of household wealth have not been collected by Statistics Canada for over a decade, nor are there any data connecting the large aggregate pools of private pension fund wealth to the distribution of individual incomes. Still, other data suggest that this dramatic growth in the aggregate volume of tax-assisted savings is based on a highly skewed pattern of contributions. Figure 4 provides new data on this point, drawn from detailed samples of income tax returns. Three time points are compared: 1972, 1981, and 1992.[2] In each case, only taxable returns were considered.

FIGURE 3: Income by Source as a Percentage of Total Income, Selected Years

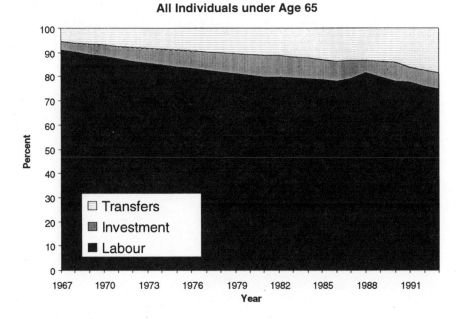

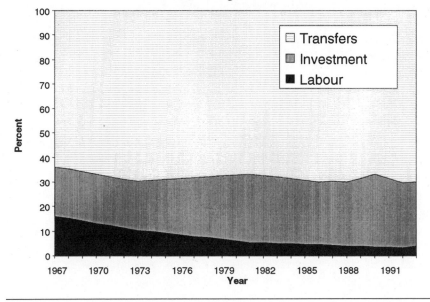

Source: Statistics Canada, selected *Surveys of Consumer Finance*, Special Tabulations.

FIGURE 4: Distribution of Private Pension Contributions by Labour Income
Decile: All Taxable Filers

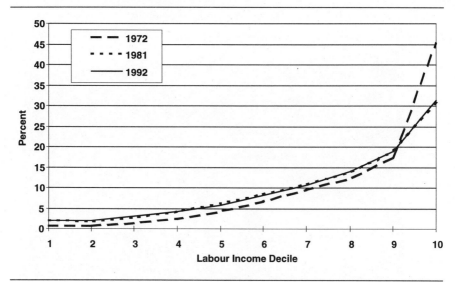

Source: Statistics Canada, selected Tax Return Files, Special Tabulations.

The taxfilers in each of these three years were first sorted in ascending order of
wages and salaries plus self-employment income, the base for RPP or RRSP contributions. Next, each of the three taxfiler populations was divided into ten equal
sized groups — earnings deciles. The curves in Figure 4 then show the proportion
of each year's aggregate individual contributions provided by each earnings decile.

For example, the top decile of earners with taxable returns in 1972 provided
about 46 percent of all RRSP+RPP contributions. This share dropped to about 32
percent in 1981, but has since risen closer to 35 percent in 1992. Other than these
changes in the top decile, the curves spanning two decades are almost identical.
Thus, even though RRSP and RPP assets have more than doubled as a percentage
of GDP over the second half of this period, the growth in private tax-assisted
retirement savings has not been associated with a broadened base of private pension plan contributions across the income spectrum. This latter point is also evident in the data on membership in RPPs (Statistics Canada 1992) which has been
roughly level at about 40 percent of the paid workforce, or even dropping somewhat, over recent decades.[3] As a result, a summary characterization of the trend in
private tax-assisted retirement savings is "pension deepening," where the future
cohorts of the elderly will have more income from private sources, but the increase

is most likely to be in the hands of those segments of the elderly population who already receive such income, namely the upper tail of the income distribution.

## SIMULATION APPROACH AND SCENARIOS

Given this brief retrospective, the main part of the analysis is a set of projections of the costs and distributional impacts of public pensions and other major public sector activities. These projections are in turn based on a special analytical tool, Statistics Canada's Social Policy Simulation Database and Model (SPSD/M; Bordt *et al.* 1992; Wolfson *et al.* 1989).

The SPSD/M has two main components, a database (SPSD), and a simulation model (SPSM). The database brings together data from several sources in order to create a "best estimate" of the household distribution of income, building on the comparative strengths of the different constituent datasets. The starting point for the SPSD is the 1988 *Survey of Consumer Finance*. It has been augmented with data from a sample of personal income tax returns, a sample of Unemployment Insurance (UI) claim histories, and expenditure patterns from the Family Expenditure Survey. The SPSD also includes a sample to represent the institutionalized elderly population.

The populations reporting receipt of specific sources of income on the SPSD, and their individual amounts, are adjusted (e.g., via imputation) to assure alignment with beneficiary count data and public accounts data on total program expenditures for CPP, QPP, GIS/SPA, UI, provincial Social Assistance, and tax return data on income from sources such as investments. For purposes of this analysis, detailed age-specific imputations to the SPSD of the monetary values of in-kind benefits from government expenditures on health care and education have also been included (Cameron and Wolfson 1994).

As a result of these statistical processes, the SPSD is a representative microdata sample of about 190,000 individuals in about 70,000 households. However, it should be noted that the individuals and households on the SPSD sample are synthetic, since their full microdata descriptions have each been pieced together from several separate and largely non-overlapping data sets.

The simulation modeling capacity of the SPSM has then been used to create a series of projection scenarios, starting with a base year of 1994 and three projection years:

- 2006 before any of the baby-boom reaches retirement,

- 2016 when the leading edge of the baby-boom birth cohorts has reached age 65, and

- 2036 when all baby-boomers are seniors, and C/QPP payouts are projected to peak.

All scenarios have:

- C/QPP employer contributions in addition to the 1994 combined rate of 5.4 percent netted from wages, equivalent to an assumption that all legislated payroll tax increases after 1994 will be fully shifted back onto employees' wages;

- fully phased-in Employment Insurance reforms as recently proposed (Canada 1995); and

- fully imputed in-kind publicly funded heath care and education benefits, based on detailed age/sex specific utilization data.

Beyond these common elements and target years, the specific scenarios are as follows:[4]

*Base1994*. The Social Policy Simulation Database is "aged" from 1988 to represent 1994:

- population projections by age, sex and province;

- Labour Force Survey employment estimates (weeks worked) for 1992 by age and sex; and

- income levels by source to reflect National Accounts and program expenditure aggregates.

Other characteristics generally remain as they were in the source 1988 data.

*MPPR: Maturation, Population and Participation Rates*. This set of scenarios for the years 2006, 2016, and 2036 makes adjustments to account for:

- maturation of the C/QPP, including full phase-in and higher benefits in the hands of women;

- population composition according to Statistics Canada's middle population projection series (Statistics Canada 1995) for individuals by age/sex/province;[5] and

- the chief actuary's (Canada. Office of the Superintendent of Financial Institutions 1995a) projections of labour force participation by sex and age.

*Economic Growth and Indexation*. We follow the chief actuary's most recent actuarial report for the CPP and assume CPI inflation of 3.5 percent, and then explore three real per capita economic growth scenarios: zero, 1, and 2 percent per annum. It may be noted that the chief actuary's economic growth assumption is 1 percent[6] while the 1995 OECD (Leibfritz *et al.* 1995) main assumption was 1.5 percent.

*Deeper Private Pensions.* The major increase in assets held by trusteed pension plans and RRSPs noted above suggests that the future elderly are likely to have much larger amounts of private pension and annuity income. However, the adage "beware of the mean" is particularly applicable in this case. The analysis related to Figure 4 above suggests that the most likely prospect is larger private pensions for the segment of the elderly who already have pensions (i.e., those with higher incomes), but not appreciably more elderly with private pensions.

As a result, one scenario has been created to explore the sensitivity of the projection results to the default assumption that private pension and annuity income will remain relatively unchanged in coming decades (i.e., bear the same relationship to average real wages as today). The alternative assumption we have chosen to simulate, in line with the data just cited, is one of private "pension deepening," but not private pension broadening. As a rough approximation to this scenario, incomes received from private pensions and annuities were (arbitrarily) doubled relative to wages. All other assumptions in this "pension deepening" scenario were the same as the medium (i.e., 1 percent) real economic growth scenario.

It is difficult to judge whether or not this is an "outer limit" assumption of the likely effects of trend increases in the volume of assets accumulated in private RRSPs and RPPs. The substantial increase in these assets is due to a mix of factors. In the case of defined benefit RPPs, it certainly reflects an enrichment of promised pension benefits, but a careful analysis of Ontario plans suggests that such benefit improvements over the period from 1970 to 1984 were on the order of one-fifth valued in terms of employer costs as a percentage of payroll (Wolfson 1988). Since 1984, the data suggest no significant defined benefit plan improvements. Some of the asset increase may represent fuller or even overfunding, especially given the exceptionally high recent real rates of return, and possible constraints on employers extracting private plan surpluses. But even more of the increase could be due to the aging of the workforces covered by defined benefit plans. It remains unclear whether current volumes of accumulated assets and their recent growth should be taken as a signal that future private investment incomes of the elderly will double, triple, or only increase by about half.

*Unit Costs.* In the past, publicly provided unit health-care costs (i.e., costs per age/sex-specific person year) and unit education costs (i.e., costs per pupil) have been rising faster than average wages. As noted above, these increases have almost nothing to do with aging, and are mainly attributable to higher intensity of servicing within age/sex groups.

This scenario builds on the assumptions of the medium economic growth (1 percent) scenario. Instead of holding unit costs fixed relative to average wages, unit costs for health and education have been assumed to grow 1 percent per year faster then average wages.[7]

*Policy Changes.* Finally, two projections have been simulated based on broad and generic policy changes under general discussion. One, denoted "big GIS," builds on discussions about income testing and universality (e.g., Battle in this volume). The OAS is assumed to be merged with the GIS into a larger GIS-like program. The basic income guarantee of this big GIS is equal in 1994 to the current OAS+GIS guarantee. But there are two main changes. One is that the guarantee is assumed to be taxed back or reduced at a 33 percent rate. This compares to a 50 percent reduction rate or effective tax rate in the current GIS, and effective income testing rates for OAS at basic income tax rates (since the current OAS is included in taxable income) plus 15 percent for the "clawback" rate at higher incomes. The other major change is to assume that this big GIS is "super-indexed" — the benefits are linked to average wages rather than the CPI. Thus, if real per capita wages grow at 1 percent per annum, the big GIS basic guarantee is also assumed to grow 1 percent per year faster than the CPI, and hence 1 percent per year faster than provided by the current OAS and GIS indexing.

The second policy change, denoted *Age 70*, raises the age of entitlement to age 70. This is simulated mechanically by zeroing all OAS, GIS/SPA, and C/QPP income received by individuals under age 70.[8] The choice of 70 as the age of entitlement in this scenario is arbitrary — it is simply a round number. It implies roughly two and a half times the reduction in public pension benefits that would occur had the age of entitlement been raised to 67, an option set out in the government's recent discussion paper on the CPP (Canada. Minister of Finance 1996).

PROSPECT

Tables 1 to 3 below present the main results of the simulations. The columns in these tables correspond to the various projection scenarios just described. The rows are the same for each of the three tables. They all present aggregate amounts for various taxes and transfers. In all cases, these amounts are expressed as percents of aggregate wages. Such a relative method of presenting aggregate dollar magnitudes is typical in actuarial analyses, and effectively standardizes for the major changes in the overall size of the economy that can be expected over this span of decades.

To assist interpretation of the numbers, it may be noted that over the past three decades, aggregate wages have been about half of GDP. Thus, halving each of these numbers in the tables gives a rough indication of its likely magnitude as a percentage of GDP.

The first main block of rows in each of the three tables presents results for transfer programs. This is followed by a block for taxes. The last two rows present summary measures of government net balances. The first, "net cash balance," is the sum of the federal-provincial taxes shown less the total of the cash transfers shown. The second, "net fiscal balance" is the "net cash balance" less in-kind transfers (i.e., health care and education). It should be noted that these balances are not the government's actual annual deficit.[9] Moreover, no account is taken in the analysis of accumulated debt.

Table 1 shows the "base 1994" scenario plus the three selected projection years where the only changes are maturation of the C/QPP and changes in the population age structure and labour force participation — the MPPR scenarios. The table therefore highlights effects that can be attributed purely to expected aging of the population, and the trends in labour force participation projected by the chief actuary, particularly increases among females.

These scenarios have the expected effects. Public health-care expenditures would increase by about one-third by 2036, driven mainly by the increasing proportion of the population that is elderly, and their higher than average rates of health-care utilization.[10] However, the "purest" indication of the effects of population aging are shown by OAS costs. These almost double, reflecting the close to doubling of the proportion of elderly in the population.

Meanwhile, there is a decline in the proportion of children in the population. As a result, education expenditures would drop by about 1 percent of aggregate wages (or about one-half of 1 percent of GDP). While population aging means a decline in the relative costs for "youth" expenditures, as far as the public sector is concerned, not very much money is likely to be "freed up" for demographic reasons alone.

The C/QPP behave somewhat differently, because different factors are at work. They more than double in cost, due to the combined effects of the increasing proportion of elderly (the only factor driving health care and OAS costs), plus the maturation of the program (due to the phasing-in period being long past), plus increased pensions to women in their own right and not just as surviving spouses.

Finally on the spending side, GIS/SPA are roughly stable in their relative costs. This is contrary to earlier expectations that the program would shrink substantially with the maturation of the C/QPP. One reason has been the enrichment of the GIS up to the early 1980s. Now, even if an elderly individual or couple has a full CPP or QPP retirement pension, but no other income, they will still be eligible for a partial GIS benefit.

TABLE 1:   Taxes and Transfers as a Percent of Aggregate Wages
Demographic Impact

| | Base 1994 | MPPR: Projected Population and Labour Force Participation Rates Only | | |
|---|---|---|---|---|
| | | 2006 | 2016 | 2036 |
| Federal/Provincial Transfers | 43.3 | 43.5 | 47.0 | 56.7 |
| In-Kind | 23.0 | 22.4 | 23.1 | 25.7 |
| Health | 13.5 | 13.7 | 14.8 | 17.2 |
| Education | 9.5 | 8.7 | 8.2 | 8.4 |
| Cash Transfers | 20.3 | 21.0 | 23.9 | 31.0 |
| Elderly Related | 10.7 | 11.6 | 14.4 | 21.1 |
| C/QPP | 5.2 | 6.5 | 8.0 | 11.6 |
| OAS | 4.1 | 4.1 | 5.1 | 7.9 |
| GIS/SPA | 1.4 | 1.0 | 1.2 | 1.6 |
| Child Tax Benefit | 1.3 | 1.2 | 1.1 | 1.2 |
| Sales Tax Credit | 0.7 | 0.7 | 0.8 | 0.9 |
| UI | 3.1 | 3.0 | 3.0 | 3.0 |
| Other | 4.6 | 4.5 | 4.7 | 4.8 |
| Federal/Provincial Taxes | 42.6 | 43.8 | 45.5 | 48.9 |
| Payroll Taxes | 4.0 | 5.0 | 5.7 | 7.6 |
| C/QPP | 1.7 | 2.8 | 3.5 | 5.4 |
| UI | 2.2 | 2.2 | 2.2 | 2.2 |
| Income Taxes | 27.2 | 27.2 | 27.9 | 28.3 |
| Income Taxes | 27.1 | 27.2 | 27.8 | 28.2 |
| OAS Repayments | 0.1 | 0.1 | 0.1 | 0.2 |
| Sales Taxes | 11.4 | 11.4 | 11.9 | 12.8 |
| Net Cash Balance | 22.3 | 22.7 | 21.6 | 17.8 |
| Net Fiscal Balance | −0.7 | 0.3 | −1.5 | −7.9 |

Note: Aggregate wages less supplementary labour income account for roughly one-half of GDP

Source: Statistics Canada, SPSD/M v5.3, Special Tabulations.


The remaining rows of Table 1 show the revenue side and net cash balances. Federal plus provincial income, payroll and sales taxes rise from almost 43 percent to just under half of aggregate wages, or about one-quarter of GDP. The main source of this overall tax increase is the legislated increase in CPP contributions (assumed identical for QPP).

For the "bottom line," these taxes roughly balance all the cash transfers plus publicly funded education and health-care expenditures in 1994. This net fiscal balance is projected to improve by about one percentage point of aggregate wages over the first decade (i.e., to 2006), then reverse somewhat when the leading edge of the baby-boom cohorts reach age 65 (i.e., 2016). By the time the baby-boom have all become seniors (2036), demographic factors will result in a more marked deterioration of this balance.

It should be emphasized that these projections in Table 1 are just the first in a series of scenarios. They mainly reflect demographic aging. Unfortunately, this is also where many analyses also stop, sometimes with messages of gloom with respect to the future affordability of public pensions and health care. However, there are a number of other factors that are likely to be as important to the future of these government expenditure programs, as well as the tax revenues on the other side of the ledger.

Table 2 begins the exploration of these additional factors. To provide ready points of comparison, the first two columns of Table 2 are copied from the first and last columns of Table 1 (i.e., "base 1994" and "MPPR"). The last three columns of Table 2 then show the effects of different assumptions on nominal and real economic growth, all for the furthest year of the projections, 2036.

Implicitly, Table 1 (and therefore the first two columns of Table 2) makes an assumption of zero inflation, and zero real per capita economic growth. In contrast, the last three columns of Table 2 all assume inflation at 3.5 percent per annum, and real per capita economic growth at rates of zero, 1 percent, and 2 percent respectively. Thus, the second last column corresponds to the chief actuary's (Canada. Office of the Superintendent of Financial Institutions 1995a) economic assumptions, and the columns on either side constitute a sensitivity analysis to his assumption regarding the real per capita economic growth rate.

The effects of existing legislation with respect to indexing provisions in the income tax and cash transfer systems are highlighted by the differences between the scenarios in columns two and three. In the third "zero real growth" column, wages rise at 3.5 percent, as does inflation. Hence only those tax and transfer program provisions indexed below CPI (i.e., either unindexed or indexed to CPI minus 3 percent) are affected.

The most dramatic effects on the spending side of the ledger are for the child tax benefit and refundable sales tax credit. They virtually disappear, each falling to about one-tenth of 1 percent of aggregate wages. For similar reasons, but not as dramatically, "other" non-indexed or partially indexed transfers decline by 0.4 percent of wages.

Meanwhile on the revenue side of the federal and provincial governments' ledgers, the CPI — 3 percent partial indexing of income tax brackets and other elements (e.g., the basic non-refundable personal tax credit amount) increases income tax revenues by close to two-thirds, to 45.1 percent of wages. In effect, the relative decline in the value of the tax brackets results in taxpayers moving to higher tax brackets, until most are in the top bracket[11] — almost a flat tax system

TABLE 2:  Taxes and Transfers as a Percent of Aggregate Wages:
Impacts of Economic Growth

| | Base 1994 | 2036 3.5% Inflation and Real Economic Growth at: | | | |
| --- | --- | --- | --- | --- | --- |
| | | MPPR | Zero | 1% | 2% |
| Federal/Provincial Transfers | 43.3 | 56.7 | 54.3 | 48.5 | 44.9 |
| In-Kind | 23.0 | 25.7 | 25.7 | 25.7 | 25.7 |
| Health | 13.5 | 17.2 | 17.2 | 17.2 | 17.2 |
| Education | 9.5 | 8.4 | 8.4 | 8.4 | 8.4 |
| Cash Transfers | 20.3 | 31.0 | 28.6 | 22.8 | 19.2 |
| Elderly Related | 10.7 | 21.1 | 21.1 | 15.6 | 12.1 |
| C/QPP | 5.2 | 11.6 | 11.6 | 9.8 | 8.4 |
| OAS | 4.1 | 7.9 | 7.9 | 5.2 | 3.5 |
| GIS/SPA | 1.4 | 1.6 | 1.6 | 0.5 | 0.2 |
| Child Tax Benefit | 1.3 | 1.2 | 0.1 | 0.0 | 0.0 |
| Sales Tax Credit | 0.7 | 0.9 | 0.1 | 0.0 | 0.0 |
| UI | 3.1 | 3.0 | 3.0 | 3.0 | 2.9 |
| Other | 4.6 | 4.8 | 4.4 | 4.3 | 4.2 |
| Federal/Provincial Taxes | 42.6 | 48.9 | 65.9 | 68.9 | 71.2 |
| Payroll Taxes | 4.0 | 7.6 | 7.5 | 7.5 | 7.5 |
| C/QPP | 1.7 | 5.4 | 5.4 | 5.4 | 5.4 |
| UI | 2.2 | 2.2 | 2.2 | 2.2 | 2.2 |
| Income Taxes | 27.2 | 28.3 | 46.3 | 50.1 | 53.1 |
| Income Taxes | 27.1 | 28.2 | 45.1 | 48.9 | 51.9 |
| OAS Repayments | 0.1 | 0.2 | 1.2 | 1.2 | 1.1 |
| Sales Taxes | 11.4 | 12.8 | 10.9 | 10.1 | 9.5 |
| Net Cash Balance | 22.3 | 17.8 | 37.3 | 46.1 | 52.1 |
| Net Fiscal Balance | −0.7 | −7.9 | 11.6 | 20.4 | 26.4 |

Source: Statistics Canada, SPSD/M v5.3, Special Tabulations.

by stealth! For corresponding reasons, the income level at which OAS repayments begin steadily falls, so that the OAS "clawback" increases roughly sixfold.

The net result is that there is a complete turn around in the government's net fiscal balance — from a deficit of almost 8 percent of aggregate wages on this set of expenditures and revenue sources, to a surplus of almost 12 percent. This surplus is even higher to the extent that there is any real economic growth.

Moving to the last two columns where there is some real economic growth as well as inflation, the relative size of public pensions begins shrinking. This is most dramatic for the OAS which falls by over half from the third to the fifth column, and GIS/SPA which almost disappear in the face of 2 percent per annum real average wage growth. This is because their basic dollar amounts are fully price-indexed, but not "super-indexed" to average wages (which, unlike the recent past, are assumed to be growing in real terms). Moreover, C/QPP benefits fall as well. The reason is that even though these earnings-related pension benefits are effectively indexed to average wages at the time they start being paid (via a complex formula using the YMPE = years maximum pensionable earnings), once they come into pay they are indexed to the CPI, and therefore shrinking relative to a growing real average wage.

It is precisely these kinds of scenarios that underlie the more sanguine conclusions of the IMF and OECD studies cited at the outset. While the results may appear unrealistic, they are an accurate working out of the implications of currently legislated indexing provisions under broadly accepted assumptions of modest inflation and real economic growth, just as Table 1 illustrated the working out in a widely accepted manner of the expected impacts of demographic aging.

To finish the discussion of the results in Table 2, with inflation-induced higher income and payroll taxes, and lower cash transfers, disposable income falls substantially. As a result, sales taxes drop by one-seventh to 10.9 percent of wages. Overall, the net cash balance for the federal-provincial public sector (for the taxes and transfers explicitly included in the analysis) improves by roughly a factor of two (from 17.8 to 37.3 percent of aggregate wages). The net fiscal balance, including public health and education expenditures, swings to a surplus (column two to three), and this surplus more than doubles as the scenario moves from zero to 2 percent per annum real per capita growth.

We turn now to the projection scenarios for pension deepening, and continuing relative unit cost increases in education and health care. Again to provide points for comparison, the first three columns of Table 3 correspond to the first, second, and fourth columns of Table 2. The last two columns represent these two new scenarios.

The results shown in the table for the deeper pension scenario reinforce the discussion at the outset. There, it was shown that private pension income is skewed towards the upper income ranges. This relationship is also embodied in the SPSD which lies at the heart of these simulations. As a result, when private pension incomes are arbitrarily doubled, GIS/SPA benefits do not fall noticeably. The reason is that even though the GIS/SPA programs reduce benefits by $.50 for every extra dollar of private pension income, almost no one who is receiving GIS/SPA benefits has any private pension income. On the other hand, the doubling of private pension income induces a one-quarter increase in OAS repayments, from 1.2 to 1.5 percent of aggregate wages, and about a 10 percent increase in personal income tax revenues.

This increase in personal income taxes raises an interesting perspective on the discussion of intergenerational equity. Much of the concern expressed about the aging of Canada's population, and the resulting increase in costs of public pensions, assumes that these increased costs will simply translate into an increased

TABLE 3:   Taxes and Transfers as a Percent of Aggregate Wages: Pension and In-Kind Unit Cost Impacts

| | Base 1994 | MPPR | 2036 Real Growth at 1% | 2036 Deeper Pensions | 2036 Unit Costs |
|---|---|---|---|---|---|
| Federal/Provincial Transfers | 43.3 | 56.7 | 48.5 | 48.5 | 61.7 |
| In-Kind | 23.0 | 25.7 | 25.7 | 25.7 | 38.8 |
| Health | 13.5 | 17.2 | 17.2 | 17.2 | 26.1 |
| Education | 9.5 | 8.4 | 8.4 | 8.4 | 12.8 |
| Cash Transfers | 20.3 | 31.0 | 22.8 | 22.8 | 22.8 |
| Elderly Related | 10.7 | 21.1 | 15.6 | 15.5 | 15.6 |
| C/QPP | 5.2 | 11.6 | 9.8 | 9.8 | 9.8 |
| OAS | 4.1 | 7.9 | 5.2 | 5.2 | 5.2 |
| GIS/SPA | 1.4 | 1.6 | 0.5 | 0.5 | 0.5 |
| Child Tax Benefit | 1.3 | 1.2 | 0.0 | 0.0 | 0.0 |
| Sales Tax Credit | 0.7 | 0.9 | 0.0 | 0.0 | 0.0 |
| UI | 3.1 | 3.0 | 3.0 | 3.0 | 3.0 |
| Other | 4.6 | 4.8 | 4.3 | 4.2 | 4.3 |
| Federal/Provincial Taxes | 42.6 | 48.9 | 68.9 | 74.7 | 68.9 |
| Payroll Taxes | 4.0 | 7.6 | 7.5 | 7.5 | 7.5 |
| C/QPP | 1.7 | 5.4 | 5.4 | 5.4 | 5.4 |
| UI | 2.2 | 2.2 | 2.2 | 2.2 | 2.2 |
| Income Taxes | 27.2 | 28.3 | 50.1 | 55.2 | 50.1 |
| Income Taxes | 27.1 | 28.2 | 48.9 | 53.6 | 48.9 |
| OAS Repayments | 0.1 | 0.2 | 1.2 | 1.5 | 1.2 |
| Sales Taxes | 11.4 | 12.8 | 10.1 | 10.5 | 10.1 |
| Net Cash Balance | 22.3 | 17.8 | 46.1 | 52.0 | 46.1 |
| Net Fiscal Balance | −0.7 | −7.9 | 20.4 | 26.3 | 7.3 |

Source: Statistics Canada, SPSD/M v5.3, Special Tabulations.

burden on future working age generations. In other words, it is implicitly assumed that the higher costs of benefits for the future elderly will be borne by the future working age generation. However, this kind of argument is based on an overly simple analysis which focuses on intercohort redistribution, while ignoring the very large volume of intracohort redistribution that occurs within successive birth cohorts.

More specifically, it is true that the elderly will become a substantially larger share of the population, and therefore receive public pension benefits that are a larger share of the economy, as has been shown in the tables of simulation results so far. However, it is also the case that the elderly will pay a larger share of taxes, thereby providing general tax revenues to finance their own OAS and GIS/SPA benefits and those of their age cohort peers.[12] The simulation methodology being used, based on the SPSD/M, allows us to delve beneath the aggregate figures to shed some light on this question.

If we focus on the first and fourth columns of Table 3, we see that elderly-related cash transfers (C/QPP, OAS, GIS/SPA) increase from 10.7 to 15.5 percent of aggregate wages. There is a similar-sized increase in health expenditures, most of which is attributable to the elderly. At the same time, income taxes increase by about a factor of two, a result mainly of the CPI-3 percent indexing of rate brackets and other amounts. Moreover, the share of income tax revenues accounted for by the elderly almost triples, from about 8 percent of aggregate revenues to about one-quarter. Similarly, the share of GST and other sales tax revenues paid by the elderly rises from over 13 percent to almost 23 percent. In the case of the increased share of income tax revenues, about half of this increase is attributable to demographic aging, hence a greater number of elderly taxpayers, and the other half to the tax revenue from the increased volume of private investment income, in turn based on the assumed magnitude of "pension deepening."

The magnitude of the overall income tax increases projected under the assumption that currently legislated indexing provisions will remain unchanged may appear unrealistic. However, the increased shares of income and sales taxes that are projected to be paid by the elderly are not that sensitive to this assumption. Therefore, concerns about the intergenerational "unfairness" of the projected pension burden on future working age cohorts are likely substantially overstated. They should be tempered by the realization that increased costs for public pensions and health care will be accompanied by substantially increased income and sales tax revenues from this same set of baby-boom birth cohorts. Indeed, under the legislated indexing scenario in the fourth column of Table 3, the same kind of scenario underlying the baseline projections in the IMF and OECD analyses cited earlier, these extra tax revenues are on the same order as the increase in public pension and health-care costs. In other words, the future elderly in this (possibly unrealistic) scenario are paying fully for the projected increased costs of their future public pensions and health care via increased taxes.

In the last column of Table 3, we turn to the projection scenario intended to explore the sensitivity of aggregate costs to long-term trends in unit costs for in-kind public health care and education benefits. The only changes from the third column are for health care and education. Again this is a rather mechanical simulation, this time working out the impacts of 1 percent per annum faster growth in the unit costs of education (i.e., per pupil) and health care (i.e., per average "visit" or service encounter, assuming a constant rate of "visits" within age/sex groups).

The results are significant. Allowing unit costs to continue rising faster that real average wages results in public expenditures on education and health care that are half again as high as otherwise simulated for 2036. As a proportion of aggregate wages, the 13 percent increase is about the same magnitude as the increase in both public pensions and in-kind public health and education benefits attributable purely to demographic aging (based on comparing the first and second columns of the table). The implication is straightforward. A long-term absence of control on unit costs can cause increases in future public sector burdens on the same scale as demographic aging. Fortunately, unit costs in the two largest public in-kind benefit programs, health care and education, are within the power of government to control, unlike demographic aging.

DISTRIBUTIONAL IMPACTS

So far, the analysis has focused on aggregate effects. However, underlying the simulated changes in taxes and pensions are important changes in the distribution of disposable income, both for the population generally and among the elderly. Table 4 presents general results on changes in the distribution of income for a number of the projection scenarios, while Figure 5 focuses on three projection scenarios for the elderly population.

In all cases, family income is measured in a standardized manner. Each family's income is first adjusted for family size and composition, and then expressed as a proportion of the median-adjusted family income.[14] Thus, an "adjusted" income of 1.2, say, means that the family has an income equal to 120 percent of the median (in both cases adjusted to account for differences in family size and composition).

Table 4 shows the proportions of family units in various ranges of adjusted income across the columns. The first set of rows is for all families, while the second focuses on the elderly. Then within each block of rows, results are shown for the 1994 base-case scenario, and then four scenarios for the year 2036. These five scenarios correspond exactly to the columns of Table 2. The second column incorporates projected C/QPP maturation, demographic aging and changes in participation rates (denoted MPPR), while the last three scenarios all include the chief actuary's 3.5 percent inflation rate. The only difference among these last three scenarios is the assumed rate of per capita real economic growth — at zero, 1, and 2 percent per annum. Figure 5 displays the first, second, and fourth scenarios for elderly family units from Table 4 in graphical form.

Comparing the 1994 base-case to the 2036 projection which includes only C/QPP maturation; demographic aging and changed labour force participation (i.e., the first two rows in each set), the more pronounced effects are among the elderly. There is a considerable equalization of incomes as those below 75 percent of the median move to income ranges nearer the median. This is mainly attributable to the maturation of the C/QPP. In turn, the effects for the population as a whole reflect mainly these changes among the elderly subpopulation.

TABLE 4:  Distribution of Disposable Income Among All Families and Among the Elderly for 1994 and Selected Projection Scenarios to 2036

| | Income as a Proportion of Median Income | | | | | |
| | 0 – .5 | .5 – .75 | .75 – 1.25 | 1.25 – 1.75 | 1.75 – 2.5 | 2.5+ |
|---|---|---|---|---|---|---|
| *All Families* | | | | | | |
| 1994 | 9.61 | 20.74 | 36.38 | 11.71 | 17.70 | 3.86 |
| 2036: MPPR | 6.28 | 21.28 | 38.99 | 11.28 | 17.73 | 4.44 |
| Zero Growth | 5.84 | 19.56 | 40.44 | 11.02 | 17.84 | 5.31 |
| 1% Growth | 8.99 | 24.33 | 31.07 | 10.00 | 19.06 | 6.55 |
| 2% Growth | 18.32 | 17.10 | 27.86 | 9.80 | 19.49 | 7.43 |
| *Elderly Families* | | | | | | |
| 1994 | 3.56 | 40.74 | 35.12 | 7.66 | 10.46 | 2.47 |
| 2036: MPPR | 1.04 | 34.46 | 42.73 | 8.01 | 10.86 | 2.89 |
| Zero Growth | 0.99 | 28.39 | 50.70 | 7.33 | 9.56 | 3.04 |
| 1% Growth | 11.33 | 43.14 | 27.59 | 5.22 | 9.19 | 3.52 |
| 2% Growth | 37.16 | 23.99 | 21.56 | 4.75 | 8.80 | 3.74 |

Source: Statistics Canada, SPSD/M v5.3, Special Tabulations.

The differences in the next pair of rows (denoted "2036: MPPR" and "Zero Growth") highlight the effects of currently legislated partial CPI indexing in various parts of the tax/transfer system. This results from the fact that the only difference between these two projection scenarios is that the CPI growth rate has increased from zero in the second row to the chief actuary's long-run 3.5 percent assumption in the third. As seen in Table 2 above, the main aggregate impact of this scenario change is large increases in income taxes and OAS repayments. In turn, higher taxes lower the median disposable income, so somewhat fewer family units (both overall and elderly) are in the bottom income range (here defined as less than half the adjusted median). The main effect is a general compression of the income distribution, with more family units having near median incomes. In other words, even though the partial indexing induces considerable "bracket creep" as families find themselves in ever higher marginal tax brackets, the overall progressivity of the income tax system results in a generally more equal distribution of disposable income.

However, this result changes with the addition of 1 or 2 percent real per capita economic growth in the next two rows. In these scenarios, the main effects are substantial shrinkage of public pensions, and even more "bracket creep" causing higher income taxes. For the elderly, the shrinkage of public pensions is associated with a dramatic increase in the proportion with low incomes, particularly below half the (adjusted) median. For the population as a whole, bracket creep

FIGURE 5: Distribution of Elderly Economic Family Units by Adjusted Family
Income, Selected Scenarios for 2036

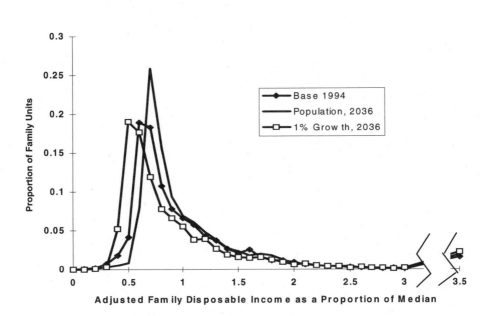

Source: Statistics Canada, SPSD/M v5.3, Special Tabulations.

and the associated rise in income taxes gets to the point that there is effectively a
flat tax system for the top 62.5 percent, so that the income tax structure begins
losing its overall progressivity. As a result, inequality in disposable income begins to rise at the upper end of the income spectrum.

Figure 5 shows these results graphically for the elderly, and for scenarios corresponding to the first (Base 1994), second (2036 MPPR) and fourth (2036 1%
Growth) rows. One key point is the importance of the basic income guarantees
provided by the OAS/GIS. Unlike income distribution curves for the non-elderly,
the federal public pension system has been highly effective in providing a floor
income for virtually all elderly. All three curves in the graph are close to the
horizontal axis until the income level associated with the basic guarantee is reached.
At that point, there is a sharp peak of elderly clustered at or just above this

guarantee. In turn, the three scenarios have their main differences in the location of this peak. Compared to the "Base 1994" scenario, aging and maturation of the C/QPP (the "2036 MPPR" scenario) move the peak up relative to the overall median family income, so that almost no elderly families have incomes below half the median. However, inflation and real growth ("2036 1 percent Growth") shrink the basic public pension income guarantee relative to the median, moving the elderly population peak significantly to the left.

These leftward and rightward shifts in the population peak in Figure 5 help explain the major changes in the incidence of low income among the elderly associated with these various projection scenarios. These low-income incidence projections are shown in Table 5. Two-income cut-points have been used:

- the LICO figures are based on before-tax incomes using 1992 Statistics Canada Low Income Cut-Offs differentiated by family size and urbanization; and

- the LIM (low income measure) figures use a cutoff at 50 percent of median-adjusted family income, where the adjustment is the same as that used in Table 4 and Figure 5.

In both cases, the cutoff income levels have been updated over time in line with the projected growth in the average wage. The estimates of low-income incidence for 1994 are somewhat smaller than those published directly from the SCF due to the many adjustments made in constructing the SPSD to account for underreporting of various income sources.

TABLE 5: Incidence of Low Income for Individuals, Various Projection Scenarios, Two Low-Income Measures and Age

|  | All Persons | | Elderly Persons | |
|---|---|---|---|---|
|  | LICO | LIM | LICO | LIM |
| *Base 1994* | *13.7* | *7.3* | *21.2* | *2.8* |
| *2036* |  |  |  |  |
| *MPPR: Maturation Population & Part Rates* | 12.5 | 5.1 | 14.9 | 0.9 |
| 3.5% Inflation and Zero Economic Growth | 15.3 | 5.7 | 19.5 | 0.9 |
| 3.5% Inflation and 1% Economic Growth | 21.0 | 6.9 | 41.7 | 8.7 |
| 3.5% Inflation and 2% Economic Growth | 23.5 | 12.1 | 50.7 | 30.3 |
| Deeper Pension | 20.2 | 8.9 | 39.0 | 14.0 |

Source: Statistics Canada, SPSD/M v5.3, Special Tabulations.

The extremely low incidence of low income among the elderly in "Base 1994" using the LIM is not an error! Rather, it is the result of the level of the OAS/GIS income guarantee falling just above half the adjusted median family income. As is evident from Figure 5 above, even relatively small movements in the OAS/GIS minimum income guarantee can have rather large effects on the head count of individuals falling below the LIM. For this reason, the erosion of the relative value of OAS/GIS under the real economic growth scenarios results in sharp increases in the incidence of low income measured by the LIM.

While the levels of incidence of low income are different, the patterns of response to the various projection scenarios of the LIM and LICO head count proportions are generally similar. One difference is between the second and third rows, where the addition of the 3.5 percent inflation assumption to the scenario has its main effect on income taxes. Since the LICOs apply to before-tax incomes, this effect is irrelevant, so other changes like the relative devaluation of GIS/SPA and the reduction in the child benefit and in refundable sales tax credits are more important factors.

Finally, the last row in the table shows the projected results for the deeper pension scenario. It has the expected effect on low-income incidence measured by the LICOs, a rather modest fall from 41.7 to 39.0 percent. However, the assumption of a relative doubling of private pension and annuity income by 2036 has an apparently perverse effect on low-income incidence measured by the LIM, causing it to rise from 8.7 to 14.0 percent. The reason is that the increase in private pension and annuity income raises the adjusted median income by more than it raises the incomes of those among the elderly with relatively low incomes.

TWO GENERIC POLICY SCENARIOS

We turn in Table 6 to the last two projection scenarios, those for two generic policy options. Again to provide ready points for comparison, the first three columns are identical to those in Table 3. The fourth *Age 70* column simulates the impact of raising the age of entitlement to public pensions to age 70. The last column gives results for the "big GIS" scenario, where OAS and GIS have been combined into a single large GIS-like program.

The Age 70 simulation, it must be emphasized, is very mechanical. Incomes from public pensions accruing to those between age 60 and age 69 were simply set to zero. The result is a reduction in public pension costs of about one-sixth compared to the scenario in the third column, real 1 percent growth. At the same time, since no one is assumed to have made any offsetting revisions to their private sources of post-age 65 income plans (a highly unlikely assumption), the incidence of low income ("LIM") rises by almost one-third.

TABLE 6:  Taxes and Transfers as a Percent of Aggregate Wages:
          Policy Scenarios

| | Base 1994 | 2036 | | | |
|---|---|---|---|---|---|
| | | MPPR | Real Growth at 1% | Age 70 | Big GIS |
| Elderly Related | 10.7 | 21.1 | 15.6 | 13.0 | 15.8 |
| C/QPP | 5.2 | 11.6 | 9.8 | 8.6 | 9.8 |
| OAS | 4.1 | 7.9 | 5.2 | 4.0 | 0.0 |
| GIS/SPA | 1.4 | 1.6 | 0.5 | 0.4 | 6.0 |
| Elderly Below LIM | 2.8 | 0.9 | 8.7 | 11.4 | 3.2 |

Source: Statistics Canada, SPSD/M v5.3, Special Tabulations.

It may be noted that the age 70 entitlement assumed here for purposes of analysis involves a significantly greater delay from the current age 65 than the 67 age of entitlement illustrated in the recent discussion paper on the CPP (Canada. Minister of Finance 1996). However, moving to an age of entitlement of 70 by 2036 would likely result in pensions payable for almost the same length of time as was the case at the inception of the C/QPP in 1966. Life expectancy at age 65 was 15.3 years in 1966, while in 1995, it had risen to 18.4, and by 2030 the chief actuary is projecting it to be 19.8 years (Canada. Minister of Finance 1996, p. 17), a projected increase of 4.5 years from 1966 to 2036.

The big GIS with its generalized income testing and super-indexing is interesting on two main counts. First, its projected cost is almost the same as the current system, including as it does the relative decline in OAS and GIS/SPA. Second, it is associated with almost no increase in the incidence of low income compared to the present. This latter result is primarily due to the assumption of super-indexing. Compared to the "Real Growth at 1 percent" scenario, this option effectively reallocates monies from the upper half of the income spectrum provided by the substantially universal OAS to the lower end of the income spectrum via a basic income guarantee for the elderly that is more dynamic.

The discussion of these two scenarios provides a convenient basis for a somewhat broader contemplation of the intergenerational sustainability of Canada's public pension system. There is broad agreement on the need for placing the system on such a footing, but little agreement or even serious exploration of the means for doing so. The calls to cut back substantially on the public system, and to turn responsibility over to individual initiative and private savings, are not an answer to this issue. The data on private investment income and private tax-assisted saving shown earlier clearly indicate that such a strategy will not help the majority of the future elderly, and will leave many more at much higher risk of retirement years with inadequate incomes.

A much more promising line of development involves a different approach to indexing and well-specified prior agreements for the continuous and gradual adjustment of the public pension system over the span of decades. This kind of proposal was put forward by the Frith Parliamentary Committee (Canada. House of Commons 1983, ch. 2), and is being considered in Sweden (Sweden. Ministry of Health and Social Affairs 1994).

The Frith committee called for a "sustainable intergenerational agreement" in respect of public pensions. They recommended that public pensions be indexed not to the CPI, but to aggregate wages adjusted for the demographic size of the working age population. This recommendation was made fully cognizant of the fact that in periods of declining real wages, or population aging, the real incomes of seniors would also have to decline. In effect, the committee's members concluded that seniors should not be immune from the vicissitudes of economic growth, or long-run trends in the productive capacity of the economy. But also over the long term, the elderly should be able to share through their publicly provided pensions in the fruits of any real economic growth.

The proposed Swedish system also includes a form of wage indexing. In addition, it includes an automatic linking of the age of entitlement to projected longevity. As life expectancy increases in future, Swedes would have to attain higher ages before they could begin claiming public pensions at the same level as cohorts born earlier.

The Age 70 and big GIS scenarios represent projected outcomes in 2036 and are not directly related to these ideas. However, they both have structures and outcomes that could be the result of a sustainable intergenerational agreement entered into in the near future, where the agreement itself embodied central features of the proposals in the Frith report, and the recently proposed Swedish reforms.

CONCLUSIONS

This paper has briefly traced the historical magnitudes of public pensions, the demographically sensitive public expenditures on health care and education, and the sources of income of the elderly. Then, in the main part of the analysis, a series of projection scenarios have been simulated in order to explore the major factors likely to affect the economic position of the future elderly.

The factor of greatest concern to the general public is the aging of the population, which will likely see a doubling of the proportion of the population age 65+ by 2036 when all of the baby-boom cohorts will have become seniors. However, demographic aging is not the only important factor, nor even the most quantitatively significant. Other factors of at least similar magnitude include the indexing provisions for the income tax system and public pensions, and the growth of unit costs in publicly funded health care and education. If any credence is attached to the prospect of real per capita economic growth over coming decades at levels on the order of 1 percent per annum, then public pension costs will be much smaller than widely thought, and income tax revenues much higher. Thus, in a rather mechanical working out of the implications of current legislation, there is no particular affordability problem with current programs.

However, this is likely an unrealistic scenario. The reason, simply, is that it is also associated with major increases in the incidence of low income among the future elderly. We are faced, therefore, with a choice, but one that does not start from the position usually assumed. If the legislation governing the current public pension and tax structures remains basically unchanged, then low income among the elderly, not affordability or deficits, will be the emergent problem.

If the projected scenarios are considered unrealistic, then fundamental policy changes will be required. An implication of the range of scenarios presented is that those embodying a more realistic balance among levels of taxation and public benefits can be contemplated. Moreover, it would be most useful to explore methods by which these scenarios could evolve, more or less automatically, based on explicit and prior agreement on the main parameters of the system that should be gradually adjusted, and the basis of such adjustment. Examples include the age of entitlement to full public pensions, and the indexing of various monetary levels in both the public pension and the income tax system. The goal would be an intergenerationally sustainable agreement, based in turn on broad agreement on the principles for both intragenerational and intergenerational equity.

## NOTES

The views expressed herein are those of the authors, and should not be taken necessarily to reflect those of Statistics Canada.

1. In effect, the overall aggregate income shares shown in the first column of Figure 2 are a weighted average of proportions of income by source for each individual, where the weights are the amounts of total income, thereby giving more weight to the income composition of those with higher incomes. The averages of proportions in the last two columns give each individual a weight of one. (Since the data are from a complex sample survey, the sampling ratio also has to be taken into account, and the same sample weights have been used for both kinds of estimates).
2. The specific years chosen were somewhat arbitrary. The general intent was to have a recent year plus time points about one and two decades earlier.
3. A few further technical points should be noted. First, the data from individual income tax returns shown in Figure 4 do not give any indication of coverage by non-

contributory RPPs. However, the data mentioned on RPP membership do cover these plans. Second, the contribution shares shown in Figure 4 include individual contributions that are well over the normal statutory limits (e.g., amounts over $25,000 and even $500,000 in even the lowest earnings deciles, when the contribution limit was $3,500 or $5,500). The most likely explanation is that these were retiring allowances or severance payments which can be legally rolled over into an RRSP. For example, an individual who had been earning $50,000 per year who retired in January with a retiring allowance of $25,000 might have had earned income for the taxation year of only $5,000 but an RRSP contribution of $25,000. Various adjustments to exclude such amounts do not appreciably affect the impression given in Figure 4; if anything, contributions appear more skewed to the upper end of the earnings spectrum. Third, it is true that the *number* of contributors at lower earnings levels has increased somewhat. But so have the numbers at higher incomes. Moreover, the point of the data in Figure 4 is that any increase in numbers of contributors with low incomes involves relatively small dollar amounts, such that the overall contribution shares have been virtually unchanged.

4. As noted at the outset, this analysis is largely an update and extension of Murphy and Wolfson (1991). The main differences are: (i) use of a 1988 micro database updated to 1994 rather than 1986 data updated to 1990; (ii) more detailed imputation of health and education in-kind benefits; (iii) projections to 2006 as well as 2016 and 2036; (iv) improved C/QPP base year and projected data, including explicit matching to the chief actuary's projections (Canada. Office of the Superintendent of Financial Institutions 1995*b*); and (v) addition of scenarios exploring sensitivity to real per capita economic growth rates, higher private pension income in the future, and two broad policy options. Other scenarios related to changing family size, and to trends towards increased polarization of earnings were examined. Since they did not have significant effects, they have not been reported here.

5. Murphy and Wolfson (1991) showed that the effects of high- and low-growth population projections are relatively small when compared to the impacts of other factors such as economic growth and indexing. Similar results were found in this analysis. Therefore, we focus only on the middle population growth scenario.

6. The chief actuary's 1 percent assumption in the CPP *Fifteenth Actuarial Report* (Canada. Office of the Superintendent of Financial Institutions 1995*a*) is down from 1.3 percent in the CPP *Eleventh Actuarial Report* (Canada. Office of the Superintendent of Financial Institutions 1988). The 1.3 percent figure was used in Murphy and Wolfson (1991). The actual revision first occured in the *Fourteenth Actuarial Report.*

7. This assumption is substantially the same as that made by the Canadian Institute of Actuaries (1996). Note that the downstream impacts of such an assumption have not been modeled (i.e., the effect of higher average wage growth for doctors, nurses, and teachers on overall wage growth, income and payroll taxes, etc.). Implicitly, this is equivalent to assuming that the wages of non-health-care/education sector employees have been growing relatively somewhat less quickly.

8. CPP disability, survivors, death and childrens benefits received by persons under age 60 are assumed to remain unchanged.

9. The SPSD/M does not account for all taxes or in-kind transfers. Absent are corporate taxes, municipal level taxes and in-kind public benefits in areas such as housing and transportation. However, the model does account for over 60 percent of the National

Accounts estimate of total federal plus provincial direct and indirect taxes and the coverage of cash transfers, health and education spending amounts to over 80 percent of government spending (exclusive of debt service charges). Moreover, the taxes and transfers covered by the model are those most sensitive to demographic changes. Thus while the net cash balance figures do not reflect the overall deficit, they do reflect the magnitude of the impact on the deficit from the major age sensitive federal and provincial programs.

10. According to the underlying age/sex-specific imputation of public health-care spending, just over one-quarter of these benefits accrued to the elderly in 1994. With the aging of the population to 2036, this proportion increases to about 40 percent.

11. The proportion of taxable filers who pay taxes at the top federal rate of 29 percent increases nearly tenfold from 6.7 percent in 1994 to 62.5 percent in 2036 under the middle economic growth scenario (1 percent) assumptions.

12. We are indebted to Dr. Thomas Courchene of Queen's University for highlighting this question.

13. The family size adjustment is based the scale of equivalent adult units used for Statistics Canada's Low Income Measures or LIMs. This is 1.0 for the first person, 0.4 for second and subsequent adults, and 0.3 for each child.

## REFERENCES

Barer, M., I.R. Pulcins, R.G.Evans, C. Hertzman, J. Lomas and G.M. Anderson (1989), "Trends in Use of Medical Services by the Elderly in British Columbia," *Canadian Medical Association Journal,* 141, 1:39-45

Bordt, M., G. Cameron, S. Gribble, B. Murphy, G. Rowe and M. Wolfson (1992), "The Social Policy Simulation Database and Model: An Integrated Tool for Tax/Transfer Policy Analysis," *Canadian Tax Journal,* 38:48-65.

Cameron, G. and M. Wolfson (1994), "Missing Transfers: Adjusting Household Incomes for Non-Cash Benefits," presented at the twenty-third general conference of the International Association for Research in Income and Wealth, August.

Canada (1995), "A 21st Century Employment System for Canada, Guide to the Employment Insurance Legislation," Ottawa: Supply and Services Canada.

Canada. Department of National Health and Welfare (1982), *Better Pensions for Canadians* (Green Paper), Ottawa: Supply and Services Canada.

Canada. Health and Welfare (1989), *Social Security Statistics: Canada and Provinces 1963-64 to 1987-88*, Ottawa: Supply and Services Canada.

Canada. House of Commons (1983), *Report of the Parliamentary Task Force on Pension Reform* (Frith Report), Ottawa: Supply and Services Canada.

Canada. Human Resources Development Canada (1994), *Social Security Statistics: Canada and Provinces 1968-1969 to 1992-1993*, Ottawa: Supply and Services Canada.

Canada. Minister of Finance (1996), *An Information Paper for Consultations on the Canada Pension Plan*, Ottawa: Ministry of Finance.

Canada. Office of the Superintendent of Financial Institutions (1988), *Canada Pension Plan: Eleventh Actuarial Report,* Ottawa: Supply and Services Canada.

_____ (1995), *Canada Pension Plan: Fifteenth Actuarial Report as at December 1993*, Ottawa: Supply and Services Canada.

Canada. Task Force on Retirement and Income Policy (1980), *The Retirement Income System in Canada: Problems and Alternative Policies for Reform* (Lazar Report), Ottawa: Supply and Services Canada.

Canadian Institute of Actuaries (1996), "Health Care Financing," Ottawa: CIA.

Fellegi, I. (1988), "Can We Afford an Aging Society," *Canadian Economic Observer*, Ottawa: Statistics Canada.

Gendron, F. (1994), "Does Canada Invest Enough in Education," *Education Quarterly Review*, 1, 4, STC-CAT81-003, Ottawa: Statistics Canada.

Heller, P.S., R. Hemming and P.W. Kohnert (1986), "Aging and Social Expenditures in the Major Industrial Countries, 1980-2025," Occasional Paper No. 47, Washington, DC: International Monetary Fund.

Leibfritz, W., D. Roseveare, D. Fore and E. Wurzel (1995), *Ageing Populations, Pension Systems and Government Budgets: How Do They Affect Savings?* Economics Department Working Papers No. 156, Paris: OECD.

Murphy, B. and M. Wolfson (1991), "When the Baby Boom Grows Old: Impacts on Canada's Public Sector," Ottawa: Statistics Canada.

Robson, W.B. (1996), *Putting Some Gold in the Golden Years: Fixing the Canada Pension Plan*, Commentary No. 76, Toronto: C.D.Howe Institute.

Statistics Canada (1992), *Pension Plans in Canada*, STC-CAT 74-401, Ottawa: Supply and Services Canada.

_____ (1995), *Population Projections for Canada, Provinces and Territories 1993-2016*, STC-CAT 91-520, Ottawa: Supply and Services Canada.

Sweden. Ministry of Health and Social Affairs (1994), "Pension Reform in Sweden, a short summary"; proposal of the Working Group on Pensions in 1994, Jakobsgaten 26, S-103 33 Stockholm.

Wolfson, M. (1988), "Pension Plans in Ontario: A Statistical Overview," in *Report of the Task Force on Inflation Protection for Employment Pension Plans*, Toronto: Queens Printer for Ontario.

Wolfson, M., S. Gribble, B. Murphy and M. Bordt (1989), "The Social Policy Simulation Database and Model: An Example of Survey and Administrative Data Integration"; *Survey of Current Business*, 69 (May):36-40.

# Comments

## Gordon Betcherman

Wolfson and Murphy consider the future costs of Canada's retirement income system by providing a detailed set of scenarios that situate public pension costs within a comprehensive framework that includes other expenditure areas, tax revenues, and demographic trends. The informational value of the analysis, which has been carefully and systematically carried out, is evident. But, in a sense, the major contribution of this paper is to force us to be very careful about uncritically accepting what passes for conventional wisdom in the pension policy, or indeed any policy, debate. Thus, this article provides a very important foundation for a grounded discussion on the reform of Canada's retirement income system.

First, the conventional wisdom. It is widely assumed that the existing pension system will be unsustainable once the enormous baby-boom generation reaches retirement age and starts to collect Canada Pension Plan (CPP) and other old age benefits. The current fiscal situation, of course, only serves to strengthen this conviction. The assumption that present arrangements are unsustainable not only has popular currency but, as Wolfson and Murphy point out in their introduction, it also represents the starting point for the current policy debate on retirement income. And, when this is accepted as the starting point, the debate is inevitably headed in a specific direction — that is, that the status quo is not an option.

Before looking at the analysis and its implications, it is worth noting parenthetically that the methodology used by Wolfson and Murphy in constructing their scenarios is based on simulations generated by Statistics Canada's Social Policy Simulations Database and Model (SPSD/M). This is probably the most sophisticated tool Canadian researchers have had at their disposal to systematically consider the economic implications of various social policy options. The mechanics of the SPSD/M have been well documented (Bordt *et al.* 1992) but readers who are unfamiliar with it should understand that this is a "mechanical" model in the sense that it does not incorporate behavioural adjustments.

Turning to the results — the simulations appear, at first blush, to tell a "good news" story. The analysis demonstrates that the cost burden of the current retirement income programs — and the other existing public obligations including health care — are affordable over the long run. The pessimism associated with the conventional wisdom turns out be unjustified. There will be money after all to pay for our pensions.

The other part of the good news is that the variables that really matter in determining long-term affordability may not be beyond our control. The particularly discouraging aspect of the conventional wisdom is that the lack of affordability will be driven primarily by demography which is something that is not easily manipulable except in the very long run or through quite drastic measures. However, an important feature of the Wolfson-Murphy results is that demographic trends are not as critical to the story as one would have thought. Despite the fact that the 65-year and over group will have doubled in size by the year 2036, the aging of the baby-boomers turns out to be a less important factor in determining the balance sheet than either economic growth or program design. While the track record of governments in these areas is not unblemished, these are obviously more subject to influence than is demography.

In the final analysis, though, the implications of the scenarios cannot be as favourable as they initially appear. The positive fiscal balances are achieved at the expense of adequate retirement income, largely because of indexing features that have been built into the tax-transfer system. The fact that we do not have full indexation on either side means that public coffers build up over time through bracket creep and through the erosion of real benefits. I should point out that neither the observation nor its import is lost on the authors who write in their introduction that "[t]he main area where conventional wisdom continues to go astray is in its failure to appreciate the longer run implications of current tax/transfer indexing provisions."

So, in a sense, although the conventional wisdom may be wrong, we still wind up asking the same question: How do you design a retirement income system that is fiscally sustainable while, at the same time, providing adequate retirement income?

I wanted to focus the remainder of my remarks on one important contextual factor that cannot really be handled by the SPSD/M analysis but that can have a major effect on the retirement income system — namely, changes in the operation of the labour market. The lifetime work experience of a given generation will have an important impact on both that generation's need for and its ability to support a public pension system.

The design of a public plan presumably will differ a great deal depending on the other legs of retirement income — private savings and private pensions. It is my guess that the last time that there was a comprehensive review of retirement income policy, there was an assumption that these other two legs, and especially private pensions, would strengthen over time. A generation ago, when the last full debate took place, Canada was still riding the crest of the postwar boom and the maturation of industrial capitalism. It was reasonable to project then that greater and greater numbers of Canadians would be employed in sophisticated corporate and government organizations increasingly offering "full-service" employment packages, including company pensions. While the public system could provide a sound base, it might be anticipated that these private plans, plus RRSPs, would be a major source of income for most seniors of the future.

Events of the past 15 years raise doubts about what we can actually expect from these other sources, especially private pensions. As Figure 1 shows, the coverage of these plans has not increased over the past decade. Employer pension plan participation, scaled either by the labour force or by paid employment, has remained relatively constant. In the United States where, it might be argued, the postindustrial employment contract has evolved the furthest, private pension plan

FIGURE 1: Employer Pension Plan Coverage 1983-1993

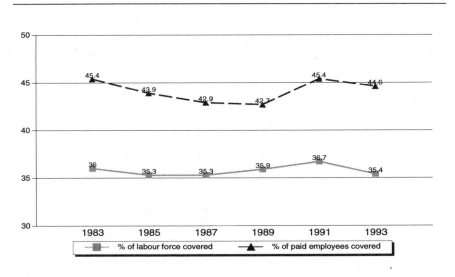

Source: Statistics Canada (1996).

coverage actually has been on a downward trend since the late 1970s (Hinz, Turner and Fernandez 1994). In both countries, coverage has declined significantly for men while it has increased for women. There is also evidence in both countries that the types of plans have been changing in ways that reduce employer risks including, for example, an increase in defined contribution plans.

Most observers would attribute the stagnation in coverage rates (or the decline in the US case) to a number of interrelated developments that began to appear in the late 1970s and early 1980s. Each of these trends, listed below, marks a shift towards an economic structure where pensions traditionally have not been prevalent:

• the growing share of employment in small firms;

• the structural shift to the commercial service sector;

• the increase in self-employment and non-standard workforms; and

• the apparent adoption by many corporations of low-commitment, "just-in-time" human resource strategies.

It is uncertain whether these trends will intensify or whether they mark out a transition period to a new labour market equilibrium. Indeed, there have been differing interpretations of these recent developments, resulting in a range of views on the future of work. In thinking about the likely course of employment, I have discerned three very different scenarios. While it is impossible, of course, to evaluate which of these scenarios will be the "right" one, this is a useful exercise for thinking about what might unfold and how we should be responding. Certainly, each of these views on the future of work has distinct implications for pension policy.

One perspective, which I call the "almost business as usual" scenario, recognizes that we are going through an important period of change driven by technological innovation and globalization. However, this is not a revolutionary scenario and the structural and behavioural trends noted above are seen as examples of how the economic system is responding to the changes. In this view, the resulting stagnation or decline in pension coverage rates is something to be addressed cautiously. A period of strong economic growth, along with appropriate program design reforms, could solve any potentially serious problems. It is interesting to note that these are the critical factors identified in the Wolfson-Murphy analysis. For the most part, the "almost business as usual" scenario underlies the thinking of the present generation of policymakers in Canada and other advanced industrial countries.

There are two other scenarios that take a much more extreme view on the future of work. Both see us in the midst of a postindustrial revolution, characterized by rapid technological change and globalization. Each scenario, then, foresees radical changes in the labour market and, by extension, in terms of appropriate public policy. However, one interprets the changes in a very optimistic manner while the other is decidedly pessimistic.

The optimistic scenario emphasizes the potential of new technology and the global marketplace for stimulating a new era of knowledge-based growth. A key thread in this scenario is the reorganization of the way that economic activity is carried out. To be more specific, the optimistic view emphasizes a process that Bridges (1994) has called "dejobbing" whereby the bundling of tasks into relatively permanent and stable jobs (which has characterized the industrial era) will be increasingly replaced by new contractual arrangements that are project-based and will typically be carried out by individuals who are self-employed or in some other type of contractor relationship. The rise in self-employment and non-standard work, the optimists would argue, is early evidence of this dejobbing. In this scenario, a reliance by policymakers on employer pension plans as a source of retirement income would be a mistake since the long-term contracting arrangements that are pre-condition for these plans are largely absent. Instead, the optimistic scenario — which typically leads to individualistic and market-oriented solutions — would direct policymakers towards RRSPs and other individual savings mechanisms.

As noted already, the pessimistic scenario also starts with the proposition that we are in the midst of an economic revolution fuelled by technology and globalization. In this scenario, however, the emphasis is not on the opportunities but on the human costs: technological displacement coupled with a global "race to the bottom," it is argued, will lead to mass unemployment and acute income polarization in all industrialized societies. Given those outcomes, not only will employer pensions not be widespread but most workers will be unable to accumulate savings for their retirement. The pessimistic scenario, then, inevitably leads to the conclusion that adequate retirement incomes will depend heavily on a strong public pension system.

Ultimately, of course, it is not possible for policymakers today to sort out what the labour market will look like a generation from now. This is unfortunate because employment experiences will be a critical factor in determining the long-run requirements of the pension system. At a minimum, though, decisionmakers in the current round of policy reform should think carefully about the implications of the reforms they are considering under various future labour market scenarios.

REFERENCES

Bordt, M., G. Cameron, S. Gribble, B. Murphy, G. Rowe and M. Wolfson (1992), "The Social Policy Simulation Database and Model: An Integrated Tool for Tax/Transfer Policy Analysis," *Canadian Tax Journal*, 38:48-65.

Bridges, W. (1994), *Jobshift: How to Prosper in a Workplace Without Jobs,* New York: Addison Wesley.

Hinz, R., J. Turner and P. Fernandez, eds. (1994), *Pension Coverage Issues for the 1990s,* Washington, DC: US Government Printing Office.

Statistics Canada (1996), *Canada's Retirement Income Programs: A Statistical Overview*, Catalogue 74-507-XPB, Ottawa: Statistics Canada.

# CHAPTER FIVE

# The Canada Pension Plan: Retrospect and Prospect

*Newman Lam,*
*James Cutt and*
*Michael Prince*

## INTRODUCTION

The retirement income system in Canada has four layers, the first two public and the others private. The Old Age Security (OAS) pension and the income-related Guaranteed Income Supplement (GIS) form the first layer, paid by the federal government from general tax revenue. Anyone who meets the residence requirement (ten years), whether he/she has contributed to the tax system or not, is eligible for benefits after the age of 65. The second layer, the Canada Pension Plan (CPP), is also publicly run, but is a contributory, occupational, pension plan financed by employer contribution and payroll deduction from employees. Participation in the CPP is mandatory for persons employed by others. Self-employed persons can also participate by making the required contribution. The CPP supplements the basic income offered by the OAS and the GIS for those who have been employed for an aggregate of ten years or more. The third layer consists of private occupational pension plans offered by employers (e.g., superannuation). Some union contracts stipulate mandatory participation in these plans. The last layer consists of voluntary saving schemes such as Registered Retired Savings Plans (RRSPs). The current tax law provides incentives for participation in some of these schemes. This paper addresses the contribution of the CPP to the retirement income system in Canada.

Although the CPP was conceived as a contributory pension plan to supplement the basic retirement income provided by the OAS and GIS, it also provides a number of survivor and disability benefits. There are three types of survivor benefits: surviving spouse's pensions, orphan's benefits, and death benefits. These benefits are paid to family members of deceased contributors. In 1987, a legislative amendment was passed to continue the payment of survivor's pensions after remarriage of the surviving spouse and to reinstate those whose survivor's pensions had been suspended due to remarriage. Although only one survivor's pension is payable to a surviving spouse disregarding the number of times he or she may have been widowed, a surviving spouse who has contributed to the CPP may be entitled to a combined retirement-survivor pension or a combined disability-survivor pension. Orphan's benefits are payable to children of deceased contributors until age 18, or age 25 if the children continue full-time attendance at school or university. Death benefit is a lump-sum benefit payable to the estate of the deceased contributor. There are two types of disability benefits, one to disabled contributors and the other to their children. The disability pension is payable to contributors who have a prolonged physical or mental impairment. Their children are entitled to receive the disabled contributor's child's benefit.

In the mid-1970s, survivor and disability benefits accounted for almost half of the total benefit expenditures. In the early 1990s, they dropped to approximately one-third of the benefit expenditures, probably as a result of improved health and safety standards. However, these types of expenditures are projected to rise again due to liberal interpretation of the rules for benefit entitlement. These benefits, strictly speaking, are not retirement pensions, despite the fact that recipients may be retired persons. On the surface, the purpose of these benefits is to provide income support to contributors and/or their family members in the event of disability or death. If this is the reason, then these benefits should be more appropriately grouped with and financed like the GIS, especially, as we will show later, since these benefits place a heavy burden on the CPP contributors. Currently, these benefits confuse the role of the CPP, a contributory pension plan, with that of the GIS, an income support program, in the scheme of retirement income security.

There are two themes that will be addressed in this paper. A vitally important part of the "data" on pension policies and pension politics is the public opinion culture of Canadians — people's attitudes, beliefs, and expectations regarding matters of personal life chances, general economic opportunities, public policies, and public finances. The first theme, therefore, deals with this pension culture as a critical element in effectively reforming the retirement income system. The second deals with the financial condition of the CPP and changes that are necessary to make it equitable and viable.

PENSION APPREHENSION: AN EMERGING PUBLIC OPINION CULTURE

Canadians' opinions of the pension system seem to have changed significantly since the last major phase of pension reform in the late 1970s and early 1980s. The change we are interested in concerns the national public pension programs, in particular the Canada Pension Plan (CPP). Paradoxically, while the CPP has grown in importance as a source of retirement income and a key pillar in the retirement income system over the last 30 years, we can observe a growing anxiety over, and faltering belief in, the CPP's future among many young and middle-aged Canadians. Compared to only a generation ago, fewer Canadians believe that their children will be better off than themselves in economic and social terms.

This anticipation of adverse circumstances ahead for public pensions represents a new apprehension for old age. Traditionally, retirement in industrial societies has been seen as a risk to the security of individuals and older families. The fear, of course, was of poverty in old age with a sharp decline in income and living standards upon retirement or widowhood. Canada's social security system developed over much of the twentieth century to provide protection to people against the loss of income due to retirement among other contingencies. In their recent report on consulting with Canadians about reforming social programs, the Standing Committee on Human Resources Development commented:

> Though programs for seniors were outside the scope of the Discussion Paper, several seniors' groups appeared before us, and other groups also touched on such matters as retirement savings and pensions. Senior citizens, many of whom grew up in the 1920s and 1930s and experienced life before the modern social security system, reminded us of the historical importance of our network of social programs. They expressed concern about the future of all Canadians — their children, grandchildren, friends and neighbours — and strong support for maintaining a comprehensive social safety net (Canada 1995, p. 7).

To deal with the risks of unemployment, sickness, and old age, a distinctive feature of social policy making in Canada has been, "the adoption of social insurance and payroll financing. These areas involve the collective pooling of individual risks by drawing on the resources of the community and, through public administration, providing basic income support" (Canada 1995, p. 13). With the introduction of the Old Age Security program, the Guaranteed Income Supplement, the Canada Pension Plan, and other developments in public and private measures, one of the more notable achievements in social policy has been the impressive reduction in poverty among seniors over the last three decades.

Despite this social policy history and relative success in tackling the original income concern of old age, a new anxiety about retirement has emerged in the 1990s. Canadians have worries about the future incomes of the elderly and doubts about the public sector's role in the retirement income security system. Many people, perhaps most, are troubled about the sustainability of the public pension plans in providing an adequate retirement income. A widespread sense exists that financial problems with public pensions are just around the corner. In short, Canadians have pension apprehension on a mass scale. Consider the following indications and events:

- A national survey by Gallup Canada in October 1994 found that nearly seven out of ten Canadians think that public pension programs such as the OAS or C/QPP will *not* be there for them when they retire. People do not expect to receive these benefits at all or not to receive what they had paid for through taxes and contributions (Markham 1995, p. 25).

- In the February 1995 budget, the Chrétien government spoke of the retirement income system in terms of cost concerns, demographic pressures and restraint imperatives. With respect to the social security system more generally, the Liberals have stated firmly that the status quo is not an option and that far more than tinkering at the edges of social policy is required (Canada 1995, p. 11). On the CPP, OAS, and GIS the Liberals have said they will take steps to make these programs sustainable; that is, affordable both now and in the future. The Chrétien government has already taken a number of measures that pertain to retirement income and pension reform, such as truly ending the universal character of the OAS program, resulting overall in modestly increased revenues for the federal purse (Prince 1995).

- The September 1995 issue of *Policy Options* was devoted to the theme of "Canada's public pensions in crisis" and asked: Will the next generation pay for your pensions? Articles by several experts, though not all (Baldwin 1995; Townson 1995), contended that the retirement income security system "is under strain" (Markham 1995, p. 25), has "serious financial trouble" (James 1995, p. 8), is facing major "demographic difficulties" (Davis 1995, p. 8), and "will come under considerable pressure as the ratio of retirees to workers rises (most sharply after 2015)" (Brown 1995, p. 17).

- A November 1995 *Maclean's*/CBC News year-end poll reported that a large majority of Canadians are expecting the worst for the CPP in the near future. Of those surveyed, 27 percent said they thought the CPP will be bankrupt by the year 2000; 54 percent indicated they thought the plan would have somewhat worse or significantly worse funding while only 11 percent believe it will have the same funding; and just 6 percent think it will have better funding. On a related question, 53 percent think the quality of life for senior citizens will be worse in Canada in the year 2000; 27 percent think it will be the same; and only 18 percent think it will be better (*Maclean's* 1995/96, p. 32).

There are, then, low expectations among Canadians of having stable pension-based incomes in their later years of life; and little confidence, as individuals or as generations, that there will be a close relationship between the pension contributions they make and the benefits they receive, resulting in what economists call a negative lifetime transfer.

This contemporary apprehension relates, it seems, more to certain parts of the retirement income system than to others. The focus of concern by the general public and federal government centres not so much on the tax-assisted savings vehicles like the RRSPs nor on private occupational pension plans, but rather on the public plans including the CPP. "It's clear," Townson notes (1995, p. 16), "that policy makers are facing something of a crisis of confidence in the CPP at the present time." Canadians are not too certain or hopeful that they will actually obtain a guarantee of income from the CPP (or, for that matter, the OAS). For many, the CPP seems a certain responsibility today of payroll deductions, yet a doubtful reward of pension benefits in the future. A British observer has noted of state pension plans across industrial countries: "Measures to reduce eligibility for social security benefits, and associated expectations of further action mean that in many countries, individuals themselves now anticipate promises will be scaled down in the light of the burden of such schemes on future wage earners and/or government borrowing" (Davis 1995, p. 8).

Intergenerational relations embody the implicit social contract underlying public pensions, and are a crucial consideration in the current unease and policy debate. Elsewhere we have written that, "we do not expect the CPP to collapse for as long as the federal government is willing to sustain it by the power of taxation or the power [shared with the provinces] to raise contribution rates. The question is really not whether the CPP will go broke but how much the public will have to spend to keep it financially afloat. Is the Canadian public willing and able to keep the CPP afloat?" (Lam, Cutt and Prince 1995, p. 28). Will the relatively smaller group of workers of the next few generations accept paying 14 percent or more of pensionable earnings into the CPP to fund the benefits of the relatively larger group of "baby-boom" retirees? Contribution rates to the CPP must be continually raised over the next 25 years just to keep the plan solvent and to maintain existing benefits. This much was and is known by public policymakers. To expand the plan's level or scope of benefits would require even greater increases in the contribution rates. This prospect has prompted some commentators to wonder whether it would spark intergenerational conflict between younger workers and the boomer pensioners (Courchene 1994; Deaton 1989; and Markham 1995). The real political constraint and issue of the CPP's future involves the sharing of national income, in the form of pension benefits and burdens, across generations, and in the context of prevailing levels of taxation, public services, and personal opportunities in Canada. To renew the social contract on pensions, the challenge will be reforming the retirement income system so that it meets the needs of the present retired and working generations, without compromising the ability of future generations of workers and retirees to meet their pension needs and goals. This, too, is what sustainable social policy means.

Canadians' deep concerns over the sustainability and survival of the CPP have been shaped by a number of factors. One reason for the weak public confidence, that Townson (1995) emphasizes, is the impact of some myths about the plan. These include beliefs and claims that the CPP is broke; that it has huge "unfunded liabilities"; that the CPP is a drain on federal revenues; that we can no longer "afford" the plan; that the contribution rates are going up in a sudden and unexpected way; and, that Canadians would be better served by a privatized pension scheme. Such myths, Townson argues, are perpetuated by alarmists, neoconservatives and *The Globe and Mail*. Whatever the sources and whether they have any substance or not, such myths are a part of the public opinion culture on pensions. On their own, they unfortunately ignore the many advantages of the CPP and lead to lopsided debates about how to cut the plan. Townson notes, rightly in our view, that little has been done by governments to challenge and counteract these myths. Moreover, many people appear not to appreciate the nature of the CPP as a social insurance-based, pay-as-you-go plan meaning that benefits are intentionally not linked actuarially to costs as they are in pre-funded private plans. The public's pessimism about the CPP is also affected by "the current conservative mood and related perceptions of what is required by the debt and deficit situation of the federal government" (Baldwin 1995, p. 43; see also Markham 1995; and Prince 1995). A related factor may well be the symbolic impact of recent cuts to social programs and related public services, suggesting that there are no "sacred trusts" in pension policy anymore. If governments regularly break campaign promises, fueling distrust towards our governing elites, why not pension promises?

The crisis of faith in Canada's pension plan, however, is by no means confined to policy myths and political ideology. As with the eroded consensus around contemporary welfare states (Mishra 1984), general confidence in public pension programs have weakened primarily for material reasons rather than mythical and ideological ones. That we live in an increasingly insecure world — economically, politically, and socially — is clear from trends at the level of society and economy, local communities, and personal lives. As Judith Maxwell (1995, p. 1) has noted, economic, political, and social forces "are polarizing Canadian society, marginalizing some people and creating opportunity for others." To take one example, changing labour market conditions for many people are adversely affecting their ability to obtain a stable living wage and thus provide for a decent retirement through personal savings, a pension plan at work, the CPP, or by tax incentives. In real terms, wages have grown little over the past 15 years for households, while personal taxation rates and burdens have risen significantly.

Along with these constraints on individual resources for retirement, doubts about the future capacity of government to finance the "pension promise" are likely linked to the aging structure of the Canadian population. "It is the shift in the ratio of expected retired-beneficiaries to worker-contributors (a consequence of enhanced life expectancy among the elderly, the coming retirement of the baby boomers and the declining number of live births) that is the biggest concern for anyone contemplating the future viability of western PAYGO schemes" (Brown 1995, p. 18).

Canadians' uneasiness about social programs and well-being is not limited to public pension policy. The *Maclean's*/CBC News poll found that 82 percent of respondents believe that, over the rest of 1990s, other social benefits like welfare and unemployment insurance will become "less generous"; 65 percent think the gap between the haves and the have-nots within Canada will be widened; and 62 percent expect "free access" to health care and Medicare not to be available to all (*Maclean's* 1995/96, p.32). Apprehension over pensions and other public programs is surely influenced by federal and provincial government restraint measures. "The current political landscape certainly features little to inspire optimism among those concerned about the possible erosion of Canada's social safety net. On the contrary — with governments across Canada taking up arms against budget deficits, the pain is hitting home" (Kopvillem 1995/96, p. 21).

If these gloomy beliefs about the CPP (and other elderly benefit programs) endure, they could have consequences of some weight for workers, seniors, and the retirement income system. Such concerns might result in one or more of the following trends:

- encourage precautionary retirement savings by those able to do so in "good jobs" and upper income levels (Davis 1995). This could be welcome since numerous working Canadians, particularly in the private sector, are not saving enough on their own for retirement (Markham 1995, p. 25);

- slow down (or, more significantly, reverse) the trend towards early retirement and, by extending the work life, increase the contributory period for the CPP;

- put tomorrow's seniors at greater risk of being poor than today's seniors (Baldwin 1995; James 1995);

- provoke political action by groups representing seniors, women, and other groups to defend pension entitlements and advocate for improvements (Prince 1995); and

- make pension reform somewhat easier to pursue if there are general expectations that further restraint measures are inevitably coming.

We now turn to examine the condition of the CPP and policy options for its reform against the backdrop of this pension culture. Our thesis is that reforms can and must be made to improve the financial position of the CPP; and that these reforms need to enhance the political acceptance of the plan, that is, the intergenerational social contract, in order to ensure its continued place in Canada's retirement income system.

## FINANCIAL CONDITION OF THE CPP

Is there any substance to public apprehension over the CPP? A quick analysis of the data provided by the Office of the Superintendent of Financial Institutions (1991), which is responsible for projecting the financial future of the CPP, surely indicates cause for concern. According to the official projection, the CPP would have a growing account balance for the next 30 years (Figure 1).

FIGURE 1: Projected Changes in the CPP Account, 1996-2025

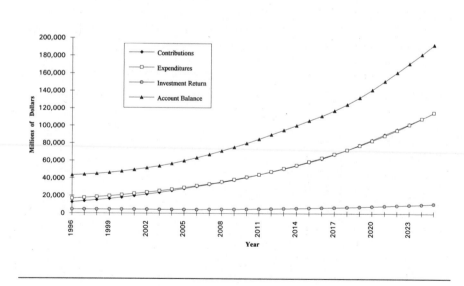

Source: Canada. Office of the Superintendent of Financial Institutions (1991).

This projection, however, is based on a continuous contribution rate increase of approximately 0.2 percentage point a year. The projection also indicates that the rate will reach 13 percent in 2030 and would remain between 13 to 14 percent until the end of the next century. It is a legitimate concern whether the public is willing to accept such high contribution rates. To employers, the contribution is essentially a payroll tax and, as the Board of Trade of Metropolitan Ontario (1993) has pointed out, the rate increases could have severe economic consequences. Without the rate increases, the CPP would exhaust its account in 2008 and would accumulate a deficit as high as a trillion dollars by the quarter mark of the next century (Figure 2).

FIGURE 2: Projected Changes in the CPP Account, 1996-2025, Based on a Constant 5.4 Percent Contribution Rate After 1995

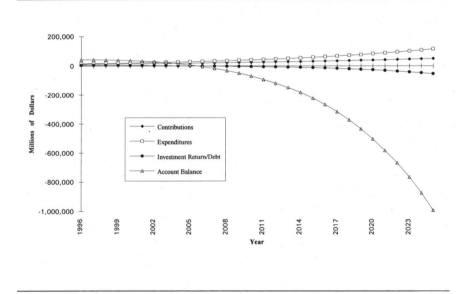

Note: Projections were made by reducing contributions, as shown in Figure 1, in proportion to the reduction in contribution rates from the proposed to 5.4 percent.

Source: Canada. Office of the Superintendent of Financial Instituions (1991).

## FACTORS CAUSING THE PROBLEM

It is a popular belief that CPP's financial problem was caused by demographic changes, specifically, that the baby-boom will create a large population of retirees. This is an inadequate explanation for two reasons. First, the management of the CPP should have foreseen this problem since it was set up (1966) long after the baby-boom had begun. However, their lack of foresight could, to a certain extent, be understood because during the 1970s and 1980s, when contributions exceeded benefit payments, public debate on pension reform was dominated by suggestions to improve and expand benefits. Nonetheless, the CPP should have realized that growing contributions meant a growing liability to be paid in the future, especially when the birth rate began to drop. Second, expenditures have exceeded contributions since 1984, at a time when the workforce was still growing. This indicates that there must be some structural problem in the CPP: either revenues are insufficient or expenditures are too high.

The CPP receives revenue from two sources: contribution and investment. At its inception in 1966, the contribution rate was set at 3.6 percent of pensionable earnings, that is, the earnings from which the contribution is deducted. Contributions were placed in a general fund from which investments were made and benefits and expenses paid. There were no individual accounts for employees and neither was any sinking fund designated for future obligations. This type of system pays one group with revenues received from another as it goes along, and is referred to as pay-as-you-go (PAYGO).

It is typical of PAYGO systems to set the initial contribution rate at a low level because there are few benefit recipients to begin with. The 3.6 percent initial rate set by the CPP, without exception, was very low. The low initial rate makes the system "very attractive to the early participants and thus to the politicians who introduce such a system" (Brown 1993). As the plan matures and the number of benefit recipients increases, the contribution rate would have to increase if the same level of benefits were to be maintained. Otherwise, benefits would have to decrease (Schwartz 1995). In 1982, it was recommended that the contribution rate be reviewed and raised (Canada 1982). The CPP rate, however, was not raised until 1987, since then it has been increased by 0.2 percentage point every year.

It is the nature of a PAYGO system to benefit early participants disproportionately (in relation to their contributions) and carry the cost of financing the early benefits indefinitely into the future. In theory, when the plan is terminated, the cost would have to be paid. If the system lasted for a sufficiently long period of time, with inflation the cost would become negligible at the end. The CPP, however, might have kept the contribution rate at the initial level for too long (21 years). According to our findings (based on historical data supplied by Human

Resources Development Canada, 1967/94), an average person who has contributed to the CPP since 1966 and just retired at age 65 in 1996 would receive approximately $8,650 of retirement pension. If the real rate of investment return after 1995 were between 2 to 4 percent per annum, the funds accumulated through contribution and investment (accumulated funds) would be enough for five years of pension. Life expectancy in 1992 was 72.1 years for males and 78.2 years for females. Assuming an average life expectancy of 75 years, the accumulated funds would be short by five years. The shortfall, spread out through the ten years of retirement, was estimated to be $3,480 per year, approximately 40 percent of the pension. Since the CPP is self-financed, future generations would have to subsidize 40 percent of the pensions paid today. The subsidy would be higher for those who retired earlier; this does not include benefits for survivors, disability, death, and children of contributors, which account for one-third of the total expenditure.

Investment return is the other source of revenue. The CPP funds are invested in public sector securities. While public sector securities may be more secure, they also provide lower returns. For example, a dollar placed in the CPP, according to the interest it had earned, would amount to $5.41 at the end of 1989. The dollar, based on investment fund data (Canada, 1967 to 1989, discontinued after 1989), would amount to $8.60 over the same period of time, 59 percent more than the CPP's. Investment funds diversify their portfolios to balance the trade-off between risk and return, and generally achieved a higher return. The CPP's investment strategy appears to be too limited and too conservative.

One contentious aspect of pension agreements is who should bear the risk and take the rewards of investment. If the investment return had been higher than expected, this means that either the contribution rate could be reduced or benefits increased. Conversely, if the investment return had been lower than expected, the contribution rate would have to be raised or benefits reduced. This leads to another contentious issue — who should be responsible for the governance of the plan? Based on a report by the Task Force on the Investment of Public Pension Funds (1987), pension agreements can be classified into a number of models (Appendix A). The models indicate that those who assume the risk and reward should assume also the responsibility for governance. Since the CPP is financed by employers and employees, they are the people who bear the risk, and should also take the rewards and govern the plan. However, this is not the case. Most pension agreements are between employers and employees. The CPP is an agreement between the government and the people, which includes employers and employees. The CPP was established by the *Canada Pension Plan Act* which gives it the mandate to collect contributions, invest the contributions, and disburse benefit payments. The administrative structure of the CPP does not provide much room for input from employers and employees. The minister of human resources development Canada (formerly Health and Welfare Canada) is by legislation responsible for all parts of the *Canada Pension Plan Act*, with the exception of Part I which concerns the coverage of persons under the plan and the collection of contributions. Part I is under the jurisdiction of the minister of national revenue. The minister receives advice and recommendations from an advisory board of no more than 16 members representing employees, employers, self-employed persons, and the public. Members on the advisory board are not elected but appointed by the governor-in-council. In addition, a number of federal departments, such as the Department of Finance and the Office of the Superintendent of Financial Institutions assume various duties in the administration of the plan (Canada. Health and Welfare 1990).

Despite the fact that there is an independent advisory board, it is questionable how well this board represents the interest of employers and employees, since its members were appointed rather than elected. It has been observed that public sector pension plans managed by the federal government did not always serve the interest of contributors (Management Board of Cabinet 1988*a*, 1988*b*). The CPP is a huge source of capital for the provinces. Federal-provincial politics have certainly played a role in CPP's investment decisions. From a contributor's perspective, a more diversified investment portfolio would be more profitable.

On the expenditure side, the CPP, since its inception, has increased the maximum allowable pensionable earnings, guaranteed full indexing of benefits to the Consumer Price Index, eliminated retirement and earning tests, and added a dropout provision (Canadian Institute of Actuaries 1993). These measures have increased the amount of pension and consequently increased the financial burden. In addition, as mentioned earlier, the CPP has extended survivor's benefits to the surviving spouse after remarriage.

POLICY OPTIONS

As indicated earlier, the funds accumulated by current retirees are insufficient to finance their retirement pensions. This could be the result of an insufficient contribution rate, a conservative investment strategy, or a gratuitously high pension. We do not consider $8,600 of pension per year to be gratuitously high, and therefore do not consider the direct reduction of the retirement pension rate as a viable policy option for improving CPP's financial condition. In addition, the general public has become aware of CPP's problem only in the last few years, and many retirees will have planned their retirement with heavy reliance on the pension. Benefit reduction, however, could be implemented in an indirect way, such as raising the retirement age or eliminating the dropout period provision — to be explored below.

The income level of retirees has been improving over the years. A case could be made that benefits be reduced for those who can afford a cut. However, the CPP is a pension plan with defined benefits, and there could be legal consequences for direct benefit reduction.

As for the survivor and disability benefits, we also do not recommend direct reduction. The reason is that recipients in these categories might have a more urgent need for resources. However, certain socio-economic trends, such as increased participation by women in the workplace, suggest that survivor benefits could be reviewed and, if appropriate, reduced gradually.

From a financial point of view, it would be more effective to increase revenue than to reduce benefits. Mathematically, the amount of funds accumulated to the time of retirement through contribution and investment ($S$) is equal to:

$$\sum_{j=1}^{n} R_j (1+i)^{n-j}$$

where $n$ is the length of the contributory period (from the first job to retirement), $R_j$ the contribution in the $j$th period, and $i$ the rate of investment return.

After retirement, the accumulated funds ($S$) would continue to earn interest if they are not depleted by pension payments.

$$F = S(1+i)^m$$

where $F$ is the funds accumulated to the end of life expectancy, $S$ the funds accumulated to the time of retirement, and $m$ the retirement period (from retirement to death).

Since the accumulated funds will indeed be depleted by pension payments, the accumulated funds will decrease by:

$$\sum_{k=1}^{m} P_k (1+i)^{m-k}$$

where $P_k$ is the pension payment at the $k$ period after retirement.

Since pension payments would eventually use up all the funds, $F$ would finally equal 0.

$$S(1+i)^m - \sum_{k=1}^{m} P_k (1+i)^{m-k} = 0$$

or

$$\left( \sum_{j=1}^{n} R_j (1+i)^{n-j} \right)(1+i)^m - \sum_{k=1}^{m} P_k (1+i)^{m-k} = 0$$

If we use real rate of investment return and assume contributions ($R$) and benefit payments ($P$) to be constant over time, the above equation can be rewritten as follows:

$$R\left(\frac{(1+i)^{n}-1}{i}\right)-P\left(\frac{1-(1+i)^{-m}}{i}\right)=0$$

Or, to equate contributions with benefit payments, we will say that

$$R\left(\frac{(1+i)^{n}-1}{i}\right)=P\left(\frac{1-(1+i)^{-m}}{i}\right)$$

As shown in the above equation, contribution ($R$) and pension payment ($P$) are linear factors, while investment return ($i$) is exponential. Increasing the investment return, therefore, would be the quickest way to improve CPP's financial condition.

For a given life span and a given age to begin contribution, a decrease in retirement period ($m$) will increase the contributory period ($n$). Another effective approach, therefore, would be to raise the retirement age. By doing so, we would have increased the number of contributions, decreased the number of pension payments, and also changed the exponential factors in favour of improving revenues.

Logically, retirement period ($m$) should be shorter than contributory period ($n$). Although changing the amount of contribution ($R$) or pension payment ($P$) would only have a linear effect, the effect of changing the contribution would be stronger than changing the benefit payment because the contribution has a larger exponent for its investment factor (i.e., $n>m$).

Therefore, from social, logical, and economic points of view, the order of reform options should be: (i) diversify investment to improve investment return; (ii) raise the retirement age to improve revenue and reduce expenditure; (iii) increase contribution rates; and (iv) reduce benefits.

The first two options are straight-forward. As far as the third option is concerned, there are two convenient ways to increase revenues. The simplest way is to increase the contribution rate, which was proposed by the CPP. Revenue can also be increased by eliminating the basic exemption. The retirement pension benefit can be reduced indirectly by eliminating the dropout provision or by increasing the contributory period for full pension entitlement. We will explain these in turn.

The CPP has a ceiling for pensionable earnings, referred to as the Year's Maximum Pensionable Earnings (YMPE). The pensionable earnings are either the YMPE or the actual earnings, whichever is less. The first 10 percent of the YMPE is exempted from contribution, referred to as the Year's Basic Exemption (YBE). The actual amount from which contribution is deducted (contributory earnings), therefore, is pensionable earnings less the YBE. The retirement pension, on the other hand, is based on the full amount of YMPE. The pension, starting at retirement, is equal to 25 percent of the average YMPE for the three years before retirement, multiplied by an average earnings ratio. An earnings ratio is the earnings in a month divided by one-twelfth of the YMPE for that year. The average earnings ratio is the earnings ratios averaged over the contributory period. Since retirement pension is based on the full YMPE, this provides a strong argument to eliminate the YBE. Eliminating the YBE should bring in about 10 percent more revenue.

Under the current policy, limited periods of low income can be excluded from the pension calculation. Since low income means low earnings ratios, the exclusion will improve the average earnings ratio and in turn increase the pension amount. These low-income periods are referred to as dropout periods. Since this provision arbitrarily increases the pension amount, it should be eliminated. However, there are certain conditions under which dropout periods or similar provisions should be considered.

First, there are periods in which a person is ineligible for full-time employment (e.g., academic training, pregnancy). However, by working part-time, they contribute to the economy as well as the CPP. There is no reason why they should get a smaller pension because of part-time employment. In this case, the YMPE should be prorated to reflect the part-time status. One way to implement this would be to consider 35 or more hours of work as full-time. For any week that employment were less than 35 hours, the YMPE would be adjusted proportionately.

Second, an employee might decide to postpone retirement after the age of 65. The CPP consequently would benefit from receiving more revenue and making fewer payments. However, elderly persons might be unable to earn as much income as before their retirement, and it would be unfair for them to receive a smaller pension because of postponed retirement. In this case, the dropout provision should apply.

The CPP requires an aggregate of ten years of contribution for full pension entitlement. As shown in Figure 2, at the historical contribution rates, even 30 years of contribution would be insufficient to finance the current level of pension. It is therefore reasonable to increase the contributory period required for full pension.

FINANCIAL ANALYSIS OF POLICY OPTIONS

The effects of the aforementioned policy options were examined using computer simulations. The simulations were based on a person with the average income of all CPP contributors. It was assumed that this person was 21 years of age in 1995 and may retire at age 65. This person represents an average contributor who is going to carry the financial burden of the CPP in the near future. By calculating what the average plan member would pay and receive from the CPP, we can assess the impact of the policy options on the CPP. The contributions to be made by this person depend on his or her earnings. The annual incomes of this person were projected using the following procedures:

1.  Average income by age group was obtained from *Canada Pension Plan Contributors* (Canada. Human Resources Development 1994). The data represent the current income distribution by age group among CPP contributors.

2.  The data provided by the *Canada Pension Plan Contributors* are divided into age groups of five-year intervals. Incomes within each age group were estimated by straight-line averaging. For example, the average income for the age group between 20 to 24 years, inclusive, was $13,881. This amount was assumed to be the income for the 22-year old, the median age within the group. The income was then adjusted by year in equal proportion, forward and backward, to match income figures in adjacent age groups.

3.  The income figures were compounded using the rates of earnings increase projected in the *Canada Pension Plan Fourteenth Actuarial Report* for future years, which were assumed to be 4.5 percent after the year 1999 (Canada. Office of the Superintendent of Financial Institutions 1991).

4.  The earnings adjusted figures were then discounted back to the 1995 value using the inflation rates projected in the *Canada Pension Plan Fourteenth Actuarial Report,* which were assumed to be 3.5 percent after 1999.

The Year's Maximum Pensionable Earnings (YMPE) for future years were compounded and discounted back using the same earnings increase and inflation rates mentioned in 3. and 4. above. Appendix B shows the projected incomes of this average contributor and the corresponding YMPE. Simulation results will be shown in constant 1995 dollars, in order to render results of different simulations comparable. Since the simulations were based on the rates of earnings increase and inflation projected by the CPP, significant deviations from the projections will render the results less reliable.

RAISING THE CONTRIBUTION RATE

Raising the contribution rate will increase revenue; this has been proposed by the CPP. We agree that the current rate is too low. As shown in Table 1, where a 2-percent real rate of investment return, 40 years of contribution, and 85 years of life expectancy (retirement period of 20 years) were assumed, a 7- percent contribution rate could sustain an annual pension of $8,629, which is very close to the current level of pension payment for the average person. This finding is consistent with our theoretical understanding. If we assume that annual pension benefit is 25 percent (.25) of annual earnings ($E$), for a contributory period of 40 years and a retirement period of 20 years, a contribution ($R$) equaling 6.8 percent of the annual earnings ($E$) is required to finance the benefit payments (.25$E$).

$$R\left(\frac{(1+2\%)^{40}-1}{2\%}\right)=.25E\left(\frac{1-(1+2\%)^{-20}}{2\%}\right)$$

$R=.068E$ or 6.8% of $E$

As far as the assumptions are concerned, from 1966 to 1989, the real rate of return was 1.5 percent for the CPP and 3.5 percent for the capital market; we therefore chose 2 percent as a conservative but realistic rate. According to projections made by the Office of Superintendent of Financial Institutions (1991), life expectancy will improve to 80.3 years for males and 86.9 years for females, suggesting an average of 83.6 years. We assume a slightly higher life expectancy to ensure that the required contribution rate would not be underestimated. We expect the average person to spend a few years unemployed or in training. By assuming a contributory period of 40 years, we make allowance for approximately seven years of "idle time."

TABLE 1:   Effects of Varying the Contribution Rate

| Contribution Rate | Actuarially Based Pension | Accumulated Funds | Increase | Cumulative Increase |
|---|---|---|---|---|
| % | | | % | % |
| 4 | 4,930 | 83,873 | | |
| 5 | 6,163 | 104,846 | 25.0 | 25.0 |
| 6 | 7,396 | 125,820 | 20.0 | 50.0 |
| 7 | 8,629 | 146,793 | 16.7 | 75.0 |
| 8 | 9,861 | 167,756 | 14.3 | 100.0 |
| 9 | 11,094 | 188,716 | 12.5 | 125.0 |
| 10 | 12,327 | 209,690 | 11.1 | 150.0 |
| 11 | 13,559 | 230,659 | 10.0 | 175.0 |

Assumptions: 2 percent real rate of investment return, 40 years of contributions, retirement at age 65, and life expectancy of 85 years.

Source: Authors' compilation.

In Table 1, the actuarially based pension indicates the amount of CPP pension that could be sustained by the respective contribution rate, given the assumptions. The accumulated funds indicate the amount accumulated at the time of retirement through contribution and investment. The table indicates that the percentage increase in accumulated funds is at a decreasing rate. This, however, is an illusion. As the contribution rate goes up, the accumulated funds grow, causing the increased amount to become a smaller percentage of the funds. The cumulative increase is a better indicator of the rate of increase. As indicated, the increase from percentage point to percentage point is roughly 25 percent. For example, an increase in the contribution rate from 5 to 6 percent represents an additional 25 percent (from 25 to 50 percent) in cumulative increase, and this is true of other percentage point increases. This confirms that the increase is linear, as suggested in our discussion.

Since we do not advocate cutting benefits directly, a 7-percent contribution rate would be required and will be used for other simulations. We would like to stress that this contribution rate can only support the retirement pension; it would not be sufficient to support the survivor and disability benefits. If we assume that survivor and disability benefits continue to consume one-third of the total benefit expenditures (equaling one-half of the expenditure on retirement pension), our calculation, as shown below, indicates that a contribution rate of 10.15 percent would be required. If these expenditures were to increase due to a liberal interpretation of the entitlement rules, the contribution rate would have to be higher.

$$R\left(\frac{(1+2\%)^{40}-1}{2\%}\right) = 1.5 \bullet .25E\left(\frac{1-(1+2\%)^{-20}}{2\%}\right)$$

$R=.1015E$ or $10.15\%$ of $E$

DIVERSIFYING INVESTMENT TO IMPROVE RETURN

Having established that a 7-percent contribution rate is needed, the next set of simulations explore the effect of varying the rate of investment return. The results (Table 2) indicate that for every percentage point increase in return, the accumulated funds would increase by 20 percent or more. The cumulative increases indicate that the increase is at an increasing rate. This confirms the exponential nature of this variable, as shown in the theoretical explanation. The results provide strong support for diversifying the CPP's investments into the capital market.

TABLE 2: Effects of Varying the Rate of Investment Return

| Real Rate of Investment Return | Increase in Accumulated Funds | Cumulative Increase |
|---|---|---|
| % | % | % |
| From 1 to 2 | 21.0 | 21.0 |
| From 2 to 3 | 22.2 | 47.8 |
| From 3 to 4 | 23.3 | 82.0 |
| From 4 to 5 | 24.3 | 126.2 |
| From 5 to 6 | 25.3 | 183.3 |
| From 6 to 7 | 26.2 | 257.5 |

Assumptions: 7 percent contribution rate, 40 years of contributions, retirement at age 65.
Source: Authors' compilation.

RAISING THE RETIREMENT AGE

Raising the retirement age would increase revenue as well as reduce expenditure. The results (Table 3) indicate a modest effect. For every year of postponed retirement, the accumulated funds would increase by about 3 percent and the funds required for CPP pensions would decrease by 3 to 5 percent. However, if the retirement age were postponed by five years, the accumulated funds would increase by 17.1 percent while the funds required for a CPP pension would decrease by 18.8 percent. The two effects would interact to provide a 46.5 percent improvement in the fund balance at the time of retirement. This finding is also consistent with our theoretical understanding. If we assume that retirement occurs at age 65 and hold all other assumptions constant, the accumulated funds would amount to 4.23 times the annual earnings (4.23E).

$$.07E\left(\frac{(1+2\%)^{40}-1}{2\%}\right)=4.23E$$

From age 65 to 70, the accumulated funds would continue to earn interest but at the same time would be reduced by pension payments equaling 25 percent of the annual earnings (.25E). At age 70, the accumulated funds would drop to 3.37 times the annual earnings.

$$4.23E(1+2\%)^{5}-.25E\left(\frac{(1+2\%)^{5}-1}{2\%}\right)=3.37E$$

On the other hand, if retirement were postponed until age 70, the accumulated funds would equal 5.03 times the annual earnings. This amounts to a 49.3 percent improvement (5.03E/3.37E).

$$.07E\left(\frac{(1+2\%)^{45}-1}{2\%}\right)=5.03E$$

TABLE 3:   Effects of Raising the Retirement Age for Full Pension Entitlement

| Change in Retirement Age | Reduction in Funds Required CPP Pensions | | Increase in Accumulated Funds | |
|---|---|---|---|---|
| | Per Year | Cumulative | Per Year | Cumulative |
| | % | % | % | % |
| From 65 to 66 | 3.5 | 3.5 | 3.4 | 3.4 |
| From 66 to 67 | 3.8 | 7.2 | 3.3 | 6.7 |
| From 67 to 68 | 4.1 | 11.0 | 3.3 | 10.2 |
| From 68 to 69 | 4.1 | 14.7 | 3.1 | 13.7 |
| From 69 to 70 | 4.8 | 18.8 | 3.0 | 17.1 |

Assumptions: 7 percent contribution rate, 2 percent real rate of investment return, and 40 years of contributions before age 65.

Source: Authors' compilation.

## ELIMINATING THE YEAR'S BASIC EXEMPTION (YBE)

A simulation indicates that eliminating the YBE would increase the accumulated funds by 12.7 percent. The YBE is 10 percent of the YMPE. The increase in accumulated funds is more than 10 percent because earnings in some years were below the YMPE, resulting in the YBE being more than 10 percent of pensionable earnings.

## ELIMINATING THE DROPOUT PROVISION

Eliminating the dropout provision would reduce the funds required for CPP pension by 3 to 6 percent, depending on the contributory period (Table 4). The reduction is higher for a longer contributory period. This is because people with shorter contributory periods tend to be highly trained (e.g., medical doctors, engineers) and would have fewer periods of low income, resulting in fewer and shorter dropout periods.

TABLE 4:   Effects of Eliminating the Dropout Provision

| Contributory Period | Reduction in Funds Required for CPP Pensions |
|---|---|
| % | % |
| 30 years | 3.7 |
| 35 years | 4.3 |
| 40 years | 6.2 |

Assumptions: 7 percent contribution rate, 2 percent real rate of return, retirement at age 65.
Source: Authors' compilation.


## RAISING CONTRIBUTORY PERIOD FOR FULL PENSION ENTITLEMENT

It is difficult to assess the effect of this option because we do not know the number of contributors who would have short contributory periods. The simulation results indicate that, for a 2-percent real rate of investment return, 40 years of contribution would be required to finance the current level of pension (Table 5). For a contributory period of 30 years, a 3-percent real rate of return would be needed. For someone who has contributed for only ten years, a 14-percent real rate of return would be needed. Although there will be few who have such a short contributory period, the findings still present a strong case for increasing the contributory period requirement.


TABLE 5:   Contributory Period and Investment Return for $8,600 of Pension

| Contributory Period | Required Real Rate of Investment Return |
|---|---|
| % | % |
| 40 years | 2 |
| 30 years | 3 |
| 25 years | 4 |
| 10 years | 14 |

Assumptions: 7 percent contribution rate, retirement at age 65.
Source: Authors' compilation.

To examine the effect of contributory period from another perspective, Table 6 shows that for every reduction of five years, the accumulated funds will drop by 10 to 23 percent.

TABLE 6:   Effects of Varying the Contributory Period

|  | Reduction in Accumulated Funds | |
| Change in Contributory Period | Every 5 Years | Cumulative |
| --- | --- | --- |
|  | % | % |
| From 40 to 35 years | 10.6 | 10.6 |
| From 35 to 30 years | 14.4 | 23.5 |
| From 30 to 25 years | 18.2 | 37.4 |
| From 25 to 20 years | 23.0 | 51.8 |

Assumptions: 7 percent contribution rate, 2 percent real rate of return, retirement at age 65.
Source: Authors' compilation.

CONCLUSIONS

We have assessed the financial impact of several policy options for reforming the CPP. From that analysis, we conclude and recommend that the following changes be made:

- *Remove survivor and disability benefits from the CPP and combine them with the GIS.* In order to finance the retirement pension as well as the survivor and disability benefits, a contribution rate of more than 10 percent is required. Even at this rate, there will not be enough funds to cover the unfunded liability which eventually has to be absorbed. Since the CPP is a contributory pension plan rather than a income support program, we recommend that survivor and disability benefits be removed from the CPP and grouped with the GIS, and appropriately financed through general revenues.

- *Raise the contribution rate, employee and employer combined, quickly (say, over a four- or five-year period) to 8 percent.* Even if survivor and disability benefits were removed, increases in the contribution rate would still be inevitable. The analysis clearly indicates that the current rate is too low and that a 7-percent contribution rate would be able to finance the current level of retirement benefits. Since the unfunded liability needs to be gradually absorbed, we recommend that the contribution rate be raised to 8 percent. Hopefully, with other measures for improving revenues and reducing costs, the financial problem could be solved. An additional simulation reveals that, at a 5.4-percent contribution rate, the accumulated funds would amount to $113,241 on average for each recipient. Since an 8-percent contribution rate would result in $167,756 of accumulated funds (see Table 1), raising the contribution rate from 5.4 to 8 percent would increase the accumulated funds by 48.1 percent.

- *Invest member contributions through the capital market.* The simulation results indicate that for every percentage point increase in real return on investment, the accumulated funds would increase by more than 20 percent. It is hard to predict how high the investment return would become if investments were extended into the private sector. Historical evidence indicates that the capital market will provide higher returns than public sector securities. Additional simulations indicate that an increase in the real return rate from 1.5 percent (achieved by the CPP) to 3.5 percent (achieved by investment funds) would increase the accumulated funds by 49.1 percent. Investing through the capital market is therefore a very effective strategy to solve the problem. It does not impose an additional cost on contributors but the provinces will lose a secure source of capital. However, the CPP was not set up to serve the capital needs of the provinces, although it may have happened that way. If the CPP were to invest through the capital market, an independent authority could be set up to regulate investment activities and to protect the interest of contributors.

- *Gradually raise the retirement age for full pension entitlement to 70 years.* Raising the retirement age would increase revenues and reduce costs. For every year of delayed retirement, expenditures would be reduced by about 3 to 5 percent while revenues will increase by about 3 percent. By raising the retirement age to 70, the combined effect would be a 46.5 percent improvement in the fund balance. Since the current trend is to retire early, early retirement should be allowed but with lower pensions. In addition, it is important to ensure that the OAS, GIS, and SPA combined together will provide adequate incomes for those who cannot prolong their career to meet basic needs. The retirement age should be raised very gradually over the next 20 to 30 years.

Individually, each of the above policy options would have dramatic effects on improving the fund balance. If implemented together, the interaction among the policies would make the effects even more dramatic. Assuming that the status quo is represented by a 1.5-percent real rate of investment return, a 5.4-percent contribution rate, and retirement at 65, additional simulations indicate that the combined effects of the recommended options, if a 3.5-percent real rate of return could be achieved by investing through the capital market, would increase the fund balance from the status quo by 323 percent. Even assuming that only a 2-percent real rate of return could be achieved, the simulation results indicate a 196-percent improvement in the accumulated funds. Since the contribution rate is destined to increase, the results of the above comparisons, though astonishing, are not very meaningful. It would be more meaningful to compare the combined effects of our recommendations with the effects of the CPP's proposed rate increases (0.2 percentage point increase per annum). Additional simulations indicate that our recommendations would provide 72 percent more funds than the CPP's proposed rate increases for a 3.5 percent real rate of return. For a 2-percent return rate, our recommendations would provide 20 percent more funds.

It is obvious that the combined effects of our recommendations would provide better results than the proposed rate increases. Theoretically, if the real rate of investment return were 2 percent per annum, an 8-percent contribution rate with 45 years of contribution (retirement at age 70) would accumulate funds equaling 5.75 times the annual earnings (5.75E) at the time of retirement.

$$.08E\left(\frac{(1+2\%)^{45}-1}{2\%}\right) - 5.75E$$

The retirement pension for 15 years (life expectancy of 85 years) less real investment returns earned during that period would equal 3.21 times the annual earnings. The contributions, therefore, would be sufficient to support the pension for 1.79 persons (5.75E/3.21E=1.79).

$$25E\left(\frac{1-(1+2\%)^{-15}}{2\%}\right) = 3.21E$$

If the real rate of return were 3.5 percent, the accumulated funds would amount to 8.46 times the annual earnings at retirement.

$$.08E\left(\frac{(1+3.5\%)^{45}-1}{3.5\%}\right) = 8.46E$$

The pension payments less earned real returns would be 2.88 times the annual earnings. This means that the contributions could support the pensions of 2.94 persons (8.46E/2.88E=2.94).

$$.25E\left(\frac{1-(1+3.5\%)^{-15}}{3.5\%}\right) = 2.88E$$

As shown in the above calculations, the four recommended options would generate enough funds to cover the retirement pension as well as to absorb the unfunded liability. At a 2-percent real rate of return, each contributor could absorb an unfunded liability equaling 79 percent of his or her retirement pension. At a 3.5-percent return rate, each contributor could absorb an amount equaling 184 percent of the retirement pension.

In addition to the above three recommendations, the following options should also be considered:

- *Eliminate the Year's Basic Exemption (YBE).* Eliminating the YBE would increase the accumulated funds by 12.7 percent. Since retirement pensions are based on pensionable earnings which include the exempted amount, it is generous of the CPP to provide this exemption. If the CPP cannot afford to be generous, the YBE should be eliminated.

- *Increase the contributory period for full pension entitlement.* The analysis indicates that at least 40 years of contributions are required to finance the current level of benefits. The retirement pension of those who contributed for a shorter period of time should be reduced accordingly. It is difficult to assess the effect of this option, since we are unsure how many contributors will have a shorter contributory period.

- *Eliminate the dropout provision.* Eliminating the dropout provision will reduce expenditures by a few percentage points. The effect is not as significant as for other policy options but is still interesting.

Although we do not recommend direct reduction in pension benefits, it does not mean that such reduction is not justifiable. In fact, the analysis indicates that the current benefits are too high for the contributions received. We do not recommend direct benefit reduction, first, because it would be politically difficult to implement, and, second, because a large proportion of current retirees may have planned their retirement with reliance on the continuation of benefits at their current level.

The CPP is an important part of Canada's retirement income system. Reforms are necessary if it is to play its role as a contributions-based supplement to OAS and GIS. We have suggested a combination of options as an alternative to the monolithic preoccupation of the CPP administration with increasing the contribution rate. We believe that our more broadly based proposal would be more effective and efficient, would avoid the potential serious economic disincentives of significant, continuing rate increases and would restore public confidence in the CPP.

# APPENDIX A

## Nature of Pension Agreement

There are a number of pension models with varying degree of risk, reward and responsibility shared by employers and employees (Task Force on the Investment of Public Pension Funds 1987). These models are explained below.

*Pure Defined Benefit.* As mentioned above, employers assume all the responsibility in this model. They provide all required contributions and employees are not required to pay into the system. The contributions are spread over the working careers of employees and are invested. Employees are guaranteed a level of pension usually based on the amount of earnings and years of service (defined benefit). Since pension benefit is unaffected by investment returns, employers assume the risk and reward of investment. If the return had been higher than expected, employers could reduce the contribution in subsequent years. Otherwise, they would have to contribute more to make up the difference. Since employers assume all the risk, they take sole responsibility in investment decisions.

*Contributory Defined Benefit.* This model is very similar to the pure defined benefit model with the exception that employees are also required to contribute to the pension plan. The contribution is usually a fixed percentage of their wages or salaries (defined contribution). Employees are guaranteed a defined benefit. This means that employers assume the investment risk and logically should take the rewards. However, if the investment return had been lower than expected, employers might attempt to pass some of the cost to employees during contract negotiation. They might try to negotiate for a lower level of benefit or a higher level of contribution from employees. Conversely, if the return had been higher than expected, employees might try to negotiate for a higher benefit or a lower contribution rate. Employers generally assume the responsibility for investment decisions.

*Shared Risk and Reward.* As the name of this model suggests, the risk and reward of investment are shared between employers and employees. Similar to the previous models, the pension benefit is defined. Contribution, however, would vary from time to time depending on previous investment returns. Since the risk and reward of investment are shared, the decision-making responsibility should also be shared. Employees, current, former or retired, should participate in making investment decisions. In practice, an employee-elected committee could represent employees in the governance of the plan.

*Hybrid.* In this model, contributions made by employers and employees are fixed (i.e., defined), usually as a percentage of earnings. An account is set up for each employee into which contributions and investment returns will be credited. Employees are guaranteed a minimum level of defined benefit. At retirement, if the amount accumulated in an employee's account had a higher actuarial value than the guaranteed benefit, the employee would get a higher level of benefit appropriate for the amount accumulated. Otherwise, the employee would receive the guaranteed benefit. The guaranteed benefit is usually set at a sufficiently low level so that the funds accrued to the employees would be enough to finance the benefit. In this model, employers forego the reward of investment and would logically prefer investments with no risk. Conversely, employees prefer high risk investments that have higher returns. Since employers assume the risk, they should be responsible for investment decisions.

*Multi-Employer.* This model arises from situations where a collective agreement is negotiated between a union and an association of employers (e.g., National Hockey League). A multi-employer plan allows employees to move from employer to employer without having to withdraw from the plan. In this model, contributions to the plan are usually based on the length of service (e.g., $X per hour) rather than the amount of earnings. The contributions and investment returns are credited to a general pension fund from which all benefits are drawn. The pension plan is governed by a uniform benefit formula which is also based on length of service ($X for Y hours of contributory service). The benefit formula could be revised over a period of time to reflect the actual investment returns. Since employees collectively assume the risk and reward of investment, they should be involved in the decision-making process.

*Pure Defined Contribution.* In this model, pension plans function mainly as saving mechanisms. Contributions are fixed, usually as a percentage of earnings (defined contribution). An account is set up for each employee into which contributions and investment returns are credited. The amount of pension varies from employee to employee depending on the funds accumulated in the individual accounts. Since employees assume all the risk and reward of investment, they should have input in investment decisions.

# APPENDIX B

## Projected Average Income and YMPE, 1995-2044
## (in 1995 dollars)

| Age | Year | Income | YMPE | Age | Year | Income | YMPE |
|-----|------|--------|------|-----|------|--------|------|
| 21 | 1995 | 12,027 | 34,900 | 46 | 2020 | 45,800 | 45,800 |
| 22 | 1996 | 14,702 | 35,800 | 47 | 2021 | 46,200 | 46,200 |
| 23 | 1997 | 16,834 | 36,100 | 48 | 2022 | 46,700 | 46,700 |
| 24 | 1998 | 19,037 | 36,400 | 49 | 2023 | 47,200 | 47,200 |
| 25 | 1999 | 21,282 | 37,000 | 50 | 2024 | 47,600 | 47,600 |
| 26 | 2000 | 23,567 | 37,600 | 51 | 2025 | 48,100 | 48,100 |
| 27 | 2001 | 25,893 | 38,100 | 52 | 2026 | 48,500 | 48,500 |
| 28 | 2002 | 27,243 | 38,500 | 53 | 2027 | 48,229 | 49,000 |
| 29 | 2003 | 28,617 | 38,900 | 54 | 2028 | 47,806 | 49,500 |
| 30 | 2004 | 30,014 | 39,300 | 55 | 2029 | 47,369 | 50,000 |
| 31 | 2005 | 31,436 | 39,700 | 56 | 2030 | 46,920 | 50,400 |
| 32 | 2006 | 32,882 | 40,000 | 57 | 2031 | 46,457 | 50,900 |
| 33 | 2007 | 33,978 | 40,400 | 58 | 2032 | 46,308 | 51,400 |
| 34 | 2008 | 35,092 | 40,800 | 59 | 2033 | 46,151 | 51,900 |
| 35 | 2009 | 36,224 | 41,200 | 60 | 2034 | 43,971 | 52,400 |
| 36 | 2010 | 37,375 | 41,600 | 61 | 2035 | 45,321 | 52,900 |
| 37 | 2011 | 38,545 | 42,000 | 62 | 2036 | 45,636 | 53,400 |
| 38 | 2012 | 39,540 | 42,400 | 63 | 2037 | 44,968 | 54,000 |
| 39 | 2013 | 40,550 | 42,800 | 64 | 2038 | 44,799 | 54,500 |
| 40 | 2014 | 41,577 | 43,200 | 65 | 2039 | 33,831 | 55,000 |
| 41 | 2015 | 42,619 | 43,600 | 66 | 2040 | 32,811 | 55,600 |
| 42 | 2016 | 43,678 | 44,100 | 67 | 2041 | 34,501 | 56,100 |
| 43 | 2017 | 44,429 | 44,500 | 68 | 2042 | 31,275 | 56,600 |
| 44 | 2018 | 44,992 | 44,900 | 69 | 2043 | 30,132 | 57,200 |
| 45 | 2019 | 45,398 | 45,300 | 70 | 2044 | 28,963 | 57,700 |

Source: Based on Canada. Human Resources Development (1967-94, esp.; 1992); and
Office of the Superintendent of Financial Institutions (1991).

REFERENCES

Baldwin, B. (1995), "Maintain Retirement Incomes," *Policy Options*, 16, 6:41-43.

Board of Trade of Metropolitan Ontario (1993), "Strategies for the Long Term Survival of the Canada Pension Plan," unpublished letter to the Minister Designate of Human Resources and Labour.

Brown, R. (1993), "Canadian Retirement Income Social Security Programs Review and Prognosis," unpublished paper, University of Waterloo.

Brown, R.L. (1995), "Achieving Stability and Equality with Paygo Financing," *Policy Options,* 16, 6:17-21.

Canada (1982), *Better Pensions for Canadians*, Ottawa: Supply and Services Canada.

Canada. Health and Welfare (1990), *Report for the Year Ending March 31, 1989, Income Security Program*, Ottawa: Supply and Services Canada.

_____. Human Resources Development (1967-94), *Canada Pension Plan Contributors*, Ottawa: Supply and Services Canada.

_____. Office of the Superintendent of Financial Institutions (1991), *Canada Pension Plan Fourteenth Actuarial Report,* Ottawa: Supply and Services Canada.

_____. Standing Committee on Human Resources Development (1995), *Security, Opportunities and Fairness: Canadians Renewing their Social Programs*, Ottawa: House of Commons, Queen's Printer.

Canadian Institute of Actuaries (1993), *Canadian Retirement Income Social Security Programs*, Ottawa: Canadian Institute of Actuaries.

Courchene, T.J. (1995), *Social Canada in the Millennium*, Toronto: C.D. Howe Institute.

Davis, E.P. (1995), "The State of Public Pensions in the OECD," *Policy Options*, 16, 6:3-8.

Deaton, R.L. (1989), *The Political Economy of Pensions*, Vancouver: University of British Columbia Press.

James, E. (1995), "The Old Age Crisis in International Perspective," *Policy Options*, 16, 6:8-12.

Kopvillem. P. (1995/96), "Unemployed, Without a Safety Net," *Maclean's,* December 25/January 1:20-22.

Lam, N., J. Cutt and M. Prince (1995), "Contain CPP Rate Increases," *Policy Options,* 16, 6:28-32.

*Maclean's* (1995/96), "Maclean's/CBC News Poll: Taking the Pulse," December 25/January 1:32-33.

Management Board of Cabinet (1988*a*), *Comments and Advice in Respect of the Rowan Report on the Investment of Public Sector Pension Funds*, Ottawa: Queen's Printer.

_____ (1988*b*), *Rowan Task Force Report on the Investment of Public Sector Pension Funds*, Ottawa: Queen's Printer

Markham, I. (1995), "Pensions Pit One Generation Against Another," *Policy Options,* 16, 6:25-28.

Maxwell, J. (1995), "The Social Role of the State in a Knowledge-Based Economy," in *Redefining Social Security*, ed. P. Grady, R. Howse and J. Maxwell, Kingston: School of Policy Studies, Queen's University.

Mishra, R. (1984), *The Welfare State in Crisis*, Brighton: Wheatsheaf Books.

Prince, M. (1995), "From Expanding Coverage to Heading for Cover: Shifts in the Politics and Policies of Canadian Pension Reform," paper presented at the Gerontology Summer Institute, McMaster University.

Schwartz, A.M. (1995), "Pension Schemes: Trade-Offs Between Redistribution and Savings," *Finance and Development,* (June):8-11.

Task Force on the Investment of Public Sector Pension Funds (1987), *The Nature of the Pension Agreement,* Toronto: Frank Russell Canada Limited.

Townson, M. (1995), "Expose Myths Behind CPP Proposals," *Policy Options*, 16, 6:13-16.

# CHAPTER SIX

# A New Old Age Pension

*Ken Battle*

## INTRODUCTION

The Liberal government of Jean Chrétien and Paul Martin is transforming Canadian social policy. It has thrown out the rule book that social policymakers, researchers, and advocates learned and generally lived by over the past 50 years.

Unemployment Insurance has had its belt cinched tighter and given a new, more hopeful title, Employment Insurance, though readers of George Orwell may detect a strong whiff of newspeak in the name change. Under proposed legislation, not only will the usual levers of UI restraint be pulled — tougher eligibility requirements, lower benefits for most recipients and a reduction in the maximum duration of payments — but some upper income repeat users will lose all their benefits to the clawback and low-income parents will receive a Family Income Supplement that could increase their total benefit to as much as 80 percent of insurable earnings. The 100-percent clawback severs the visible link between premiums and benefit eligibility, one of the tenets of social insurance, and will provide a revenue windfall to the federal government which no longer contributes to the financing of the program. The new Family Income Supplement should, by the former rules of the social policy game, be part of the already existing Child Tax Benefit and financed through general revenues rather than UI/EI premiums levied on employees and employers.

Federal social transfers to the provinces for health and postsecondary education under Established Programs Financing (EPF) and welfare and social services under the Canada Assistance Plan (CAP) will be thrown into a single pot — the Canada Health and Social Transfer (CHST) — that will be substantially smaller and may even boil off within 15 years or so, depending upon whether or not the finance minister decides to heed the urgings of his critics (including some members of his own caucus and Cabinet) to stabilize the federal block fund transfer. If the CHST follows current practice and is only partially indexed, federal cash transfers will dissipate and eventually disappear and along with them Ottawa's capacity to enforce the conditions of the *Canada Health Act* that maintain universal health care.

But even if the federal government maintains a sizable transfer to the provinces, certainly welfare and most likely social services will suffer from the competition for smaller federal transfers from more powerful provincial health ministries, warring within the bosom of a single block grant. Not only have welfare and social services lost the designated federal and provincial funding they had under the Canada Assistance Plan, but two of the three conditions imposed by CAP — welfare must be made available to all in need, regardless of category or cause of need and welfare systems must provide an appeals mechanism — will be jettisoned by the CHST. The sole remaining condition that will be carried over in the CHST — the prohibition of residency requirements for welfare — already has been challenged both politically and now legally by the British Columbia government. The federal government's *de facto* abandonment of a welfare safety net throughout Canada is an extraordinary and lamentable change in the rules of social policy (Battle and Torjman 1995).

These changes come on the heels of equally momentous measures put in place by the Mulroney Conservatives. The Tories' changes, left in place by the Liberals, include: the replacement of universal Family Allowances and the refundable and non-refundable child tax credits by a single income-tested program, the Child Tax Benefit and its component Working Income Supplement for the working poor; partial indexation of the personal income tax system, child benefits and the refundable GST credit; cuts to and partial indexation of federal transfer payments to the province for health and postsecondary education; the "cap on CAP," which put a 5 percent ceiling on increases in federal costsharing of welfare and social service expenditures for Ontario, Alberta, and British Columbia and rang the death knell of CAP; and two rounds of cuts to Unemployment Insurance, including withdrawal of federal funding which put the full cost burden on employees and employers.

What, you might well ask, has all this to do with pensions? There are several good reasons to preface a paper on old age pensions with a reference to changes in other major social programs.

This paper argues that, as with other social policies, the transformation of elderly benefits that is occurring under the Liberals was started and well advanced by the Tories and is being guided by the same new rule book. Key to the Conservatives' political success in changing elderly benefits was their practice of social policy by stealth, which they applied with equal efficacy to other areas of social and tax policy (Battle 1990). The primary motivation for changing old age pensions, as with the other social programs, is to reduce the federal government's costs. One of the key criticisms of the transformation of elderly benefits — that it represents a step backward to the bad old days rather than forward to the brave new world — has been levelled as well against the Conservative/Liberal changes to child benefits, federal social transfers to the province, Unemployment Insurance, and the tax system.

Moreover, public pensions have played a pivotal role in the development of the Canadian welfare state: Old Age Security (1952), the Canada and Quebec Pension Plans (1966), the Guaranteed Income Supplement (1966) and the Spouse's Allowance (1975) were major additions to our social security system and greatly strengthened its fundamental anti-poverty and earnings-replacement capacities. The last major attempt to expand the welfare state was during the so-called Great Pension Debate of the early 1980s, when proposals were put forward to substantially increase the Canada and Quebec Pension Plans or to mandate private pension plans for the entire workforce. Those proposals failed, and instead governments chose the politically safer path of more modest changes to the C/QPP, Guaranteed Income Supplement, Spouse's Allowance and federal and provincial legislation regulating employer-sponsored pension plans. The sole exception was the decision taken by the Mulroney government and upheld by the present Liberal government (with minor changes in scheduling) to substantially boost tax deduction limits for contributions to Registered Retirement Savings Plans. Defenders of the universalist welfare state will contend that the Conservatives' and Liberals' changes to elderly benefits over the past ten years are playing a significant part in the rapid erosion of Canada's social security system that took many decades and hard-won battles to build.

This paper attempts three major tasks. First, it explains the transformation of elderly benefits over the past decade. Second, it tries to decode the five principles of pension reform set forth in the 1995 Budget. Finally, it runs a concrete proposal for a family income-tested elderly benefit up the flagpole to give critics something to shoot at, supporters something to support, and debaters something to debate.

## THE TRANSFORMATION OF ELDERLY BENEFITS: 1985-1996

Canada has a layer-cake retirement income system made up of a mix of various public and private programs which, in varying fashion, are intended to serve its two basic objectives — providing a basic income floor so that no senior need live in poverty (anti-poverty) and ensuring the maintenance of an adequate living standard when Canadians retire from the labour force (earnings-replacement). The foundation layer is furnished by three federal programs — Old Age Security (OAS), the Guaranteed Income Supplement (GIS) and the Spouse's Allowance (SPA) — and by provincial/territorial income supplementation programs for low-income seniors. In addition, there are two tax-delivered benefits, the non-refundable age credit and pension income credit, that can be considered as part of the first tier of the pension system. This collection of direct spending and tax-delivered programs, which serve both the anti-poverty and earnings-replacement objectives, are the subject of this paper.

Two social insurance programs, the Canada Pension Plan and (virtually identical) Quebec Pension Plan, make up the second layer of the pension system. Employer-sponsored (occupational) pension plans and individual retirement savings plans (Registered Retirement Savings Plans or RRSPs) constitute the third tier. Together, the C/QPP, occupational pension plans and individual savings plans are intended to serve the earnings-replacement needs of the majority of pensioners. To ease the financial burden on members of employer pension plans and workers who are saving individually for their retirement, the income tax system provides a tax credit for contributions to the Canada and Quebec Pension Plans and tax deductions for contributions to employer pension plans and RRSPs.

## The Elderly Benefits System in 1985

By "elderly benefits," I mean the federal troika of Old Age Security, the Guaranteed Income Supplement, the Spouse's Allowance as well as two tax-delivered benefits, the age credit (an exemption before 1988) and the pension income credit (a deduction before 1988). Ottawa and the provinces share the cost of the two tax benefits, which reduce both federal and provincial income taxes, so in that sense they are joint federal-provincial programs. Five provinces and the two territories provide income supplements for low-income seniors; these will be discussed later in terms of their contribution to the anti-poverty objective and the potential impact upon them of reforms to federal old age pensions, but the paper focuses on federal programs.

Figure 1 shows the distribution of federal elderly benefits in 1985 for single Canadians 65 and older. Old Age Security was a universal program that benefited seniors at all income levels, but its taxability produced a progressive distribution of benefits — the higher the income, the smaller the after-tax OAS, and vice-versa. The Guaranteed Income Supplement was (and remains today) a non-taxable program geared to low-income seniors; its high benefit reduction rate of 50 percent (of non-OAS income) ensured that it was targeted to the poor and steeply progressive in its distribution of benefits. (The Spouse's Allowance, which serves some but not all low-income persons aged 60 to 64, is also sharply targeted like

FIGURE 1: Elderly Benefits System, Single Pensioners, by Income, 1985

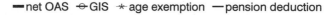

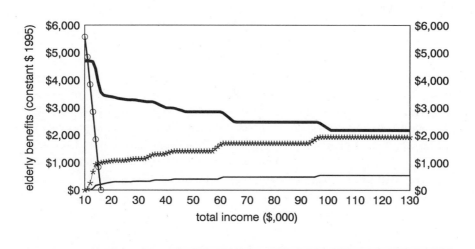

total income ($,000)

Source: Caledon Institute of Social Policy.

the GIS. The age exemption (for taxfilers 65 or older) excluded the poorest sen-iors below the taxpaying threshold and was regressive in impact, providing fed-eral and provincial income tax savings that increased with rising marginal tax rates; the income tax system in those days had ten brackets, with marginal tax rates ranging from 6 percent to 34 percent. The pension income deduction al-lowed taxfilers to deduct from taxable income up to $1,000 in private pension income (from employer-sponsored pension plans and RRSPs) and was, for the same reason as the age exemption, regressive in impact.

These programs had varying, though in some cases similar, rationales. Old Age Security provided a universal foundation for the retirement income system; it was a "demogrant" paid to all seniors, no matter what their level or sources of income, their economic circumstances or their experience in or not in the paid labour force. OAS played a role in both of the retirement income system's basic objectives: with GIS and SPA, it served the anti-poverty objective. But OAS also contributed to the earnings-replacement objective for seniors at all income levels, though of course in inverse proportion to income.[1]

The universal nature of Old Age Security was justified as a way for society (through an income benefit provided by the state) to recognize the contribution that all elderly women and men — regardless of income — made to Canada. Universalists argue that universal programs like OAS and Family Allowances are required to provide a solid foundation for the social security system, upon which income-targeted programs can be erected; without some social programs that benefit all income groups, so the argument goes, the middle-class and well-off Canadians will have no stake in the welfare state and so will be less willing to pay taxes to support programs for the poor. The argument for universal child benefits is similar to that advanced for universal old age pensions: Universal Family Allowances recognized the contribution that all parents make to society by raising future taxpayers, workers, and citizens (National Council of Welfare 1983, pp. 26-31; Mendelson 1981, pp. 62-67). Universal programs were touted as safer from cuts and tampering from cost-cutting governments because they supposedly enjoy broad public support. The three pillars of the universalist welfare state — Old Age Security, Family Allowances and Medicare — helped foster a sense of social solidarity that is a distinctive element of the Canadian (non-American) national identity and helped offset the divisive effects of the country's deep regional, ethnic, and linguistic cleavages.

First paid out in 1952, OAS on its own provided a relatively meagre benefit for seniors with little or no income from other sources. The Guaranteed Income Supplement and the Spouse's Allowance were added in 1966 and 1975, respectively, to bolster Old Age Security's capacity to ensure a basic income for all seniors. The new programs considerably boosted the elderly benefits system's anti-poverty capacity. OAS alone currently amounts to just 27.8 percent of Statistics Canada's low-income cutoff for a single person living in a metropolitan centre of 500,000 or more; OAS and GIS together provide a basic income equal to 60.8 percent of the low-income cutoff. For elderly couples, OAS represents 44.5 percent of the low-income cutoff for a metropolitan centre, but OAS and GIS together raise the basic income to 78.9 percent of the low-income cutoff.[2]

The age exemption's rationale was that seniors typically must live on less income when they retire, often much less, and so merit some tax relief to improve their disposable income; the "societal recognition" argument used for OAS also was advanced for the age exemption, that is, that the elderly deserve special treatment in recognition of their long contribution to society and the economy. The pension income deduction, which gave an income tax break to taxfilers with private pension income, was intended to provide an incentive for Canadians to save for their retirement and also to help maintain the purchasing power of (usually unindexed) private pensions (Ontario Fair Tax Commission 1993, pp. 323-26).

The argument in favour of providing such tax assistance in the form of a deduction from taxable income hinged on the concept of horizontal equity. The age exemption ensured that elderly taxpayers paid proportionately less income taxes than non-elderly taxpayers at the same income level throughout the income range. The non-refundable age credit, which replaced the age exemption in 1988, is a weaker method of achieving the objective of horizontal equity because its value in terms of income tax savings declines proportionately with increasing income. As a result, higher-income elderly taxpayers' tax advantage over non-aged tax-payers with the same income declines with rising income. The same argument holds for the pension income deduction, which also was converted to a non-refundable credit in 1988.

The overall effect of these programs was to create a universal system that was progressive only for the poor and basically flat for all other seniors. Figure 2 shows the distribution of combined elderly benefits for a single pensioner in 1985; figures have been converted to constant 1995 dollars to allow comparison to the current system, discussed later. OAS and GIS combined to provide a maximum benefit of $10,264 for the poorest seniors; eligibility for GIS ended at total income of $16,000. But above this relatively low income level, total elderly benefits remained virtually flat at around $4,600. The regressive age exemption and pension income deduction offset the progressive taxable OAS, so that in effect

FIGURE 2: Total Elderly Benefits, Current (1995) and Old (1985) System, Single Pensioners, by Income

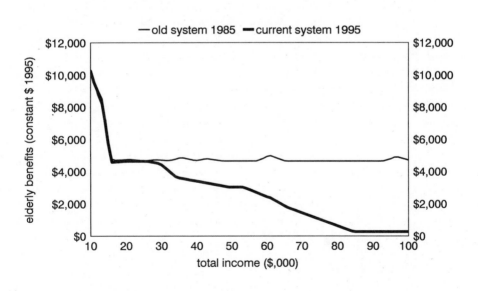

Source: Caledon Institute of Social Policy.

gross and net OAS ended up the same. As a result, a senior with an income of $16,000 received $4,762 in elderly benefits or little more that someone at the opposite end of the income spectrum ($4,634 at $130,000). The "old" elderly benefits system was universal not only in reach, but in impact as well for all but the poor.[3]

## The Tory Transformation of Elderly Benefits: 1985-1991

The first attempt to change the elderly benefits system was a spectacular flop. Finance Minister Michael Wilson's first budget, in 1985, attempted to index partially the OAS to the amount of inflation over 3 percent. Seniors and their lobby organizations, which remembered the bad old days before OAS was fully indexed in 1973, got the government to back down when they won widespread support from other groups and public sympathy for their cause. The prime minister was embarrassed for the first time in his mandate on national television when castigated by a near-senior named Solange Denis, whose small stature added a David-and-Goliath flavour to the episode, and the media and the government's critics had a field day.

The partial indexation proposal was a ham-fisted attempt at cost control of OAS, an increasingly expensive program because of the steady increase in the number of seniors. If the Conservatives had taken a page from the Trudeau Liberals' book, when as part of the 6 and 5 program they partially indexed OAS but made up the difference for low-income seniors by super-indexing GIS, they might have got away with partially indexing OAS by protecting the poor — and still would have reaped sizable savings.

To underscore the importance of indexation, I calculated the value of OAS over the past ten years if the Tories had managed to impose the partial indexation formula. Figure 3 traces the value of OAS since the program began in 1952. Between 1952 and 1967, OAS was not indexed but was adjusted only on an ad hoc basis — in 1957, 1962, 1963, and 1967, dates which by no coincidence were just before or soon after federal elections. Between 1968 and 1972, Old Age Security was indexed according to various formulas, including (from 1968 to 1970) the Canada Pension Plan's Pension Index which fixed a 2-percent ceiling on increases; in other words, it was only partially indexed. In 1973, the federal government fully indexed OAS on a quarterly basis (i.e., rates are adjusted every January, April, July, and October) in order to adjust responsively for changes in the cost of living; if inflation fluctuated rapidly, a quarterly-indexed benefit can respond more quickly than one indexed only once a year. Indexation was limited temporarily to 6 percent in 1983 and 5 percent in 1984 as part of the federal government's anti-inflation program, but inflation came down sufficiently as to render these measures

FIGURE 3: Old Age Security Benefits Per Pensioner, With and Without Full
Indexation After 1986, 1952-1995

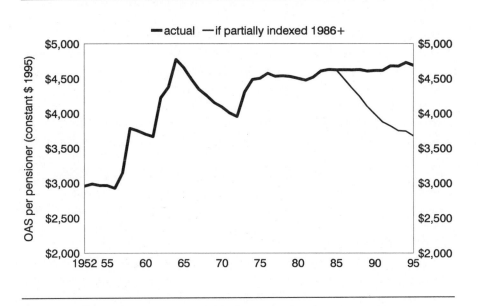

Source: Canada. Human Resources Development; Caledon Institute of Social Policy.

unnecessary (i.e., OAS benefits would have been much the same under full indexation).

OAS amounted to $2,956 in 1952 (in 1995 dollars) and stayed around that level until 1956 because inflation was virtually zero; the cost of living decreased a bit in 1953 and was only 0.6 percent in 1954, 0.1 percent in 1955 and 1.5 percent in 1956. OAS payments increased in value to $3,146 in 1957 because rate increases in July and November exceeded the rate of inflation. Though inflation remained low, OAS declined in value from 1958 through 1961 because benefits were frozen. Ad hoc adjustments in 1962 and 1963 raised OAS to $4,775 by 1964, but benefits eroded again until 1972 because indexation methods used between 1968 and 1972 were not adequate. OAS payments were boosted by 20.6 percent in April 1973 and fully indexed starting October 1973, so benefits have remained around $4,600 ever since; in 1995, OAS amounted to $4,690.

Figure 3 also shows what would have happened if OAS benefits had been partially indexed in 1986. OAS benefits would have fallen to an estimated $3,679 by 1995 — $1,011 less or 22 percent below their actual value of $4,690. If OAS had been partially indexed in 1995 the federal government would have spent an estimated $3.5 billion less than it actually did. Partial indexation is a powerful mechanism for cutting program spending, as Ottawa discovered in other areas of social spending where it did succeed in applying the technique — the OAS clawback, child benefits, the GST credit and federal social transfers to the provinces.

Partial indexation of the tax-transfer system is a regressive measure because it falls heaviest on the poor, for whom OAS constitutes a large part of their limited income. Had the Conservatives gone ahead with their plan to partially index OAS, the poorest single pensioners — who are wholly reliant on OAS and GIS — would have suffered a hefty 9.8 percent cut in income (i.e., comparing their fully indexed OAS in 1986 with the partially indexed value in 1995) as opposed to 6.6 percent for those with $5,000 in other income (e.g., from C/QPP, private pensions, annuities), 5.1 percent for seniors with $15,000 in other income and just 1.9 percent for those with $50,000 in other income.

The partial indexation debacle was the Tories' one and only reversal on pension policy and, for that matter, social policy. The same budget that failed to partially index OAS succeeded in partially indexing the personal income tax system — tax brackets, personal exemptions (including the age exemption) and deductions. Partially indexing the income tax system was an astute revenue-enhancing move that steadily and surreptitiously eroded the value of exemptions and deductions and moved some taxpayers into higher tax brackets (it worked best when there were a lot of tax brackets, as there were before tax reform in 1988). The finance minister's inflation-over-3 percent formula, which he also applied to child benefits, meant that the value of tax exemptions and deductions as well as Family Allowances automatically lost at most 3 percent of their value each year if inflation ran 3 percent or more, and at least the amount of inflation if the latter were less than 3 percent. The pension income deduction, which allowed taxfilers to deduct up to $1,000 in private pension income, had been frozen since 1983.

The partial indexation of tax brackets, exemptions, and deductions had three significant effects. First, it imposed a hidden and regressive annual tax increase on taxpayers, including the aged. Second, partial indexation also had the effect of gradually lowering the income tax threshold each year, adding increasing numbers of low-income Canadians to the income tax rolls each year. Some modest-income seniors had to pay taxes for the first time; the federal taxpaying threshold for single pensioners fell from $9,887 in non-OAS income in 1980 (in constant 1995 dollars) to $6,541 in 1995. Finally, partial indexation means that the after-tax value of taxable social benefits, such as OAS, C/QPP and Unemployment Insurance, will decline steadily over time as income taxes take an ever-increasing bite.

I coined the term "social policy by stealth" to characterize the Tories' style and technique of policy reform (Battle 1990). Largely through the use of technical changes such as partial indexation, they imposed hidden increases in both income taxes and the GST and cuts to child benefits and federal social transfers to the provinces that proved to be as politically successful as they were fiscally potent because few Canadians understood what was going on. Try to explain (as I have, repeatedly and with no success over the years) why what appear to be increases in benefits are in fact reductions because of the difference between current and constant dollars. Try explaining how the partial indexation of income tax brackets moves some taxfilers into higher tax brackets. Try explaining how the partial indexation of the threshold for the GST credit imposes a hidden, automatic GST increase on the one group in society least able to bear it — the poor — and is steadily shifting the regressivity of the GST from middle-income to lower-income consumers.

The next change to elderly benefits came in 1988, with the income tax reforms that broadened the base of taxable income by converting personal exemptions and most deductions to non-refundable tax credits, and lowered tax rates (though not in all cases) and reduced their number from ten to three. The age exemption was $2,640 in 1987, though its value in terms of federal and provincial income tax savings varied according to the taxfiler's marginal tax rate (there were ten before the 1988 reforms). The age exemption was converted to a non-refundable credit of $550, calculated as 17 percent (the lowest marginal tax rate in the new system) of what became known on the income tax return as the "age amount" of $3,236. The increase in the age amount was intended to help compensate for the abolition of the interest income deduction, which had helped many seniors (including those with relatively modest incomes) who have some income from savings and investments. Non-refundable credits with a ceiling (as is the case for both the age credit and pension income credit) provide equal federal and provincial income tax savings to all taxpayers who qualify for the maximum amount. Of course, the change from exemption to non-refundable credit affected seniors differently, depending on their level and sources of income; another factor to be taken into account is the fact that tax rates changed as well (e.g., the top marginal tax rate was reduced from 34 to 29 percent).

Although the age credit does not vary in value as much as the age exemption it replaced, and is not regressive overall, it is worth less than the maximum for low-income seniors with little tax liability. For elderly taxfilers with incomes low enough that they do not require the full amount of the age credit to reduce their taxes to zero, the age credit is worth the amount of their basic federal tax. The age credit is worth its maximum amount for elderly taxfilers who still owe taxes after factoring in the age credit. Married spouses whose incomes are not high enough to require the full age credit can transfer the unused portion to their spouse, up to the maximum amount.

The Tories also converted the $1,000 pension income deduction to a non-refundable credit worth up to $170 (17 percent of $1,000) in federal income tax savings and, on average, $94 in provincial income tax savings, for a combined federal-provincial income tax savings of $264, though, of course, taxfilers with less than $1,000 in private pension income receive a smaller tax break. Under the old pension income deduction, the maximum federal-provincial tax savings varied from $93 to a claimant in the lowest tax bracket in 1987 (with taxable income under $1,295) to $527 for a taxfiler in the highest tax bracket (with taxable income over $62,160). Like the age credit, any unused portion of the pension income credit can be transferred from the lower-income spouse to the higher-income spouse.

The age credit in 1995 was worth $592 in federal tax savings and, on average, $349 in provincial income tax savings, for a total maximum tax savings of $941. The age credit has lost value over the years because it is only partially indexed. If it had been fully indexed, it would now be worth $667 in federal income tax savings and $393 in average provincial income tax savings, for a total $1,060. Most seniors are paying $119 more in income taxes than they would have if the age credit had not been partially indexed. The pension income credit is not indexed at all, not even partially, so its value has declined even more than the age credit over time. If the pension income credit had been fully indexed, it would now be worth a maximum $328 in federal/average provincial income tax savings rather than its actual $270.

Universality fell not with a bang but a clawback in 1989. The finance minister announced that OAS recipients with net incomes over $50,000 (the "threshold") would have to repay 15 cents of their OAS for every dollar of income above the threshold, over and above their normal federal and provincial income taxes; to complicate matters further, the amount of the clawback is treated as a deduction. (Actually, it took until 1991 for the full clawback to come into effect and universality to disappear, because the change was phased in one-third at a time over three years.) Once net income exceeded a certain point — $72,521 when the clawback was introduced — seniors would have to pay back at income tax time all of the OAS they had received the year before, which struck me at the time as a peculiar way to run a social program. The federal government insisted that Old Age Security was still a universal social program because every senior received a monthly cheque; critics pointed out that a program that makes some recipients pay back all of their benefits is not universal.

The beauty of the clawback from the federal government's point of view is that it is a prime example of social policy by stealth — a technical measure so arcane and complex that few Canadians outside of a handful of social policy wonks and seniors' groups understood what was going. Another stealthy feature is that the clawback is only partially indexed, which means that it falls steadily each year in value, reaching more and more seniors and recouping an ever-increasing amount of money for the federal treasury as the gap between gross and net OAS expenditures widens. The falling clawback means that more and more seniors repay their entire OAS, and more and more are hit by the partial clawback. By 2000, the clawback will reach down to pensioners with incomes above an estimated $41,400, and those with incomes above $61,886 will receive no OAS.

In a report I wrote while Director of the National Council of Welfare, I calculated that a 35 year-old Canadian earning $40,000 when the clawback was announced in 1989 (the average male worker earned $39,000 that year) would end up at age 65 with only one-quarter of his/her Old Age Security benefits (an estimated $1,001) after taxes and clawback, as opposed to 60 percent ($2,358) under the old system when benefits were subject to normal taxation but no clawback (National Council of Welfare 1989, pp. 16-19). These estimates assumed that the clawback threshold remained partially indexed and so declined steadily over time; I also modelled three other options in which the threshold was partially restored. While it can be argued that future governments would not allow the threshold to decline as low as my worst-case estimate, I am not so sanguine about such a prospect. In the absence of potentially controversial "up-front" reform of OAS, such as the Liberal government is contemplating now, the steadily-declining clawback might be seen to offer a politically easier and still fiscally potent way of restraining future OAS increases. Of course, the government could decide to change OAS and maintain a partially indexed threshold, which would give it larger future savings than under the current system.

The OAS clawback was set high enough that it is affecting relatively few seniors in its early years. The 1989 Budget estimated that it would hit only 4 percent of OAS recipients at first. The measure will save the federal government "only" about $400 million in 1995-96, which is peanuts in terms of the total cost of OAS ($16 billion-plus) but still real money at a time when there is no "new" money to be had.

The clawback on OAS, applied as well to Family Allowances, was a milestone in the history of Canadian social policy. It spelled the end of the universal foundation of the child and elderly benefits systems, one of the sacred principles of the universalist welfare state. In 1993, the Mulroney government went all the way with Family Allowances and replaced that universal program, along with the refundable and non-refundable child tax credits, with a single family income-tested Child Tax Benefit.

The Conservatives made no more changes to elderly benefits, leaving it to the Liberals to complete their transformation to a family income-tested system as the Tories did to child benefits. But the Mulroney government paved the way for further changes under the Liberals: the Tories established the direction, substance, and mechanisms of change and bequeathed to their Liberal successors the political momentum for further reform. The political climate for pension reform, and public policy generally, changed significantly under the Conservatives. Perhaps the same would have happened under a different (e.g., Liberal) administration, as the Canadian government, like those in many other countries, struggled with the collision between pay-as-you-go public pension programs and demographic pressures and with the growing strains on the welfare state in general. Sacred trusts in Canadian social policy became fatted calves, as the politics of stealth and the government's successful campaign to raise public concern about the deficit enabled it to make paradigm-shifting changes to the welfare state with relative political ease. Seniors, women's, and social policy groups shouted just as loudly against the clawback on OAS and Family Allowances as they had about the attempt to partially de-index OAS and Family Allowances, but to no avail. This time around, the government stood firm. By the end of the Tories' second term, Family Allowances were extinct and universal Old Age Security was gone in all but name.

## Changes Under the Liberals: 1994-1996

Jean Chrétien inherited from Brian Mulroney and left intact the well-oiled and powerful machinery of stealth — partial indexation of the personal income tax system, of the refundable GST credit, of federal social transfers to the provinces and of the Child Tax benefit — which invisibly generates revenues and cuts social benefits. The Liberals have made changes of their own to elderly benefits, though these have gone largely unnoticed, perhaps because they were overshadowed by Human Resources Development Minister Lloyd Axworthy's travelling circus Social Security Review and Paul Martin's tough talk about the fiscal targets for reform of Unemployment Insurance and social transfers to the provinces.

The Liberals' first (1994) budget announced that the age credit would be income-tested. Only taxfilers with net incomes under $25,921 (the tried and true income threshold for the refundable GST credit and the Child Tax Benefit) can claim the maximum age credit. The credit is reduced at the rate of 15 percent of income above the $25,921 (the same reduction rate as the clawback), which means that it disappears once a senior's net income reaches $49,134. Since lower-income seniors cannot qualify for the full age credit, it shows an up-flat-down distributional pattern. Income-testing the age credit will save the federal government an estimated $300 million a year when fully phased in by 1996-97 (Canada. Department of Finance 1994, p. 43).

The 1995 Budget made two changes to elderly benefits. In order to correct an inequity and plug a revenue leak, seniors who live outside Canada will have to report their worldwide income (i.e., their income from all sources, inside and outside Canada) in order to receive OAS benefits; up to this point, they have not been required to report either their Canadian or non-Canadian income and so have not been subject to the clawback. Effective July 1996, OAS will be income-tested before rather than after the fact, based on seniors' incomes for the previous year as reported on their tax form. This change will complete the conversion of OAS from a universal to income-tested program, since upper-income seniors will not be eligible for benefits. Eligibility for OAS benefits will be determined on the basis of level of income, like other income-tested programs including GIS, SPA, the Child Tax Benefit, and the refundable GST credit; however, for the time being OAS will remain tested according to individual income, not family income as is the case with the other programs.

## The Distribution of Elderly Benefits: 1985 versus 1996

Figure 4 shows the amount and distribution of elderly benefits for a single senior today, after the various changes made by the Conservative and Liberal governments. OAS is progressive and phases out a relatively high ($85,000) income. GIS is the same steeply targeted program as it was in 1985. The age credit is

FIGURE 4: Elderly Benefits, Single Pensioners, by Program and Income, 1995

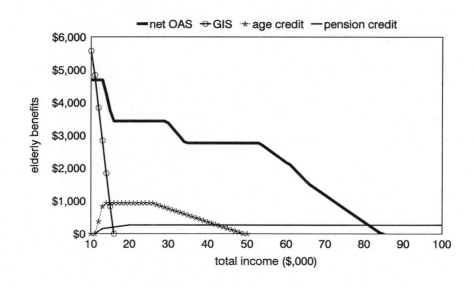

Source: Caledon Institute of Social Policy.

moderately income-tested, phasing out at around $50,000, while the pension in-
come credit is the only benefit available to upper-income seniors (providing they
have private pension income, which is a safe bet).

Figure 2 compares elderly benefits under the old (1985) and current (1995)
systems. Only poor seniors are in the same position now as they were a decade
ago, since they receive the same total benefit from OAS and GIS; the various
changes to OAS do not affect the poor and GIS remains unchanged both in design
and value of benefits. However, the majority of seniors, with modest, average or
high incomes, have experienced a significant decline in their elderly benefits,
though the cuts are distributed in a progressive fashion. Figure 5 shows the dollar
change in benefits between 1985 and 1996, and Figure 6 the percentage change.
Losses are only a few percentage points for seniors with incomes as low as $14,000
to 94 percent for those in the upper-income range.

I did a seat-of-the-pants calculation of the cost of the 1985 system if it were
still in effect in 1995. By rough and conservative estimate, the federal government is spending $784 million less than it would have if the old system were still
operating. The total savings to the federal and provincial governments is about
$1.6 billion.

FIGURE 5: Change in Elderly Benefits, Current (1995) versus Old (1985)
System, Single Pensioners, by Income

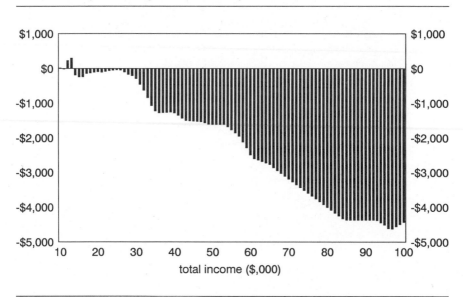

Source: Caledon Institute of Social Policy.

FIGURE 6: Change in Elderly Benefits, Current (1995) versus Old (1985) System, Single Pensioners, by Income

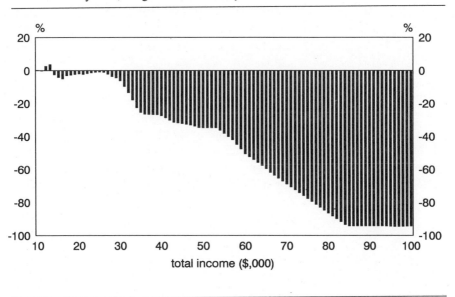

Source: Caledon Institute of Social Policy.

Today's elderly benefits system distributes its benefits in a much more progressive fashion than it used to, but progressivity has come at a price for most seniors — lower benefits for all but the poor. There have been no increases in benefits since the 1984 increase in the GIS for single pensioners. The reforms over the past decade have created a progressive but also leaner elderly benefits system with a built-in money-saver in the form of partial indexation of the clawback on OAS and the age credit and the non-indexation of the pension income credit.

Because I think the fiscal and political pressures on the public pension system necessitate changes to stem future expenditure increases and restore public confidence in the fairness and viability of the system, I regard the outcome of the various changes made over the last decade in a positive light. The one large caveat is the use of stealthy mechanisms to achieve this result, which are undemocratic and eventually could undermine public support for the social security system.

## DECODING THE FIVE PRINCIPLES OF REFORM

The 1995 Budget said that the minister of finance and human resources development will release a paper "on the changes required in the public pension system to ensure its affordability with the goal of legislating changes to take effect in 1997" (Canada. Department of Finance 1995, pp. 57-58). The 1994 Budget also had announced a discussion paper, but it got side-tracked by the Social Security Review (dealing with other major social programs) and the Quebec referendum. The 1995 Budget set forth five "basic principles" for the reform of OAS and GIS: undiminished protection for all seniors "who are less well-off," continued full indexation of benefits, family income-testing of OAS, greater progressivity of benefits and control of costs.

I will examine each of the principles in turn, using them as criteria to gauge the changes made over the past decade and to assess the elderly benefits system's performance in achieving its twin objectives. I also will use the five principles to predict the elderly benefits redesign that Ottawa likely has up its sleeve and to explore some of the trade-offs that confront policymakers in designing a new system.

## Undiminished Protection for Less Well-Off Seniors

Canada has made significant progress against poverty among the aged thanks largely to improvements in its retirement income system, mainly its public elements — OAS, GIS, SPA, C/QPP and provincial income supplements for the aged. The incidence of poverty among families led by Canadians 65 or older fell from 41.1 percent in 1969 (double the 20.8 percent rate for all families) to 7.1 percent in 1994 (half the 14.1 percent rate for families with non-elderly heads and close to half the 13.5 percent rate for all families). Single seniors also have seen a significant reduction in their risk of poverty over the years, from 69.1 percent in 1969 (42.8 percent for all unattached individuals) to 47.6 percent of the elderly unattached (40.6 percent for all singles). However, single pensioners still have a higher rate of poverty than those under 65 (40.6 percent versus 38.0 percent) and single elderly women fare worse (52.9 percent) than single aged men (31.8 percent).

The anti-poverty performance of the federal elderly benefits system has not improved since the increase in GIS benefits for single seniors in 1984. But over the long term, federal elderly benefits have increased considerably with the addition of income-tested programs geared to poor seniors (GIS and SPA), periodic increases in benefits and the full indexation of benefits (which maintains but does not enhance the income guarantee). In 1952, Old Age Security (GIS did not exist) paid $2,956 (in constant 1995 dollars) or just under 18 percent of Statistics Canada's low-income cutoff for single person living in a metropolitan centre; in 1995 OAS and the GIS provide a maximum benefit of $10,264 or 61 percent of the low-income line. OAS guaranteed elderly couples $5,912 or 28 percent of the low-income cutoff for a metropolitan centre in 1952 and OAS and GIS together amounted to $16,642 or 79 percent of the low-income line in 1995.

The "poverty gap" — the difference between elderly benefits and the low-income cutoff — varies because the latter vary according to size of community. The maximum benefit in 1995 from OAS ($4,690) and GIS ($5,574) for a single person came to $10,264, which falls below the low-income line for all communities. The poverty gap for single pensioners in 1995 ranged from $6,610 below the line for a metropolitan centre to $4,209 for a large city (100,000-499,999), $4,108 for a small city (30,000-99,999), $3,109 for an urban area under 30,000 and $1,397 for rural areas. Maximum OAS/GIS for couples was $16,642 in 1995, which is below the low-income line for all communities except rural areas — $4,450 below the low-income cutoff for metropolitan centres, $1,449 below for large cities, and $1,323 for small cities and towns. OAS/GIS virtually matches the poverty line for couples living in urban communities under 30,000 (just $74 under) and raises couples in rural Canada $2,060 above the low-income line.

Five provinces (Ontario, Manitoba, Saskatchewan, Alberta, British Columbia) and Yukon and the Northwest Territories provide income supplements for their low-income elderly residents, ranging from $446 for singles and $959 for couples in Manitoba to $2,350 for single renters and $3,500 for couples renting in Alberta. However, combined federal-provincial-territorial benefits cannot provide single seniors an income guarantee equal to the low-income cutoff for all communities throughout Canada — with the exception of single pensioners in rural Alberta (who are a few hundred dollars above the poverty line) and in rural areas in the Northwest Territories. Federal and provincial/territorial elderly benefits ensure couples an income that is several thousand dollars above the low-income cutoff for rural areas everywhere, for communities under 30,000 in all regions except Atlantic Canada, and in small cities of 30,000-99,999 and large cities of 100,000-499,999 in British Columbia, Alberta, Saskatchewan, and Ontario. The federal-provincial income guarantee for aged couples falls below the poverty line for metropolitan centres throughout Canada as well as large cities in Manitoba and Atlantic Canada.

Thus it can be argued that the retirement income system fails to achieve fully its anti-poverty objective. Federal and (where available) provincial/territorial elderly benefits leave the large majority of single pensioners and many elderly couples below the low-income line if they have no other source of income. The income guarantee is better for couples than it is for single seniors; federal benefits from OAS/maximum GIS for couples are 79 percent of the low-income cutoff for a metropolitan centre and only 61 percent for singles.

I qualify the above assertion with "may" be argued because there is no consensus about how to measure the anti-poverty capacity of the elderly benefits system. Statistics Canada has steadfastly warned that its low-income cutoffs are not official government poverty lines or, for that matter, measures of poverty. The federal government, like everyone else, uses the low-income cutoffs as *de facto* poverty lines, but to my knowledge has never sanctioned their use as standards by which to assess the adequacy of social benefits.

One way to "improve" elderly benefits' anti-poverty capacity is simply to use a different, lower measure of poverty. For example, if we use as our yardstick Statistics Canada's alternative low-income measures (LIMs) instead of the conventional low-income cutoffs (LICOs), then we will arrive at a more favourable assessment of the elderly benefits system's income guarantee. LIMs define poverty in purely relative terms as incomes below 50 percent of the median income; they vary by family size but not by community size. In 1995, the LIM for a single person is an estimated $12,000 and $16,800 for a couple. If we use the LIM instead of the LICO for a metropolitan centre, the poverty gap for single seniors is $4,389 as opposed to $6,610 and OAS/GIS guarantees them 86 percent of the poverty line rather than 61 percent. The poverty gap for senior couples is a mere $158 using the LIM as opposed to $4,450 using the metropolitan LICO; the federal income guarantee is 99 percent of the poverty line rather than 79 percent.

LICOs, LIMs, and other income-based poverty lines are relatively crude measures of the contribution of social programs to living standards. Ruggeri, Howard and Bluck argue that seniors have an advantage over the non-aged because many of them benefit from non-taxed social programs (GIS, SPA, provincial income supplements for the aged); pay no payroll taxes or other work-related expenses; enjoy tax breaks (e.g., the age credit and pension income credit) that reduce their federal and provincial income taxes; and often benefit from school tax exemptions, property tax rebates, and rental assistance (Ruggeri, Howard and Bluck 1994). Many elderly Canadians own their homes mortgage-free. Seniors, including those with low incomes, are in this sense better off than their incomes might lead us to believe, indicating the need for better measures of poverty.

During the "Great Pension Debate" of the early 1980s, labour, seniors organizations, women's groups and social advocates argued that the elderly benefits system does not adequately meet the anti-poverty objective; the typical proposal was a sizable increase in the GIS to close the gap. The GIS was boosted by $500 in 1984, but for single seniors only and nowhere near the amount required to raise the OAS/GIS income guarantee to the low-income line. Since then, there have been no enhancements to OAS/GIS benefits; to the contrary, the Mulroney government tried to partially index OAS, which would have weakened elderly benefits' anti-poverty capacity steadily over time.

What does this all mean for the 1995 Budget's principle that elderly benefits redesign should provide "undiminished protection" to "less well-off seniors, including those now receiving the Guaranteed Income Supplement"? It will strongly influence the design of the new elderly benefit system.

For one thing, prospects for a sizable increase in the income guarantee are unlikely. To help "sell" its proposed changes and counter accusations that it is out to cut old age pensions, the federal government would be wise to provide a modest improvement in benefits for the elderly poor (or, at least, to include an option that does so, if its forthcoming proposals take the form of several possible options). Modest increases in the GIS (e.g., in the several hundreds of dollars range) could be financed through savings from upper-income senior households, which would lose some or all of their benefits (depending upon their income level and the design of the new system). Increases could be restricted to or weighted in favour of single pensioners, since their income guarantee is substantially further below the poverty line than that of couples; on the other hand, confining increases to single seniors is open to the criticism that couples would see themselves as treated unfairly and might be tempted to present themselves as singles in order to qualify for a larger benefit. If the finance minister wants to save some money in the process, then increases to low-income seniors will have to be very modest; but even if he decided that immediate savings are not in the political cards (for reasons I will discuss later), a revenue-neutral design still could not deliver the very large increase in benefits required to raise single seniors up to the poverty line, however the latter is defined. In 1994, the total poverty gap as measured by the low-income cutoffs for senior households was $1.7 billion; a workable elderly benefit that raised all seniors to the poverty line would cost much more than this, for reasons discussed later.

"Undiminished protection ... for the less well-off, including those now receiving the Guaranteed Income Supplement" certainly must mean no reduction in benefits for low-income seniors. I cannot imagine the Liberal government or any government wanting to reduce the income guarantee for the elderly poor, and I doubt they could get away with it politically in any event. Eligibility for the GIS ends once a single person's non-OAS income reaches $11,280 in the first quarter of 1996, or $16,017 including OAS, which is close to the low-income cutoff for a metropolitan area (an estimated $17,111) and higher than the cutoffs for other community sizes. A GIS recipient married to a pensioner no longer qualifies for GIS once the couple's income exceeds $24,162 ($14,688 in non-OAS income and $9,474 in OAS), which is several thousands of dollars above the low-income cutoff for all community sizes (e.g., ranging from an estimated $21,389 for metropolitan centres to $14,781 for rural areas).

The question, then, is what is meant by the vague term "less well-off." The average income for elderly unattached individuals at last count (1994) was only $18,780 and the median income was $14,596, reflecting the heavy concentration of single seniors on the bottom rungs of the income ladder (because many rely on OAS/GIS for the large part of their income); by way of comparison, the low-income cutoff for single people in 1994 ranged from $15,511 to $11,410. The average income of families with aged heads was $40,183 and the median income was $32,099. I suspect that the $40,000-$45,000 range will be the rough dividing line between the less well-off and the rest ("more well-off"?).

There are three reasons why I think Ottawa will design the new elderly benefit in such a way as to ensure that senior households with average incomes and below end up no worse off, and preferably a bit better off, than they are under the current system. One reason is to prevent a middle-class backlash against its proposals; middle-income Canadians are subjected to a media barrage about the "declining middle class" and do not need experts to tell them about their substantial tax increases over the last decade, so any suggestion that the government wants to "take away their old age pension" would not sit well. In other words, I do not think that the new system will be simply a "super-GIS," sharply targeted to the poor. A for-the-poor-only elderly benefits system also would be subject to the common criticism from economists that it would have an undesirable effect on behaviour, influencing some working-age Canadians not to bother saving for their retirement because private pension income would simply offset their old age pension.

A second reason, which I trust at least some policymakers have in mind, is to maintain the important role of OAS in helping achieve the earnings-replacement objective of the pension system overall; OAS forms a significant part of the retirement income of middle-income and modest-income seniors, though its contribution varies inversely with income. A third reason is to ensure that a new elderly benefit produces a high percentage of winners/no changers and a low percentage of losers amongst single seniors, most of them women, who typically are viewed as "the deserving poor."

The latter consideration calls for either a single threshold for maximum OAS benefits for singles and couples, or a relatively high threshold for singles that is not far below that of couples. For example, the new OAS could use the $25,921 family income threshold already in place for the age credit, the refundable GST credit, and the Child Tax Benefit. I will demonstrate later that such a design would leave most single seniors better off or no worse off and ensure that elderly couples begin to lose benefits only over the $40,000-$45,000 range. While the use of a $25,921 threshold means that OAS would decline above that income level, it should not be interpreted to mean that households with incomes over $25,921 will get less from a new system; the proper comparison is their total elderly benefits (including the age and pension income credits) under the current system and under any proposal. Obviously, different thresholds could be selected — e.g., $25,921 for single seniors and $30,000 for couples, or $20,000 for singles and $25,000 for couples, whatever — that would have different costs and distributional consequences. Whatever parameters are chosen, I think they will have to ensure that losers begin only above the average income level for senior couples, and substantially above the average income of seniors (which was $18,780 in 1994 or only $3,269 above the $16,511 low-income cutoff for a metropolitan centre).

"Less well-off," then, likely means average income and below for couples (around $40,000). To help sell its proposals, I think the federal government will design its options(s) so that only households with incomes substantially above average lose significantly. Ottawa will want to assure Canadians that the low- and middle-income majority of seniors will suffer no loss in benefits from reform, and indeed that some will come out ahead; only the affluent will see fewer or no benefits. Let me say it again: I do *not* recommend that elderly benefits redesign cut the old age pensions of the middle class; nor do I believe the federal government will propose options that do so.

## Continued Full Indexation of Benefits

Before I am accused of being a social policy Pollyanna or having turned my back on my previous work, let me explain that a new elderly benefit which on the face of it offered both undiminished protection for the less well-off *and* continued full indexation of benefits still could be unacceptable. (Of course, any change in the directions outlined in the 1995 Budget will be regarded by some as unacceptable, but I do not include myself in this school.)

The social policy landscape has changed considerably over the past decade, but I cannot imagine the federal government risking a repeat of the Solange Denis episode by trying to partially index the new elderly *benefit*. However, I can well imagine Ottawa partially indexing the income *threshold* for a family income-tested OAS. It has encountered little political flack over its practice of partially indexing the threshold for the clawback on OAS, the Child Tax Benefit, and the refundable sales tax credit, not to mention the personal income tax system's tax brackets and credits. Most Canadians just don't get it, and the government's critics have been unsuccessful in raising public awareness of/or concern about the politics of stealth.

One possibility is that the discussion paper simply will ignore the issue and not tell the public that it intends to partially index the threshold, since that is simply "accepted practice" in the brave new tax-transfer system. Or the federal government may anticipate criticism and seek to counter it by saying that the threshold will be reviewed and adjusted from time to time as necessity and financial circumstances permit, which is the line the Tories used.

Partial indexation of the threshold for a new OAS is objectionable for several reasons. It continues social policy by stealth, which I do not think is healthy public policy. It undermines the federal government's credibility and integrity, because the evidence they will present concerning the impact of its elderly benefits options will be false: it will be true only for the first year the system is put in place. As the years go by, inflation will gradually lower the threshold and erode the OAS of every senior with incomes above the (falling) threshold; eventually, even modest-income seniors will suffer. Partial indexation of the threshold will weaken the earnings-replacement capacity of OAS for middle-income and eventually modest-income seniors and thus will undermine a vital objective of the retirement income system.

Why, then, would the federal government choose to partially index the threshold for a new OAS? In order to save money surreptitiously, since a gradually declining threshold will affect increasing numbers of seniors and thus yield increasing real savings.

The other political advantage of partial indexation is that it allows governments to announce "increases" in social benefits or "cuts" in taxes which are nothing more than partial catch-up for past losses.

Partial indexation could creep up on a new old age pension in another way. If the new OAS were, like the current program, a taxable benefit, then the hidden income tax grab resulting from partial indexation would erode the net value of OAS over time. But the new OAS probably will be a non-taxable benefit, like other income-tested programs. In that case, the only threat from inflation is a partially-indexed threshold.

## Family Income-Testing of OAS

The most controversial aspect of the government's forthcoming proposals probably will be family income-testing OAS. Wherever one comes down on the issue, one has to recognize that it represents a major change in the philosophy of public pensions. Family income testing surely will stir up a hornet's nest of protest.

The first part of this paper chronicled the evolution from a universal to income-tested elderly benefits system. The clawback converted OAS from a universal to an income-tested social program. The age credit also is income-tested, though the transferability of the credit between spouses is not. GIS always has been income-tested on the basis of family income. Only the pension income credit is not income-tested, in the sense that it provides a tax savings to all taxpayers with private pension income (though it excludes those with incomes below the taxpaying threshold).

Family income testing rests on the assumption that the family is an economic unit as well as a social and emotional partnership — that its members pool their resources and share their financial needs — and thus is an appropriate vehicle for delivering social benefits geared to need. The GIS, for example, assumes that low-income aged couples are deserving of assistance based on their level of total income, and that the contribution of each spouse to that income is not a relevant factor. Family income testing of social programs can be seen as subscribing to the traditional marriage vow — in sickness and in health, for better or worse.

One can take the argument a step farther and argue that income testing logically should be levied on the basis of household income, not just family income. In other words, two adults living together who are neither legally nor common-law married might be deemed to be benefiting from the same economies of scale of living under the same roof as spouses, and thus also should have their entitlement for social benefits based on their combined income. There are two counter-arguments that come to my mind. One is that people who are married knowingly enter into a contract that (or so it can be argued) assumes a shared economic status, whereas adults who live together as roommates do not enter into such a contract. (According to an argument levelled against family income testing that will be discussed later, some married people apparently do not accept the notion of being in an economic unit.) The other is that such an approach would not be accepted by a large portion of Canadians and thus would be widely evaded and impossible to administer. Household income testing is, in fact, used in the Netherlands. Nonetheless, household income testing is an intriguing argument.

*Con.* A key argument against family income-testing OAS can be levelled equally against the current individually income-tested program: it allegedly converts (subverts?) a pension entitlement into what amounts to a form of social assistance or "state charity" in the words of the Canadian Labour Congress (Canadian Labour Congress 1995, p. 6), in the process doing severe damage to the retirement income system overall.

According to this school of thought, universal OAS was intended to provide a foundation to the entire retirement income system. Universal social programs like OAS and Family Allowances recognized the contribution that all seniors and parents, respectively, make to society, regardless of their income or economic circumstances. They fostered a sense of social solidarity and support for the welfare state and for Canada, crossing class, regional, ethnic, and linguistic lines. Universal OAS ensured that every senior received a basic retirement benefit of his/her own (Coalition of Seniors for Social Equity 1995, p. 6). Universal programs like OAS were touted as avoiding the stigma that comes with means-tested programs, since everyone benefits regardless of socio-economic class or income level. Universal programs also were viewed as more secure than selective programs with a smaller constituency, especially those geared to the poor. And without universal social programs, broad public support for the welfare state generally — including programs for the poor — will weaken, in the end hurting the poor as well.

Another argument that has been proffered for universal OAS and against income-testing the program (whether on an individual or family basis) is that it is intended to contribute to the earnings-replacement objective of the retirement income system (Baldwin 1995b, p. 14). OAS provides a base on which to build other sources of pension income — C/QPP, employer pension plans, RRSPs, and other forms of savings — necessary to maintain a reasonable standard of living in retirement for non-poor seniors, including the affluent. Granted, OAS also makes a vital contribution to achieving the anti-poverty objective, along with the income-tested GIS and SPA programs. But the 1991 move to an individually income-tested OAS, and the prospect of going all the way to a family income-tested program, is criticized as jeopardizing OAS's earnings-replacement role and a lamentable shift in emphasis from the earnings-replacement to the anti-poverty objective. One critic accused the 1995 Budget of "effectively eliminating [OAS's] role in income replacement and converting it to a strictly anti-poverty program" (Townson 1995, p. 3).

OAS is a particularly important source of retirement income for women, who still earn less on average than men and who are less likely to belong to employer-sponsored pension plans or to contribute to RRSPs. (The same argument holds for the C/QPP). Family income-testing OAS, if done in a highly targeted manner, would reduce or even remove many women's OAS; a more gradually targeted OAS, on the other hand, would affect far fewer women. Especially hard hit would be the current generation of elderly women, because many worked wholly or mainly in the home and thus have little or no retirement income from earnings-linked programs (C/QPP, employer pension plans): OAS is their only independent source of income, which they could lose if their husband's income disqualified the couple for an income-tested OAS. It is argued that some men block wives' access to family income, especially in cases where there is spousal abuse; not sharing family income is seen as a form of abuse in itself (Women and Taxation Working Group 1992, p. 7).

Homemakers are not the only women who could lose out in the change to a family income-tested OAS. So also could some women who worked in the paid labour force part-time or full-time for wages and so qualified for C/QPP (and maybe even an employer pension). If their (typically lower) retirement income and their husband's (usually higher) retirement income raised the couple above the income threshold for OAS, such women could lose part or all of their OAS. Of course, the same holds for the man, unless his income is high enough that it disqualified him for OAS under the existing system.

Critics of family income-testing OAS can also dispute what they see as the real motive behind the proposal — to cut costs. As we shall see next, some people do not swallow the argument that the upward rise of expenditures on the aged is unaffordable. Individual income testing has cut middle-income and upper-income seniors' elderly benefits but done nothing to improve the lot of the elderly poor, being used instead for deficit reduction or to pay for boosting the tax deduction limit for RRSP contributions, as it were.

*Pro.* One argument in favour of family income-testing OAS is that such a change would correct the "horizontal inequity" of the present system that arises from the interaction of benefits that are income-tested on different bases (i.e., individual income for OAS and the age credit, family income for GIS). The amount of elderly benefits for couples varies as between couples with the same total income but different proportions of income from the spouses. Throughout most of the income range, what can be termed "two-income couples" — i.e., elderly couples in which both spouses have part of the family's non-OAS/GIS income — receive more benefits than do "one-income couples," meaning senior couples in which one spouse has most or all of the family's non-OAS/GIS income. One-income couples have the advantage over two-income couples at the low and high ends of the income spectrum. Figure 7 illustrates the differences.

FIGURE 7: Average Elderly Benefits, One-Income and Two-Income Elderly Couples, Current System, 1995

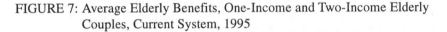

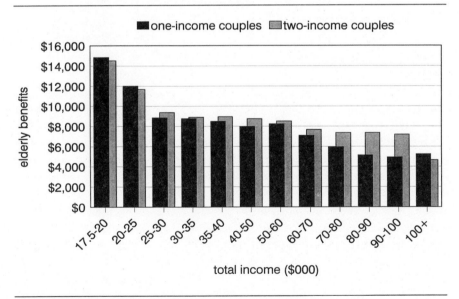

Source: Caledon Institute of Social Policy.

The precise reasons for the differences in benefits between one-income and two-income couples at different rungs of the income ladder are too tediously complex to recount here in painstaking detail. (Readers so masochistically inclined can contact the author for further information.) At the heart of the matter is the fact that each of the two types of family has two income recipients who receive varying benefits from as many as four different programs, depending upon their share of the family income. At every income level, the difference between the elderly benefits for one-income and two-income couples depends upon the complex interplay among each spouse's individual level of income (for OAS, the age credit and the pension income credit) and type of income (for the pension income credit), the couple's level of income (for GIS) and the particular design (e.g., benefit level, reduction rate, income threshold if applicable) of each program.[5]

Only a family income-tested elderly benefits system can deliver the same amount to all couples with the same total income. This most easily could be achieved by eliminating the age credit and pension income credit and folding their expenditures into a simpler, two-program system made up of a family income-tested OAS to complement the existing family income-tested GIS. Technically speaking, such a system would be a single program with two different benefit levels, thresholds, and reduction rates. But for political purposes, it would be easier and better to treat them still as two separate programs and keep their same names.

Another important argument that can be made in favour of a family income-tested OAS is that it will help achieve a more progressive distribution of benefits, according to the fourth commandment of pension reform. A family income-tested benefit will better target benefits to those below the threshold (whatever that may be) than an individually income-tested program with the same threshold. The existing clawback on OAS, which is based on individual income, means that a single senior or an elderly spouse with most of a couple's income will be hit by the clawback if his or her income is above the threshold, which is $53,215 in net income. However, a senior couple with total income of $53,215 made up of two smaller incomes escapes the clawback. If the clawback were based on the spouses' combined income, it would capture such two-income couples and thus both save the federal treasury more money and produce a more progressive distribution of benefits.

Of course, in theory an individually income-tested OAS could be designed to produce as progressive a distribution of benefits as one could want. It could be as steeply targeted as GIS, or it could be re-universalized and still made progressive (e.g., by going back to the pre-1988 days of ten tax rates and a higher top tax rate). However, a family income-tested OAS will always be more progressive than an individually income-tested OAS of comparable benefits because it will deliver less to many two-income senior couples than they would get from the latter.

Family income testing is linked to the fifth and final objective of pension reform — cost control. A family income-tested OAS will appeal to a government worried about the rising curve of public pension expenditures. Combine a family income-tested OAS with a partially-indexed threshold, and you achieve an attractive reform for finance ministers and their officials. However, it is not just finance ministers who favour such an approach; so too will Canadians who believe that demographically-inevitable rising expenditures on seniors must be better targeted to seniors with low or modest incomes.

*Rebuttals.* Proponents of family income-testing can marshall some counter-arguments to those aimed against the concept. The allegation that a family income-tested OAS will amount to a form of "social assistance" is based on a lack of understanding of the difference between income testing and needs testing in social policy, which many people typically and wrongly lump together under the rubric "mean testing." An income-tested program is based on a simple and anonymous test of level of income as measured by the income tax system or on some other application form. A needs-tested program, like welfare, involves a complex, intrusive and detailed one-on-one assessment of applicants' resources, assets, family composition, age of children, employability, and other indicators of need, as well as periodic re-tests to ensure there have been no changes in welfare recipients' circumstances. There is a world of difference between an income-tested program like GIS or the Child Tax Benefit and needs-tested welfare; in fact, universal and income-tested programs are much closer together than are income-tested and needs-tested programs. The argument that income-tested programs are stigmatizing or marginalizing, like needs-tested welfare, is nonsense.

The universalists' claim that universal programs that benefit a broad swath of the population are more secure than income-targeted programs looks pretty feeble, now that the federal government has done away with two of the most popular and well-known social programs — OAS and Family Allowances! The political ease with which the Tories' knocked down the walls of universality was extraordinary. Stealth played a significant role in the demise of universality, but social advocates had little success in mobilizing seniors or parents, let alone the general public, in the way they had back in the 1985 defeat of partial indexation of OAS.

The empirical evidence suggests that universal social programs are no more or less immune to benefit reductions or outright demolition than are income-tested programs. To help pay for the income-tested refundable child tax credit introduced in 1978, the Trudeau Liberals cut universal Family Allowances by six dollars a month. The Liberals raised the GIS for single seniors in 1984 but also temporarily partially indexed OAS during the 6 and 5 campaign, albeit with an offset to GIS to protect low-income seniors. Neither OAS nor GIS suffered benefit reductions under the Mulroney Conservatives or the current Liberal government, with the exception of upper-income seniors caught by the clawback on OAS. Universal Family Allowances were partially indexed and later abolished, while the income-tested refundable child tax credit was substantially increased under the Tories. Unemployment Insurance, a universal social insurance program, has been whacked several times over the past decade, hardest by the Liberals' 1994 Budget; under proposed new legislation to convert UI to Employment Insurance, upper-income repeat users could lose all of their benefits to a clawback.

That a family income-tested program will reduce or deny OAS for some Canadians, including wives with little or no income of their own, is true. However, the number of seniors who will lose from a family income-tested OAS depends on the design of the program; a sharply-targeted program will hit a lot, while a moderately-targeted program will affect far fewer pensioners. The "poor wives with rich husbands" argument raises the question as to whether social programs should be asked to try to solve the problem of income sharing between spouses. At a time of rising expenditures on the aged and a federal government committed to reducing the deficit and at least slowing the rise in the debt, is it justifiable to keep paying out elderly benefits amounting to a small portion of well-off couples' incomes while 635,000 elderly Canadians, 1,362,000 children and 2,944,000 women and men between the ages of 18 and 64 remain thousands of dollars below the low-income line?

The argument that family income-testing OAS would damage the program's earnings-replacement capacity cannot be tested in the absence of a concrete proposal. A family income-tested program can be designed to augment, maintain or diminish benefits to middle-income seniors. I for one certainly would not advocate a design that gutted elderly benefits for middle-income seniors or below, and doubt that the federal government will try to do so either — although it could sow the seeds for an erosion of the earnings-replacement function if it partially indexes the threshold for the new OAS. As to upper-income seniors, who would lose some or all of their OAS (and, under my proposal, the age and pension income credits too) to a family income-tested program, the issue is how much they would lose and how high up the income ladder the significant losses would begin. The current elderly benefits system accounts for a small and diminishing share of the income of affluent seniors, so further losses in benefits would have little impact on their economic status.

Critics of family income-testing OAS are unlikely to be swayed by arguments and counter-arguments from the other side. Anti-family income-testers believe that Old Age Security properly should be regarded as a pension entitlement belonging to the individual, regardless of his or her income level or the income of his or her spouse. They see family income testing as wrong-headed and unfair, serving as a smokescreen to rationalize further unwarranted cuts in the elderly benefits system. Further reductions to elderly benefits are all the more galling to them when contrasted to the expensive boost under way to the tax deductions for RRSP and RPP contributions, a plush feather for upper-income Canadians who least need to feather their retirement income nests.

## Greater Progressivity of Benefits

Changes made by the Conservatives and Liberals already have achieved a much more progressive distribution of elderly benefits. The evident motive and effect were cost control, since the considerable savings that resulted from reducing benefits for all but the poor were not used to boost benefits for the poor. The 1995 Budget calls for an even more progressive elderly benefits system which, if my prediction is right, will mean cuts for upper-income senior households.

It would be interesting to debate the issue of progressivity of elderly benefits. The old system provided a *de facto* uniform OAS payment to all seniors, including the wealthy. This offends my sense of fairness, since I believe that income-security programs should be progressive. On the other hand, one could argue that a preferable outcome from the changes over the last decade would have been an even more progressive distribution of benefits, which could have been achieved by redirecting some or all of the savings from cuts to middle-income and upper-income seniors to the poor by boosting the GIS.

Elderly benefits play a small but not completely trivial role in achieving the earnings-replacement objective for upper-income seniors. Single pensioners with an income of $50,000, for example, get just 9 percent of their disposable income from elderly benefits, most (8 percent) from OAS. Two-income elderly couples with incomes of $80,000, twice the average income, receive only 12 percent of their disposable income in the form of elderly benefits, 10 percent from OAS. The results are similar for one-income couples. Would a new old age pension system that substantially reduced or removed their benefits seriously harm the living standard of such affluent seniors? Indeed, is it even legitimate to charge the elderly benefits system with helping achieve the earnings-replacement objective — a goal that some experts see as the proper role for the C/QPP, employer pension plans and RRSPs?[6]

A more important issue, to my mind, is the harm that will be done to the earnings-replacement role if the threshold for the new OAS is partially indexed, which is a strong possibility. Gradually lowering the real level of the threshold will depress the disappearing point — the income level above which seniors do not qualify for benefits — which over the years will eventually reach middle-income territory. But partial indexation of the threshold also will have the effect of reducing OAS benefits for everyone above the threshold, which likely will include most non-poor seniors. If the threshold remained partially indexed and were never adjusted, eventually it would begin to affect poor pensioners as well.

Critics have every reason to be concerned about the earnings-replacement issue — even without a new old age pension. In 1952, OAS benefits came to 17 percent of the average wage. The average moved up and down during the 1950s and 1960s depending on ad hoc adjustments in OAS and changes in average wages. In 1964, OAS reached 20 percent of the average wage, but fell to 12.8 percent of the average wage by 1972. The substantial increase in benefits in 1973 increased OAS to 14 percent of the average wage, where it has remained ever since because real wages have pretty much stagnated since the mid-1970s. Future real growth in average wages would reduce OAS's earnings-replacement role, even if the program were left as is; the ever-declining clawback compounds the problem (Ascah 1994, pp. 9-10).

Another criticism of the move towards a more progressive, income-tested OAS is that it will have the undesirable result of jacking up marginal tax rates for seniors with incomes in the diminishing-benefit range. The steeper the reduction rate for the new OAS, the more serious will be the marginal tax rate problem. High marginal tax rates, so the argument goes, will create a disincentive for Canadians to save for their retirement during their working years through RRSPs and other investments because they will see their private pension income offset by reductions in their OAS. Moreover, a steep reduction rate means that seniors with relatively similar incomes can end up with significantly different elderly benefits, which is unfair. A related criticism is that a family income-tested OAS will encourage elderly people to cheat the system by hiding income and will discourage them from working.

One way to keep out of the high marginal tax rate woods is not to have high marginal tax rates: a relatively mild reduction rate (e.g., in the 10-12.5 percent range) would not appreciably raise marginal tax rates, as I will show in the final section of the paper. The contention that an income-tested OAS will discourage private savings for retirement assumes that Canadians are more irrational than I can imagine; would the potential loss of some or all of a $4,690 OAS benefit really drive people not to save anything for their retirement? An interesting twist is the new conventional wisdom amongst younger Canadians that there will be no public pensions when they retire. Would this not suggest that they will save more in RRSPs than their parents and that the marginal tax rate issue is a red herring, since they do not think any of them will get OAS period? Indeed, the myth that there will be no public pensions in future could be useful, to the extent that it encourages workers to save more for their retirement and so reduces OAS and GIS costs.

## Control of Program Costs

The various changes made to elderly benefits under the Tories and now the Liberals have reduced costs over what they would have been under the old system, as explained in the first section of the paper. Nonetheless, expenditures on OAS have mounted steadily, as they have for the C/QPP, causing concern on the part of the federal government and others (myself included) who preach the need to control public spending. The 1995 Budget noted that combined OAS and C/QPP expenditures were 5.3 percent of GDP in 1993 and are projected to rise to more than 8 percent of GDP by 2030 (Canada. Department of Finance 1995, p. 56). The reason for rising elderly benefit expenditures is no secret; demographic pressure has far outweighed restraint measures. Public pensions have increased in total real and per capita terms and measured as a percentage of GDP and federal program spending.

There is a difference between what a program costs and whether it is affordable. The former is a pretty straightforward accounting-cum-demographic projection exercise. OAS expenditures have risen steadily since the program began in 1952 and will continue to do so until around 2035, after which the baby-boomers will pass from this vale of tears and the OAS curve will rise much more slowly. In constant 1995 dollars, OAS expenditures went from $2 billion in 1952 to $16 billion in 1995 and will reach a projected $39 billion by 2035 . The actual cost to government will be somewhat less than the usual projections, which are based on gross payouts, might lead one to believe; partial indexation of the personal income tax system is taking a growing bite out of taxable OAS benefits, and partial indexation is steadily lowering the real level of the clawback and so recovering increasing amounts over time. But even in net terms, demographic pressures will keep pushing up OAS costs until well into the next century.

The affordability of OAS, C/QPP, and other social programs (e.g., medicare and social services) under pressure from the aging population is a much more contentious issue that involves at least as much political as economic judgement. One widely-used measure, the OAS-to-GDP ratio, shows the expected increase over time; OAS rose from 1.28 percent of GDP in 1952 to 2.03 percent in 1995. But does this mean that OAS will be "unaffordable" in future?

My projections of the OAS-to-GDP ratio find that, even assuming low real rates of average GDP growth, the sky will not fall. With only 1.5 percent real growth in GDP, the OAS-to-GDP ratio will rise from 2.03 percent in 1995 to 2.79 percent in 2030, but will fall steadily after that, subsiding to its 1995 level in 2060 and lower still thereafter. A 2-percent assumption of average annual real GDP increase produces a similar curve in the OAS-to-GDP ratio, though the peak will be lower in 2030 than under the 1.5 percent scenario (2.37 as opposed to 2.79) and the decline after that will be greater. Under more robust assumptions of economic growth — 3 and 4 percent — the OAS-to-GDP ratio will decline after 1995 and throughout the next century because OAS expenditures are projected to rise less than 3 percent a year. Figure 8 illustrates the scenarios. Indeed, the rate of increase in OAS costs has been decelerating over the past few years and will continue to slow until early in the next century because of a slowdown in the rate of increase of the elderly population; the Great Depression and World War II produced relatively small cohorts (which are now aging) compared to the baby-boom generation that followed (Desjardins and Dumas 1993, p. 19).

Neither does the future growth of OAS suggest a doomsday scenario if we use employment earnings as our denominator. The chief actuary has projected that Old Age Security costs will actually decline from 4.19 percent of total employment earnings in 1995 to 3.91 in 2005 because earnings will increase at a somewhat faster rate than OAS expenditures. The OAS-to-earnings ratio then will rise with the aging of the baby-boom generation to peak at 5.59 percent in 2030, after which it will fall to a projected 3.13 percent by the year 2100 (Canada. Health and Welfare 1991, p. 4).

FIGURE 8: Projected Old Age Security Expenditures, as Percent of GDP
Under Different Assumptions of Real GDP Growth, 1995-2100

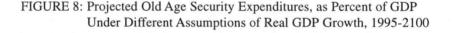

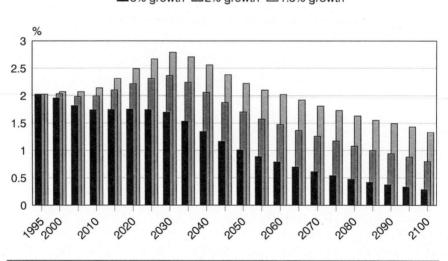

Source: *Old Age Security Program Statutory Actuarial Report*, and Caledon Institute of Social Policy.

On the other hand, labour market developments — such as the growth of non-standard jobs, continued high unemployment and underemployment, tough job prospects for many young Canadians, displacement of middle managers, the decline of blue-collar jobs in traditional manufacturing sector workers, and wage polarization — will have a significant impact on the pension system of the future. Many of today's unemployed, underemployed, and non-standard workers will have little if any private pension income when they retire, leaving them mainly or wholly dependent on public pension programs. Trends in the coverage of employer pension plans are not encouraging: the proportion of paid employees in employer pension plans was lower in 1993 (44.6 percent) than 1983 (45.4 percent) because the declining coverage of men more than offset the improved coverage of women; only 36 percent of the entire labour force belonged to private pension plans in 1983 and 35.4 percent in 1993.[7] These labour market and employer pension coverage trends, combined with substantial growth of the elderly population, will place heavy pressure on the public pension system in the coming decades, including OAS, GIS, and SPA; indeed, it is possible that GIS costs, which have pretty much levelled off since 1985, could increase again in future. An elderly benefits system that better targets its payments will be in a stronger position to sustain its support for the rising number of low- and modest-income seniors in future.

Moreover, population aging is increasing not just elderly benefits costs. The C/QPP, health care, and social services also are caught in the demographic meat-grinder. The Canadian Institute of Actuaries used the Office of the Superintendent of Financial Institutions projections to forecast OAS, C/QPP and Medicare expenditures for seniors, which will rise from a total 8.5 percent of GDP in 1995 to 14.8 percent by 2030 (Canadian Institute of Actuaries 1995, p. 19).

There is a political argument that can be made in favour of a more income-targeted OAS. Younger Canadians may see themselves as getting a raw deal on the intergenerational equity index. They are dubious that the welfare state will be able to afford to pay them public pensions when they retire, yet their income and payroll taxes (if they are lucky enough to have job) go to support today's aged and will have to increase in future to pay for the baby-boomers' pensions, health care, and social services. To the extent that the government can sell its new old age pension as sustainable and fair, it may restore confidence in and generate public support for the public pension system.

However, the finance minister does not have his gaze fixed on OAS-to-GDP and OAS-to-earnings ratios or the trend in GIS expenditures in the middle of the next century. Instead, he and his Cabinet colleagues see rising OAS expenditures taking a growing share of federal program spending, in the process making it harder to reduce the deficit and slow the debt, let alone contemplate desirable improvements to other social programs such as child benefits. While partial indexation of the personal income tax system and the clawback will ease somewhat the rising real cost of OAS, the 1995 Budget's principle of "control of program costs" clearly signals that Ottawa wants to save some money out of reform. Otherwise, why take the political risks involved?

Cost control is not the same as cost cuts. I do not think that the federal government is contemplating the kind of elderly benefits redesign that could slash spending enough to effect an absolute reduction in OAS expenditures. The aim is to "slow the steamroller," to borrow Terrance Hunsley's apt phrase applied in another context (Hunsley 1990, p. 194), which will continue to drive up spending even with the impending reforms.

There are several reasons why I think that Ottawa's scope for cost control is constrained or at least challenged by political realities.

The new OAS will not be a sharply-targeted *de facto* GIS that will turn the elderly benefits system into an anti-poverty program and abolish OAS's earnings-replacement role for non-poor seniors. Losers likely will be restricted to upper-income seniors, of which there are simply not enough to yield massive cost savings. If the GIS is increased somewhat to sweeten the reform pot, then that extra cost will (depending on the size of the increase) at least partly offset the savings from reducing benefits to the well-off. Granted, the joker in the deck is indexation of the threshold for the new OAS. If Ottawa partially indexes the threshold for the new OAS, it will impose gradual and growing cuts to benefits; however, the real savings would be some years down the road.

Another tempting reform to policymakers around the world is to raise the age of eligibility for public pensions, which several countries are doing. The United States, for example, is raising the age of eligibility for Social Security from 65 to 67. Seniors between the ages of 65 and 70 make up almost one-third of the elderly population in Canada, so serious money could be saved by making Canadians wait longer for their OAS (and CPP).

However, there are solid arguments that will be levelled against the option of raising the age of entitlement for OAS and CPP. Such a move would go in the opposite direction of the trend to early retirement, and could increase competition for scarce jobs. It would make life even harder for Canadians who are forced into early retirement because of layoffs and job restructuring. It would continue the catch-22 tradition of Canadian social policy of offloading clients and costs to Unemployment Insurance/Employment Insurance and welfare, though cuts to each of those programs are making the safety net harder to jump onto and stay on.

Others counter that there may well be labour shortages as the baby-boom generation retires, and that many seniors have valuable skills and experience built up over their working lives and a desire to keep working, if only part-time. The traditional notion that old age means retirement may fade away. Robert Brown argues that work should be seen as a fourth layer of the retirement income system (Brown 1995, p. 61).

One of the selling points of a family income-tested elderly benefits system is that, with some adaptations, it could be extended downwards to cover all low-income persons aged 60 to 64. This would end the inequity of the Spouse's Allowance which denies benefits to never-married, divorced, and separated low-income 60-64 year-olds, an issue that is the subject of a Charter challenge. Unfortunately, the costs involved — it would require in the order of $2 billion more to extend the SPA to all lower-income near-seniors — closes out that option, at least for the immediate future.

The Americans are implementing their age increase very gradually; it will reach 66 in 2005 and 67 in 2022. The reason for such a slow phase-in is to minimize the impact on older workers who have planned their affairs on the basis of receiving Social Security once they turn 65. Any major reform of a pension system, such as the shift to a family income-tested OAS, ideally should be phased in over a reasonably long period, and should "grandparent" the measure so as not to change the rules on the current elderly. Of course, changes to the elderly benefits system and other social programs over the past decade have not been phased in gradually; the clawback on OAS, for example, was phased in over just three years.

The 1995 Budget said that the federal government wants to legislate its changes to elderly benefits to take effect in 1997. However, this does not necessarily mean that a new scheme would be imposed in one fell swoop. More likely, the legislation will provide for a gradual phase-in over time, including a higher age of entitlement should Ottawa decide to go this route as well as family income-testing OAS. The slower the phase-in, the smaller the immediate savings, if any, from a new old age pension. Politics is another important factor: by gradually phasing-in changes to elderly benefits, the prime minister could claim he did not go back on his commitment during the referendum campaign not to reduce old age pensions for Quebec seniors. By grandparenting its pension changes, the federal government might to some extent lessen the ferocity of the attack from the seniors' lobby, though probably not much.

A MODERATELY-TARGETED OPTION FOR A NEW OLD AGE PENSION

It is impossible to have an informed debate about pension reform in the absence of options which allow us to gauge the various effects of reform and test the validity of the criticisms that have been made in the abstract. This final section presents an option for reform.

My proposal involves a rationalization of elderly benefit programs into a family income-tested OAS and GIS. The age credit and pension income credit would be eliminated and their budgets folded into the new system. Ideally, the Spouse's Allowance would be replaced by a variant of the new old age pension extended downwards to serve all low-income Canadians aged 60 to 64. However, such an option would be so costly (in the $2 billion range) as to be a political non-starter at this point, so I deal only with persons 65 and older.

I have called my proposal a "moderately-targeted system" to distinguish it from the super-GIS that rears its ugly or handsome head, as the case may be, in some people's minds when we talk about a family income-tested elderly benefit. Of course, one could build a sharply-targeted system that focused on the anti-poverty objective at the expense of the earnings-replacement objective. However appealing it might be to boost the income guarantee up to the poverty line, such a lopsided model would be enormously expensive and would cripple the earnings-replacement capacity of the elderly benefits system for middle-income seniors. A GIS-only elderly benefits system would impose very high marginal tax rates on modest- and middle-income seniors and would deliver sharply different amounts of benefit to seniors with relatively similar total incomes.

I have modelled a "giant-GIS" option that eliminates OAS and increases the maximum GIS for both singles and couples to the low-income cutoff for cities of 500,000 and larger. Such an option would cost $9 billion more than the present system and would impose sharp cuts in benefits on seniors with average incomes and above. The high cost results from the increase in the maximum benefit, and the fact that the "disappearing point" (i.e., the income above which eligibility for GIS ceases) would be pushed high up the income scale and thus extend GIS benefits to a larger number of seniors. Of course, one could reduce this massive extra cost somewhat by granting a lower maximum benefit, but then that would leave some seniors (i.e., those in metropolitan centres) short of the low-income line, if we employ the community size-variable low-income cutoffs as our measure of low income. One way around this problem would be to vary the giant-GIS according to community size, but this would raise other problems, since low-income cutoffs have never been used to design social programs; for example, seniors on the border between different community sizes would receive different amounts of elderly benefits.

I modelled several variants of the moderately-targeted option, but will present only one here to save space and because the results are similar. GIS operates the same as it does now except for a $300 increase in the maximum payment for single pensioners (from $5,574 to $5,874) and a $500 increase for couples (i.e., $250 per person) from the current $7,261 to $7,761; remember that GIS is reduced by 50 percent of income from C/QPP, private pensions, investments, employment, and other sources, as under the present program. OAS pays its current benefit ($4,690.29 per person or $9,381 per couple) but is income-tested on a family income basis (i.e., the combined income of the spouses); benefits are reduced at the rate of 12.5 percent of other income above a threshold of $25,921 in other income.

In designing this and other options, I used a Caledon tax-transfer microsimulation model, but relied upon Statistics Canada's Social Policy Simulation Database and Model (SPSD/M) to cost and test options. The SPSD/M runs were performed by Richard Shillington of the Centre for International Statistics at the Canadian Council on Social Development. A word of caution is in order here: the Finance Department uses another model, so there would be some minor differences in estimates of cost and impact if they were to run my option. However, I am confident that our estimates are in the same ball park.

This moderately-targeted option would save the federal government an estimated $578 million if it were implemented all at once. Yet it would still manage to boost benefits by $300 for low-income single pensioners and by $500 for low-income pensioner couples. If a revenue-neutral outcome were on the table, which seems unlikely these days, then a somewhat larger increase in elderly benefits for low-income seniors would be possible, though we are still talking in the hundreds of dollars, not the thousands that would be required to close the poverty gap.

Note that I specified that this option would save Ottawa about half a billion dollars if it were put in place immediately. In reality, I would hope that the federal government phased such a new program in over a number of years, perhaps even "grandparenting" it so as not to affect current seniors. In that case, the reform would not generate immediate savings of the magnitude estimated for this option.

Figure 9 illustrates how the new system would work for single seniors. GIS is sharply targeted on low-income pensioners, disappearing at $12,148 in non-OAS income. OAS pays its maximum benefit up to the threshold of $25,921 then declines and disappears at $63,411 in non-OAS income. Figure 10 adds GIS and OAS to show total elderly benefits under the new system (a maximum of $10,564), which are steeply targeted at the low end of the income spectrum as GIS phases out quickly (as in the present system), remain flat at $4,690 between the disappearing point for GIS ($11,748 and the threshold ($25,921) and then decline to phase out at what for single seniors is a high income — $63,441.

Figure 11 uses SPSD/M to compare benefits under the current system with the moderately-targeted option. The x-axis shows total income, including elderly benefits. Figure 12 indicates the average impact of the option on single seniors in different income groups. Single elderly Canadians with incomes under $40,000 (more than twice the average income) would see, on average, increases in their elderly benefits in the $200-$600 range for three reasons. The first is the $300

FIGURE 9: Elderly Benefits, Single Seniors, Moderately-Targeted Option, 1995

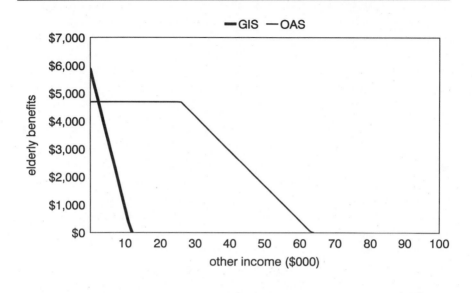

Source: Caledon Institute of Social Policy.

FIGURE 10: Elderly Benefits, Single Seniors, Moderately-Targeted Option, 1995

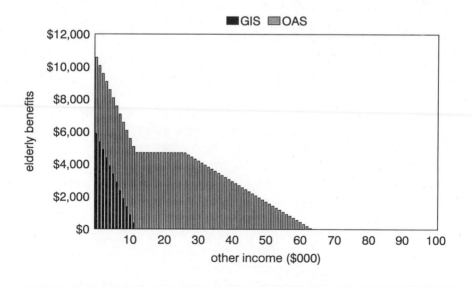

Source: Caledon Institute of Social Policy.

FIGURE 11: Average Elderly Benefits, Single Seniors, Current System and Moderately-Targeted Option, 1995

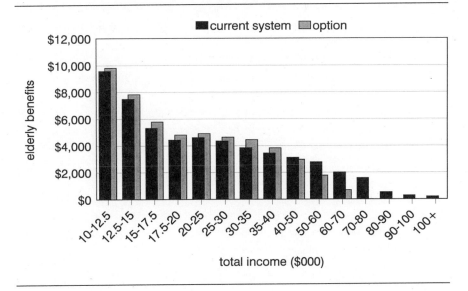

Source: Caledon Institute of Social Policy.

FIGURE 12: Average Change in Elderly Benefits, Single Seniors, Moderately-Targeted Option, 1995

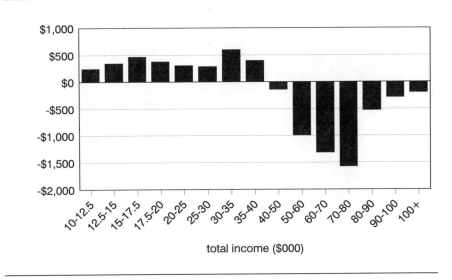

Source: Caledon Institute of Social Policy.

increase in the GIS maximum payment for single seniors, which increases benefits for the poorest pensioners. The second reason is that the $300 boost will extend the reach of the GIS, since its disappearing point would rise from $11,148 to $11,748 in non-OAS income. Finally, the new OAS would for some seniors exceed what they now get from taxable OAS and the age and pension income credits. Losses would begin above $40,000, reaching on average a high of $1,573 for seniors with income between $70,000 and $80,000. In other words, only well-off seniors would see a substantial decline in their elderly benefits, and the loss would amount to a very small percentage of their total income.

Figure 13 expresses the change in benefits as a percentage of total income. Low-income single seniors' average gain would be in the 2 to 3 percent range, while the largest loss (for upper-income seniors in the $70,000-$80,000 range) would amount to only 2 percent of income. A new old age pension designed along these lines, then, would do little damage to the earnings-replacement capacity of the elderly benefits system for affluent seniors; to the contrary, the elderly benefits system would modestly improve its earnings-replacement capacity for the large majority of single elderly Canadians.

FIGURE 13:  Average Change in Elderly Benefits as Percent of Income, Single Seniors, Moderately-Targeted Option, 1995

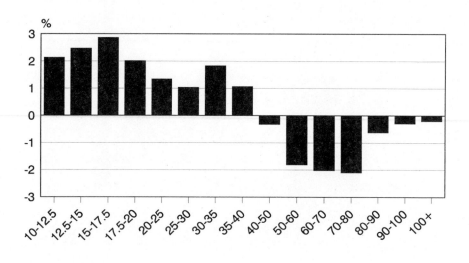

Source: Caledon Institute of Social Policy.

The $300 increase in the maximum GIS for singles would provide a welcome albeit modest improvement in the anti-poverty power of the federal elderly benefits system. Maximum OAS and GIS for single seniors would rise from $10,264 to $10,564. The income guarantee for single pensioners would rise from 60.8 percent to 62.6 percent of the low-income cutoff for metropolitan centres (which have the highest low-income cutoff). The income guarantee for single seniors in cities of 100,000 to 499,999 would increase from 70.9 percent to 73.0 percent of the poverty line, from 71.4 percent to 73.5 percent for seniors in communities of 30,000 to 99,999, from 76.8 percent to 79.0 percent for those in centres under 30,000 and from 88.0 percent to 90.6 percent for seniors living in rural areas.

Figure 14 gives the percentage of elderly households that under this option would get less than, the same as or more than the present system. Only 6.3 percent of single seniors would receive less from the moderately-targeted option; 14.6 percent would get about the same and 79.1 percent would come out ahead. In

FIGURE 14: Seniors With Less, More and the Same Elderly Benefits, by Type of Household, Moderately-Targeted Option, 1995

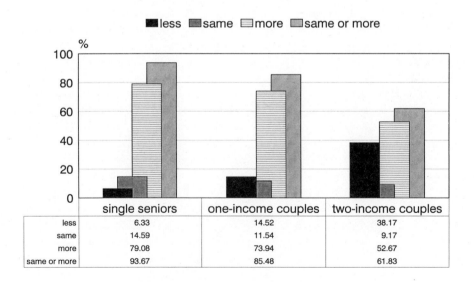

| | single seniors | one-income couples | two-income couples |
| --- | --- | --- | --- |
| less | 6.33 | 14.52 | 38.17 |
| same | 14.59 | 11.54 | 9.17 |
| more | 79.08 | 73.94 | 52.67 |
| same or more | 93.67 | 85.48 | 61.83 |

Source: Caledon Institute of Social Policy.

total then, 93.7 percent of single Canadians 65 and over would be either better off or no worse off under the new old age pension. The reason is that the large majority of single seniors have low or modest incomes and so would qualify for the larger maximum benefit of the moderately-targeted option. Single elderly women would constitute a larger proportion of winners than men from this option because they have lower average incomes than men and because there are more single women than men over 65. In 1994, the average income of unattached elderly women was $17,106 compared to $23,782 for single elderly men; there were 783,000 women in this category as opposed to 261,000 men.

Figure 15 shows the total distribution of elderly benefits for elderly couples under the moderately-targeted option. The maximum benefit from OAS ($9,381) and GIS ($7,761) totals $17,142; GIS disappears at $15,522 in non-OAS income, as opposed to $14,522 under the present system. OAS pays its maximum benefit of $9,381 up to the threshold of $25,921, then declines and disappears at $100,969 in non-OAS income.

FIGURE 15: Elderly Benefits, Elderly Couples, Moderately-Targeted Option, 1995

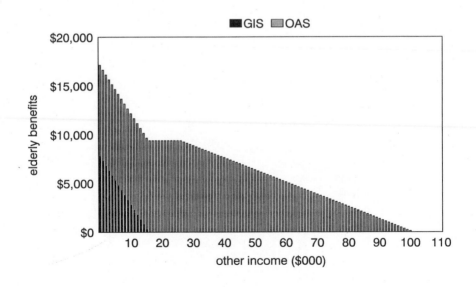

Source: Caledon Institute of Social Policy.

Figure 16 shows the average impact of the moderately-targeted option on one-income and two-income couples (in which both spouses are 65 or older) at different income levels. One-income couples with incomes up to $50,000 (which is $10,000 above the average $40,000 income for aged couples) would generally get more than they do now, with estimated average increases ranging as high as around $900 for couples with incomes between $30,000 and $35,000; losses would be as high as about $4,500 for those with incomes above $100,000. Two-income couples with incomes under $40,000 (average income) would generally get more as well, though the increase would be somewhat smaller (as much as around $550 for couples in the $30,000-$35,000 group), and losses would go as high as $5,000 or so for couples in the $90,000-$100,000 range. The reason for the slightly different pattern of wins and losses is that, though one-income and two-income couples at the same total income mark would get the same elderly benefits under the new family income-tested system, they get different amounts from the present system, so the impact of the option will vary to some extent.

FIGURE 16:  Average Change in Elderly Benefits, One-Income and
Two-Income Aged Couples, Moderately-Targeted Option, 1995

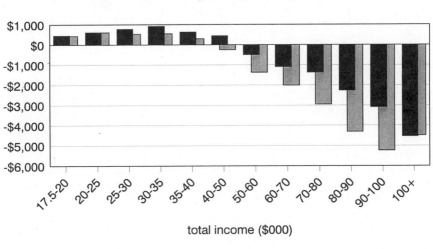

Source: Caledon Institute of Social Policy.

Figure 17 shows the change in benefits for elderly couples as a percentage of their total income. The largest gain for one-income couples would amount to 2.8 percent of income for those in the $25,000-$35,000 range, while the biggest loss would amount to around 4.5 percent of income for those in the $100,000-plus group. For two-income couples, the largest average increase would represent about 2.7 percent of total income for those in the $20,000-$25,000 group and the largest loss would be 5.5 percent of total income for the $90,000-$100,000 range. A moderately-targeted option like the one illustrated here would have a negligible negative impact on the earnings-replacement objective for upper-income couples and in fact would improve the system's earnings-replacement capacity for couples with average incomes and below.

Figure 14 gives the winner/loser/no change profile for couples. Among one-income couples, 14.5 percent would get less, 11.5 percent the same and 73.9 percent more under this moderately-targeted option; thus 85 percent would receive the same or see an increase in elderly benefits. Two-income couples fare somewhat less well because they generally get more from the current system than do one-income couples; 38.2 percent would get less, 9.2 percent would get much

FIGURE 17:  Average Change in Elderly Benefits as Percent of Income,
Elderly Couples, Moderately-Targeted Option, 1995

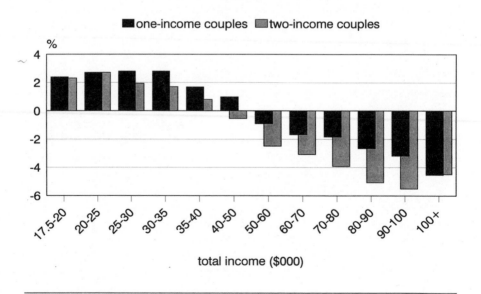

Source: Caledon Institute of Social Policy.

the same and 52.7 percent would come out ahead; however, 62 percent would get the same as or more than they do now.

Figure 18 shows the impact of the option on elderly women and men. Overall, 14 percent of aged women would receive less elderly benefits than under the current system, 13 percent would see no change and 72.9 percent would get more. Among elderly men, 27.8 percent would get less, 10.2 percent would stay the same and 61.9 percent would get more. Figure 19 illustrates the impact of the moderately-targeted option on single and married elderly women. Only 6.3 percent of single elderly women would get less, 14.5 percent would stay where they are now and 79 percent would get more. Among women in one-income aged couples, 14.5 percent would get less, 11.5 percent the same and 73 percent more. In two-income couples, 38.2 percent of women would get less, 9.2 percent the same and 52.7 percent more from the option. In total, then, 93.6 percent of single elderly women, 85.4 percent of women in one-income couples and 61.8 percent of women in two-income couples would get more than or the same as they do now.

FIGURE 18: Seniors With Less, More and the Same Elderly Benefits, by Sex, Moderately-Targeted Option, 1995

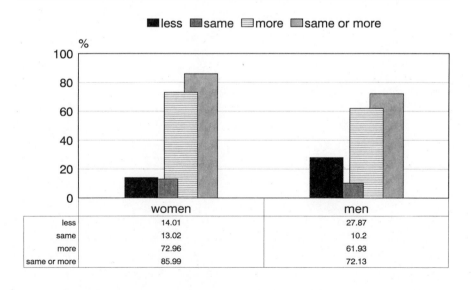

Source: Caledon Institute of Social Policy.

FIGURE 19: Women With Less, More and the Same Elderly Benefits, by Type of Household, Moderately-Targeted Option, 1995

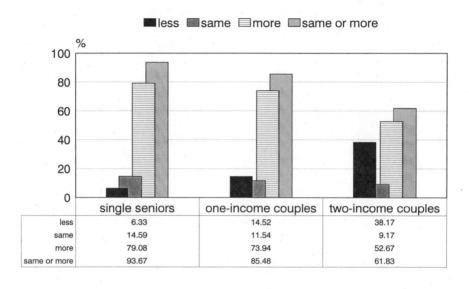

| | less | same | more | same or more |
|---|---|---|---|---|
| single seniors | 6.33 | 14.59 | 79.08 | 93.67 |
| one-income couples | 14.52 | 11.54 | 73.94 | 85.48 |
| two-income couples | 38.17 | 9.17 | 52.67 | 61.83 |

Source: Caledon Institute of Social Policy.

Figure 20 ranks the provinces in terms of the proportion of their elderly households (i.e., single and couples together) that would get more from the targeted option. The results range from 85 percent of senior households in Quebec to 60 percent in Ontario. Quebec fares best of all the provinces. Two factors occur to me that help explain this result. One is that Quebec's seniors have lower average incomes; the average income for families with aged heads in 1994 was $36,113 in Quebec as opposed to $40,183 in Canada, and the average income for elderly individuals in Quebec was $17,265 as opposed to $19,067 for Canada. Since lower-income households generally get more from this option, then proportionately Quebec does better. A related factor is that Quebec has an above-average proportion of single seniors (as a percentage of all senior households); the option favours lower-income singles.

FIGURE 20: Elderly Households With More Benefits, by Province,
Moderately-Targeted Option, 1995

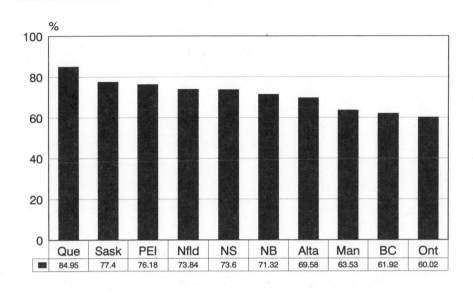

| | Que | Sask | PEI | Nfld | NS | NB | Alta | Man | BC | Ont |
|---|---|---|---|---|---|---|---|---|---|---|
| ■ | 84.95 | 77.4 | 76.18 | 73.84 | 73.6 | 71.32 | 69.58 | 63.53 | 61.92 | 60.02 |

Source: Caledon Institute of Social Policy.

A moderately-targeted option also would not cause the problem of significant increases in marginal tax rates, discussed earlier. Figure 21 illustrates marginal tax rates for single seniors under the present elderly benefits system and as they would be under the option. Seniors in the $30,000-$50,000 other income range would see a relatively small increase in their marginal tax rate (e.g., at $40,000, the marginal tax rate would increase from 46 to 54 percent) because they have their OAS reduced by 12.5 cents for every dollar of other income, which is more than what they currently lose from the taxation of and clawback on OAS. Seniors in the $53,000-$84,000 other income range would face lower marginal tax rates under the new old age pension than they do under the current system because their OAS is small or (above $61,000) nil, so the taxability of OAS is not adding to their marginal tax rate as it does under the existing system. At non-OAS income of $85,000, the marginal tax rates are the same because OAS under the existing system is subject to the 100 percent clawback.

Raising the age of eligibility for elderly benefits would save the federal government a lot of money. Making Canadians wait until age 67 would slice an

FIGURE 21: Marginal Tax Rates, Single Seniors, Current System and
Moderately-Targeted Option, 1995

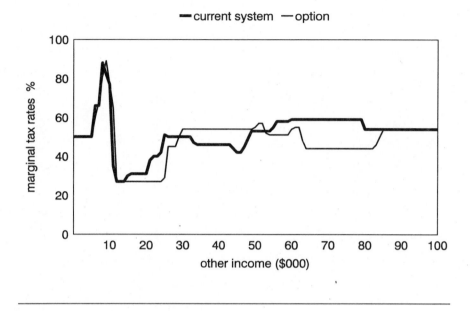

Source: Caledon Institute of Social Policy.

estimated $492 million from the initial cost of the proposal, while raising the age
of eligibility to 70 would save an estimated $844 million.

Finally, any option should ensure a fully-indexed threshold for the OAS. Figure 22 shows what would happen if the threshold for the moderately-targeted
option were only partially indexed according to the tried and true inflation-over-
3 percent formula. By 2015, the $25,921 threshold would have fallen to an esti-
mated $17,478 in constant 1995 dollars. The disappearing point for elderly ben-
efits would have declined from $63,441 in other income to $54,998. More seniors
would be disqualified from elderly benefits, fewer would receive maximum benefits and all seniors with incomes above the threshold ($17,478) would suffer a
reduction in their elderly benefits. By my estimate, the federal government would
save $820 million as a result of partial indexation (i.e., would spend $820 million
less in 2015 than it would if the threshold were fully indexed to the cost of living).

The reform of elderly benefits has implications for federal-provincial relations
and for the unity issue. Some provinces would fare better than others, as shown

FIGURE 22: Elderly Benefits With Partially-Indexed Threshold, Single
Seniors, Moderately-Targeted Option, 1995 and 2015

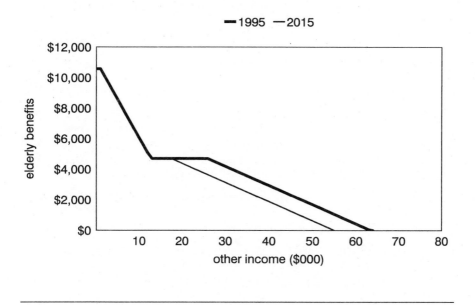

Source: Caledon Institute of Social Policy.

above. Quebec would do best under this moderately-targeted option. This is somewhat ironic in light of the controversy during the Quebec referendum campaign
in the autumn of 1995 when separatist leaders argued that seniors' pensions were
in jeopardy from a cost-cutting federal government and the prime minister coun-
tered that pensions were secure.

But changes to federal elderly benefits also will have revenue impacts on the
provinces because elderly benefits are intertwined with provincial income tax
systems. The provinces receive revenues from the income taxation of OAS but
forego revenues as a result of the age credit and pension income credit. They
collect an estimated $1.2 billion from taxation of OAS and forego an estimated
$1 billion in revenue losses from the age and pension income credits, so they
would be net losers as a result of the change to a system that provided an untaxed
income-tested OAS and eliminated the age credit and pension income credit. Since
five provinces and the two territories provide income supplements to their low-
income seniors, conceivably they could make up for their revenue losses by

reducing their provincial income supplements for the aged, which of course could leave seniors in such provinces no better off and perhaps even worse off after reform. In this way, the reform of elderly benefits would add yet another issue to be resolved by Ottawa and the provinces in their remaking of Confederation.

## SUMMARY

Cost control is the primary motive behind the numerous changes made to the elderly benefits system since 1985, first by the Conservatives and now the Liberals. The changes also have created a more progressive elderly benefits system, and have converted universal Old Age Security to an income-tested program that excludes upper-income seniors. Progressivity has come at a price — a substantial loss of elderly benefits for middle- and upper-income pensioners. Partial indexation of the threshold for the clawback and the personal income tax system has given the federal government a politically invisible means of cutting expenditures on OAS, the age credit, and the pension income credit, but clearly the finance minister wants to do more to control costs.

Pension commentators and experts are sharply divided on whether or not such reductions and changes are necessary or warranted. Rising costs are one thing; whether such demographically-driven expenditures are affordable or not is quite another matter. Some critics see in the 1995 Budget's five principles of reform a further devolution of old age pensions from a universal entitlement that promoted social solidarity, bolstered support for the welfare state and helped define the Canadian identity, to an anti-poverty scheme that will pull the rug out from middle-income seniors retirement income and hurt their standard of living. The shift to family income testing is a controversial change that, wherever one comes down on the issue, marks a major shift in the underlying philosophy of Canada's pension system.

One problem with the whole debate, such as it is, has been the absence of concrete proposals. However, the critics have not been constrained by the lack of a clear target to shoot at, having launched their volleys already. They should keep their powder dry in preparation for the forthcoming proposals from the federal government (assuming, of course, that Ottawa doesn't get cold feet because of the unity issue and the not-that-so-distant federal election and forget its commitment to reform old age pensions).

This paper presents a fiscally attractive and socially desirable proposal to redesign elderly benefits. My "moderately-targeted" option would cost more than half a billion dollars less than the present system — while providing a larger benefit to 79 percent of single seniors, 74 percent of one-income couples, and 53 percent of two-income couples. Overall, 94 percent of single pensioners, 85 percent of one-income couples and 62 percent of two-income couples would get more than or the same as they do under the present system. The majority of elderly women, 73 percent, would come out ahead under this proposal, and 86 percent would be better off or no worse off. Quebec would fare best of all the provinces: 85 percent of elderly households in Quebec would get more elderly benefits and 92 percent would get either more or the same.

This is a win-win-win-win proposal for a new old age pension.

CODA

Subsequent to the writing of this paper, the federal government announced a new Seniors Benefit in its March 1996 Budget (Canada. Department of Finance 1996, pp. 64-66). While the Seniors Benefit is more targeted than the proposal I put forward in this paper, its other design features are strikingly similar to mine.

The Seniors Benefit is carefully constructed to ensure that no senior or near-senior will lose benefits. The new program will not take effect until 2001. All Canadians age 60 by 31 December 1995 will be able to choose either the Seniors Benefit or the old system — whichever provides the better benefit — for the rest of their lives.

The Seniors Benefit employs the same two-step, family income-tested design as my proposal, combining a GIS-style component (with the same steep 50 percent reduction rate as the current Guaranteed Income Supplement) and an OAS-like component (with a $25,921 threshold and a 20-percent reduction rate). We differ only on the amount of the maximum benefit and the reduction rate for the OAS component. The Seniors Benefit will pay $120 more than the current maximum OAS/GIS for both singles and couples, providing an income guarantee of $11,420 for single seniors and $18,440 for elderly couples in 2001. The option illustrated in this paper adds $300 to the maximum benefit for single seniors ($11,600) and $500 for elderly couples ($18,820), expressed in the same 2001 terms as the Seniors Benefit. Where the two designs differ most is in the reduction rate for the OAS component — mine is 12.5 percent as opposed to the Seniors Benefit's 20 percent. As a result, the Seniors Benefit will disappear at a lower income level than my proposal — for single seniors, at $51,721 (versus $67,201 for my option) and $77,521 (versus $108,481 for mine) in 2001. However, the large majority of elderly Canadians, who have low or modest incomes, will receive much the same from the Seniors Benefit as they would from my option.

Like my proposal, the Seniors Benefit will pay the majority of seniors either more than or the same as they get under the current system: three in four elderly households will receive more or the same. Elderly households with incomes under $40,000 — about the average income for couples and more than double the average income for single seniors — will be better off or no worse off under the new program. Some couples in the $40,000–$50,000 income range will receive somewhat more and some will get less, depending on the income mix of the spouses. Couples with income over $45,000 (above the $40,000 average income) will get less, and those above $78,000 (almost double the average income) will no longer receive elderly benefits.

Critics who *kvetch* that the Seniors Benefit will deny payments to the poor wives of rich husbands living in such poverty zones as the British Properties, the Bridal Path and Westmount should pause and consider that nine in ten single aged women will come out ahead under the new program. For every archetypal "banker's wife" who will not qualify for the Seniors Benefit, 50 lower-income single elderly women will receive a larger benefit.

Like the reform proposed in this paper, the Seniors Benefit will feature a fully-indexed benefit and income threshold. This is an unexpected and welcome improvement over the present elderly benefits system, with its partially indexed OAS clawback threshold and age credit and unindexed pension income credit.

The critics have taken their predictable, well-rehearsed swings at the Seniors Benefit as the final stake through the heart of universality (how many times can we kill it?), an assault on the middle class (not true, but the allegation makes good media copy) or a usurious tax that will drive better-off Canadians to stop saving for their retirement. However, the Seniors Benefit was cleverly crafted, packaged, and sold to seniors and the public. In their coverage of the 1996 Budget, the newspapers showed a photo of Paul Martin with his arm around the shoulders and hand in the hand of a smiling 73 year-old woman. She was Solange Denis, the erstwhile Joan of Ark of the fight against partial indexation of Old Age Security in 1985.

NOTES

I want to acknowledge the invaluable assistance of Richard Shillington in modelling the paper's elderly benefits option using Statistics Canada's Social Policy Simulation Database and Model. I also benefited greatly from the helpful comments of William Robson, Melanie Hess, Ed Tamagno, and Sherri Torjman.

1.  The earnings-replacement objective of Old Age Security is not accepted by all observers. William Robson of the C.D. Howe Institute, a discussant of this paper, argues that OAS has a legitimate role to play in providing income support but not earnings replacement. Unlike earnings-replacing pension programs such as the C/QPP and employer pension plans, OAS is not earnings-related in design and does not hinge upon participation in the paid labour force. Presumably by "income support," Mr. Robson means providing a basic floor of income upon which earnings-replacement pension programs build. In this sense, income support is akin to the anti-poverty objective, though it could be construed to provide income to a wider group of

pensioners than just those with low incomes. At the end of the day, I am not sure if there is much difference between saying that an income-tested OAS (proposed in this paper) would help achieve the earnings-replacement objective for lower- and middle-income pensioners and that it would achieve an income support objective. Much more important than the choice of the terms "income support" and "earnings replacement" are the amount and distribution (by income level) of OAS benefits.

2.  In 1995, OAS for a single person totalled $4,690 and GIS a maximum $5,574 for a total of $10,264; the low-income cutoff for a city of 500,000 or more was $16,874. OAS for an aged couple was $9,381 and maximum GIS $7,261 for a total $16,642; the low-income cutoff for two people in a metropolitan centre was $21,092.

3.  One can arrive at a progressive distribution if elderly benefits are expressed as a percentage of total income.

4.  My thanks to Ed Tamagno for pointing this out to me.

5.  A research paper prepared by the Caledon Institute for the National Advisory Council on Aging gives a detailed analysis and explanation.

6.  See William Robson's comments above.

7.  Unpublished data on employer pension plan coverage provided to the author by Statistics Canada.

## REFERENCES

Ascah, L. (1994), *The Pension Gap*, Ottawa: Canadian Centre for Policy Alternatives.

Baldwin, B. (1995*a*), "Overview of the Retirement Income System," in *Roundtable on Canada's Aging Society and Retirement Income System*, Ottawa: Caledon Institute of Social Policy.

_____ (1995*b*), *The Adequacy and Cost of Retirement Incomes in Canada, Now and in the Future*, Ottawa: Canadian Labour Congress.

Battle, K. (under the pseudonym Grattan Gray) (1990), "Social Policy by Stealth," *Policy Options*, 11, 2:17-29.

_____ (1993), *Thinking the Unthinkable: A Targeted, Not Universal, Old Age Pension*, Ottawa: Caledon Institute of Social Policy.

Battle, K. and S. Torjman (1995), *How Finance Re-formed Social Policy*, Ottawa: Caledon Institute of Social Policy.

Brown, R. (1995), "Canada Pension Plan: Financing," in *Roundtable on Canada's Aging Society and Retirement Income System*, Ottawa: Caledon Institute of Social Policy.

Canada. Department of Finance Canada (1994), *Budget Plan: Including Supplementary Information and Notices of Ways and Means Motion*, Ottawa: Department of Finance Canada.

_____ (1995), *Budget Plan: Including Supplementary Information and Notices of Ways and Means Motion*, Ottawa: Department of Finance Canada.

_____ (1996), *Budget Plan: Including Supplementary Information and Notices of Ways and Means Motion*, Ottawa: Department of Finance Canada.

Canada. Health and Welfare (1991), *Old Age Security Program: Second Actuarial Report as at December 31, 1991*, Ottawa: Supply and Services Canada.

Canadian Institute of Actuaries (1995), *Troubled Tomorrows: The Report of the Canadian Institute of Actuaries' Task Force on Retirement Savings,* Ottawa: Canadian Institute of Actuaries.

Canadian Labour Congress (1995), *The Upcoming Debate on Public Pensions: Issues as Seen by the Federal Government, the Reform Party and the CLC*, Ottawa: Canadian Labour Congress.

Coalition of Seniors for Social Equity (1995), *Seniors' Income*: *What Next?* Submission to the Finance Committee of the House of Commons.

Desjardins, B. and J. Dumas (1993), *Population Ageing and the Elderly: Current Demographic Analysis,* Ottawa: Industry, Science and Technology.

Hunsley, T. as quoted in A. Moscovitch (1990), "Slowing the Steamroller: The Federal Conservatives, the Social Sector and Child Benefits Reform," in *How Ottawa Spends 1990-91: Tracking the Second Agenda,* ed. Katherine Graham, Ottawa: Carleton University Press.

Mendelson, M. (1981), *Universal or Selective? The Debate on Reforming Income Security in Canada,* Toronto: Ontario Economic Council.

_____ (1995), *Looking for Mr. Good-Transfer: A Guide to the CHST Negotiations,* Ottawa: Caledon Institute of Social Policy.

Myles, J. (1994), *Old Wine in New Bottles: Privatizing Old Age Pensions,* Ottawa: Caledon Institute of Social Policy.

_____ (1995), *The Market's Revenge: Old Age Security and Social Rights,* Ottawa: Caledon Institute of Social Policy.

National Council of Welfare (1983), *Family Allowances For All?* Ottawa: Supply and Services Canada.

_____ (1989), *The 1989 Budget and Social Policy,* Ottawa: Supply and Services Canada.

Ontario Fair Tax Commission (1993), *Fair Taxation in a Changing World,* Toronto: University of Toronto Press in cooperation with the Ontario Fair Tax Commission.

Ruggeri, G.C., R. Howard and K. Bluck (1994), "The Incidence of Low Income Among the Elderly," *Canadian Public Policy* 20, 2:138-151.

Townson, M. (1995), *Our Aging Society*: *Preserving Retirement Incomes into the 21st Century,* Ottawa: Canadian Centre for Policy Alternatives.

Women and Taxation Working Group (1992), *Women and Taxation,* Toronto: Ontario Fair Tax Commission.

# Comments

## Bob Baldwin

My comments have four parts to them. I will begin with several general observations on public pensions in Canada. These comments will establish a context for my comments on the papers by Ken Battle and Newman Lam, James Cutt and Michael Prince. I will then discuss, in turn, historical and political, and analytical and technical dimensions of the papers. Finally, I will offer some concluding comments.

My comments are more of an elaboration on issues raised in these papers than they are a critical commentary on them.

### GENERAL OBSERVATIONS ON PUBLIC PENSIONS IN CANADA

#### OAS and CPP as a Source of Income

Bearing in mind that so much is being said about program expenditures associated with Old Age Security (OAS) and the Canada and Quebec Pension Plans (C/QPP) in the future, it is important to balance the discussion by noting the role that these programs play as a source of income for Canadians over 65. (It is also important to note that program expenditures are *not* costs to the economy.)

For all Canadians 65 and over in 1992 (individuals and family units), OAS accounted for 30 percent of all income received, and C/QPP for 18 percent. Even for Canadians over 65 in the income range of $41,500 to $63,000 (the fourth quintile for the entire population), OAS accounted for 16 percent of income received, and C/QPP for 15 percent. Thus, even for moderately "well-off" Canadians over 65, OAS and C/QPP are very important sources of income.

Given the important role that OAS and C/QPP play as sources of income, the prospect of cutting their benefits has to be accompanied by an assessment of what that means for the incomes of the elderly and the overall distribution income. In addition, it should be noted that most of the so-called "private" pension arrangements have been designed on the assumption that full OAS and C/QPP benefits are available. The impact on the "private" arrangements of changing OAS and C/QPP needs to be explored.

## Share of National Income Claimed by the Elderly Through OAS and CPP

In February 1995, the supplementary documents tabled with the federal budget raised the question of whether current public pension programs were sustainable over the long run and appeared to give a negative answer in noting that OAS and C/QPP expenditure would increase from roughly 5.3 percent of national income in 1993, to roughly 8 percent in 2030. Eight percent of national income is less than the *current* average expenditure on comparable programs in the OECD area.

The relatively small share of GDP to be accounted for by OAS and CPP in 2030 speaks to two points. First, it reflects the modest level of benefits provided by OAS and CPP. Second, it begins to raise doubts about whether the increased OAS and CPP expenditures should be viewed as a "crisis" of affordability or sustainability.

## Immediate Priorities Associated with Population Aging

Between now and the year 2015, there will be a steady but undramatic increase in the portion of the population over 65. After 2015, the pace at which the aging of the population increases will accelerate somewhat as the baby-boom grows old. Pay-as-you-go CPP contribution rates will hit a temporary peak in 2035. They will subside somewhat through 2050, and then begin a long, slow escalation.

There are two key conclusions that might be drawn from what we know about the impact of aging on OAS and CPP expenditures. First, the increase in program expenditures is driven primarily by the baby-bust, not by the baby-boom. Second, the one issue that requires a fairly quick resolution is whether fuller funding of CPP will be chosen as one of the means of trying to limit increases in CPP contribution rates. Bearing in mind that there are pros and cons of fuller funding, the potential benefit in the future will only materialize if the decision is taken in the near future.

## HISTORICAL AND POLITICAL DIMENSIONS

It is refreshing to deal with papers that explicitly introduce historical and political dimensions to the discussion of public pensions. I could not agree more with the general concern expressed in both papers about the lack of public knowledge of public pension programs. In the future, more research effort might usefully be focused on what people actually know about pension programs and how they acquire information about pensions.

I was also pleased to see that the Lam, Cutt and Prince paper raised the issue of the governance of the CPP. Raising the issue from the perspective of the Rowan Task Force may not be the best way to get at the issue. Nonetheless, the manner in which the program has been governed warrants much more attention than it gets. Current arrangements are far too closed to public scrutiny and accentuate distrust.

Both papers offer perspectives on the recent political history of public pensions. The perspectives they provide are worthwhile, but neither discusses this history in the context of wider developments in the political arena.

It is important to see the recent debate on public pensions in the context of the wider swing to the political right and the positive currency that is associated with liberalizing market forces. The interest that is being shown in downsizing public pensions is hardly a stand-alone event. Public pensions are merely taking their place in the lineup of social programs, and other government programs as well, that are going through the downsizing ringer.

There is one aspect of liberalizing market forces in the field of social security that we see a little more clearly in the public pension area than we do in some others. That is the constraining of public programs in order to increase the scope for "private," "market-based" solutions to social needs; in this case, the need for retirement incomes. Thus, the "virtues" of RRSPs and workplace pensions are extolled in the critique of public pensions, notwithstanding the manifest inability of the "private" solutions to provide good pensions for many people.

There are three quick, specific points to add here:

- the downsizing and liberalizing of Canada's social security system pre-dates the Mulroney era by nearly a full decade;

- when the CPP was introduced in 1966, and again when the federal government finally announced its position on pension reform in February 1984, the Liberal governments of the day emphasized that they wanted to leave plenty of room for private sector pensions, that is, at its zenith, the system that is currently being downsized always was a "liberal" system in Esping-Anderson's sense; and,

- the current moment is not the first time that the political right wing has argued that the CPP is bankrupt, but it is the first time that the federal government has refused to confront the false claim.

The paper by Lam, Cutt and Prince includes the comment that the people who designed the CPP should have foreseen the merits of more fully funding the CPP.

When I first read this comment, I thought it was quite unreasonable. On reflection, I find it even more unreasonable.

At the time the CPP was founded, all available evidence suggested that a pay-as-you-go contribution rate would be lower than a fully funded rate. Even during the great pension debate of the late 1970s and early 1980s, when virtually every aspect of Canada's pension system was subject to close scrutiny, there was no demand for a more fully funded CPP. The creators of the CPP would have been prescient, indeed, had they foreseen today's economic and demographic circumstances.

Indeed, the original intention of the federal government was to have a contribution that would have been lower than the 3.6 percent rate that was originally established. The higher 3.6 percent rate emerged from the series of compromises that were made to accommodate Quebec's desire for a separate parallel plan. Quebec wanted a reserve fund to invest in the province's social and economic future.

Finally, it should be noted that throughout all but the most recent history of the CPP, business organizations and spokespeople have argued vociferously against a more fully funded CPP. They have not wanted Canadian governments to have large investment funds at their disposal. (Their past history has not stopped some of today's business commentators from criticizing the absence of fuller funding of the CPP.)

Part of my purpose in dwelling on the funding issue is to highlight some of what gets lost if our political focus is preoccupied exclusively with the attitudes and behaviours of politicians and bureaucrats, and the wider political and ideological forces are ignored.

## ANALYTICAL AND TECHNICAL DIMENSIONS

Much of the current discussion of public pensions revolves around the question of whether they are sustainable or affordable in the future. The terms "sustainability" and "affordability" are not given great prominence in the papers but these concepts have a powerful, implicit presence in the way that the issues they address are framed. Unfortunately, like so much public commentary, both papers show a tendency to move quite directly from a discussion of expected program expenditures in the future, to conclusions (both implicit and explicit) about what is sustainable or affordable, as if the conclusion was self-evident.

It is not hard to find papers that are much more remiss than the ones under review in not being clear about what is meant by sustainability or affordability. But, it is a matter of some importance to demand greater clarity in these key terms. Sometimes, these terms seem to refer to negative impacts on the economy. At other times, they seem to refer to impacts on public finances. And, at other times, to impacts on the living standards of the working age population. In the specific case of the CPP, there is often a lack of clarity on whether the issue is the contribution rate or the amount of income that is channelled through the program. If it is the former, there is a much broader range of options for dealing with the issue than if it is the latter.

In fairness, there will always be some degree of "political judgement" in deciding what is affordable or sustainable. But, more in the way of precise definition can and should be expected of pension commentators who want to invoke these terms.

A second issue relates more to Ken Battle's paper than to the other.

There are two distinct sets of circumstances that are seen as contributing to the affordability issues. One is the financial situation of the federal government. The other is longer term demographic change. Each of these sources of affordability issues has its own distinct time horizon, unless one assumes that debt-service charges will continue to account for large portions of federal government spending well into the next century. If debt-service charges as a percentage of GDP were to return to the levels typical of the 1920s through to the early 1980s, about $20 billion per year would be "freed up" on the expenditure side of the federal budget (coincidentally, the approximate expenditure under OAS, GIS, and SPA). I detect a tendency to confuse the two sources of affordability concerns and to enhance the image of impending financial doom by doing so. People who want to comment on the long-term affordability of public programs should clarify their assumptions about debt-service charges and, of course, about productivity increases in the future.

Commentators on the longer term implications of an aging population should also be asked to note the consequences for both public and private transfers to the young of a declining youth share of the population.

In context, it should be noted that the Battle paper avoids one of the other great shortcomings of so much current discussion. It does not ignore the impact on incomes of what it says about costs.

The paper by Lam, Cutt and Prince raises a number of issues that revolve around the possibility that the CPP should be more fully funded. It is argued that a more fully funded CPP could have a lower contribution rate. (I should add that while I have a number of concerns about the quantitative dimension of the case made in the paper, qualitatively I accept the argument.) An argument is also made that a change in investment policy could lower the contribution rate, although this seems to presume a change in funding policy.

There are some other issues associated with the possibility of fuller funding of the CPP that should be taken up in future work.

Attention needs to be focused directly on transitional issues associated with moving from a largely pay-as-you-go plan to a more fully funded plan. There will clearly be a generation that will be asked to maintain the tradition of paying the pensions of predecessor generations, while paying for more of its own pensions than the predecessor generations paid for. This reality alone imposes a serious constraint on how far one can go in moving towards a more fully funded CPP.

It is also important to think through the kinds of disciplines that will apply under a more fully funded CPP when fund assets and liabilities depart from their expected path. Departures from the expected path are inevitable, especially when one bears in mind the volatility of investment returns over relatively short time frames. It is possible that the need for short-term contribution rate increases to offset poor investment returns might be more problematic than a higher pay-as-you-go contribution rate that has more short-term stability.

In its general form, the debate on the impact of pay-as-you-go pension plans on savings, investment, and economic growth has been exhausted. No firm conclusions can be drawn on this issue. However, if a more fully funded CPP is contemplated, it is worth focusing attention on the changing role of the plan in generating internal savings as one moves from a "phasing-in" period to a "mature" version of a more fully funded CPP, and as the population ages. The short-term macroeconomic effects of a more fully funded CPP also need to be assessed.

Finally, the paper by Lam, Cutt and Prince draws attention to the fact that the CPP contribution rate can be reduced by measures that do not involve benefit reductions. Attention is drawn to the potential for achieving this objective through changes to funding and investment policy, and through changes to the tax base. The exploration of possible changes to the CPP tax base is limited to eliminating the year's basic exemption (YBE). Clearly, other possibilities with a much bigger potential impact exist.

It is important to know that there are options for reducing the contribution rate that do not involve lower benefits. It is striking, though, that these options do not reduce the share of GDP flowing through the program and remind us of the need to be as clear as possible about the nature of the issue with which we are trying to deal.

There are a pair of complementary themes in the Battle paper on which I will comment: progressivity is a desirable characteristic of social programs; and implicitly, people with incomes over a certain amount do not really need income from OAS.

With regard to the role of progressivity:

- it is only one of a number of virtues one might look for in social security programs, yet, it seems to be the only virtue recognized in the Battle paper; other virtues might include providing: stabilization of income; horizontal equity; and economic autonomy for women;

- the progressivity of the OAS is questioned in the Battle paper, yet the OAS is highly progressive as it represents a much larger share of low incomes than high incomes; and

- the sphere within which the progressivity of public arrangements are considered should include tax support for so-called private arrangements and not just the sphere of OAS and an income-tested alternative — maybe resources should be reallocated from tax support to a universal OAS.

Regarding the possibility that people with incomes over some amount do not need OAS, I am struck by the incredible discrepancy in the way this issue is dealt with on the tax versus the expenditure side of government budgets. If somebody has a six figure income that includes OAS, why is it only the OAS income they do not need? Why is an OAS recipient with a high income in less need of every last dollar they receive than some with the same income, none of which comes from OAS?

In a debate on the OAS clawback with Department of Finance officials some years ago, these questions were raised and the answer that came back from Finance officials was that the "special treatment" of OAS income is justified because it is "the government's" money. Ever since, I confess to taking admittedly perverse delight in applying the logic of the answer to the Finance officials' incomes.

CONCLUSION

Unless one can develop a much more convincing case than has been developed to date that there is a real "affordability" or "sustainability" problem with OAS and CPP, then Canadians are likely to be dragged into an exercise of fixing what ain't broke. Indeed, not only are these programs not broke, they have been a remarkable success story — only part of which is reflected in the progress in reducing poverty among the elderly in recent decades. For many moderate- and low-income Canadians, OAS and CPP are the institutions that make retirement a real possibility. Most workplace pensions presume the existence of full OAS and CPP benefits.

Then again, the future of OAS and CPP will not be resolved in isolation and the winds of market liberalization are blowing strongly.

# Comments

*William B.P. Robson*

## INTRODUCTION

A comment on these two papers can usefully begin by emphasizing the distinction between income support and income replacement as objectives. Following Ken Battle's opening comments about changes in unemployment insurance, I would observe that confusion between these objectives can lead to incoherent design and evolution of programs. The rationales for state involvement in income support are different from those regarding income replacement, and the standards for judging the success, or justifying the existence, of a program of either type are different as well.

Distinguishing between income support and income replacement is all the more important in connection with programs for the elderly, because the pressure of these programs on the living standards of the non-elderly population is intensifying. If it proves politically impossible to maintain the total of various transfers and in-kind benefits such as medical care to the elderly at current levels in real per-recipient terms as time goes by, the task of choosing which programs to protect and which to erode will be aided by clear thinking about their objectives.

## The Strong Case for Income-Support Programs for the Elderly

Income-support programs — or, as they should more properly be termed, consumption-support programs — are safety-net programs that protect their recipients from destitution. Despite some wild statements about the motivations of government budget-cutters, the consensus in favour of the state's role in preventing destitution among citizens with limited past opportunities and current prospects for helping themselves appears solid. This type of safety net is available to anyone who needs it. Since the less well-off elderly are foremost on most people's lists of such citizens, the political durability of a commitment to income support for seniors seems high.

Commitment in principle is, of course, not the same as commitment to any particular system. As the Battle paper shows, there are several issues open to debate. Determining eligibility involves trade-offs between economically meaningful measures — which, in a system aimed at safeguarding potential consumption would ideally relate to net worth — and measures that are practical and palatable — which, at present, means age and declared annual income. Generosity is necessarily a political decision: targets for recipients' living standards, which involve both absolute concepts of comfort and dignity and relative measures (with the latter being a function of the relative size and prosperity of the non-elderly population) must be weighed against the frictions and deadweight losses of taxation. And structure — how graduated the implicit tax-back of benefits should be; whether benefits should be on an individual or family basis — is clearly an open question. It is inconceivable, however, that even when Canada's elderly dependency ratio reaches its baby-boom-driven height, there will be no seniors benefits providing access to basic food, clothing, shelter, and medical care.

## The Weaker Case for Income-Replacement Programs

Income-replacement programs, on the other hand, are concerned with preventing abrupt declines in income when employment ends. In contrast to the safety net of income support, the logic of income replacement links benefits to previous income: over a range, those with higher employment incomes will receive higher benefits. The public finance motivation for state-run programs of this sort for the elderly is to prevent their falling upon income-support programs, either because they failed to anticipate their needs after retirement, or because they decided not to save, knowing that income support was available. These considerations, though important, are less compelling than the general case for income support. The choice between income-replacement programs and the risk that an improvident or free-ride-seeking portion of the population will strain the safety net is less stark than that between income-support programs and the risk that destitute elderly will starve in the street. Their urgency, moreover, will be greater or less depending on the generosity and terms of access of the income-support programs.[1]

If the case for state-run income-replacement programs is weaker than that for income-support programs, one might expect the political consensus in their favour to be less solid. And analysts of a given program's design can be more demanding in setting standards of performance that would justify its existence in the first place. In particular, if the public-finance motivation is reflected less strongly in an income-replacement program's design than a public-choice motivation that stresses redistribution towards politically influential groups, both analysts and the general public ought to criticize it more forcefully than in the case of an income-support program. Such criticism is evident in attitudes towards Unemployment Insurance (UI). And it ought — and may be coming — to be in connection with the CPP.

THE BATTLE PAPER

That preamble requires me to get past a terminological obstacle in order to get to my fundamentally favourable assessment of Ken Battle's paper. Battle is ambivalent about the purpose of what he terms the "foundation layer" of Canada's system of elderly benefits, tending to describe it as in income-replacement system. And indeed the bundle he starts with — OAS, GIS, the Spouse's Allowance, and the age and pension credits — is a mixture of income-support-oriented (the first three) and income-replacement-oriented (the latter two) measures. My reading of his discussion, however, with its heavy focus on the low-income cutoff and other measures generally associated with poverty, is that he is dealing with income support. If it is true that the case in principle for state involvement in income support is stronger than that for state involvement in income replacement, then the hurdle that a given income-support program needs to clear for a favourable assessment is lower than that for an income-replacement program. The Battle proposal would appear to clear it with room to spare.[2]

## In Praise of Better Targeting

Indeed, its clear focus on income support is the proposal's principal strength. Its benefits are more completely and more coherently directed towards those with low incomes than are those of the current system. There is a key criticism to be levied in this connection — that is, that net worth, rather than declared annual income, ought to determine the level of benefit. Under such a proposal, even more than today, senior homeowners will fare better than senior renters whose annual consumption, including housing services, is identical; and dishonest seniors will fare better than their honest counterparts. But solutions to these problems require changes to aspects of Canada's approaches to taxes and transfers that lie well beyond the borders of this discussion.

Battle will undoubtedly come under fire for his efforts to contain the overall cost of his proposal from those who would urge something less targeted and more generous. Let me then weigh in on the other side. When it comes to targeting, I would underline Battle's comments about the lack of opposition to the ending of universality: public acceptance of the OAS clawback did not signify indifference to income support for the elderly; it signified indifference to income support for the well-off.[3] And a more expensive system, even if it initially got past a less bottom-line oriented government than the present one, would simply be subject to greater ad hoc erosion as time passes and the strain on the rest of the population of transferring resources to the elderly grows. Battle-type proposals will likely prove more durable than less targeted and more expensive alternatives.

Another differently motivated criticism of targeting focuses on the adverse incentives of steep implicit tax-back rates that arise when the basic benefit is high and the vanishing point is low. One of the Battle proposal's merits is that the 12.5 percent reduction rate exacerbates the very high marginal tax rates facing seniors less than easily plausible alternatives.[4] It is common to dismiss incentive problems with regard to specific groups for specific reasons; in the case of seniors, for example, work effort may not appear important. But this tendency is too careless: bad incentives often distort behaviour in ways that are hard to predict beforehand. A durable system needs, moreover, to survive the entry into the seniors population of a generation whose reluctance to cheat in pursuit of benefits may be less than their predecessors. And if greater labour force participation by future seniors is desirable, it would be foolish to put in place a tax-transfer system that confiscates far more than half of every dollar that they earn.

## In Praise of Incremental Changes

Battle's objections to "social policy by stealth" as embodied in the 3-percentage-point indexation deductible in the tax and transfer system is a suitable leadoff for a final observation on the paper and the proposal. I agree wholeheartedly that deliberately using incomplete indexation to rejig taxes and benefits is dishonest and should be dispensed with.[5] But both in looking back and in looking forward, it is important to be clear about the alternatives.

On a quasi-technical level, even if we accept that the consumer price index (CPI) reflects seniors' cost of living as well as that of the population generally, full CPI indexation of seniors' benefits may not make sense. For one thing, quite intractable measurement biases may cause the CPI to overstate inflation: if the bias is in the order of 0.5 percent per year (see Fortin 1990; Crawford 1993), the cumulative overcompensation for inflation since the OAS was fully indexed in 1973 would now amount to over 12 percent. In addition, indexation to the CPI automatically protects recipients against increases in consumption taxes, a privilege necessarily reflected in disproportionate burdens on everyone else.[6] On these grounds, a smaller indexation deductible applied to a net price index might seem preferable to a return to full CPI indexation.

More fundamentally, however, the alternative to steady incremental changes such as those produced by partial indexation is not no changes at all, but large, lumpy ones. In a sense, it was because the Conservatives failed to partially de-index OAS in 1986 that the clawback came when and in the form that it did. Ideally, one would like a seniors' income-support system that adjusted benefits incrementally up or down as suggested by demographics and changes in the relative prosperity of the non-elderly population. The alternative is periodic larger shifts that are more disruptive to recipients and risk creating major unfairness between similarly situated people with, for example, slightly different dates of birth.[7] Phasing-in a higher eligibility age for elderly benefits — perhaps allowing continued earlier access at reduced rates — is one eminently sensible approach. Ongoing small adjustments to the benefits schedule are also a possibility. One way or another, it would be nice if the doing away with partial indexation could be accompanied by the establishment of something less arbitrary and more honest, but equally incremental.

## THE LAM-CUTT-PRINCE PAPER

Some sorting out of income-support and income-replacement objectives also seems apt in launching a discussion of the paper by Lam, Cutt and Prince. The CPP is often discussed as though its primary purpose was progressive redistribution, and it has many such features. This design owes more to the stronger consensus for income-support programs and the related bias against benefits for the better off, however, than to the logic of an employment-related pension plan. Despite its redistributive wrinkles, the CPP is at bottom a plan whose benefits are earned by working and which provides — up to the maximum covered earnings — benefits that are larger for those whose pre-retirement income was larger. In short, it is an income-replacement program.

As an income-replacement program, the CPP appears to an individual participant at the beginning of a career as one — albeit mandatory — option among many others: occupational defined-benefit plans, RRSPs, annuities, and various types of insurance. Given the many effective alternatives, the hurdle that an income-replacement program like the CPP must clear to be judged desirable is relatively high. To someone like me, who views the CPP as currently falling well short of that hurdle (Robson 1996), the proposals in the Lam-Cutt-Prince paper may appear insufficient to push it over.

## Ambiguity about the CPP's Design

When it comes to the CPP's objectives, the paper's assessment is ambiguous. Early on, the authors appear to endorse a pay-as-you-go approach, with no or minimal prefunding. Yet major elements in their critique are that CPP contribution rates were too low for too long and that full pensions became payable after too short a period — features central to the pay-as-you-go structure. And the first priority in their reforms goes to improving the investment returns in the CPP account — not a fruitful course in a pay-as-you-go plan that maintains a tiny (currently less than 7 percent of the present value of its obligations) precautionary inventory of funds. Forced by the paper's ambiguity to pick and choose a little, I would endorse raising the plan's funding ratio with higher contribution rates and investing through capital markets as essential for an income-replacement scheme in a world where investment returns exceed economic growth rates.

This ambiguity is, however, reflective of a broader contextlessness in the paper that heightens my reservations about its recipe for CPP reform. Some comments — such as the one about inflation eroding the real value of CPP benefits — suggest imperfect understanding of the plan's provisions (benefits are indexed to wage growth as they accrue and to the CPI after they become payable). Other observations about raising contribution rates, enhancing investment returns, and increasing eligibility age are sound in principle, and would be useful considerations in the process of establishing an income-replacement plan. They appear rather disjointed and inadequate, however, when set against a program that has been running — and storing up big trouble — for 30 years.[8]

## The Scale of the CPP's Problems

The CPP's unfunded liability — the gap between the present value of obligations accrued to date and funds on hand — is growing at around $50 billion a year, and is approaching $600 billion. Put another way for the sake of avoiding controversy over the 2.5 percent real interest rate used in the present-value calculation, meeting the obligations already accrued by CPP participants, before allowing for those accruing now and in the future, would require a contribution rate of over 8 percent of covered earnings for the next decade, and over 7 percent for the following two decades (McCrossan 1995). If new entrants to the plan were to be charged a contribution rate that, maintained through their working lifetimes, would cover the benefits projected for them and their dependents, moreover, they would now pay more than 10.5 percent (Canada. Office of the Superintendent of Financial Institutions 1995, pp. 99-101). The gap between these figures and the 5.6 percent rate now being charged is a measure of the size of the adjustment that needs to be made if the (likely unsuccessful) attempt to collect 15-percent-plus contribution rates in 30 years' time is to be avoided.

In that context, the Lam-Cutt-Prince suggestion, based largely on calculations related to retirement pensions, to raise the contribution rate to 8 percent looks inadequate. At 8 percent, new plan entrants would not even cover the benefits that will accrue to them — benefits extending well beyond retirement pensions — let alone begin to amortize the unfunded liability of the benefits promised to their predecessors. Higher investment returns in a better funded plan would, over time, lower future contribution rates, but before that can happen, funds need to be put into the plan in the first place — which, to repeat, requires a bigger hike in contribution rates. And while raising the retirement age to 70 is a useful element in a CPP reform, such a step taken in isolation and over the several-decade time frame presumably involved in implementing it would make little impact on the CPP's financial problems.[9] An investigation that took the CPP's current state as a starting point for more explicitly modelled changes would be more helpful — and would, moreover, lead to more dramatic conclusions about the changes that are needed if the CPP is to survive to replace any incomes at all by the time the baby-boom's successors are in line for benefits.

CONCLUSION: THE NEED TO CHOOSE

Discussions of the tax and transfer system in Canada as it affects the elderly are hampered by confusion among the general public — and even among recipients themselves — about the differences between the OAS and the GIS on the one hand and the CPP on the other. The confusion is worsened by the tendency of experts in the debate to adopt similar positions with regard to both categories of the program: both should be enriched, both should be rolled back, both should be more targeted, and so on. So let me close by reemphasizing the merit of distinguishing between the objectives of income support and income replacement.

The Battle paper starts from an implicit premise that anti-poverty programs are a legitimate object of political compromise. His proposal reflects a balance between considerations of what is an appropriate standard of living for recipients, what is the appropriate reduction in standard of living of payers into the system, and what implicit marginal tax rate should apply as benefits are reduced to the better off. Enthusiasm for the specifics will vary from person to person — I find the proposal attractive — but Battle's approach is consistent with a view of income-support that sees it as part of a social contract carried on through the state.

The Lam, Cutt and Prince paper is less obviously grounded in a firm vision of how an income-replacement system ought to work, and is less clear about what to do with one that is not working well. Their proposals for greater prefunding are inadequate in relation to the scale of the CPP's unfunded liability, which has grown to its current size because the plan's political masters disregarded such logic in pursuit of their main aim: to transfer considerable purchasing power to current and soon-to-be recipients. Far from guarding against today's younger workers falling on the income-support system, the CPP is increasing the likelihood that they will do so, by dipping ever more heavily into the paycheques from which they must save for their own retirement. I am not sure whether, seeking to safeguard their own projected benefits, younger baby-boomers and Generation Xers will try to maintain the CPP and force their own children into it. But I would bet that, if they do try, they will fail. The CPP exhibits defects of a type that tend to plague state-run income-replacement programs, and it is doubtful whether even more vigorous reforms along the lines suggested by Lam, Cutt and Prince will fix it.

In view of the mounting pressure on the non-elderly population's living standards as seniors' programs expand in scale, the contrast between the solid case for state provision of income support and the shakier case for state provision of income replacement points towards protecting the former at the expense of the latter. Financial and political support for a system of elderly benefits along the lines suggested by Battle will be stronger if the attempt to collect CPP premiums as large as are currently forecast is never made. But the proposals for CPP reform from Lam, Cutt and Prince appear inadequate to rein them in much. A more vigorous attack on the CPP's future obligations, motivated by recognition of the relatively weak case for state-run income-replacement programs, would be better. Otherwise, by seeking to play a major role in both income-support and income-replacement programs for the elderly, Canadian governments may end up doing neither well.

## NOTES

1. It may be a distinctly second- or third-best solution to respond to bad incentives built into an income-support program by adding an income-replacement program, instead of fixing the bad incentives.
2. The similarity of the proposal for a new elderly benefit in the March 1996 federal budget (Canada. Department of Finance 1996) to that in Battle's paper suggests that the government thinks so too. Much of what is said here applies to some extent to the budget proposals; in order to maintain the integrity of this discussion as a contribution to a conference held before the budget, points relevant to the budget proposals will be relegated to footnotes.
3. In this context, I must register an objection to his including the clawback under the "social policy by stealth" heading. Partial de-indexation of parts of the tax and transfer systems fully deserves this label, but the clawback does not: it was widely described by experts and in the media at the time as signifying an end to universality.
4. Such as the proposal in the March 1996 budget, which reduces benefits by 20 cents/ dollar of other income.

5.  Battle's difficulties in explaining the difference in current and constant dollar benefits are only the tip of a much larger iceberg of serious confusion when inflation renders money untrustworthy as a stable measure of purchasing power (Laidler and Robson 1993). Price stability reduces that confusion, and eliminates incentives for governments to take advantage of it through devices such as partial indexation.

6.  To those who feel that heavier consumption taxes are a good way to set about righting the tilt of fiscal policy against the young, this objection would have particular appeal.

7.  As appears to be the case in the March 1996 proposals which, as written, will mean that differences of minutes in birth dates (30 December 2000 as opposed to 1 January 2001) will result in middle-to-upper-income elderly couples receiving benefits differing by as much as $6,000 annually for the rest of their lives.

8.  This is in part, but only in part, because the paper uses outdated projections from the *Fourteenth Actuarial Report* in 1991, rather than the more recent *Fifteenth Actuarial Report*, which documented further deterioration in the CPP's prospects.

9.  If no changes are made to the CPP's disability provisions, the high incidence of disability among the older population and the relative generosity of CPP disability benefits would reduce the net savings on retirement pensions resulting from higher eligibility ages by roughly 50 cents on the dollar.

## REFERENCES

Canada. Department of Finance (1996), *The Seniors Benefit: Securing the Future,* Ottawa: Supply and Services Canada; Canada Communications Group.

Canada. Office of the Superintendent of Financial Institutions (1993), *Canada Pension Plan: Fourteenth Actuarial Report as at 31 December 1991,* Ottawa: Supply and Services Canada.

_____ (1995), *Canada Pension Plan: Fifteenth Actuarial Report as at 31 December 1993,* Ottawa: Supply and Services Canada.

Crawford, A. (1993), "Measurement Biases in the Canadian CPI: A Technical Note," *Bank of Canada Review,* (Summer):21-36.

Fortin, P. (1990), "Do We Measure Inflation Correctly?" in *Zero Inflation: The Goal of Price Stability,* ed. R.G. Lipsey, Toronto: C.D. Howe Institute.

Laidler, D. and W. Robson (1993), *The Great Canadian Disinflation: The Economics and Politics of Monetary Policy in Canada, 1988-93,* Toronto: C.D. Howe Institute.

McCrossan, P. (1995), "Replacing the Canada Pension Plan: The Problems of Transition," paper presented to the Fraser Institute conference *Replacing the Canada Pension Plan,* 15 November.

Robson, W. (1996), *Putting Some Gold in the Golden Years: Fixing the Canada Pension Plan,* C.D. Howe Institute Commentary no. 76, Toronto: C.D. Howe Institute.

# CHAPTER SEVEN

# Private Provision of Retirement Income: Tax Policy Issues

*Jack M. Mintz and Thomas A. Wilson*

## INTRODUCTION

Over the years, Canada has developed a complex but important set of provisions that allow individuals to accumulate savings on a tax-free basis for retirement purposes. Under the Canadian *Income Tax Act,* individuals may deduct contributions to registered pension and savings plans, subject to certain limits. Income earned by the plans are tax free and the withdrawals of savings from these plans are taxable. Canadians have grown accustomed to these plans as annual contributions to Registered Pension Plans (RPPs) and Registered Retirement Savings Plans (RRSPs) are now $35 billion or over $1,000 per return (Revenue Canada 1995).

Despite the popularity of RPPs and RRSPs as mechanisms for individuals to save for retirement, the plans are politically controversial. Given the fiscal constraints faced by federal and provincial governments, some analysts have advocated a reduction in RPP and RRSP contributions limits, if not the virtual elimination of the tax-free status afforded to income earned in these plans. According to *Government of Canada Tax Expenditures* accounts (December 1994), the 1992 revenue loss from RPPs has been $8.1 billion and from RRSPs $5.5 billion for a total of $13.6 billion. Given the federal deficit of over $30 billion, it seems tempting for some advocates to eliminate altogether tax assistance for retirement in order to accommodate the fiscal needs of the federal government.

It would be oversimplistic to point out that the elimination of tax assistance for retirement purposes would increase personal income taxes by almost 15 percent, clearly at odds with an almost universally held "truism," regardless of its validity, that income taxes are too high in Canada. Instead, one could consider the trade-off of tax assistance for retirement income as a price for a significant reduction in personal income tax rates. A move to broaden the annual income base in favour of lower personal tax rates might be argued by some to be good policy (Ontario Fair Tax Commission 1993) under the argument that it would be fair and efficient.

However, the evaluation of these questions of fairness and efficiency in public policy debates are always more difficult than they might first seem. As is well known (Kaldor 1955), the taxation of capital income can result in inequities and inefficiencies whereby savers are more highly taxed then consumers. This is referred to as the *intertemporal distortion*. Under an income tax, a consumer is only taxed once when income is earned while a saver is taxed twice, once when income is earned and a second time when capital income is generated on the earnings saved for future consumption purposes. Thus, it is by no means clear that a broad-based income tax with low rates is efficient or fair, given the intertemporal distortion associated with the taxation of savings. Instead, one could argue that not only should RPP and RRSP treatments be continued but also enhanced since all forms of savings should be exempt from taxation (United States Treasury 1977; Institute for Fiscal Studies 1978).

To understand the issues associated with the private provision of retirement savings, one must deal not only with questions of tax policy but also with social policy. Retired Canadians have three important means of support: accumulated savings or wealth, monetary or in-kind transfers from children, and public pensions. In Canada, public pensions include the Old Age Security (OAS) benefit (a demogrant, subject to a clawback under the income tax, available to the elderly), the Guaranteed Income Supplement (a payment available to the elderly poor) and the Canada Pension Plan (a pay-as-you-go system, based on past contributions whereby benefits paid during the year to the retired population are effectively financed by payroll contributions of the working population). One could also include the non-refundable age and pension credits under the personal income tax if it is viewed that these credits have little to do with ensuring fair taxation as much as providing special income support.[1]

The relative importance of public and private[2] sources of retirement income is presented in Table 1 below. In 1993, public pensions accounted for about half of total retirement income. Surprisingly, this share has declined by only 1.1 percent points over the previous 20 years. The stability of the share of public pensions is explained by the rapid growth of C/QPP benefits. Since these plans were established in 1966, rapid growth would occur until the plans matured. OAS pensions experienced much slower growth than C/QPP benefits, with "other pensions or superannuation" in between.

Given the more rapid growth of RPP/RRSP contributions than C/QPP contributions in recent years, however, we should anticipate that pension and annuity income from these sources should represent a growing share of future retirement income.

The role of public-provided pension plans as social policy has been evaluated in the literature (see, e.g., Diamond 1977) — our task is neither to provide rationales for nor evaluate the public pension system. Instead, we are only concerned with how private and public pension systems relate to each other. Indeed, many private pension plans already take into account the public pension system by integrating public benefits with payments under the private insurance plan. Any reform of the public pension plan may therefore affect the current private pension benefits paid to the retired population.

TABLE 1:  Public and Private Pension Benefits and Contributions

| | ($Million) | | Average Annual Growth Rates (%) | | |
|---|---|---|---|---|---|
| | 1973 | 1983 | 1993 | 1973-83 | 1983-93 |
| A. Benefits | | | | | |
| OAS Pension | 1,184,705 | 4,278,226 | 12,678,541 | 13.70 | 11.48 |
| CPP or QPP Benefits | 277,466 | 3,812,992 | 16,673,365 | 29.96 | 15.90 |
| Subtotal Public | 1,462,171 | 8,091,218 | 29,351,906 | 18.66 | 13.75 |
| Other Pensions or Superannuation | 1,283,291 | 6,014,901 | 21,910,912 | 16.71 | 13.80 |
| Annuity Income | 74,225 | 969,122 | 2,146,238 | 29.30 | 8.28 |
| RRSP Income | n/a | n/a | 4,356,802 | n/a | n/a |
| Subtotal Private | 1,357,516 | 6,984,023 | 28,413,952 | 17.80 | 15.06 |
| TOTAL | 2,819,687 | 15,075,241 | 57,765,858 | 18.25 | 14.38 |
| B. Contributions | | | | | |
| CPP or QPP Contributions | 659,931 | 2,318,006 | 5,914,825 | 13.39 | 9.82 |
| RPP Contributions | 1,093,146 | 4,057,687 | 6,908,504 | 14.01 | 5.47 |
| RRSP Contributions | 922,595 | 4,997,187 | 17,499,790 | 18.41 | 13.35 |
| Subtotal Private | 2,015,741 | 9,054,874 | 24,408,294 | 16.21 | 10.42 |
| TOTAL | 2,675,672 | 11,372,880 | 30,323,119 | 15.57 | 10.30 |

Source: Revenue Canada, *Taxation Statistics*.

A common way of relating public and private provision of pensions is to consider the role of government policy and its impact on the distribution of income in society. It is argued that the tax assistance for private pensions is primarily a benefit for the rich (under the assumption that the income base is the "right base for taxation" and tax assistance is a "tax expenditure") while the public pension system is a benefit primarily to ensure a reasonable level of income support for all members in society. This connection between the two systems seems somewhat forced. After all, one could have a income tax without any tax assistance for the private provision of pensions and still operate a public pension plan system. Also, one could conceivably not operate a pension plan system but still reduce the level of tax on savings for other reasons besides supporting the private provision of pensions. Nonetheless, there is an important relationship between tax-assisted private and public pensions. Both are important to Canadians when they retire. Also, the development of state pensions and the tax system has always recognized the relationship between these public and private provision of retirement income.

Our primary task is to consider what options for reform could be undertaken to improve the tax treatment of private savings, keeping in mind the role of the public pension system as a mechanism to deliver social benefits to the population. Given that resources available at the time of retirement could depend on both tax-assisted as well as non-tax-assisted savings, one might ask how the tax system affects both the savings and retirement decisions made by individuals and whether tax measures can be improved.

In the next section of the paper, we discuss the economic role of the private pension and retirement systems in Canada. The thrid section describes the current tax system with respect to the taxation of savings for retirement. The final section considers reform options.

## ECONOMIC ROLE OF TAX-ASSISTED PENSION AND SAVINGS PLANS

As discussed above, tax-assisted private pension and savings plans have been important vehicles for the provision of wealth for retirement purposes. Many of the arguments stated in favour of providing tax assistance for retirement purposes also apply to other purposes for which savings are held, such as to insure against future contingencies during one's lifetime. It therefore begs the question as to why savings for retirement purposes should be specially treated compared to other types of savings. Indeed, since RRSPs can be withdrawn at anytime prior to retirement without penalty,[3] the RRSP has become an important savings instrument for other purposes besides retirement.

There are a number of important rationales given for special tax provisions that accommodate this form of savings. These rationales include the need for individuals to accumulate wealth to retire, average their tax base over time, and insure against future uncertainties, including early retirement or longevity.

## Retirement

During a person's lifetime, annual consumption will diverge from annual income. At the beginning of a career, consumer expenditures may often be greater than earnings as a person borrows funds to finance the purchase of consumer durables, education, and other non-divisible forms of consumption. During the rest of one's working career, past loans may be repaid and one may begin to accumulate wealth for retirement. During retirement, consumption needs are typically greater than earnings so that a person begins to dissave.

The description of the above process for savings has been referred to as the "lifecycle" motivation for savings (Ando and Modigliani 1963). Individuals basically save for only one purpose and that is to provide savings for retirement. Although lifecycle considerations are an important motive for accumulating wealth, it is not the only explanation for savings. Individuals may wish to accumulate savings to bequeath wealth to heirs or to ensure that they have sufficient wealth to offset any risk associated with fluctuations in income or expenditure commit-, ments. The latter motivation for savings is referred as to the precautionary motive for savings, and will be further discussed below.[4]

As is well known, an annual income-tax system discriminates against savings for retirement purposes (see, e.g., Bradford 1986). When an individual receives earnings and consumes the earnings immediately, the earnings are taxed once. However, should the same individual save some of the earnings and invest it in an asset, the taxation of capital income earned on the asset results in a larger amount of tax owed on savings compared to consumption. As Feldstein (1978) has pointed out, the taxation of the return on savings is equivalent to taxing future consumption more heavily than current consumption. Indeed, the rate of interest, which governs the normal return on savings, is the "price" by which individuals exchange current for future consumption. A tax on the return to savings increases the price of future consumption relative to current consumption. Thus, an annual income tax becomes a non-uniform consumption tax by taxing more heavily consumption in the future, relative to consumption, dated today.

The argument in favour of exempting the return on pension and retirement savings is to eliminate double taxation of savings. Under this argument, the elimination of taxes on the return to savings is not a "tax expenditure" since the annual income is not the appropriate benchmark for measuring the lifetime welfare of an individual. One might therefore suggest that governments in Canada have chosen a "uniform" consumption tax for pension and retirement savings and a "non-uniform" consumption tax for other assets that might bear some tax. In the next section, we will consider which forms of savings are taxed or exempt in Canada.

As mentioned above, the lifecycle approach to savings has been criticized for not explaining vast amounts of wealth accumulated for other reasons. One particular motivation is bequeathing wealth to children. Under an annual income tax, inheritances received by children would be subject to taxation, at least in principle. However, in practice, inheritances in Canada are exempt. It has been suggested that a tax on the return to savings is a rough way to ensure that a tax is imposed on the transfer of wealth. This equivalency, however, is very rough (Mintz 1991). Since it is impossible for governments to determine which assets are accumulated for lifecycle (and precautionary) reasons and which ones are accumulated for bequests, then a tax on the return to savings will fall on both types of savings. Thus, if wealth transfers should be subject to taxation, a specific wealth transfer tax is advisable rather than an annual income tax that discriminates against all forms of savings regardless of the motive.[5]

## Averaging

As a result of progressivity in the tax system, individuals with growing, declining, or fluctuating income may pay more tax over time than those with an equivalent but stable level of income. Moreover, when there is a mismatch between the timing of deductions and income, an individual may deduct expenses at a low rate, even at a zero rate, compared to the rate of tax on income generated by the expense at a later time. For example, a person may have an inadequate level of income to obtain the non-refundable tuition fee and education expense credit (assuming an inability to transfer the credit to a related taxpayer) yet pay significant amounts of tax on the incremental income resulting from education. This can result in a relatively high effective tax rate on human capital.

Governments have tried to provide relief for individuals by allowing averaging of a tax base over time. In Canada, averaging was once permitted to enable individuals to reduce the tax penalty on income that shifts over time.[6] Such relief is no longer explicitly granted in the tax system. However, through the RRSP system, some averaging is possible. A person who expects income to decline or fluctuate is able to reduce the tax base when income is high and withdraw from plans when income is low without penalty. Thus, the RRSP allows for some averaging of the tax base that would otherwise not be available.

One should point out, however, that the RRSP system does not allow perfect averaging. If incomes are growing, an individual cannot borrow from registered loan accounts, pay tax on amounts borrowed and deduct the repayment of principal and interest at a later time. Also, limits on RRSPs make it difficult for individuals to average fully their tax base over time especially those who receive pensions that are locked-in until retirement.

## Risk

A significant problem faced by individuals is with respect to uncertain outcomes. Individuals may unexpectedly become unemployed, forced to retire early, required to retrain or change occupations, or face the possibility of bankruptcy due to low income. Savings may thus be accumulated to guard against future contingencies that might impair a person's ability to meet commitments. Also, as discussed by Yaari (1964), uncertainty over death is also a factor influencing savings behaviour, particularly with respect to the demand for annuities. As mentioned above, wealth accumulation in the face of these uncertainties is referred to as the precautionary motive for savings.

Taxation of savings affects the ability of individuals to save for precautionary reasons in a rather complex way (Atkinson and Stiglitz 1980). By taxing the return on savings, an income tax (or wealth tax for that matter) may encourage individuals to consume rather than save. However, through the tax system, governments may share risks faced by investors particularly if losses are refundable under the tax system.[7] Assuming that governments do not transfer back the risk to savers through expenditures, the sharing of losses may encourage savings for precautionary reasons. In addition, as stressed by Deaton (1989), the presence of liquidity constraints on individuals implies that savings are highly variable in the face of uncertainty. Taxes have quite complicated impacts on individual savings behaviour in the presence of such liquidity constraints.

Another role of RPP and RRSPs in the tax system is to encourage individuals to save wealth for precautionary reasons. Tax-assisted savings may allow individuals to better fund retraining, changes in occupation, and retirement. In fact, the deductibility of contributions and taxation of withdrawals from savings plans provides a natural way for governments to share risks through the tax system with investors. Risk is therefore not penalized under the RPP or RRSP system. This will be particularly important since the income tax system does not otherwise provide full refundability of tax losses for other assets not held in the RRSP or RPP.

These interesting aspects of the link between tax-assisted savings, precautionary savings, and the flexibility in labour markets in the presence of uncertainty has not received detailed analysis, especially with respect to empirical work (see Engen and Gruber [1995] for a recent effort that suggests that the existence of social insurance programs has a significant impact on precautionary savings).

## THE CURRENT SYSTEM

### Private Retirement Income

Since the pension reform of 1990, contributors to defined contribution (money purchase) Registered Pension Plans and Registered Retirement Savings Plans have been subject to the same total contribution limits. Last year the limit was $14,500, but it dropped to $13,500 this year as a result of changes introduced in the 1995 federal budget. By 1999 the limit is scheduled to be $15,500, and it will be indexed thereafter to the average industrial wage.[8]

Defined benefit plan accruals are valued according to the 9 x formula: each percentage point of income accrued for future pension benefits is treated to the equivalent to an RRSP contribution of 9 percent of income.

Contributions to Deferred Profit Sharing Plans (DPSPs) are counted as equivalent to money purchase RPPs.

The stated purpose of the 1990 pension reforms was to eliminate inequities between taxpayers who were members of RPPs and those who were not. Prior to the reforms, RPP participants could effectively shelter more retirement savings than taxpayers who relied only on RRSPs.

While levelling the playing field between money purchase RPPs and RRSPs, the 1990 reforms may actually have tilted the system to the detriment of many participants of defined benefit RPPs. The 9 x rule would appear appropriate only for "Cadillac" RPPs, with pensions based on final three-year averaging, full indexation, and generous spousal and early retirement benefits. Many, perhaps most, RPPs do not have all of these features, so the 9 x rule overvalues the accrued benefit.

Contributions to RRSPs are subject to two limits: 18 percent of last year's qualifying income, and an absolute dollar limit (currently $13,500). Members of RPPs have their RRSP contribution room reduced by their Pension Adjustments (PA) which measure the value of their pension accruals (employee plus employer contributions to money purchase plans; the 9 x rule for defined benefit plans). Unused RRSP contribution room may be carried forward seven years.[9]

Withdrawals from RRSPs are fully taxable in the year of withdrawal, with the exception of certain amounts withdrawn for purchases of housing. At retirement or age 71 at the latest, RRSPs must be converted to annuities or Registered

Retirement Income Funds (RIFs). Except for rollovers to a surviving spouse, any remaining funds in an RRSP, RIF, or term-certain annuity from these plans are taxable at death.

Contributions to RRSPs within the limits specified are deductible from income. In addition to these "normal" RRSP contributions, there are a number of special rollovers permitted to RRSPs from RPPs and DPSPs. Furthermore, retiring allowances (up to specified limits) may be rolled over into an RRSP without tax.

The distribution of contributions to RRSPs and PAs by age and income are presented in Table 2.

Not surprisingly, participation in RRSPs and RPPs varies with age. Only 40 percent of taxpayers under 45 participate in either or both types of plans, whereas 53 percent of those between 45 and 65 participate. After age 65, participation drops sharply to 7 percent.[10]

Within each broad age group, participation rises with income. Typically, 90 percent of taxpayers with income over $50k participate in one or other type of plan. An inspection of the first two sections of Table 2 reveals that the apparent association of age with participation (below age 65) is almost completely related to income effects. Except for the three lowest income groups (income below $30k) participation is very similar for individuals above and below age 45.

The pattern of participation in RRSPs and RPPs also varies by age and income. Participation in RRSPs only is bimodal, with local peaks at income of $30-40k and in the highest income groups. By contrast participation in RPPs rises into the middle- to uppermiddle-income brackets, with peak participation in the $50-60k and $60-80k groups.

Combined RRSP Contributions and Pension Adjustments expressed as a percentage of total income are also shown in Table 2. These combined contribution rates are somewhat higher for the age 45-65 group than for the younger group. The combined contribution rate varies by income within each broad age group. For the 45-65 age group, the peak combined contribution rate of 13.3 percent is reached in the $60-80k income bracket. The contribution rate declines sharply for the top income group, reflecting the impact of the absolute dollar limits on combined contributions.

Table 3 shows the average dollar amount of contribution to RRSPs and PAs by broad age group and income. Average absolute contribution rises monotonically with income within each broad age group, and increase with age for each income class.

TABLE 2:   RPP and RRSP Contributions by Income Class and Age, 1993

| | Contribs. to RRSP Only | | Returns with PA Only | |
|---|---|---|---|---|
| | % of Returns | % of Total Income | % of Returns | % of Total Income |
| *Under 45* | | | | |
| Under 10K | 2.56 | 0.58 | 2.26 | 0.42 |
| 10-20K | 13.05 | 1.33 | 7.68 | 0.50 |
| 20-30K | 21.98 | 1.67 | 21.69 | 1.48 |
| 30-40K | 22.10 | 1.84 | 31.16 | 2.38 |
| 40-50K | 19.91 | 1.79 | 30.81 | 2.60 |
| 50-60K | 17.91 | 1.80 | 29.49 | 2.74 |
| 60-80K | 22.31 | 2.58 | 21.99 | 2.08 |
| 80-100K | 36.32 | 4.06 | 11.88 | 1.03 |
| 100K+ | 60.66 | 3.87 | 6.46 | 0.34 |
| TOTAL | 13.81 | 1.91 | 14.22 | 1.69 |
| | | | | |
| *Age 45 to 65* | | | | |
| Under 10K | 4.76 | 1.26 | 2.51 | 0.78 |
| 10-20K | 19.15 | 2.54 | 8.10 | 0.80 |
| 20-30K | 24.79 | 2.90 | 19.82 | 1.46 |
| 30-40K | 24.40 | 2.79 | 26.34 | 2.09 |
| 40-50K | 20.76 | 2.40 | 26.30 | 2.42 |
| 50-60K | 18.14 | 2.14 | 25.13 | 2.50 |
| 60-80K | 19.28 | 2.43 | 21.26 | 2.27 |
| 80-100K | 27.64 | 3.28 | 14.27 | 1.43 |
| 100K+ | 48.21 | 3.03 | 9.08 | 0.46 |
| TOTAL | 18.61 | 2.63 | 15.18 | 1.64 |

TABLE 2 (cont'd.)

| Contribs. to RRSPs on Returns with PA | | Contributions to RPPs on Returns with RRSP Contribs. | | Returns with RRSP Contribs. &/or PA Amount | |
|---|---|---|---|---|---|
| % of Returns | % of Total Income | % of Returns | % of Total Income | % of Returns | % of Total Income |
| 0.15 | 0.04 | 0.15 | 0.04 | 4.97 | 1.09 |
| 2.04 | 0.18 | 2.04 | 0.13 | 22.78 | 2.14 |
| 10.73 | 0.67 | 10.73 | 0.74 | 54.40 | 4.56 |
| 23.75 | 1.39 | 23.75 | 1.75 | 77.01 | 7.36 |
| 36.34 | 2.05 | 36.35 | 3.02 | 87.07 | 9.46 |
| 44.27 | 2.43 | 44.26 | 4.05 | 91.66 | 11.02 |
| 48.36 | 2.74 | 48.35 | 4.50 | 92.66 | 11.90 |
| 42.25 | 2.48 | 42.25 | 3.41 | 90.45 | 10.97 |
| 22.76 | 0.68 | 22.76 | 0.93 | 89.88 | 5.81 |
| 11.74 | 1.31 | 11.74 | 1.88 | 39.77 | 6.79 |
| | | | | | |
| 0.38 | 0.08 | 0.38 | 0.13 | 7.65 | 2.24 |
| 3.70 | 0.44 | 3.70 | 0.32 | 30.96 | 4.09 |
| 15.03 | 1.22 | 15.03 | 1.13 | 59.64 | 6.72 |
| 26.91 | 1.99 | 26.91 | 2.11 | 77.65 | 8.99 |
| 38.68 | 2.61 | 38.69 | 3.39 | 85.74 | 10.82 |
| 48.28 | 3.08 | 48.28 | 4.61 | 91.55 | 12.33 |
| 52.73 | 3.32 | 52.73 | 5.29 | 93.27 | 13.31 |
| 50.23 | 3.15 | 50.23 | 4.56 | 92.14 | 12.42 |
| 31.18 | 1.38 | 31.18 | 1.36 | 88.48 | 6.23 |
| 19.26 | 2.04 | 19.26 | 2.65 | 53.04 | 8.98 |

... continued

TABLE 2 (cont'd.)

| | Contribs. to RRSP Only | | Returns with PA Only | |
|---|---|---|---|---|
| | % of Returns | % of Total Income | % of Returns | % of Total Income |
| *Age Group 65+* | | | | |
| Under 10K | 0.35 | 0.05 | 0.20 | 0.02 |
| 10-20K | 1.21 | 0.17 | 0.38 | 0.05 |
| 20-30K | 8.45 | 1.14 | 1.56 | 0.12 |
| 30-40K | 16.07 | 2.00 | 1.96 | 0.20 |
| 40-50K | 19.99 | 2.36 | 1.92 | 0.15 |
| 50-60K | 22.98 | 2.45 | 2.33 | 0.18 |
| 60-80K | 26.86 | 2.82 | 1.79 | 0.13 |
| 80-100K | 24.90 | 2.53 | 1.40 | 0.13 |
| 100K+ | 30.41 | 2.11 | 1.65 | 0.09 |
| TOTAL | 5.68 | 1.32 | 0.83 | 0.11 |
| | | | | |
| *Total – All Ages* | | | | |
| Under 10K | 2.86 | 0.67 | 2.15 | 0.45 |
| 10-20K | 10.68 | 1.24 | 5.56 | 0.43 |
| 20-30K | 20.67 | 1.91 | 18.15 | 1.27 |
| 30-40K | 22.20 | 2.15 | 26.74 | 2.07 |
| 40-50K | 20.21 | 2.05 | 26.99 | 2.35 |
| 50-60K | 18.36 | 1.98 | 25.88 | 2.47 |
| 60-80K | 21.25 | 2.53 | 20.18 | 2.02 |
| 80-100K | 30.69 | 3.50 | 12.03 | 1.14 |
| 100K+ | 49.86 | 3.15 | 7.09 | 0.36 |
| TOTAL | 13.83 | 2.08 | 12.42 | 1.47 |

Source: Revenue Canada (1995, Table 12).

TABLE 2 (cont'd)

| Contribs. to RRSPs on Returns with PA | | Contributions to RPPs on Returns with RRSP Contribs. | | Returns with RRSP Contribs. &/or PA Amount | |
|---|---|---|---|---|---|
| % of Returns | % of Total Income | % of Returns | % of Total Income | % of Returns | % of Total Income |
| 0.00 | 0.00 | 0.00 | 0.00 | 0.55 | 0.08 |
| 0.09 | 0.01 | 0.09 | 0.01 | 1.68 | 0.24 |
| 1.11 | 0.11 | 1.11 | 0.08 | 11.12 | 1.46 |
| 2.07 | 0.20 | 2.07 | 0.17 | 20.10 | 2.58 |
| 2.76 | 0.30 | 2.76 | 0.18 | 24.67 | 2.99 |
| 3.96 | 0.38 | 3.96 | 0.34 | 29.28 | 3.36 |
| 4.86 | 0.49 | 4.86 | 0.38 | 33.51 | 3.82 |
| 5.25 | 0.43 | 5.25 | 0.37 | 31.55 | 3.47 |
| 4.19 | 0.22 | 4.19 | 0.17 | 36.26 | 2.60 |
| 0.77 | 0.16 | 0.77 | 0.12 | 7.27 | 1.71 |
| 0.19 | 0.05 | 0.19 | 0.06 | 5.20 | 1.22 |
| 1.78 | 0.18 | 1.78 | 0.14 | 18.02 | 1.99 |
| 10.40 | 0.74 | 10.40 | 0.74 | 49.22 | 4.67 |
| 22.54 | 1.45 | 22.54 | 1.70 | 71.48 | 7.38 |
| 34.51 | 2.11 | 34.51 | 2.92 | 81.70 | 9.42 |
| 42.92 | 2.53 | 42.92 | 4.00 | 87.17 | 10.98 |
| 47.18 | 2.84 | 47.18 | 4.56 | 88.62 | 11.95 |
| 42.55 | 2.61 | 42.55 | 3.69 | 85.27 | 10.94 |
| 24.34 | 0.97 | 24.34 | 1.03 | 81.29 | 5.52 |
| 12.05 | 1.40 | 12.05 | 1.91 | 38.30 | 6.85 |

TABLE 3:   Average RPP and RRSP Contributions by Income Class and Age, 1993

| | Contribs. to RRSP Only | | Returns with PA Only | | Contribs. to RRSPs on Returns with PA | |
|---|---|---|---|---|---|---|
| | # of Returns (000) | Avg. Contrib. ($000) | # of Returns (000) | Avg. Contrib. ($000) | # of Returns (000) | Avg. Contrib. ($000) |
| *Under 45* | | | | | | |
| Under 10K | 95.5 | 0.993 | 84.4 | 0.809 | 5.7 | 1.239 |
| 10-20K | 338.0 | 1.484 | 199.0 | 0.957 | 53.0 | 1.278 |
| 20-30K | 426.1 | 1.883 | 420.5 | 1.696 | 207.9 | 1.557 |
| 30-40K | 307.2 | 2.890 | 433.1 | 2.647 | 330.1 | 2.023 |
| 40-50K | 170.0 | 4.007 | 263.1 | 3.758 | 310.4 | 2.510 |
| 50-60K | 90.1 | 5.480 | 148.3 | 5.072 | 222.6 | 2.989 |
| 60-80K | 77.3 | 7.785 | 76.2 | 6.367 | 167.5 | 3.817 |
| 80-100K | 30.2 | 9.859 | 9.9 | 7.610 | 35.2 | 5.167 |
| 100K+ | 59.3 | 11.808 | 6.3 | 9.641 | 22.2 | 5.539 |
| TOTAL | 1593.7 | 3.176 | 1640.7 | 2.730 | 1354.5 | 2.551 |
| *Age 45 to 65* | | | | | | |
| Under 10K | 57.0 | 1.223 | 30.0 | 1.438 | 4.6 | 0.918 |
| 10-20K | 193.7 | 1.950 | 82.0 | 1.442 | 37.5 | 1.729 |
| 20-30K | 216.0 | 2.923 | 172.7 | 1.844 | 131.0 | 2.036 |
| 30-40K | 176.5 | 3.973 | 190.5 | 2.759 | 194.6 | 2.568 |
| 40-50K | 105.2 | 5.170 | 133.3 | 4.112 | 196.0 | 3.021 |
| 50-60K | 63.9 | 6.442 | 88.5 | 5.441 | 170.0 | 3.481 |
| 60-80K | 64.7 | 8.564 | 71.4 | 7.238 | 177.0 | 4.275 |
| 80-100K | 30.7 | 10.507 | 15.8 | 8.842 | 55.7 | 5.555 |
| 100K+ | 70.1 | 12.632 | 13.2 | 10.174 | 45.4 | 8.898 |
| TOTAL | 977.6 | 4.600 | 797.4 | 3.544 | 1011.7 | 3.449 |

TABLE 3  (cont'd.)

| Contribs. to RPPs on Returns with RRSP Contribs. | | Contribs. to RRSPs on All Returns with RRSP Contribs. | | Contribs. to RPPs on All Returns with RPP Contribs. | | Returns with RRSP Contribs. &/or PA Amount | |
|---|---|---|---|---|---|---|---|
| # of Returns (000) | Avg. Contrib. ($000) | # of Returns (000) | Avg. Contrib. ($000) | # of Returns (000) | Avg. Contrib. ($000) | # of Returns (000) | Avg. Contrib. ($000) |
| 5.7 | 1.244 | 101.2 | 1.006 | 90.1 | 0.837 | 185.6 | 0.955 |
| 53.0 | 0.962 | 391.0 | 1.456 | 252.0 | 0.958 | 590.0 | 1.374 |
| 207.9 | 1.707 | 634.0 | 1.776 | 628.3 | 1.699 | 1054.4 | 2.080 |
| 330.1 | 2.554 | 637.4 | 2.441 | 763.2 | 2.606 | 1070.4 | 3.312 |
| 310.4 | 3.696 | 480.4 | 3.040 | 573.5 | 3.724 | 743.5 | 4.837 |
| 222.6 | 4.981 | 312.7 | 3.706 | 370.9 | 5.018 | 461.0 | 6.551 |
| 167.5 | 6.275 | 244.7 | 5.069 | 243.6 | 6.304 | 320.9 | 8.652 |
| 35.2 | 7.115 | 65.4 | 7.336 | 45.1 | 7.223 | 75.3 | 10.695 |
| 22.2 | 7.572 | 81.5 | 10.097 | 28.6 | 8.029 | 87.8 | 11.982 |
| 1354.5 | 3.678 | 2948.2 | 2.889 | 2995.2 | 3.159 | 4588.9 | 3.918 |
| 4.6 | 1.553 | 61.5 | 1.201 | 34.6 | 1.453 | 91.6 | 1.356 |
| 37.5 | 1.267 | 231.1 | 1.914 | 119.4 | 1.387 | 313.1 | 1.942 |
| 131.0 | 1.883 | 347.0 | 2.588 | 303.7 | 1.861 | 519.7 | 2.816 |
| 194.6 | 2.727 | 371.1 | 3.236 | 385.2 | 2.743 | 561.7 | 4.019 |
| 196.0 | 3.914 | 301.2 | 3.771 | 329.3 | 3.994 | 434.5 | 5.642 |
| 170.0 | 5.222 | 233.8 | 4.289 | 258.4 | 5.297 | 322.3 | 7.359 |
| 177.0 | 6.822 | 241.7 | 5.424 | 248.4 | 6.942 | 313.1 | 9.694 |
| 55.7 | 8.040 | 86.4 | 7.313 | 71.5 | 8.218 | 102.2 | 11.933 |
| 45.3 | 8.769 | 115.5 | 11.165 | 58.6 | 9.086 | 128.7 | 14.154 |
| 1011.7 | 4.487 | 1989.3 | 4.014 | 1809.1 | 4.072 | 2786.7 | 5.509 |

... continued

TABLE 3 (cont'd.)

| | Contribs. to RRSP Only | | Returns with PA Only | | Contribs. to RRSPs on Returns with PA | |
|---|---|---|---|---|---|---|
| | # of Returns (000) | Avg. Contrib. ($000) | # of Returns (000) | Avg. Contrib. ($000) | # of Returns (000) | Avg. Contrib. ($000) |
| *Age Group 65+* | | | | | | |
| Under 10K | 1.5 | 1.035 | 0.9 | 0.831 | 0.0 | 0.000 |
| 10-20K | 18.8 | 1.915 | 5.9 | 1.777 | 1.4 | 1.652 |
| 20-30K | 42.3 | 3.285 | 7.8 | 1.912 | 5.5 | 2.519 |
| 30-40K | 38.0 | 4.266 | 4.6 | 3.559 | 4.9 | 3.397 |
| 40-50K | 23.2 | 5.240 | 2.2 | 3.515 | 3.2 | 4.908 |
| 50-60K | 15.1 | 5.806 | 1.5 | 4.299 | 2.6 | 5.213 |
| 60-80K | 14.4 | 7.148 | 1.0 | 4.907 | 2.6 | 6.838 |
| 80-100K | 5.5 | 9.080 | 0.3 | 8.297 | 1.2 | 7.361 |
| 100K+ | 12.7 | 14.871 | 0.7 | 11.601 | 1.8 | 11.311 |
| TOTAL | 171.5 | 5.186 | 24.9 | 2.900 | 23.2 | 4.672 |
| *Total – All Ages* | | | | | | |
| Under 10K | 153.9 | 1.078 | 115.4 | 0.973 | 10.2 | 1.096 |
| 10-20K | 550.6 | 1.663 | 286.9 | 1.112 | 91.9 | 1.468 |
| 20-30K | 684.4 | 2.298 | 601.0 | 1.741 | 344.4 | 1.754 |
| 30-40K | 521.7 | 3.357 | 628.2 | 2.687 | 529.7 | 2.236 |
| 40-50K | 298.4 | 4.513 | 398.6 | 3.875 | 509.6 | 2.721 |
| 50-60K | 169.0 | 5.872 | 238.3 | 5.204 | 395.2 | 3.215 |
| 60-80K | 156.4 | 8.049 | 148.5 | 6.777 | 347.1 | 4.073 |
| 80-100K | 66.4 | 10.094 | 26.0 | 8.370 | 92.0 | 5.430 |
| 100K+ | 142.1 | 12.488 | 20.2 | 10.061 | 69.4 | 7.881 |
| TOTAL | 2742.9 | 3.809 | 2463.1 | 2.995 | 2389.4 | 2.951 |

Source: Revenue Canada (1995, Table 12).

TABLE 3  (cont'd.)

| Contribs. to RPPs on Returns with RRSP Contribs. | | Contribs. to RRSPs on All Returns with RRSP Contribs. | | Contribs. to RPPs on All Returns with RPP Contribs. | | Returns with RRSP Contribs. &/or PA Amount | |
|---|---|---|---|---|---|---|---|
| # of Returns (000) | Avg. Contrib. ($000) | # of Returns (000) | Avg. Contrib. ($000) | # of Returns (000) | Avg. Contrib. ($000) | # of Returns (000) | Avg. Contrib. ($000) |
| 0.0 | 0.000 | 1.5 | 1.035 | 0.9 | 0.831 | 2.4 | 0.956 |
| 1.4 | 1.219 | 20.2 | 1.896 | 7.4 | 1.668 | 26.2 | 1.936 |
| 5.5 | 1.785 | 47.9 | 3.197 | 13.3 | 1.860 | 55.7 | 3.194 |
| 4.9 | 2.846 | 42.9 | 4.167 | 9.5 | 3.192 | 47.5 | 4.401 |
| 3.2 | 2.866 | 26.4 | 5.200 | 5.4 | 3.132 | 28.7 | 5.389 |
| 2.6 | 4.704 | 17.7 | 5.719 | 4.1 | 4.554 | 19.2 | 6.239 |
| 2.6 | 5.347 | 17.0 | 7.101 | 3.6 | 5.228 | 17.9 | 7.759 |
| 1.2 | 6.328 | 6.7 | 8.780 | 1.5 | 6.744 | 7.0 | 9.812 |
| 1.8 | 8.794 | 14.4 | 14.440 | 2.4 | 9.588 | 15.1 | 15.328 |
| 23.2 | 3.609 | 194.7 | 5.125 | 48.1 | 3.241 | 219.6 | 5.254 |
| 10.2 | 1.382 | 164.2 | 1.079 | 125.7 | 1.006 | 279.6 | 1.086 |
| 91.9 | 1.090 | 642.5 | 1.635 | 378.8 | 1.107 | 929.4 | 1.581 |
| 344.4 | 1.775 | 1028.8 | 2.116 | 945.4 | 1.754 | 1629.8 | 2.353 |
| 529.7 | 2.620 | 1051.3 | 2.792 | 1157.9 | 2.657 | 1679.6 | 3.579 |
| 509.6 | 3.775 | 808.0 | 3.383 | 908.2 | 3.819 | 1206.6 | 5.140 |
| 395.2 | 5.083 | 564.2 | 4.011 | 633.5 | 5.129 | 802.5 | 6.868 |
| 347.1 | 6.547 | 503.5 | 5.308 | 495.6 | 6.616 | 625.0 | 9.128 |
| 92.0 | 7.665 | 158.4 | 7.385 | 118.0 | 7.820 | 184.4 | 11.348 |
| 69.4 | 8.383 | 211.4 | 10.977 | 89.6 | 8.762 | 231.6 | 13.407 |
| 2389.4 | 4.020 | 5132.3 | 3.410 | 4852.5 | 3.500 | 7595.4 | 4.540 |

*Effective Tax Rates on Different Assets.* Representative effective tax rates on income from different types of assets for taxpayers in three different rate brackets are presented in Table 4. In addition to investment in RRSPs, and RPPs, owner-occupied housing and farms and small business shares (within the $500K deduction) are taxed at a zero marginal rate.

Across the remaining assets, effective marginal tax rates vary between 14.2 and 27.4 percent for taxpayers in the first bracket, between 22.6 and 41.9 percent for middle-bracket taxpayers and between 29.0 and 52.4 percent for top-bracket taxpayers.[11]

It is clear that investment income (including accrued capital gains) is subject to taxation at a wide variety of effective marginal rates, depending on the type of asset and the tax position of the recipient.

Table 5 provides information on real assets, financial assets, and liabilities of the household sector since 1961. Table 5A provides information on assets holding in 1993 for RRSP, RPP, housing, and other assets and liabilities.

Households' holdings of assets in the different Retirement Savings Plans were over $450 billion in 1993. This represented about one-third of households' financial assets and about one-fifth of households' net worth. Owner-occupied housing represents most of the real asset holding of the households sector. In 1992 those assets totalled $725 billion, which represented 55 percent of households' real assets.[12]

Mortgage debt is the major financial liability of the household sector. In 1992, mortgage debt was $315 billion, which was 67 percent of total liabilities. The value of the owner-occupied housing less mortgage debt was $410 billion, or almost 20 percent of households' net worth.[13] For many individuals, the paying down of mortgage debt represents the best alternative to investing in RRSPs. Since mortgage interest is typically non-deductible[14] in Canada, the discharge of this debt effectively earns the tax-free rate of interest.

TABLE 4: Representative Effective Marginal Tax Rates[1] by Type of Savings, Ontario, 1993

| | Taxable Income Levels | | |
| | $25,000 | $45,000 | $100,000 |
|---|---|---|---|
| | % | % | % |
| Interest Income | 27.37 | 41.86 | 52.35 |
| Dividend Income | 7.39 | 25.50 | 35.36 |
| Capital Gains[2] | | | |
| – Shares | 17.32 | 27.03 | 34.31 |
| – Real Estate | 14.21 | 22.56 | 29.03 |
| – Small Business and Farm (under $500K)[3] | 0.00 | 0.00 | 0.00 |
| Owner Occupied Dwelling | 0.00 | 0.00 | 0.00 |
| RPP/RSP | 0.00 | 0.00 | 0.00 |

Notes:

[1] These rates do not include the social benefits repayment which become effective at *net* income levels of $58K for unemployment insurance and $53K for Old Age Security in 1993.

[2] This rate is calculated using the accrual equivalent marginal tax-rate methodology. A holding period of six years is assumed for shares and 12 years for real estate. The average annual compound total return from the TSE 300 over the six years to 1993 is used as a proxy for the internal rate of return.

[3] The $100K capital gains exemption for every taxpayer was in effect in 1993 but has since been cancelled. Thus, we do not list it here.

Source: Authors' compilation.

TABLE 5:   Canada – National Balance Sheet, Year End Outstandings, 1961-1994, Persons and Unincorporated Business, $ Billions

| | Total Assets | Real Assets | Resident Structrues | Other Real | Net Financial Assets | Total Financial Assets | Currency Deposits & Crdit | T-Bills & Short Paper | Mort-gages | Domestic Bonds |
|---|---|---|---|---|---|---|---|---|---|---|
| 1961 | 131.1 | 68.2 | 26.9 | 41.3 | 45.8 | 62.9 | 16.0 | 0.2 | 2.1 | 11.6 |
| 1962 | 138.4 | 71.8 | 28.3 | 43.4 | 47.7 | 66.6 | 17.2 | 0.3 | 2.2 | 13.0 |
| 1963 | 149.6 | 76.8 | 30.3 | 46.4 | 51.7 | 72.8 | 18.7 | 0.2 | 2.3 | 13.5 |
| 1964 | 162.3 | 83.1 | 33.2 | 49.9 | 55.2 | 79.2 | 20.7 | 0.2 | 2.5 | 14.1 |
| 1965 | 180.7 | 91.2 | 36.6 | 54.6 | 61.8 | 89.5 | 23.7 | 0.1 | 2.5 | 14.7 |
| 1966 | 199.8 | 100.7 | 40.3 | 60.3 | 69.9 | 99.1 | 26.3 | 0.2 | 3.1 | 15.3 |
| 1967 | 216.8 | 110.2 | 43.7 | 66.5 | 74.1 | 106.6 | 30.5 | 0.1 | 3.3 | 16.0 |
| 1968 | 234.3 | 119.8 | 47.3 | 72.5 | 77.5 | 114.5 | 34.3 | 0.3 | 3.6 | 15.8 |
| 1969 | 254.0 | 130.9 | 51.7 | 79.1 | 81.9 | 123.1 | 37.5 | 0.7 | 4.3 | 16.6 |
| 1970 | 271.6 | 140.7 | 56.8 | 83.9 | 85.9 | 130.9 | 41.2 | 0.1 | 5.1 | 18.6 |
| 1971 | 298.1 | 155.8 | 64.7 | 91.0 | 92.3 | 142.3 | 46.6 | 0.0 | 5.3 | 21.4 |
| 1972 | 334.3 | 179.0 | 76.3 | 102.7 | 97.5 | 155.3 | 52.4 | 0.0 | 5.8 | 22.3 |
| 1973 | 393.4 | 216.7 | 93.4 | 123.3 | 112.1 | 176.7 | 64.4 | 0.0 | 6.4 | 22.5 |
| 1974 | 465.2 | 260.7 | 110.0 | 150.8 | 130.5 | 204.4 | 74.9 | 0.4 | 6.9 | 26.1 |
| 1975 | 528.7 | 294.2 | 123.8 | 170.4 | 143.9 | 234.4 | 88.3 | 0.4 | 7.8 | 27.9 |
| 1976 | 599.4 | 329.4 | 138.4 | 191.1 | 163.0 | 269.9 | 103.6 | 0.7 | 9.1 | 28.5 |
| 1977 | 675.3 | 368.3 | 151.9 | 216.4 | 187.4 | 307.0 | 119.2 | 0.5 | 8.6 | 33.5 |
| 1978 | 774.6 | 417.8 | 169.7 | 248.1 | 218.0 | 356.8 | 138.9 | 1.1 | 8.5 | 36.6 |
| 1979 | 890.3 | 480.2 | 191.1 | 289.1 | 252.7 | 410.1 | 161.4 | 1.6 | 8.6 | 36.8 |
| 1980 | 1029.7 | 553.1 | 217.7 | 335.4 | 300.9 | 476.5 | 184.2 | 6.2 | 9.0 | 38.5 |
| 1981 | 1138.9 | 615.9 | 242.8 | 373.1 | 334.4 | 523.0 | 204.9 | 1.6 | 9.9 | 48.9 |
| 1982 | 1215.9 | 647.3 | 258.9 | 388.4 | 379.2 | 568.6 | 211.3 | 4.0 | 10.2 | 55.8 |
| 1983 | 1301.8 | 671.1 | 279.1 | 391.9 | 426.3 | 630.8 | 224.1 | 11.0 | 9.9 | 62.2 |
| 1984 | 1398.3 | 706.5 | 298.0 | 408.4 | 476.6 | 691.8 | 241.2 | 10.4 | 10.3 | 71.2 |
| 1985 | 1498.7 | 741.4 | 322.3 | 419.1 | 519.3 | 757.2 | 252.7 | 13.9 | 10.2 | 77.5 |
| 1986 | 1655.4 | 818.7 | 360.2 | 458.5 | 567.3 | 836.7 | 282.7 | 20.0 | 10.7 | 68.9 |
| 1987 | 1823.5 | 907.6 | 406.0 | 501.5 | 604.5 | 916.0 | 300.1 | 21.7 | 13.0 | 78.6 |
| 1988 | 2003.9 | 1004.3 | 451.6 | 552.7 | 646.2 | 999.6 | 344.1 | 24.2 | 15.2 | 84.8 |
| 1989 | 2203.3 | 1104.2 | 488.7 | 615.5 | 707.1 | 1099.1 | 393.9 | 35.9 | 18.6 | 64.0 |
| 1990 | 2314.4 | 11144.0 | 517.3 | 626.7 | 750.1 | 1170.5 | 420.7 | 43.8 | 21.5 | 63.8 |
| 1991 | 2440.8 | 11195.6 | 542.4 | 653.2 | 804.5 | 1245.3 | 440.2 | 34.2 | 25.2 | 73.7 |
| 1992 | 2571.7 | 11247.2 | 569.4 | 677.8 | 860.0 | 1324.6 | 468.0 | 37.3 | 31.5 | 67.4 |
| 1993 | 2702.1 | 11305.6 | 600.0 | 705.6 | 912.2 | 1396.5 | 478.2 | 29.6 | 38.3 | 63.8 |
| 1994 | 2832.4 | 11368.1 | 632.8 | 735.2 | 955.3 | 1464.4 | 487.2 | 20.3 | 41.2 | 64.5 |

TABLE 5A:   National Balance Sheet, Year End Outstandings, 1993, Persons and Unincorporated Business, $ Billions

| Total Assets | Real Assets | Net Financial Assets | Total Financial Assets | Fixed Income | Of Which RRSP | Life Ins. and Pensions | Of Which: Trusteed Pension | RRSP | Other |
|---|---|---|---|---|---|---|---|---|---|
| 2702.1 | 1305.6 | 912.2 | 1396.5 | 609.9 | 112.2 | 423.7 | 257.4 | 53.6 | 112.7 |

Source: Authors' compilation.

TABLE 5 (cont'd.)

| Life Ins. and Pensions | Stocks | Foreign Invest. | Other Financial Assets | Total Financial Liabilities | Consumer Credit | Trade | Loans & Bonds | Mortgage | Net Worth |
|---|---|---|---|---|---|---|---|---|---|
| 14.1 | 15.6 | 1.0 | 2.4 | 17.1 | 4.3 | 1.2 | 2.0 | 9.7 | 114.0 |
| 15.3 | 15.7 | 1.1 | 1.9 | 18.9 | 4.8 | 1.2 | 2.3 | 10.7 | 119.5 |
| 16.6 | 18.0 | 1.1 | 2.3 | 21.1 | 5.4 | 1.2 | 2.7 | 11.8 | 128.5 |
| 18.1 | 20.4 | 1.1 | 2.2 | 24.0 | 6.2 | 1.4 | 3.3 | 13.1 | 138.3 |
| 19.7 | 25.8 | 1.0 | 2.1 | 27.6 | 7.1 | 1.8 | 3.9 | 14.9 | 153.0 |
| 21.2 | 29.8 | 0.8 | 2.3 | 29.2 | 7.7 | 1.6 | 3.6 | 16.3 | 170.6 |
| 22.8 | 30.6 | 0.8 | 2.4 | 32.4 | 8.5 | 2.0 | 3.9 | 18.1 | 184.4 |
| 24.6 | 32.2 | 0.4 | 3.2 | 37.0 | 9.7 | 1.7 | 5.3 | 20.3 | 197.3 |
| 26.3 | 34.2 | 0.3 | 3.2 | 41.2 | 11.0 | 2.4 | 5.4 | 22.5 | 212.7 |
| 28.2 | 34.3 | 0.5 | 2.8 | 45.0 | 11.6 | 2.5 | 6.0 | 24.8 | 226.6 |
| 30.5 | 34.7 | 0.6 | 3.2 | 50.0 | 12.5 | 2.6 | 7.2 | 27.6 | 248.1 |
| 33.8 | 36.0 | 1.1 | 4.1 | 57.8 | 14.7 | 2.9 | 7.7 | 32.5 | 276.5 |
| 37.6 | 39.6 | 1.8 | 4.5 | 64.6 | 17.5 | 2.7 | 5.9 | 38.5 | 328.8 |
| 41.6 | 47.2 | 2.0 | 5.4 | 74.0 | 20.4 | 1.6 | 7.8 | 44.3 | 391.2 |
| 47.1 | 53.8 | 2.4 | 6.8 | 90.5 | 23.5 | 2.9 | 13.0 | 51.0 | 438.2 |
| 54.5 | 60.5 | 2.6 | 10.4 | 106.9 | 27.4 | 2.6 | 15.8 | 61.1 | 492.5 |
| 61.8 | 63.3 | 2.6 | 17.7 | 119.6 | 30.7 | 1.1 | 17.8 | 70.1 | 555.7 |
| 71.4 | 82.6 | 4.0 | 13.7 | 138.9 | 35.5 | 2.5 | 18.4 | 82.5 | 635.7 |
| 84.3 | 94.5 | 4.9 | 18.1 | 157.4 | 40.3 | 0.2 | 21.5 | 95.4 | 732.9 |
| 98.1 | 114.5 | 4.9 | 21.1 | 175.7 | 44.9 | 0.5 | 23.7 | 106.6 | 854.0 |
| 113.3 | 120.7 | 3.9 | 19.7 | 188.6 | 46.9 | 0.1 | 26.1 | 115.5 | 950.3 |
| 128.1 | 131.3 | 3.9 | 24.1 | 189.5 | 46.0 | 0.3 | 26.7 | 116.3 | 1026.4 |
| 146.2 | 144.4 | 4.7 | 28.2 | 204.5 | 47.8 | 2.0 | 27.6 | 127.1 | 1097.3 |
| 164.4 | 157.3 | 4.2 | 32.9 | 215.2 | 52.1 | 1.9 | 26.9 | 134.3 | 1183.1 |
| 186.9 | 175.2 | 7.0 | 33.9 | 238.0 | 59.2 | 3.6 | 28.2 | 147.0 | 1260.7 |
| 213.0 | 197.7 | 7.7 | 35.9 | 269.4 | 65.1 | 4.4 | 31.9 | 168.0 | 1386.0 |
| 237.9 | 218.4 | 10.9 | 35.2 | 311.5 | 74.6 | 4.7 | 37.9 | 194.3 | 1512.0 |
| 262.6 | 229.1 | 11.5 | 28.1 | 353.4 | 84.2 | 5.7 | 42.5 | 221.0 | 1650.5 |
| 301.8 | 238.2 | 13.6 | 33.2 | 392.0 | 92.4 | 6.4 | 44.6 | 248.6 | 1811.3 |
| 328.8 | 246.7 | 15.5 | 29.7 | 420.4 | 97.6 | 7.0 | 46.5 | 269.2 | 1894.1 |
| 360.6 | 270.7 | 13.5 | 27.1 | 440.7 | 98.8 | 6.2 | 45.3 | 290.4 | 2000.1 |
| 391.4 | 291.4 | 10.8 | 26.7 | 464.6 | 98.0 | 6.7 | 45.2 | 314.7 | 2107.1 |
| 423.7 | 333.3 | 7.8 | 21.9 | 484.3 | 103.6 | 6.5 | 44.9 | 329.3 | 2217.8 |
| 452.5 | 363.3 | 6.6 | 28.8 | 509.1 | 110.2 | 7.1 | 43.9 | 347.8 | 2323.3 |

TABLE 5A (cont'd.)

| Stocks | Of Which RRSP | Other Financial Assets | Total Financial Assets | Mortgage | Other Liabilities | Net Worth |
|---|---|---|---|---|---|---|
| 333.3 | 40.6 | 29.7 | 484.3 | 329.3 | 155.0 | 2217.8 |

REFORM OPTIONS

In this section, we discuss several options for tax reform that could be considered for the private provision of retirement income. The options that are considered are what we entitle as "harmful ideas," "less harmful ideas," and our suggested reform (which we hope is not harmful). Prior to discussing these reforms, it would be useful to outline objectives for reform of the tax system.

## Objectives for Reform

Economists highlight three objectives for policy reform:

* *Allocative Efficiency.* Government policy should improve the allocation of resources in the economy.

* *Equity.* Policies should be fair. They should treat similar individuals in the same way (horizontal equity) and be less beneficial to the rich compared to the poor (vertical equity).

* *Simplicity.* Policies should be simple for governments to administer and individuals to comply with.

It is clear that the current system regarding the taxation of savings is distortive, unfair, and not simple. Three impacts may be noted: portfolio effects, savings-leisure distortions, and occupational choice.

*Portfolio Effects.* Some assets, such as RRSPs, RPPs, certain investments yielding capital gains, and equity ownership in housing are treated on a consumption basis so that the rate of return earned on investments is exempt from taxation. Other assets such as bonds and equities earn income that is taxed while tax shelters such as flow-through shares, film shelters, and labour-sponsored venture capital investments might be taxed at negative rates. Rules limiting the proportion of RPP and RRSP funds invested in non-Canadian assets also distort portfolio decisions (some of the rules are circumvented as in the case of holding derivative security funds). Thus, the current treatment of savings can have inequitable and distortionary impacts on individuals.

*Intertemporal-Labour Distortions.* As discussed above, the taxation of the return to savings may have an intertemporal effect by discouraging savings for future consumption (see Davies, St. Hilaire and Whalley 1984). When individuals can accumulate assets on a tax-assisted basis, then they are more able to provide for retirement. In fact, as discussed above, the RPP and RRSP systems have allowed more flexibility with regard to early retirement as well.

As pointed out in the literature, the taxation of savings may be argued, however, as a way of reducing the distortive effect of other taxes, such as labour taxes. By eliminating the tax on savings, the tax system must rely more on labour taxes, given the same revenue requirement for the government. The additional tax on labour income could be more distortive than the intertemporal effect of taxing the return to saving, resulting in an efficiency loss to the economy (Auerbach and Kotlikoff 1987). However, in the usual analysis, governments are restricted to only levying capital income and labour taxes. It is possible that other taxes, such as excise taxes and user fees could be used instead to make up for losses in tax revenue resulting from the tax exemption provided for capital income.

*Occupational Choice.* The choice of occupation depends on the after-tax income earned by individuals (adjusted for risk), the cost of training, and the benefits received. As discussed above, the tax system can discourage human capital investments when the costs of education and training are not deductible from income. In addition, the tax treatment of pension plans, one of the important benefits received by workers, can also affect occupational choice. Individuals employed with companies and non-profit organizations may have pension plans vested with their organization. Small business owners, fishermen, farmers, and professionals may rely more on the RRSPs and taxable assets to accumulate savings for retirement purposes.

Defined benefit plans, the most common system, provide an income based on the number of years of service and salary (e.g., last three years) earned by recipient. These provisions encourage workers to stay with the firm until retirement. Defined contribution plans which provide benefits based on amounts contributed by the individual and firms provide more flexibility when an occupation is changed. However, both defined benefit and contribution plans may not be transferable. Moreover, they must be vested — it may be a requirement for the worker to be employed for a minimum number of years for the firm's contribution to be vested with the individual. Thus, private pension plans can reduce flexibility in labour markets. The RRSP system, however, provides more flexibility in that it is held by the individual no matter how many times his or her occupation might change.

As discussed above, the tax system in the past has provided a more favourable treatment for individuals holding defined benefit plans. The 1990 changes provided a more equitable treatment of defined benefit, defined contribution, and RRSP plans which also removes some of the distortions of the tax system associated with occupational choice.

## Some Harmful Ideas for Reform

In the interest of increasing taxes on savings instruments, two prominent reforms have been suggested: turning deductions for RPPs and RRSPs into credits (the "credit" proposal) and taxing income earned by RPPs and RRSPs.

Under the first proposal, individuals would receive a 17-percent federal credit (augmented by the provincial credit to about 25 percent) instead of deducting contributions from income. It is argued that the proposal is more fair because middle- (about $28,000 to $56,000 in taxable income) and upper-income individuals (more than $56,000 in income) would receive a smaller tax benefit since contributions may have a tax value in the range of 40 to 50 percent when deductible from income.

The "credit" proposal for reform is singularly concentrated on only one objective for policy: vertical equity. Yet, the proposal would create far greater inequities and distortions than intended. The effect of such a policy is to highly discourage savings in RRSPs and RPPs when it is expected that tax rates will increase over time. Indeed, it would be better for an individual to hold taxable assets rather than RPPs or RRSPs if the tax rate at the time of contribution is far less than the tax rate at the time of withdrawal. For example, if a person has only three years until retirement, a $1,000 contribution, yielding interest at a rate of 10 percent, with a tax credit of 25 percent and overall retirement income taxed at a 40 percent rate would be taxed at a rate equivalent to a wealth tax of 15 percent, much greater than the 10 percent return on the asset. Such taxation would be expropriation of wealth.

Although very low-income individuals would not be affected by this ill-thought out "credit" proposal, pension holders with middle or upper income would need to have the terms of their pension system changed to avoid such high levels of tax. In particular, many pension holders would prefer to invest in assets outside the pension system, especially prior to retirement.

A more reasonable but also difficult-to-implement proposal would be to tax income earned by pension and RRSP plans. Although, in principle, taxing pension income might be consistent with the treatment of some assets, it would not necessarily improve the allocative efficiency or equity since many other types of investments are either tax-free or taxed at a negative rate. Also, such taxation of income makes the intertemporal distortion worse, as discussed earlier.

Transition issues would also be particularly difficult for defined benefit plans with a pension income tax. A tax on income earned by defined benefit plans will make it more difficult for these plans to fund current or future benefits requiring an increased rate of contribution from existing contributors or reduced payments to existing beneficiaries.

## Somewhat Less Harmful Ideas

Two other ideas expressed for reform are less harmful than the ones characterized above but, in our view, are still somewhat harmful nonetheless. The first is to impose a tax penalty on early withdrawals from RRSP plans and the second is to reduce contribution limits for RRSPs.

The penalty tax on RRSP withdrawals prior to retirement may arguably be put on the same footing RRSPs and RPPs. The latter are locked-in until retirement (unless early retirement is permitted) while the former are not. This restriction on RPP funds provides a clear advantage to the RRSP system in that it is a more flexible instrument that could be used for other purposes besides retirement. As discussed earlier, the RRSP is useful for averaging the tax base and providing resources for contingencies that might arise prior to retirement.

A penalty tax on RRSP withdrawals prior to retirement is harmful precisely for the reason that it reduces flexibility for savers. With reduced flexibility, individuals may be less willing to save money through the RRSP system and provide resources for retirement since they might feel that their resources are locked-in. As shown in Table 5, many individuals hold both RPP and RRSP plans. RRSPs provide flexibility that the RPP would not otherwise provide.

Moreover, retirement dates of RPPs are well established by agreements with workers while RRSPs have no determined date for retirement.[15] A penalty tax would require the government to specify the date of retirement for an individual who might wish an earlier retirement date either as a result of layoff, disability, or choice.

The second proposal, limiting RRSP contribution limits, has been the preferred method for governments to reduce the advantages of the RRSP and RPP system for retirement savings. As discussed in the previous section, contribution limits, once adjusted for inflation, have not increased since 1972 — in fact, they have fallen significantly during the 1970s and 1980s and were only recently corrected with the reforms of the late 1980s and early 1990s.

The argument in favour of limiting contributions to RRSPs is primarily based on vertical equity: upper-income individuals are provided fewer advantages (although contributions to RPP and RRSP as a percentage of income are smaller for upper-income individuals). In addition, Ragan (1994) suggests that decreases in contribution limits could increase savings.[16]

However, a policy that would reduce contribution limits for RRSPs alone discriminates against those individuals who do not avail themselves of the RPP system. Moreover, the RRSP provides for flexibility that is important for other reasons such as averaging the tax base and providing resources in the face of contingencies such as layoffs.

## Our Own Reform Proposals

Any reform of the tax treatment of savings should improve the efficiency or equity objectives of the tax system. While the 1990 reforms redressed previous inequities of the treatment of RPP and RRSP participants, these reforms may have created some inequities in the treatment of defined benefit RPPs. Other tax changes over the 1980s — starting with the November 1981 budget and culminating in the 1987 Tax Reform — moved the PIT system towards an "income" base and away from an expenditure base. In particular, income averaging measures have been effectually eliminated for most taxpayers (aside from using RRSPs for this purpose). The 1981 budget eliminated income averaging annuities, a feature of the tax system recommended in the Carter report to redress inequities in the tax treatment of fluctuating income, and the 1987 tax reform eliminated the general averaging provision. Throughout the 1980s, measures were also taken to attack tax deferrals. The budget of 1981 introduced mandatory three-year reporting of accrued interest, and the 1989 budget mandated annual reporting of accrued interest. The investment income deduction — introduced in the budget of 1974 — was eliminated in the 1987 tax reform.

At the present time, it is fair to say that the RPP-RRSP system represents the only explicit general provisions in the income tax act which exempt savings from tax.[17]

A major improvement introduced in the 1990 reform is the seven-year carry forward of unused RRSP contribution room. This provision provides greater flexibility than the previous "use it or lose it" system and improves opportunities for the RRSP system to be used for income averaging.

However, the annual caps on the RRSP-RPP system discriminate against individuals with fluctuating incomes. Furthermore, no provision exists for rebuilding RRSP assets after withdrawal prior to retirement, imposing limitations on the use of RRSPs for income averaging purposes.

Finally, the ceiling on accrued pension benefits under RPPs has been frozen since 1976. The indexing of this ceiling, originally promised for 1989, has been deferred to 1999.

Our proposed reforms are to make the RRSP/RPP more flexible and to redress present inequities in the treatment of defined benefit RPPs, recipients of fluctuating income, and individuals who make pre-retirement withdrawals.

*Placing the RRSP-RPP System on a Lifetime Basis.* The basic principle is that the amount of tax-sheltered savings should be related to lifetime income and not annual income.

An individual whose income is less than the amount required for maximum RRSP contributions in a year should be allowed to carry forward the excess to be used in years when his/her income is above the maximum.

- Lifetime RRSP

  Limit    ≤ 18 percent of lifetime qualifying income

      ≤ Max * N

  where N is the number of years of qualifying income and Max is the annual dollar limit.

- Consistent with this lifetime approach, early withdrawal from RRSPs should create added RRSP room; that is, the allowable final total of RRSP contributions made should be net of any withdrawals through the lifecycle.

- The RRSP carry-forward period should be extended to the earlier of either the date of retirement or age 71.[18]

*Redressing Inequities in the Treatment of Defined Benefit RRPs.* At present the Pension Adjustment for participants in RPPs is based on the 9 x formula: each 1 percent of income accrued in the year for future pension payments is treated as equal to an RRSP contribution of 9 percent of income. As noted above, this factor is only appropriate for "Cadillac" RPPs, which are based on the final three-years earnings, have full indexation of pensions, 75 percent spousal benefits, and generous early retirement provisions. A more flexible formula needs to be used for defined benefit plans with less generous features.

The annual and percentage limits and the maximum annual pension accrual need to be adjusted. One unfortunate feature of the 1990 reforms was that many lower-income taxpayers saw their contribution limits reduced from 20 percent of the current years income to 18 percent of the previous years income.

We see no reason why the present limits should not be raised to the 30 percent threshold recommended by the ECC some time ago. As an interim measure, the 20 percent limit should be restored.

The maximum annual pension accrual under a defined benefit plan has been frozen since 1976. This maximum also relates to the annual limits on RRSP contributions. Originally indexation was proposed to begin in 1989. This date has been *postponed* repeatedly, (at the present time it is scheduled to take effect in 1999).

We recommend that the limits be increased to reflect changes in the average industrial wage since 1989.

*The $500K Capital Gains Deduction for Owners of Small Corporations and Farms.* Although the 1994 federal budget eliminated the $100K general capital gain deduction, the $500K deduction for gains realized on the sale of farms or shares in small businesses remain. In our opinion, the only valid reason for preferential treatment of these gains relates to possible retirement savings inequities. Owners of these businesses and farms may plough back available earnings into expanding their enterprises. With no RPP, and little room (or cash) for RRSPs they would be treated inequitably if their retirement savings — in the form of their accrued gains on farms and businesses — were fully taxed.

It is therefore appropriate, on equity grounds, to provide special treatment of these capital gains. However, the present blanket $500K deduction is far too crude a measure. It may be far too generous in some cases (e.g., the part-time farmer who has pension benefits from his full-time job) and not generous enough in others (e.g., the full-time farmer who could not afford to contribute to RRSPs over his working life).

The proposed lifetime approach provides a solution to this problem. All capital gains on farms and small businesses realized by active workers of the business should be treated as qualifying income for RRSP purposes. When the farm or business is sold before retirement, the individual could make use of any previously unused RRSP room plus the room generated by the realized gains.

*Age and Pension Credits.* Under the current *Income Tax Act,* persons over 65 can claim a credit of $592, which is subject to clawback at a 15 percent rate of income above $25,921. Up to $1,000 of pension income is eligible for a tax credit at the lowest marginal rate.

These two measures serve the important function of reducing or eliminating the amount of income overlaps of the Guaranteed Income Supplement (GIS) with the income tax, thereby avoiding near punitive marginal rates on some low-income retirees. However, *both* credits should be subject to clawback at incomes above $25,921.

*Retiring Allowances (RAs).* Individuals can roll over a portion of retiring allowances into an RRSP. The limits are $2,000 per year of employment, (plus $1,500 for years prior to 1989 when no RPP or DPSP benefits were earned). The 1995 federal budget eliminated the rollover for years of service after 1995.

Recently, retiring allowances have become more common with early retirement packages. This change in the tax treatment effectively increases the costs to employers of a given after-tax early retirement arrangement or other employee buyouts. This would not appear to be a wise policy, given the current extent of employment restructuring.

Retiring allowances could be incorporated into the lifetime RRSP system proposed above. Basically RAs should be defined as qualifying income, and individuals should be allowed to pre-pay eligible amounts into an RRSP upon retirement from a position. For individuals who have fully utilized RRSP room at retirement, the Retiring Allowance rollover would reduce future RRSP contribution room.

## NOTES

The authors wish to thank Steve Murphy of the Institute for Policy Analysis for capable research assistance.

1. In addition to the above public measures, the role of governments in supporting the disabled population forced into retirement may also be considered. The tax deductibility of disability costs, the taxation of workers' compensation benefits and the public provision of disability pensions and workers' compensation raise a whole set of policy issues as well. Even though there is some relationship between disability and retirement, we will not delve into this subject as it is deserving of a separate paper. For a recent study, see Vaillancourt (1995).

2. Note that "private" includes funded pension plans of public servants, as well as pensions of employees in the "MUSH" sector and of Crown corporations.

3. In 1993, about $4 Billion was withdrawn from RRSPs (excluding annuity payments) (Revenue Canada 1995, Table 2A).

4. Some studies have suggested that the bequest and precautionary motives may be the most important factors explaining savings behaviour. See Kotlikoff and Summer (1981) and Deaton (1989).

5. Note that transfers of RRSP wealth are subject to income tax (except for transfers between spouses and deferral of tax on transfers to minor children).

6. The 1970 tax reform instituted Income Averaging Annuity Contracts (IACCs), which permitted forward averaging of designated types of income. These were eliminated in the 1981 federal budget. In addition, general averaging provisions allowed backward and subsequently forward averaging of total income. These were eliminated in the 1987 tax reform.

7. Refundability means that the government provides the equivalent of a tax credit equal to the tax rate times the loss incurred by the investor.

8. Indexing was originally proposed to start in 1989, and has been repeatedly postponed. This has effectively eroded the real value of the maximum limit. The 1996 budget has extended the $13,500 limit to 2002, and indexing will not begin until 2004.

9. The 1996 federal budget provides an indefinite carry forward of unused RRSP contribution room.

10. As contributions to these plans must cease at age 71, a large number of taxpayers in this broad age group are not allowed to contribute.

11. This table shows effective tax rates for broad types of investment income only. Effective tax rates on specific assets that receive special tax treatment — such as flow-through shares, certain limited partnerships, and labour venture funds — would be lower (or even negative).

12. At the time of the conference we do not have 1993 data on owner-occupied housing.
13. This figure is approximate, in that some mortgage debt finances rental housing owned by unincorporated businesses.
14. The exception is where mortgage debt is increased to finance taxable investments or a business.
15. At age 71, RRSPs must be converted into a Registered Income Fund (RIF) or an annuity; otherwise the full amount is taxable.
16. The argument suggested by Ragan is that individuals holding both RRSPs and other taxable assets may reduce savings with an increase in RRSP contribution limits. If individuals increase RRSP contributions, future taxable income will rise, thereby increasing future tax rates relative to the current period. When the future tax rate is higher than the current rate, savings may be discouraged since the effective tax rate on savings increases with a higher contribution limit. This argument is predicated on three assumptions that may not be consistent with empirical data. First, it assumes that non-RRSP assets are taxable — clearly this is not true for some assets like housing. Otherwise, individuals could average tax rates over time. Second, the argument is based on a progressive rate schedule — with clawbacks, progressivity cannot be assumed. Third, the Ragan argument is based on a simple lifecycle model that predicts that individuals would oversave by shifting so much of their income to the future so that retirement income is greater than current income. It is not clear that the simple lifecycle model characterizes savings behaviour well since precautionary and bequest motives for savings have been shown to be important for explaining savings behaviour. The precautionary motive is particularly important since the RRSP and RPP systems may share risks better than the regular income tax as discussed above.
17. The exclusion of capital gains on principal residences and the absence of income tax on imputed rent prevent taxation of these assets. The $500K deduction for capital gains on farms and small businesses represents a partial exclusion of these assets from tax — partial in that current income is subject to tax.
18. The age 71 limit should also be reexamined as life expectancy and seniors' health improve.

## REFERENCES

Ando, A. and F. Modigliani (1963), "The 'Life Cycle' Hypothesis of Saving: Aggregate Implications and Tests," *American Economic Review,* 53:55-84.

Atkinson, A. and J. Stiglitz (1980), *Lectures on Public Economics*, London: McGraw-Hill.

Auerbach, A. and L. Kotlikoff (1987), *Dynamic Fiscal Policy*, Cambridge: Cambridge University Press.

Bradford, D. (1986), *Untangling the Income Tax*, Cambridge, MA: Harvard University Press.

Davies, J., F. St. Hilaire and J. Whalley (1984), "Some Calculations of Lifetime Tax Incidence," *American Economic Review*, 74 (September):63349.

Deaton, A. (1989), "Saving in Developing Countries: Theory and Review," *Proceedings of the World Bank Annual Conference on Development Economics*, Supplement to the *World Bank Economic Review*, 61-96.

Diamond, P. (1977), "A Framework for Social Security Analysis," *Journal of Public Economics*, 8:275-98.

Engen, E.M. and J. Gruber (1995), "Unemployment Insurance and Precautionary Saving," NBER Working Paper No. 5252, Cambridge, MA: National Bureau of Economic Research.

Feldstein, M. (1978), "The Welfare Cost of Capital Income Taxation," *Journal of Political Economy*, 86:S29-51.

Institute of Fiscal Studies (1978), *The Structure and Reform of Direct Taxation: A Report of a Committee Chaired by Professor James Meade*, London: Allen and Unwin.

Kaldor, N. (1955), *An Expenditure Tax*, London: Allen and Unwin.

Kotlikoff, L. And L. Summer (1981), "The Role of the Intergenerational Transfers in Aggregate Capital Accumulation," *Journal of Political Economy*, 89, 4:706-32.

Mintz, J.M. (1991), "The Role of Wealth Taxation in the Overall Tax System," *Canadian Public Policy*, 17, 3:248-63.

Ontario Fair Tax Commission (1993), *Fair Taxation in a Changing World: Report of the Ontario Fair Tax Commission*, Toronto: University of Toronto Press.

Ragan, C. (1994), "Progressive Income Taxes and the Substitution Effect of RRSPs," *Canadian Journal of Economics*, 27, 2:43-57.

Revenue Canada (1995), *Tax Statistics on Individuals, 1993 Tax Year*, Ottawa: Supply and Services Canada.

United States Treasury (1977), *Blueprints for Basic Tax Reform*, Washington, DC: Government Printing Office.

Vaillancourt, F. (1995), "The Financing and Pricing of WCBs in Canada: Existing Arrangements, Possible Changes," in *Chronic Stress: Workers' Compensation in the 1990s*, ed. J. Richards and W. Watson, Toronto: C.D. Howe Institute.

Yaari, M.E. (1964), "Uncertain Lifetime, Life Insurance and the Theory of the Consumer," *Review of Economic Studies*, 32:137-50.

# Comments

*James Davies*

This is a very fine paper. It sets our RRSP/RPP system in a broad tax policy context, approaching these elements of sheltered saving less as a component of the retirement income system, and more as an element of the Canadian tax system. These forms of sheltered saving, it is made clear, help to lend an important consumption tax aspect to our system. This approach makes evident why sheltered saving is controversial; we do not have a consensus in Canada after all that the ideal base for personal taxation is consumption. The paper also calls attention to the importance of the RRSP/RPP system as an offset to the high effective tax rates which apply to some other personal financial assets, in allowing averaging in the tax system, and in effecting risk-sharing between taxpayers and government.

In common with many public finance specialists of their generation, Mintz and Wilson see strong equity and efficiency attractions in the consumption tax approach. This approach requires the provision of two kinds of savings instruments: registered or "qualified" accounts, of which our RRSPs are an almost ideal example, and sheltered saving in "non-qualified" form. Contributions to "non-qualified" sheltered saving accounts are non-deductible, but returns are not taxed. There is no tax on withdrawals. The most important example in Canada is owner-occupied housing. Prior to the 1987 federal tax reform non-qualified sheltered saving in financial assets was also available via the $1,000 interest and dividend income deduction.

In the main, a reasonable outlook on Canada's RRSP/RPP system, I believe, is "It's not broken, so don't try to fix it." With the 1990 reforms our RRSP/RPP system is in good shape (although there is some need for fine-tuning, for example, in the treatment of defined benefit, RPPS, as the authors point out). The main task before us is to defend the integrity of the system in the face of onslaughts from those who regard deductions for RRSP/RPP contributions as an unnecessary sop to higher income groups. Often the best defence is a strong offence, and this is what Mintz and Wilson mount. They argue that contribution limits should, in fact, be raised — to 30 percent of earnings; that lifetime carry-forward of unused contribution room should be allowed; that the $500,00 lifetime capital gains exemption for farms and small businesses should be integrated with the RRSP/RPP system; and that more generous treatment for most defined benefit plans should be provided. I find this a very appealing set of recommendations, but it is certainly one that one should not endorse before satisfying one-self that it is attractive on both equity and efficiency grounds.

To begin with, there are two points which I think should be addressed in further development of the Mintz/Wilson proposals: (i) these proposals would reduce revenue in the short run, and some thought should be given to how that revenue loss would be made good, and (ii) in order to enact the full consumption tax scheme we need to restore some saving in non-qualified but sheltered financial assets. The easiest way to do this would be via a reinstituted interest income deduction. This deduction would have to be provided at more than the $1,000 level to provide equivalent protection to the former $1,000 deduction of the 1970s and 1980s, of course.

Thinking further about the central message of this paper, we should ask what we think about the efficiency argument in favour of this RRSP/RPP system. A full analysis of the welfare aspects of this system would have to look at both static and dynamic efficiency aspects. We may have no doubt that there are important dynamic efficiency gains from the additional saving, and consequent domestic capital formation which a full-blown RRSP/RPP system of the type proposed by Mintz and Wilson would create. But, suppose that such a system is politically infeasible. Then, the question arises, how large are the dynamic efficiency gains created by the *existing* RRSP/RPP system? If these are small, what defence do consumption tax advocates have against the critics who find the RRSP/RPP system an unacceptable benefit to middle- and upper-income groups (that is, aside from the response that there may be enough redistribution in Canada already)?

Standard lifecycle modelling would predict that in a system with an annual contribution limit many taxpayers will contribute at the limit. These taxpayers are provided with no saving incentive by the RRSP/RPP system *at the margin*. Could it be then, that the RRSP/RPP system does not in fact reduce savings distortions, and does not actually stimulate saving? In answering we have to take some care. Think first about the static deadweight loss. If your desired RRSP contribution is $14,501 and your contribution limit is $14,500 you face the full intertemporal distortion *at the margin*. However, the excess burden you face relative to an equal yield lump sum tax is trivial. Similarly, the amount saved is much greater than it would be under an equal present value yield income tax. So the mere fact that RRSP contributions are inframarginal does not mean that the system has no static or dynamic efficiency effects.

Other possible criticisms might attack the equity basis for the consumption tax approach. In particular, horizontal equity concerns might be raised. As Mintz and Wilson note, for example, some are concerned about the lack of taxation of gifts and bequests in Canada. I share that concern, since I lean towards an individual-based view of tax equity rather than to a dynastic view. However, as the authors note, taxing capital income is a very rough substitute for taxing gifts and bequests, since such a substantial portion of wealth in our society is accumulated over the lifecycle, rather than inherited.

A possible horizontal equity argument in favour of restrictions on RRSP/RPP contributions rests on the importance of liquidity or borrowing constraints. If two individuals have equal expected lifetime earnings in present value, but one currently has low earnings and very low consumption due to borrowing constraints, then he or she may be significantly worse off, and it could be argued that this effect needs to be taken into account in assigning tax burdens. (See Davies 1994.) How can we do this? To answer, note that the receipt of returns from liquid assets, for example, ordinary interest income, or accruing RRSP income, is a signal that one is not facing borrowing constraints. Davies (1994) shows that a capital income tax rate of 10-15 percent could be required, given our current payroll and income taxes, to provide more truly equal tax treatment of borrowing constrained and unconstrained taxpayers. Given estimates that place the fraction of borrowing constrained adults at about 20 percent of the population, this argument could provide some justification for stopping short of an increase in RRSP/RPP contribution limits to 30 percent. On the other hand, it could certainly be argued that if one-fifth of Canadians are borrowing constrained it would be appropriate to attack the root causes of that problem, which could lie in capital market imperfections, poor consumer education in personal finance, or excessive levels of taxation in the early stages of the lifecycle.

A final comment concerns the tax treatment of human capital. Mintz and Wilson note that some of the expenses of human capital formation, for example, tuition and other expenses of formal education, are not fully deductible. This tends to reduce the after-tax rate of return to investment in human capital. However, against this must be set the fact that the direct expenses of on-the-job training are fully deductible; that foregone earnings are the major cost of human capital formation and are automatically deductible; and finally that the direct costs of formal education are heavily subsidized on the expenditure side of the government's budget. Putting this all together, I would argue that human capital receives something very close to consumption tax treatment. (This is supported by calculations reported in Dupor *et al.* 1996.) Adding up then, we treat human capital, owner-occupied housing, RRSPs, and RPPs in Canada essentially on a consumption tax basis. In other words, by far the largest part of household assets are on a consumption tax basis, and the "typical" Canadian effectively faces a consumption tax world. I would argue that this has not happened by accident. Although our public debates are steeped in comprehensive income tax rhetoric, the revealed preference of Canadians seems to be for something much closer to the consumption tax approach.

## REFERENCES

Davies, J.B. (1994), "Equity and Tax Mix: Theoretical Perspectives," in *Issues in the Taxation of Individuals,* ed. A.M. Maslove, Toronto: University of Toronto Press.

Dupor, W., L. Lochner, C. Taber and M.B. Wittekind (1996), "Some Effects of Taxes on Schooling and Training," *American Economic Review* 86, (May):340-46.

# Part Three

## THE POLITICS OF POLICY REFORM

# CHAPTER EIGHT

# Recent Trends in Public Pension Reform: A Comparative View

*John Myles and Jill Quadagno*

## INTRODUCTION

Pension reform has been on the political agenda since the 1980s and significant changes have already been made in many countries. Although the specter of population aging often provides a background for these changes, reform has mainly been a response to current economic pressures resulting from slow economic growth, high rates of unemployment, and in many countries, rising deficits (OECD 1988, p. 102; Ploug and Kvist 1994, p. 16; General Accounting Office 1994).

Benefit cuts of various sorts have been the main order of the day although significant changes to improve old age provision have been made in several countries. Australia, for example, mandated employer pensions for all workers in 1992. Higher contribution rates (e.g., Denmark, Finland, France, Sweden, the United States) as well as benefit cuts have been part of the reform package in some countries.

There are several reasons that might motivate a comparative look at pension reform. One is to learn from the experience of others. Has someone else discovered the magic bullet to solve the long-term economic problems associated with population aging? We are sceptical of such a strategy, however. It is possible to identify the *intended* consequences of these reforms but virtually impossible to anticipate the actual and the unintended consequences that will only appear in the long run. This is because behavioural responses to benefit changes and future levels of major macroeconomic parameters (labour demand, interest rates, economic growth) are unknown.

Raising the retirement age, for example, will reduce the number of years during which benefits are paid, raise the number of years workers contribute to production through their labour, and reduce the number of years over which benefits are paid out. As Susan St. John (1993, p. 146) observes, however, raising the retirement age may require expansion of other public sector benefit programs. Costs may be shifted to early retirement programs or to disability and unemployment allowances. Nor does raising the retirement age automatically reduce the "burden" of supporting the elderly population by the young. Increasing the labour supply of older workers without a corresponding rise in labour demand reduces the number of jobs available to, and/or the wage levels of younger workers.

Cutting benefit levels reduces the contribution rate of future generations to the public pension system but the effects on the actual living standards of the young are unknown. Reducing *public* expenditures on the old may simply be an exercise in cost-shifting — to employer pensions, private investments, or intrafamily transfers. In all of these cases the "cost" of supporting the elderly population is borne by working age adults; only the form of payment differs.[1]

If there were a straightforward solution to the economic consequences of population aging, one might expect all countries to converge on it. In the absence of such a solution, we can think of the current round of pension reform as a set of national experiments that vary in form, content, and in their intended and unintended consequences. This hardly means that the pattern of reform is random, however. Nations do not conduct just any experiment as they retrench or rearrange their social budgets. Our review of pension reforms in the developed Western economies points to several identifiable patterns.

*The end of universality.* Universal flat rate benefits common to the Nordic and Anglo-Saxon countries (outside the US) are in decline. "Clawbacks" (to use Canadian terminology) from upper- and middle-income households have been implemented in Australia, Canada, Denmark, Finland, Holland, Iceland, Sweden, and New Zealand. Only Ireland, Japan, Norway, and the United Kingdom still provide universal flat rate benefits to all citizens who reach a specified age. "Need" is replacing "citizenship" as the criterion for eligibility.

*From defined benefits to defined contributions.* The pattern of change in earnings-related contributory schemes is in the opposite direction. Income testing weakens the link between contributions (or taxes) and benefits. In earnings-related schemes, the link between contributions and benefits is being tightened. The Europeans refer to this as a shift from a defined benefit to defined contribution model. They do not mean that pensions will now be funded. Rather, where the link between lifetime contributions and benefits has traditionally been weak, the linkage is being tightened. Traditional understandings of old age pensions as a "deferred wage" are being replaced by a savings model. "Workers," if you will, are being transformed into "savers." Italy and Sweden are the most notable examples but similar changes of a more modest nature can be observed in a variety of countries where the contribution/benefit linkage has been weak.

*Governments want people to work longer.* Efforts to raise the retirement age and reduce benefits for early retirees are widespread. In this respect, governments are working against markets. Since the 1970s, firms have been shedding older workers and the retirement age has been falling. Thus far, there is little evidence that legislative changes to public pension schemes have had much effect on this trend. The result, instead, is reduced benefits for early retirees.

The question is what determines the direction of change? Is there an identifiable patterned response, given the range of available options? In this paper, we argue that the direction of pension reform is conditioned by the institutional features of the existing system. Postwar public pension systems evolved from two distinct starting points. One form, associated with Beveridge, developed from a means-tested benefit for the aged poor and expanded into a universal flat benefit for citizens. The second associated with Bismarck was aimed at status preservation by providing income replacement for retired workers. In reviewing recent directions in pension reform, we conclude that the trend in countries with Bismarck social insurance systems is towards reinforcing the link between benefits and contributions, thus moving towards a defined contribution system. In contrast, in countries where the Beveridge model has been dominant, the shift has been away from universality and a return to "need," albeit more broadly defined, as the basis for determining eligibility for benefits.

## THE POLITICS OF RETRENCHMENT

Both the form and degree of change varies significantly among countries. As Pierson (1994) persuasively argues, conventional welfare state theory leaves us poorly equipped to understand this variation. "Conventional theory" is about the politics of welfare state expansion. The "politics of retrenchment" is rather different.

Pension reform is the result of a political process in which contending actors vie with each other to promote or resist change or to determine the form and amount of change. Who wins these debates, we argue, is heavily constrained by the institutional structure of the pre-existing pension system. The institutional features of pension systems create an opportunity structure for certain kinds of debates to take place and help determine who is likely to win them.

By "institutional structure" we mean two things. The first is the formal design of the pensions system including the financing mechanism, the method of determining benefits and the juridical basis on which pension entitlements are based. The second is the decision-making structure embedded in legislation that defines the political actors whose participation and consent is required to change current legislation. In Canada, for example, reform of the Canada Pension Plan requires the consent of two-thirds of the population representing two-thirds of the population and cannot unilaterally be decided by Ottawa. Corporatist decision-making institutions in place in many European countries require that consent be won from representatives of both labour and business to alter current practices.

Our attention in this paper is on the first component, the formal design of the pension system, turning briefly to a discussion of decision-making institutions in the conclusion. Our analysis draws heavily on the arguments developed by Pierson in this volume and elsewhere (Pierson 1994) concerning the "politics of retrenchment." Politicians seeking to restrain the growth of pension expenditures face a double challenge. First they require a rhetoric to legitimate not only cuts in general but also the distribution of those cuts. Whose benefits will be reduced and by how much? Second, they must cut in ways that minimize voter backlash. As Pierson points out, the politics of retrenchment is a politics of "blame avoidance." There is, as he observes, a profound difference between extending benefits to large numbers of people and taking those benefits away. The most likely reform is the one that alienates the smallest number of voters.

For these reasons, retrenchment is likely to be incremental in nature. Changes are made "at the margin" where, in the short run at least, they affect a small number of voters and leave the basic structure of the system more or less intact. In Canada, for example, the Conservatives failed miserably in their attempt to de-index Old Age Security (OAS) benefits for all elderly Canadians in 1985. They had little difficulty three years later, however, in "clawing back" OAS benefits from high-income seniors.

"Cutting at the margin," however, depends on where the "margin" is. There is more room to adjust the pension age in countries where workers are eligible for benefits at age 60 than at age 65 or 67. "Clawing back" benefits from high-income seniors, as we will see, is relatively easier in systems financed from general revenue than in systems where benefits are an "earned right" based on past contributions.

As Pierson notes (and as Murphy and Wolfson demonstrate in this volume) changes that appear small in the short run can have very large effects when accumulated over a long time period. But "changes at the margin" can also have large effects for two other reasons. First, a successful small change can set the stage for a subsequent new round of legislation that accelerates the change. The modest Canadian clawback of OAS benefits in 1988, for example, created a precedent for deeper cuts by subsequent governments. Second, small changes at the margin may introduce new principles for benefit eligibility and alter both the juridical basis for, and traditional understandings of, old age pensions.

## BEVERIDGE AND BISMARCK:
## THE INSTITUTIONAL DESIGN OF MODERN PENSION SYSTEMS

A useful starting point for understanding modern pension systems and the possibilities for reform is based on the points of departure from which they originated.

One group of countries, beginning with Denmark (1891) developed out of the poor law tradition, offering basic means-tested benefits to the elderly poor that were tax-financed from general revenue (Overbye 1994). Following Beveridge's lead after the World War II, means tests were relaxed and a universal flat benefit (or demogrant) was made to all citizens meeting specified age and residency requirements. This was the path followed by the Nordic countries (Denmark, Finland, Norway, Sweden), the Netherlands, and the Anglo-Saxon countries (Australia,[2] Canada, New Zealand, the UK) outside the United States.

The Beveridge countries do differ in forms of financing, however. In the UK, Ireland, Finland, Norway, Sweden, and the Netherlands, the basic benefit (or demogrant) is mainly financed from payroll contributions. Australia, Canada, Denmark, and New Zealand, in contrast, finance the basic benefit from general revenue.

The second line of development follows from the adoption of an earnings-related social insurance model in Bismarck's Germany (1889). Although those with higher earnings paid higher contributions and received higher benefits, the European understanding of the juridical basis of entitlement was not that of a retirement "savings" (or defined contribution) plan. Rather, old age pensions were understood as part of the compensation package for a lifetime of work, a "deferred wage."

The "Bismarck" countries generally include the United States and major nations of Continental Europe, including Austria, Belgium, France, Germany, Italy, and Spain.[3] Financing is based on contributions from a mix of employer-employee contributions and sometimes contributions from the state to finance non-employment based benefits (e.g., child drop-out provisions) and revenue shortfalls.

From the 1950s on, the Nordic countries plus Canada all added a second tier of earnings-related pensions to produce a Beveridge plus Bismarck model. The UK joined this group in 1975 (SERPS) but then partially abandoned it in the 1980s under Margaret Thatcher when "contracting-out" to private providers was encouraged (Daykin 1994). Australia (1992) followed a different path by making employer pensions mandatory. "Pure" Beveridge models remain only in Denmark, Ireland, the Netherlands, and New Zealand.[4]

Most countries also provide benefits based on a measure of need but their form differs in important ways. In the Beveridge (and Beveridge + Bismarck) nations, supplementary benefits are built on top of the universal flat benefit to provide what Palme (1990) calls a "basic security model" of income protection. In Canada, Denmark, the Netherlands, and New Zealand the supplement is tested against income (i.e., assets are excluded).[5] The result is a guaranteed minimum income. Finland, Norway, and Sweden use a "pension test," that is, the supplement is tested only against public pension income and the result is a guaranteed minimum pension.

In the Bismarck countries, means-tested benefits take the form of traditional social assistance based on a means test of both income and assets (and hence might be characterized as Elizabethan). They reach rather narrow sectors of the population and provide comparatively low benefits and hence are called "residual" in Palme's terms. Supplemental Security Income (SSI) in the US is an example.

## RIGHTS, RHETORIC AND AGENDA SETTING

When the issue of pension reform rises on the political agenda, say of the Cabinet, an initial question that must be resolved is what a pension "really" is or ought to be. Redesigning a public pension system hinges critically on prior assumptions concerning the juridical and moral basis on which the right to a pension is granted. For example, are old age pensions an earned right, an entitlement of citizenship, or an intergenerational transfer scheme?

Niemela and Salminen (1995) distinguish among three traditional bases on which the right to a pension has been justified: need (or social condition), citizenship, and employment. Each of these models contains both a juridical and technical calculus embedded within it: an understanding of the grounds on which a claim to a pension is justified, on the one hand, and on the other, an understanding of how a pension system ought to be designed.

Traditional social assistance programs designed in the poor law tradition were based on *social condition*, that is, indigence. Public provision was an act of charity and was stigmatized by a close examination of individual circumstances to distinguish the "deserving" from the "undeserving" poor. The transition towards a *citizenship* model of social protection — a universal right based on permanent residence — changed the criterion of indigence to that of membership in a national community. The rhetoric of charity was replaced by a rhetoric of social rights and is usually associated with the transition from the Elizabethan model of poor relief to the Beveridge model of universal flat benefits.[6]

As Niemela and Salminen point out, however, the social character of means testing also underwent a subtle transformation with the passage of time. Modern "means testing" for supplementary income-tested (Canada, New Zealand) or pension-tested (the Nordic countries) benefits for the elderly are granted to all individuals whose incomes/pensions fall below a specified level defined in legislation, not the result of a discretionary assessment of "need" or moral worthiness made by a public official or social worker. Moreover, programs of this sort acquired the character of a right to a social *transfer* paid for by the *tax* contributions of the community rather than a discretionary act of communal charity for the deserving poor.

In the Bismarck tradition, in contrast, the right to a pension is based on past employment. The underlying idea is that a pension is part of the compensation package — a deferred wage the individual has earned through a lifetime of hard work. Conceptions of equity and fairness are based on notions of status preservation: the retirement wage should enable the individual to maintain a standard of living similar to that achieved during the working years. Although those with higher earnings pay higher contributions, the notion that there should be a strict one-to-one relation between contributions and benefits is not an intrinsic part of the model. As with defined benefit plans in the private sector, the retirement wage — its terms and conditions — is negotiated at the bargaining table. How it is financed is the responsibility of the employer. This is why such great symbolic importance was traditionally attached to the notion that benefits should be financed by employer contributions even though economists would argue that both employer and employee contributions ultimately come out of the pay packet of the latter. Considerable redistribution can and does take place in both public and private sector defined benefit plans.

An alternative employment-based model rests on the premium principle in which notions of individual savings and self-help predominate. Benefits are paid on the basis of accumulated contributions plus estimated "returns." The technical and moral calculus that goes into determining pension claims is based on a strict correspondence between contributions and benefits. As in private sector "defined contribution" plans, benefits are determined by what one has put into the system.[7]

While the juridical and moral justifications regarding pension claims are usually reflected in the design of the system, the correspondence has never been exact. Legitimation of the German system has traditionally been based on the metaphor of a deferred wage, a reward for a lifetime of hard work. However, as we will see, the German model more closely approximates a defined contribution scheme than that of Italy, Sweden or even the US.

Conversely, American Social Security leaders have relied heavily on notions of personal savings (the defined contribution model) to legitimate a program in which the link between contributions and benefits is quite tenuous (Derthick 1979). Since the 1980s, critics of US Social Security have used the tax-transfer metaphor to justify proposals for redesigning the system on the basis of need (Quadagno 1996). Payroll deductions, it is argued, are taxes not contributions; benefits are "social transfers" made by the young to the old. Hence, it is claimed, there is little justification for paying benefits/transfers to high-income seniors and more should be done to help low-income seniors.

Palme's (1994) description of Swedish welfare-state debates indicates how all of these alternative policy discourses can jostle for attention at the same time, creating curious mixes of allies and enemies. The tax-transfer metaphor is used by the Conservatives who view current high levels of "taxation" as harmful for economic growth. They are joined by factions among the Social Democrats, the Centre Party (formerly the Agrarian Party) and the Left Party (formerly the Communist Party) who emphasize the basic security and redistributive, "transfer," side of the "tax-transfer" system. The Liberal Party advocates a closer link between contributions and benefits (a defined contribution model) while the unions generally favour the traditional earnings-based (defined benefit) system.

Since each of these metaphors contains within it not only a justificatory rhetoric for establishing pension claims but also an implicit model for the way in which public pensions should be designed (or redesigned), the "definition of the situation" can become real. The critical issue is who gets to "define the situation."

Our review of pension reforms in the OECD nations since the 1980s suggests the following. Among the Beveridge countries, the tax-transfer (needs-based) model has emerged as the dominant paradigm for pension reform with the result that the linkage between contributions and benefits is being weakened. This development represents both continuity ("path dependency") and change. The traditional "citizenship" model of universal flat-rate benefits is being abandoned in favour of programs based on an income or pension test. This is not a return to traditional (Elizabethan) poor law models but a shift to a modern version of testing more akin to the guaranteed income or negative income tax (NIT) model associated with Milton Friedman. The transition is "natural" or path-dependent especially in countries where citizenship entitlements were traditionally financed from general revenues ("taxes") and a weak association between benefits/transfers and contributions/taxes was recognized as an explicit part of the program design.

Conversely, reforms in the Bismarck countries have adhered strictly to an employment-based model. But here too there is change: the defined benefit/ earnings-replacement model is giving way to formulas that more closely approximate a defined contribution scheme. "Wage-earners," if you will, are being transformed into "savers."

Within each type, the amount of change is conditioned by pre-existing pension designs simply because some systems offer more room for change than others. Reform of the universal flat benefit is more dramatic in Sweden than in Finland because the flat benefit portion of the system offered much higher benefits. The shift of direction towards a defined contribution model is sharper (and more self-conscious) in Italy and Sweden than in Germany because the link between contributions and benefits in the German system has always been close relative to the other two nations.

## THE END OF CITIZENSHIP?
## MOVING FROM BEVERIDGE TO FRIEDMAN

A readily available *moral framework* for adjusting to "hard times" is the principle of need. The costs of restructuring should be borne by those most able to afford it and the weaker members of society should be protected. Benefits for high-income seniors should be reduced and the savings used to achieve a number of desirable social goals: cut deficits, raise investment, and improve benefits for low-income groups, whether old or young.

A needs-based rhetoric provides both a justificatory rhetoric and a model for pension reform. Cuts will be made by reducing or eliminating benefits for high-income families. Both the Concord Coalition in the United States and the Conservative Party in Canada have used the imagery of benefits going to "wealthy bankers" in their symbolic struggles to implement income testing for old age pensions.

Critics oppose such tests on the grounds that they undermine "the political support, the legitimacy, and ultimately the financing of Social Security" (Kingson 1994, p. 733) as well as the "broad, cross-class political coalitions that sustain and protect the policies" (Skocpol 1991, p. 63). The conventional critique of income testing in welfare state theory, however, is premised on an understanding of the politics of traditional social assistance programs in which needs-based tests exclude the majority and provide benefits to a small, powerless, minority — the "poor." Without support from the median voter, such programs are likely to erode with time.

There is nothing technical about income testing that requires this to be so, however, (see, e.g., the paper by Ken Battle in this volume). Income tests can take effect at the bottom, middle or top of the income distribution.[8] Historically, Australian labour supported means-tested social programs as a mechanism for excluding "the rich."[9] The political sustainability of programs that exclude "the rich" will depend on the size and electoral influence of those who remain in the program.

More important for our purposes is the viability of an income test as an expenditure reduction strategy that solves the problem of the politician seeking reelection. The challenge to the politician in pursuit of the median voter is to accurately gauge how far down the income distribution he/she can go with a test.

Here, politicians benefit from the flexibility provided by modern computer technology which allows a remarkable amount of fine-tuning in targeting benefits. The introduction of the income-tested Canadian Child Tax Benefit (CTB) which formally ended Canada's system of universal family allowances in 1992 provides an example. For families with incomes above $26,000 benefits are taxed back at a rate of 2.5 cents for every dollar in additional family income. As a result, the benefit only disappears when family income exceeds $70,981.

While the rhetoric of need and its related strategy for program redesign has its advocates in both the Bismarck and Beveridge nations, the only countries that have successfully implemented this strategy are those that have traditionally had well-developed Beveridge-type basic security systems.

Four countries — Australia, Canada, Denmark, and New Zealand — finance their basic security systems from general revenue and all four have abandoned the principle of universal flat benefits. After moving towards universality in the 1970s, Australia restored the assets test in 1985 (Shaver 1991). New Zealand introduced an income-tested clawback on its universal demogrant in 1985, renamed it the Guaranteed Retirement Income in 1989, and adopted a much harsher income test in 1992 (St. John 1993). Canada introduced a "clawback" on Old Age Security benefits for high-income earners in 1989 and is expected to deepen the income test in 1996. Denmark adopted an income test for the universal *folkspensionen* in 1994 (Plovsing 1994).

General revenue financing appears to facilitate the transition to a needs-based model since there is no clear link between an ear-marked "contribution" and the benefit received. Benefits are "social transfers" financed from "taxes" paid by the entire population. However, while general revenue financing appears to be a sufficient condition for implementation of more means testing, the Nordic example indicates it is not a necessary one.

In the postwar period, Finland, Norway, and Sweden introduced universal flat benefit pensions financed from payroll deductions. All three then subsequently added a second tier of very highly developed earnings-related pensions that, unlike Canada or the UK, made private retirement plans more or less redundant. However, all three also introduced *pension-tested* supplements for those who earned few or no earnings-related benefits, supplements that are analogous to Canada's Guaranteed Income Supplement.[10] As the earnings-related plans matured, the basic universal benefit has eroded, replaced with greater pension-testing (Overbye 1995, p. 20). In essence, as the Nordic countries have become more Bismarckian, the basic security elements have become increasingly selective.

The most dramatic example of this pattern is evident in the 1994 reform proposed in Sweden which essentially abolishes the universal National Pension benefit by introducing a "pension test" for the entire benefit.[11] Moreover, the guaranteed minimum will be indexed to prices while the revised contributory plan (see below) is indexed to wages implying that the aim is to reduce the minimum relative to average wages over the long run. Finland followed the Swedish path towards pension testing of the entire basic benefit in January 1996.[12] Iceland, in fact, led the way in this group, introducing a pension test in the 1970s.

Elsewhere, income testing of universal flat benefit financed from ear-marked payroll contributions has been more hesitant. A small, externally induced, shift towards greater means testing took place in the Netherlands in 1994. In 1987, the Netherlands added an income-tested "spouse allowance" equal to 30 percent of the social minimum to its universal flat benefit program. Because of the European Community's "Third Directive" on equal treatment of men and women, the 70/30 formula was changed to 50/50 in 1994, thus effectively raising the income-tested portion of the couple's basic pension from 30 to 50 percent (Groen 1994). Thus far Britain has not income-tested the basic benefit, but has substantially slowed its growth as a result of 1980 reforms that changed the indexing formula from the higher of wages or prices to a price-based index only (Pierson 1994, p. 59).

At first glance, the spread of income testing in the Beveridge countries might appear as a return to the "poor law" tradition (from Beveridge to Elizabeth). The analogy is misleading, however. Rather, the Beveridge countries could best be characterized as moving from Beveridge to Friedman, that is, towards a public system designed as negative income tax (NIT). New Zealand is now the exemplar of a pure NIT model and Denmark has begun to move in this direction. Australia combines a NIT-type design with mandatory employer pensions. Sweden has redesigned its basic security system along NIT (but pension-tested lines). Canada has moved in this direction and appears poised to move further.

Because of the interaction with earnings-related and contributory pensions (public or private), income testing of basic benefits may have a variety of consequences. For those affected by the test, income replacement rates (from basic + earnings-based pensions) will be lower in the future. Higher-income employees may well offset this reduction, however, by remaining longer in the workforce or with an increase in private retirement savings. We return to these issues in our conclusion.

The moral and juridical basis for pension claims has also changed from one based on citizenship to one based on need or, at least to a new mixture of the two. Henceforth, what is guaranteed to all citizens is not a pension but minimum guaranteed income conditioned by need.

To summarize, the tax-transfer, needs-based, model of public sector pensions is likely to enjoy most success in nations with Beveridge-type models, especially those financed from general revenue. As discussed in the following section, nations with highly developed Bismarck models face enormous difficulties moving in this direction. Instead of weakening the link between contributions/taxes and benefits/transfers, the pattern of reform in employment-based programs indicates a trend away from the deferred wage (defined benefit) model towards a defined contribution, premium-based, design and a tighter link between contributions and benefits.

## PENSION REFORM IN THE BISMARCK COUNTRIES

The tax-transfer approach to social pensions and the view that governments should increasingly confine their activity to the "basic security" function of old age pensions, as advocated by the World Bank (1994) or the Concord Coalition in the United States (Peterson 1994) is an extremely difficult one to pursue in the Bismarck countries where public employment-based pensions are well developed.

For the Bismarck countries to move in the direction advocated by the World Bank would require massive privatization of mature public sector schemes. Because public schemes are financed on a pay-as-you-go basis the transition to a private funded scheme produces a "double-payment" problem (Pierson 1994, p. 61). During the transition years employees must continue to pay into existing public schemes to finance current retirees while also making mandatory contributions to finance their own retirement in private schemes.[13]

The double-funding problem caused even employers to oppose the 1985 proposal of the Thatcher government to phase out SERPS. Because SERPS was still not mature, the government was able to pass legislation in 1986 encouraging new labour force entrants to "contract-out" of the public scheme. Britain, however, was a latecomer to the Bismarck model.[14] Program immaturity provided the Thatcher government with a "window of opportunity" that is not available to the majority of countries.

Wholesale or partial privatization of employment-based programs also threatens politicians with potentially enormous electoral costs. Employer pensions typically offer inferior benefits to well-developed public schemes and voters are well attuned to these differences (Pierson 1994). To encourage "contracting-out," for example, it was necessary for the British government to offer contributors a "bribe" in the form of an additional rebate of 2 percent of earnings for newly contracted-out employees.

Rather than adopt a needs-based model for old age provision, countries with well-developed employment-based systems appear to have chosen another route. Perhaps the most self-conscious expression of this change can be found in the official description of the Italian reform of 1995. The Italian Ministry of Labour and Social Welfare (1995, p. 5) describes the change as a shift from "il sistema retributivo" to "il sistema contributivo." Literally translated, this means a change from a benefit structure tied to previous earnings levels to a benefit structure tied to total lifetime contributions, a method to ensure that people get out of the system what they pay into it. In a similar vein, Swedish observers (Palme 1994) have characterized the 1994 reform of the Swedish employment-based pension as a change from a defined benefit (deferred wage) model to a defined contribution model.

To understand how a shift in the rhetorical basis for pension claims can reduce expenditures, it is useful to consider the elements that enter into traditional defined benefit programs (OECD 1988, p. 68). At the time of retirement, benefit determination can be conceptualized as a function of three variables: assessed earnings, the period of assessed contribution, and the accrual factor. The distinction between defined benefit contribution plans is a continuum, not a dichotomy. All three parameters can be adjusted to strengthen or weaken the relationship between total lifetime contributions and pension benefits.

The scope of what counts as assessed earnings varies considerably among countries. As in many countries, Germany has relied on average pensionable *career* earnings, Sweden on average pensionable earnings of the *best* 15 years, France on the best ten years, and Italy the average pensionable earnings of the *last* five years.

Shorter assessment periods weaken the relation between contribution and benefits and are redistributive towards employees with many years of low or zero earnings. Traditionally, the Swedish and Italian systems, for example, clearly favoured individuals with many years of low earnings (such as women) relative to the German system.

Once assessed earnings are established, the result is then multiplied by the assessment period. Shorter assessment periods favour individuals with fewer years of labour force participation. Forty years of contributions has been the most common assessment period but some countries have had more (45 years in Austria) and some less (traditionally 30 years in Sweden).

The final variable is the accrual factor, the percentage of assessed income that enters into the pension formula. In most countries, the accrual factor is between 1 and 2 percent of assessed earnings (OECD 1988, p. 68). For nations like Canada with a very low accrual factor (about 0.5 percent of annual earnings up to $25,000) and for the US (.66 for minimum wage earners, .41 for average wage earners and .23 for contribution ceiling earners) there is less room for downward adjustment.[15]

*After retirement*, benefit levels and the total cost of financing benefits until death are a function of the indexing formula applied to the initial benefit and the longevity of the beneficiary.

For countries with a relatively short period of assessed earnings, future benefits can be more closely linked to contributions by changing the formula bringing assessed earnings closer to lifetime earnings. In 1992, France changed its formula from the best ten to the best 25 years. In 1994, Sweden changed its formula from the best 15 years to lifetime earnings and Italy changed from last five years to lifetime earnings in 1995. More modestly, Finland has changed its formula from the last four to the last ten years.[16]

The Italian and Swedish reforms effectively collapse the distinction between "assessed earnings" and the "assessment period." Henceforth, total lifetime contributions will be multiplied by an accrual factor to determine benefits. The result is a sharp reduction in pension entitlements for workers with many years of low earnings and a few years of high earnings. In both cases, however, the change is muted by dropout provisions which credit periods out of the labour market for child-rearing Sweden (Italy), care of dependents (Sweden), or unemployment (Sweden).

In the more typical employment-based pension systems, both assessed earnings and the assessment period have traditionally been much closer to a lifetime of work for the average employee (e.g., 40 years). In effect, they are closer to a defined contribution model and so there is less room for adjustments of this sort (and hence less radical reforms). As a result, reforms tend to take the form of adjustments to the accrual rate, particularly in light of projected increases in life expectancy.

Expected increases in future life expectancy are a major factor affecting the ratio of benefits to contributions and many countries have taken steps to adjust initial benefit levels on these grounds. While the "packaging" of these reforms differ, the core of these reforms is similar. The US amendments of 1983 raised the "normal retirement age" from 65 to 67 to be phased in after the year 2000. What the increase in "normal retirement age" effectively means is a lower accrual rate for workers who retire before age 67.

Rather than raising the spectre of a higher "retirement age" the Italian and Swedish reformers simply lowered the accrual rate for those who retire "early." In Sweden, the accrual rate at retirement will be indexed to the average life expectancy of the retiree's cohort. As life expectancy rises, the accrual rate will fall, requiring more years in the labour force to obtain benefits equal to those of earlier cohorts.

Steps to encourage later retirement are a common element of reform legislation throughout the OECD countries. Sweden abolished the upper age limit on the contribution period used to assess benefits and from 1997 the right to carry on working until age 67 will become law. Raising actual retirement ages was a major goal of the Italian reform. Under the previous legislation many workers were able to retire on a full pension in their early fifties. Henceforth, the earliest retirement age for a pension will be 57 and accrual rates will rise sharply between age 57 and 65 to encourage continued labour force participation. However, a slightly higher accrual rate will be applied to early retirees employed in physically demanding occupations (*lavori usuranti*). Under the pressure of equal rights legislation in the European Community, women's retirement ages are being harmonized with those of men⁻ in countries where the traditional retirement age for women has been lower (e.g., Germany).

Sweden has taken the additional step of allocating 2 percentage points of the 18.5 percent contribution rate into a funded "premium reserve" account that will pay benefits on the basis of the invested capital and the yield on this capital. The result is a small shift away from "pay-as-you-go" towards partial funding. The 1996 report from the US Social Security Advisory Committee is expected to propose a similar strategy.[17]

Since the 1970s, governments have responded to two unexpected developments that affect the consequences of indexing provisions. The first was a tendency during the seventies, for prices to rise faster than wages. As a result, pensioners incomes rose faster than those of workers. Second, as taxes and contribution rates rose as a percentage of earnings, there was a growing gap between gross and net earnings in the working age population.

The response in a number of countries has been to adjust indexing provisions to track real growth in the economy and/or the real wages of the working population. The main savings from the 1992 German reforms come from changing the indexing formula for benefits from gross to net (after tax) wages (Hinrichs 1993). Japan also adopted this practice in 1994 (Takayama 1995). Before retirement, Swedish contributions will be indexed to real wage growth (nominal wage growth minus inflation) so that a decline in real wages also leads to a decline in purchasing power. Italian contributions will be indexed to real GDP (nominal GDP minus inflation) of the past five years.

As a strategy, invoking the rhetoric of the defined contribution model to legitimate cost-saving legislative changes is constrained by pre-existing legislation. Sweden and Italy could make more "radical reforms" than Germany because of the relatively loose connection between lifetime contributions and benefits. In Germany, by contrast, the link between contributions and benefits has always been very close and the room for reform of the Italian/Swedish variety very limited.

## IMPLICATIONS FOR THE FUTURE

As we emphasized at the beginning of our paper, extrapolating the implications of these policy reforms is a hazardous exercise because the consequences depend critically on the behavioural responses of individuals and firms and on unknown future values of major macroeconomic parameters. Nevertheless it is possible to anticipate likely tensions in future policy debates.

Efforts to increase the normal retirement age is now a relatively common response to rising pension costs and greater longevity. Thus far increases have been modest in countries where the normal retirement age has been 65 or older and more dramatic where the pensionable age was age 60 or younger (e.g., Italy). Whether this raises labour force participation or simply reduces benefits for those who retire early (or both) remains to be seen. Some of the savings, however, will be spurious to the extent that the result is "cost-shifting" to disability and unemployment benefits, or employer plans for early retirement. An increase in the labour supply of older workers may also exacerbate downward pressure on employment and/or wages among younger workers.

The major challenge in the "pure" Beveridge countries is meeting the income security needs of average wage-earners. Mandated employer pensions and/or strong unions appear to be meeting this demand in Australia, Denmark, and the Netherlands. Maturation of these plans will reduce demand for means-tested public benefits but tax revenues will also decline because of tax deductions on contributions and accumulated assets. As in the Nordic countries, maturation of these earnings-related plans may also exert downward pressure on basic security benefits. As employer-based plans grow in significance, one can anticipate that pension politics will focus on regulatory issues and capital-labour disputes over the level and quality of these benefits.

New Zealand is an extreme case where the public sector only provides income-tested basic security, private coverage is low, and where there are no tax subsidies for pension contributions or savings.[18] There, the politics of income security for average earners will dominate the future agenda.

Although Canada has followed the Nordic path of income testing the basic benefit the implications are rather different. Traditional replacement rates for an average worker in the Nordic countries were quite high (80 percent in Sweden). Income testing of the basic benefit (and other reforms) will result in a substantial reduction but replacement rates will stabilize at much higher levels than now exist in the Canadian system. Starting from a much lower base (about 40 percent replacement), the decline in earnings replacement that results from the OAS "clawback" over time is more serious (see the paper by Murphy and Wolfson in this volume). This development is exacerbated by the sharp decline in earnings and private pension coverage among new labour market entrants in recent years. As a result, like New Zealand, the politics of income security for average earners will dominate Canadian debates well into the future.

In the Nordic countries (Finland, Norway, Sweden), basic security benefits and replacement rates for average earners have traditionally been among the highest in the world (Kangas and Palme 1989). The main result of the Swedish reforms will be to lower replacement rates for average- and upper-income earners. The shift to a defined contribution model will be partially mitigated by provisions to credit periods of childrearing, unemployment, and illness. Since the wage gap between men and women is comparatively small in Sweden the obvious gender implications will be more muted there than would similar reforms in other countries. Nevertheless, high rates of part-time work among Swedish women mean the reforms will hardly be gender neutral. What remains to be seen is whether lower replacement rates will also stimulate expansion of private pensions.

A well-developed Bismarck model (as in Germany) works well where there is high and more or less full employment and where earnings inequality is low. Most people are earning entitlements most of the time. These favourable conditions prevailed in Europe until recently. High unemployment, however, means a growing share of the population is excluded from the social insurance system for extended periods of time. The result is what the French refer to as "les exclus" or elsewhere in Europe as the "A team and the B team." Consequently, countries that lack a strong basic security system face a possible prospect of moving in the direction of the United States where rates of low income among the elderly are exceptionally high (Smeeding, Torrey and Rainwater 1993), especially among single elderly women. The consequences of rising unemployment is avoided in Germany and Sweden since spells on unemployment insurance are credited to the pension account.

Among the countries with strong Bismarck systems, France shows some tendency of enhancing basic security benefits (Walker 1993; Bonoli and Palier 1995). Old age minimums were raised substantially in 1981. In 1990, a new tax (*Contribution sociale generalisée*) was introduced that adds general revenue financing to the social security system for the first time and in 1988 the RMI, a sort of guaranteed income, was added. Spain introduced a guaranteed minimum non-contributory pension in 1991 (Walker 1993, p. 54).

Greater reliance on funded pension schemes (employer pensions or partially funded public schemes) in some countries also suggest a new set of political debates in the next century since funded plans are vulnerable to downturns in the economy and, in the case of employer plans, to bankruptcies and mergers (Ghilarducci 1992). If the government then picks up the cost of market failure, as advocated by the World Bank (1994, p. 202) the expenses are shifted back to the public sector (Schulz 1994).

More speculatively, perhaps, are the possible political ramifications of Robert Brown's (1995) projections for equity markets and inflation rates as the babyboom begins to liquidate its assets after 2010. The negative impact on equity values will suddenly make funded pensions look like a "bad buy," particularly in light of the expected increase in inflation that will result from a changing ratio of producers to consumers. Under these conditions, governments may be faced with relearning the lessons of an earlier generation in Europe and the reasons why pre-funding was abandoned in favour of the pay-as-you-go design.

CONCLUSION

Pension reform became part of the political agenda during the 1980s. Many countries have already introduced significant changes and more changes will doubt-lessly follow in the 1990s. Our principle claim is that thus far the type and extent of reform has been largely dictated by the possibilities inherent in the design of the pension regimes put in place from the 1950s through the 1970s in the advanced capitalist democracies. Large and well-developed employment-based schemes have been trimmed by reinforcing links between contributions and benefits. There was room for change in the Swedish and Italian models because of the more tenuous link between contributions and benefits. Sweden and Italy, if you will, moved closer to Germany. Nowhere, however, have such programs been rationalized along the lines proposed by the World Bank (1994), which has advocated a three-tier arrangement for old age security based on a basic means-tested public program, a mandatory, privately managed savings scheme, and voluntary saving.

Where Beveridge-type basic security programs financed from general revenues are the only (New Zealand, Australia, Denmark) or major (Canada) source of old age pensions, rationalization has taken the form of greater income testing that weakens the linkage between benefits and contributions.

It is important to recognize the theoretical and empirical limits of our account, however. The earliest theories of welfare state development emphasized the effect of economic growth, to the exclusion of politics (Wilensky 1975). Our review of recent pension reform developments shares with the "logic of industrialism" thesis a monocausal explanation in the following sense: we emphasize the effect of declining economic growth and fiscal constraint as factors leading nations to converge in the general direction of cost-containment measures aimed at limiting future growth in public expenditures. Thus, we imply that this downward drifting trend line in the quality, generosity, and coverage of public entitlements is common among all countries, irrespective of partisan ideologies or the balance of political forces. As Stephens, Huber and Ray (1994) demonstrate, there is some evidence in favour of such a view. They show that the partisan effects (e.g., control of government by left wing parties) so evident and robust in models that account for the period of welfare state expansion, drop to insignificance in models estimated for the period since 1980. The implication is not that traditional political cleavages of left and right have disappeared (see George, Taylor-Gooby and Bonoli 1995). Rather, the internationalization of trade, and of financial, currency and capital markets, greatly restrict the range of choices open to national governments regardless of partisan preferences.

Although monocausal arguments of this sort were helpful in accounting for the trend line during the era of expansion, they proved much less useful for explaining the variations around the trend line (Pierson 1995). In evaluating recent efforts at pension reform, we must also be attuned to explaining variations. The critical question is whether there are, for example, liberal, conservative, and social democratic variants of retrenchment in the same way that there were liberal, conservative and social democratic variants of expansion (see Esping-Andersen 1990).

Part of our difficulty comes from the fact that we are in the midst of a process that is still unfolding. It is premature to begin developing *general* models to explain outcomes simply because the final outcomes of the process do not yet exist. Analytically, our position is much like that of welfare state analysts in the early 1960s. At that time, the process of welfare state expansion was already underway in some countries and scarcely begun in others. The *explanandum* of the past two decades of welfare state research — the large cross-national differences in levels and types of spending evident by the mid-seventies — were only apparent in embryo.

A related difficulty is the manner in which the *explanandum* should be theorized. Three possibilities exist. One is that we are observing a common pattern of "retrenchment," a withering away of the old welfare state. A second is that we are simply observing efforts to stabilize existing systems in public provision. Changes in the indexing formula from gross to net wages are of this sort. Third, we may be observing a case of restructuring, where the welfare state is reorganized to accomplish new and different goals. Changes of this sort may reflect the emergence of new economic risks (e.g., among the young), or changing family forms (e.g., the rise of two-earner households). The 1992 pension reforms in Germany, for example, were followed in 1994 by the introduction of long-term care insurance. A reduction in retirement income was partially offset by an increase in public services for a population that will need more such services precisely because of their longevity.

If we turn to the right-hand side of the equation — the *explanans* — the problems are equally challenging. Apart from the formal design of the pension system, there are political actors who engage the process and try to influence it. Pierson (1995) argues that the main actors who shaped the years of expansion — unions and left wing parties — are no longer so central for understanding of welfare state politics. Welfare state cutbacks, he concludes, have thus far been more moderate than the precipitous decline in labour strength and there appears to be little correlation between "left power" and the magnitude of retrenchment.

This is in part because interest groups created by welfare state programs (e.g., old age lobbies) have risen in importance, muting the significance of traditional actors involved during the period of expansion.

Pierson's neo-institutionalist argument is important in highlighting the way in which past policies affect the current distribution of political resources and structure the organization of interest group networks. But even on its own terms, the argument leads to the conclusion that classes will continue to matter in explaining cross-national differences in the restructuring process simply because of differences in the way classes have been structured into the policy-setting process across countries. The corporatist social security schemes directly administered by representatives of labour and capital — not government — build class into the institutional structure of decision making in a way not found in the "pluralist" democracies. France, as recent events attest, is not the United States. The fall of the Berlusconi government in Italy was a result of its attempt to bypass the process of neo-corporatist consensus building. In contrast, the subsequent Dini government succeeded with a pension reform package because it incorporated the social partners (Esping-Andersen, in press). Australian labour was incorporated into the restructuring process, while New Zealand labour was not. Greater targeting of benefits was a key strategy of reform in both countries. However, Australian workers got both a restoration of medicare and mandatory employer pensions as social wage offsets to wage accord agreements to slow the pace of wage increases (Castles and Shirley 1995, p. 14).

If we were to suggest a leading hypothesis to guide future welfare state research it would be this. The main division among nations is between those with "democratic corporatist" political institutions and those that do not ("pluralist" democracies). In the former, party politics are organized along class lines and political bargaining takes place among peak associations representing workers, employers, and the state. Centralized institutions create conditions for consensus building and a search for non-zero-sum compromise among competing interests (Esping-Andersen 1995). In contrast, decentralized, pluralist political systems, as in the US, create political competition among numerous fragmented groups whose influence on the political process reflects their numbers, financial resources, and degree of mobilization. The result is usually zero-sum trade-offs reflecting the power resources of the competing groups.[19] The argument is less about classes per se than about the way encompassing institutions that incorporate broad sectors of the population force decisionmakers to internalize negative side-effects of their actions (Esping Andersen 1995).[20] In the United States, old age lobbies lobby for the elderly and child lobbies promote the interests of children. As Heclo (1988, p. 386) observes for Americans, "Thinking about age cohorts as a distributional problem through stages of one life that we all share, seems distinctly foreign." In the absence of the more inclusive, corporatist, models found elsewhere, creating consensus and finding non-zero-sum solutions is difficult.

The most fruitful direction for understanding pension reform appears to be in the analysis of the structure of the existing system and in the political processes involved. Structure, defined broadly, includes both the institutional design and the decision-making procedures inherent in pension programs. Process includes the political actors mobilized and the models involved in agenda setting. The basic dichotomy laid out here between Bismarck- and Beveridge-type systems is not an end point but a take-off for more detailed appraisal of variations around the model.

## NOTES

Special thanks to Karl Hinrichs, Olli Kangas, Jon Kvist, Ted Marmor, Einar Overbye, Jim Schulz and Paola Zanon for their comments and corrections on previous versions of this paper.

1.  A common fallacy is to assume that reducing *public* costs also reduces the *total* costs of supporting the retired. Shifting emphasis from public to private pensions, however, simply moves the costs from one part of the economy to another. Rather than financing the future elderly with higher taxes and contributions, they will be supported by rising dividends paid into the funds on which private pensions depend. In either case the share of national income going to the elderly rises. Only if the shift results in higher economic growth does the "burden" on future generations decline.

2.  Australia differs from the other countries in that pensions were traditionally means-tested. However, they are means-tested largely at the top of the wealth and income distribution. In 1986 for example, 75 percent of couples and 91 percent of single females were receiving benefits (Shaver 1995, p. 18).

3.  The United States is distinct in that some "basic security" features are incorporated into the earnings-based Social Security plan. Two of these are especially important: a 50 percent supplement for dependent spouses and an accrual formula that provides higher benefits relative to contributions for low-wage earners than to high-wage earners.

4.  Among these countries, coverage by employer plans is highly developed in Denmark and the Netherlands. After failing to win a national earnings-related pension scheme, Danish unions took matters into their own hands in the late 1980s and began to negotiate separate plans with their employers. The result was a dramatic expansion in coverage between 1989 and 1991 (Overbye 1995, p. 15). By 1993, approximately 70 percent of Danish employees were covered (Hippe and Pedersen 1995). Occupational plans cover approximately 50 percent of the labour force in Ireland and 22 percent in New Zealand.

5.  Australia also tests against assets but asset exemptions are such that the test converges on an income test for most people. See note 2

6.  As Alan Zeesman has pointed out to us, the shift from means testing to universality was not necessarily in a new ethos of citizenship. Rather, in the early years following the Second World War, old age was judged to be a rough if ready proxy for indigence.

Nevertheless, *post facto*, the juridical basis for entitlement changed from need to citizenship and moral rhetoric followed suit.

7. In the Anglo-Saxon countries, the term "defined contribution" is usually applied to fully funded private sector plans. Throughout the paper we will use the term "defined contribution" to refer to the technical calculus that goes into determining benefit levels and the moral justification for pension claims irrespective of the funding mechanism. Debates over Social Security in the United States, for example, are dominated by discussions of the "windfall gains" of the first generation of beneficiaries and by calculations to determine whether the current generation of workers will "get back" what they pay into the system. In effect, a defined benefit plan is being evaluated against the standards of a defined contribution plan. In the private sector, defined benefit plans also "distort" the relation between contributions and benefits.

8. Even wealth tests can be adjusted, through exemptions, so that they have little impact on the majority of the population. The Australian asset test for old age pensions is an example.

9. Australian pensions are subject to both an income and a wealth test but in 1986 75 percent of couples and 91 percent of single females received benefits (Shaver 1995, p. 18).

10. Pension testing is a variant of income testing. Pension supplements are "tested" only in relation to earned pension entitlements, not all income. However, since most Nordic retirees receive most of their income from the public pension system and have relatively little private income the results are similar to an income test.

11. For an English language summary of the Swedish reforms, see Sweden. Ministry of Health and Social Affairs (1994).

12. Protected by revenues from North Sea oil, Norway has thus far been comparatively immune to the wave of pension reform.

13. It could also be argued that means testing of Beveridge flat-rate benefits also creates a double-payment problem. Those affected by the test will have to save more to maintain traditional replacement rates while continuing to finance the income-tested program. In systems financed through general revenue, however, the double-payment problem is less visible since "contributors" are generally unable to distinguish the taxes paid to finance old age benefits from those paid for things like highways or schools.

14. SERPS legislation was passed in 1975 and only took effect in 1978. The program was not scheduled to mature until 1998.

15. The variable accrual factor in the US system is clearly a non-insurance-like, redistributive, feature of the system that provides higher "returns" to low-income than high-income earners, a sort of hidden means test. Advocates of means testing in the US have floated proposals to increase means testing by further adjusting the "bend points."

16. Olli Kangas, personal communication.

17. Similar legislation was actually introduced in the US Senate in 1995. The Personal Investment Plan Act would allow workers the option of diverting two percent of their payroll deductions to their own personal investment plans (United States Senate 1995).

18. New Zealand is unique in taxing contributions and savings but exempting benefits paid by private plans.

19. Especially relevant in this regard is Pampel's (1994) study showing that there is an intergenerational trade-off between old and young in the pluralist democracies that does not appear in countries with neo-corporatist, consensus building, structures.
20. For a general discussion of "encompassing organizations" see Olson (1982: 47-53; 89-92)

## REFERENCES

Bonoli, G. and B. Palier (1995), "Redefining Social Policy in France: From Bismarck to Beveridge," presented at the Social Policy Association annual conference, 18-21 July .

Brown, R.L. (1995), "A Demographer's Review of the Assumptions Underlying the OASDI Trustee's Report," presented at the Annual Conference of the National Academy of Social Insurance, Washington, 25-26 January.

Castles, F. and I. Shirley (1995), "Labour and Social Policy: Gravediggers and Refurbishers of the Welfare State," presented at the meetings of the International Sociological Association, Research Committee 19, Pavia, Italy.

Daykin, C. (1994), "Occupational Pension Provision in the United Kingdom," paper presented at the Pension Research Council Symposium, "Security Employer-Based Pensions: An International Perspective," Wharton School, University of Pennsylvania.

Derthick, M. (1979), *Policy Making For Social Security*, Washington, DC: The Brookings Institution.

Esping-Andersen, G. (1990), *The Three Worlds of Welfare Capitalism*, Princeton, NJ: Princeton University Press.

_____, ed. (In Press), "Positive-Sum Solutions in a World of Trade-Offs?" in *Transforming the Welfare State*, London: Sage.

General Accounting Office (1994), *Deficit Reduction: Experiences of Other Nations,* Washington, DC: US Government Printing Office.

George, V., P. Taylor-Gooby and G. Bonoli (1995), *Squaring the Welfare Circle: The Political Limits to Growth in European Welfare States*, Canterbury: University of Kent.

Ghilarducci, T. (1992), *Labor's Capital: The Economic and Politics of Private Pensions,* Cambridge: MIT Press.

Groen, J. (1994), "The Netherlands: Recent Trends in Cash Benefits," in *Recent Trends in Cash Benefits in Europe*, ed. N. Ploug and J. Kvist, Copenhagen: Danish National Institute of Social Research.

Heclo, H. (1988), "Generational Politics," in *The Vulnerable*, ed. J. Palmer, T. Smeeding and B. Torrey, Washington, DC: The Urban Institute.

Hinrichs, K. (1993), *Public Pensions and Demographic Change: Generational Equity in the United States and Germany*, Bremen: Zentrum fur Sozialpolitik.

Hippe, J. and A. Pedersen (1995), "The Growth of Private Pensions in Two Scandinavian Welfare States. A Comparison of Denmark and Norway," presented at the Enterprise and Welfare State Project Workshop, Vienna.

Italy. Ministero del Lavoro e della Providenza Sociale (1995), *La Riforma delle Pensioni: Una Guida per Capire le Nuove Norme*. Rome: Department of Information.

Kangas, O. and J. Palme (1989), *Public and Private Pensions: The Scandinavian Countries in a Comparative Perspective*, Stockholm: Institute for Social Research.

Kingson, E. (1994), "Testing the Boundaries of Universality," *The Gerontologist,* 34(6):733-40.

Niemela, H. and K. Salminen (1995), *How to Define a Pension Scheme*, Helsinki: The Social Insurance Institution.

Olson, M. (1982), *The Rise and Decline of Nations*, New Haven: Yale University Press.

Organisation for Economic Cooperation and Development (1988), *Reforming Public Pensions*, Paris: OECD.

Overbye, E. (1994), "Convergence in Policy Outcomes: Social Security Systems in Perspective," *Journal of Public Policy*, 14(2):147-74.

———— (1995), "Different Countries on a Similar Path: Comparing Pension Politics in Scandinavia and Australia," Oslo: Institute of Applied Social Research.

Palme, J. (1990), *Pension Rights in Welfare Capitalism: The Development of Old-Age Pensions in 18 OECD Countries, 1930-1985*, Stockholm: Swedish Institute for Social Research.

———— (1994), "Recent Developments in Income Transfer Systems in Sweden," in *Recent Trends in Cash Benefits in Europe*, ed. N. Ploug and J. Kvist, Copenhagen: Danish National Institute of Social Research.

Peterson, P. (1994), *Facing Up: How to Rescue the Economy from Crushing Debt and Restore the American Dream,* New York: Simon and Schuster.

Pierson, P. (1994), *Dismantling the Welfare State? Reagan, Thatcher and the Politics of Retrenchment*, Cambridge: Cambridge University Press.

———— (1995), *The New Politics of the Welfare State*, Bremen: Zentrum fur Sozialpolitik.

Ploug, N. and J. Kvist, eds. (1994), *Recent Trends in Cash Benefits in Europe*, Copenhagen: Danish National Institute of Social Research.

Plovsing, J. (1994), "Social Security in Denmark: Renewal of the Welfare State," in *Recent Trends in Cash Benefits in Europe*, ed. N. Ploug and J. Kvist, Copenhagen: Danish National Institute of Social Research.

Quadagno, J. (1996), "Social Security and the Myth of the Entitlement Crisis," *The Gerontologist*.

St. John, S. (1993), "Income Support for an Ageing Society," in *New Zealand's Ageing Society*, ed. P. Koopman-Boyden, Wellington: Daphne Brasell.

Schulz, J. (1994), *The Economics of Aging*, Dover, MA: Auburn House.

Shaver, S. (1991), "'Considerations of Mere Logic': The Australian Age Pension and the Politics of Means Testing," in *States, Labor Markets and the Future of Old-Age Policy*, ed. J. Myles and J. Quadagno, Philadelphia: Temple University Press.

———— (1995), *Universality and Selectivity in Income Support: A Comparative Study in Social Citizenship*, Sydney: Social Policy Research Centre.

Skocpol, T. (1991), "Targeting Within Universalism: Politically Viable Policies to Combat Poverty in the United States," in *The Urban Underclass,* ed. C. Jencks and P.E. Peterson, Washington, DC: The Brookings Institution.

Smeeding, T., B. Torrey and L. Rainwater (1993), "Going to Extremes: An International Perspective on the Economic Status of the U.S. Aged," Working Paper No. 87, Luxembourg: Luxembourg Income Study.

Sweden. Ministry of Health and Social Affairs (1994), *Pension Reform in Sweden: A Short Summary,* Stockholm: Ministry of Health and Social Affairs.

Stephens, J., E. Huber and L. Ray (1994), "The Welfare State in Hard Times," presented to the conference on Politics and Political Economy of Contemporary Capitalism, University of North Carolina, Chapel Hill, 9-11 September.

Takayama, N. (1995), "The 1994 Reform Bill for Public Pensions in Japan: Its Main Content and Related Discussion," *International Social Security Review*, 48(1):45-65.

United States Senate (1995), "Kerrey, Simpson Introduce Sweeping Reform to Strengthen Retirement Entitlements, Renew National Savings Base," *News Release*, Washington, DC: US Senate, 18May.

Walker, A. (1993), "Living Standards and Way of Life," in *Older People in Europe: Social and Economic Policies*, ed. A. Walker, J. Alber and A.-M. Guillemard, Brussels: Commission of the European Communities.

Wilensky, H. (1975), *The Welfare State and Equality,* Berkeley: University of California Press.

World Bank (1994), *Averting the Old Age Crisis,* Oxford: Oxford University Press.

# CHAPTER NINE

# The Politics of Pension Reform

*Paul Pierson*

## INTRODUCTION

Even those convinced that government has a central role to play in providing economic security for the elderly must acknowledge that public pension systems are facing considerable problems in all the advanced industrial countries. Demographic changes will increase the pressures in coming years, and higher health-care costs associated with population aging will exacerbate fiscal strains. There is considerable cross-national variation in the magnitude of these pressures, but they will be formidable everywhere (OECD 1995).

The political tensions already appearing in many countries suggest just how daunting these problems are likely to become. Governments wrestle with substantial budget deficits and confront fiercely-contested trade-offs between taxes and spending. So far, the "crisis of the welfare state" generally has been met as much or more by tax increases as by spending cuts. There are, however, limits to such a strategy. Enhanced capital mobility is increasingly cited as a constraint on government's capacity to tax. Whatever the economic limits to tax levels may be, the political constraints are becoming apparent in many countries.

Problems of fiscal management are thus already difficult and are virtually certain to get worse. Given the prominence of public pensions in current and future budget projections, they will undoubtedly be a central target for savings. One can, and should, point to the major successes of public pension systems. The expansion of retirement programs and dramatic declines in poverty among the elderly have gone hand in hand. One should also recognize that many seeking to "rescue" pension systems are interested in no such thing, and are eager to exaggerate the extent of the problem to mobilize support for radical initiatives. The problems, however, remain very real. The question is not whether restrictive adjustments in pension systems will occur. Rather, it is whether reforms will take place in a timely manner so that individuals can make appropriate adjustments, in ways that both protect the most vulnerable and facilitate growth, and in ways that do not generate needless anxiety and fuel already high levels of public alienation from the political process.

Because efforts to place public pension systems on a more secure financial footing are inevitable, it is crucial to understand the political issues associated with such initiatives. Pension reform is not primarily an accounting problem; the stakes are enormous, affecting benefits that offer important, often essential, resources to millions of citizens. As recent events in France underscore, the possibilities for sharp conflict are ever present. Yet the success of recent reforms in Germany, Sweden, and elsewhere suggest that political meltdowns are not inevitable either. The goal of this essay is to analyze how adjustments in public pension programs seem likely to unfold, and to identify some of the factors that may account for cross-national variations in the adjustment process. I emphasize the difficulty of carrying out major reforms, and discuss some of the features of both pension systems and broader national contexts that have the largest impact on pension politics. There is no simple "politics of pensions." Rather, each country faces the distinctive politics of distinctively constituted systems. We can present general arguments about the nature of the problem, and identify some features common to a number of systems that are likely to matter. Beyond that, however, efforts at generalization should be offered, and accepted, with great caution.

The analysis proceeds in three steps. First, I outline some of the broad characteristics that distinguish the contemporary politics of austerity from the preceding half century of welfare state expansion. Second, I discuss some of the peculiar characteristics of pension systems, which may lead to distinctive constraints and opportunities for those pursuing reform. In the final section I bring together these two strands of argument with a brief discussion of aspects of particular national settings that seem likely to facilitate or impede reform efforts, to create particular kinds of cleavages or conflicts, or to channel reform initiatives in particular directions.

## THE POLITICS OF WELFARE STATE RETRENCHMENT[1]

The welfare state has entered a new era, an era of austerity. In contrast to our vast knowledge of the dynamics of welfare state expansion, however, welfare state retrenchment remains largely uncharted terrain. This puzzling state of affairs results in part from the very success of earlier scholarship. The quality of historical research on the welfare state has encouraged a simple process of borrowing already developed models for the examination of a new environment. There are, however, compelling reasons to reject such a straightforward extrapolation. For two reasons, the new politics of the welfare state is quite different from the old. First, the political goals of policymakers are different; second, there have been dramatic changes in the political context. Each of these points requires elaboration.

There is a profound difference between extending benefits to large numbers of people and taking those benefits away (Weaver 1986). For the past half century, expanding social benefits was generally a process of political credit claiming. Reformers needed only to overcome diffuse concern about tax rates (often sidestepped through resort to social insurance "contributions") and the frequently important resistance of entrenched interests. Not surprisingly, the expansion of social programs had until recently been a favoured political activity, contributing greatly to both state-building projects and the popularity of reform-minded politicians (Flora and Heidenheimer 1981).

In the past 20 years, a combination of economic turbulence, political shifts to the right, and rising costs associated with maturing welfare states has provoked growing calls for retrenchment. This new policy agenda stands in sharp contrast to the credit-claiming initiatives pursued during the long period of welfare state expansion. The politics of retrenchment is typically treacherous. On very rare occasions, policymakers may be able to transform retrenchment into an electorally attractive proposition. More often, the best they can hope to do is to minimize the political costs involved. Advocates of retrenchment must persuade wavering supporters that the price of reform is manageable — a task that a substantial public outcry makes almost impossible.

Retrenchment is generally an exercise in blame avoidance rather than credit claiming (Weaver 1986). A crucial reason is that the costs of retrenchment are relatively concentrated (and often immediate), while the benefits are not. That concentrated interests will be in a stronger political position than diffuse ones is a standard proposition in political science (Olson 1965; Wilson 1973). As interests become more concentrated, the prospect that individuals will find it worth their while to engage in collective action improves. Furthermore, concentrated groups are more likely to be linked to organizational networks that keep them informed about how policies affect their interests. These informational networks also facilitate political action.

An additional reason that politicians rarely get credit for program cutbacks concerns the well-documented asymmetry in how voters react to losses and gains. Extensive experiments in social psychology have shown that individuals respond differently to positive and negative risks. Individuals exhibit a *negativity bias*: they will take more chances — seeking conflict and accepting the possibility of even greater losses — to prevent any worsening of their current position (Kahneman and Tversky 1979; 1984). Studies of electoral behaviour, at least in the United States, confirm these findings. Negative attitudes towards candidates are more strongly linked with a range of behaviours (e.g., turnout, deserting the voter's normal party choice) than are positive attitudes (Bloom and Price 1975; Kernell 1977; Lau 1985).

While the sources of this negativity bias remain unclear, the constraints that it imposes on elected officials are not. When added to the imbalance between concentrated and diffuse interests, the message for advocates of retrenchment is straightforward. A simple "redistributive" transfer of resources from program beneficiaries to taxpayers, engineered through cuts in social programs, is generally a losing proposition. The concentrated beneficiary groups are more likely to be cognizant of the change, are easier to mobilize, and because they are experiencing losses rather than gains are more likely to incorporate the change in their voting calculations. Retrenchment advocates thus confront a clash between their policy preferences and their electoral ambitions.

If the shift in goals from expansion to cutbacks creates new political dynamics, so does the emergence of a new *context*: the development of the welfare state itself. As Peter Flora has noted, "including the recipients of [pensions,] unemployment benefits and social assistance — and the persons employed in education, health and the social services — in many countries today almost 1/2 of the electorate receive transfer or work income from the welfare state" (Flora 1989, p. 154). With these massive programs have come dense interest-group networks and strong popular attachments to particular policies, which present considerable obstacles to reform. To take one prominent example, by the late 1980s the American Association of Retired People (AARP) had a membership of 28 million and a staff of 1,300, including a legislative staff of more than 100 (Day 1990, pp. 25-26).

The maturation of the welfare state fundamentally transforms the nature of interest-group politics. The emergence of powerful groups surrounding social programs can make the welfare state less dependent on the political parties, social movements, and labour organizations that expanded social programs in the first place. This explains why neither the significant decline in the power of organized labour nor the rightward shift in electoral politics in many countries has led to anything like a dismantling of the modern welfare state.[2]

Nor is the political context altered simply because welfare states create their own constituencies. As I will discuss in detail, welfare state programs themselves have now become important parts of the institutional context, affecting the distribution of political resources and the incentives of political actors. The structures of social programs may, for instance, have implications for the decision rules governing policy change (e.g., whether national officials need the acquiescence of local ones). They may have major effects on how visible cutbacks will be, which in turn has a significant impact on the vulnerability of politicians. "Policy feedback" from earlier rounds of welfare state development is likely to be a prominent feature of retrenchment politics (Esping-Andersen 1985; Skocpol 1992; Pierson 1993).

In short, the shift in goals and context creates a new politics. This new politics, marked by pressures to avoid blame for unpopular policies, dictates new political strategies (Weaver 1986; Pierson 1994). Retrenchment advocates will try to play off one group of beneficiaries against another, and will often develop reforms that compensate politically crucial groups for lost benefits. Because of the political costs associated with retrenchment, policymakers will seek to spread the blame by achieving broad consensus on reform wherever possible. Perhaps most important, those favouring cutbacks will attempt to lower the visibility of reforms, either by making the effects of policies more difficult to detect or by making it hard for voters to trace responsibility for these effects back to particular policymakers (Arnold 1990).

This last point is especially important and requires some elaboration. Democratic polities are distinguished by the central role of elections in determining who wields political authority. This institutional structure provides voters with a crude but strong instrument for protecting their interests. Yet they can do so only if the relevant activities of policymakers are visible. The role of "visibility" in politics is often mentioned casually but little understood. All political actors posssess imperfect information about issues relevant to their interests. Furthermore, the distribution of information is usually highly unequal. In particular, mass publics often have limited information about the impact of changes in public policy. In this context, it may be possible for policymakers to lower the political costs of retrenchment actions by raising the costs to possible opponents of obtaining relevant information — that is to say, by lowering the visibility of their actions.

As Douglas Arnold (1990) has argued, electoral retribution against incumbents for unpopular policies requires three things. First, voters must be able to discern that they have experienced particular negative outcomes. Second, they must be able to trace those outcomes to government policies. Third, they must be able to identify the policymakers responsible for the undesired policies. These conditions are not easily fulfilled, and policymakers may possess tools to lower the visibility of their actions in each respect. As recent Canadian experience suggests, the result may be a "politics of stealth," in which significant retrenchment occurs without generating a substantial public outcry (Gray 1990).

In the contemporary era of austerity, those pursuing retrenchment will attempt to avoid blame by rallying broad support, dividing their opponents, and obscuring the negative consequences of their initiatives. Determining the likelihood of welfare state cutbacks thus requires that we identify the factors that faciliate or impede these strategies of retrenchment. Prominent among these are the characteristics of the particular area of social policy at issue, which is the subject of the next section.

## THE DISTINCTIVE FEATURES OF PUBLIC PENSION SYSTEMS

"The welfare state" is an umbrella term covering a wide range of programs, each of which has distinctive goals, clienteles, and rules. In addition to exploring the general character of contemporary welfare state politics, one needs to consider the specific factors that distinguish the politics of pension reform. Here I examine some common characteristics of pension systems, as well as a few of the important features that characterize some national systems but not others.

As is often noted, pension systems clearly gain public support from characteristics of their main constituency. The elderly represent a sizable and electorally active section of the population. Furthermore, the elderly are widely seen as deserving. In most countries, they have contributed to meeting the cost of pensions through past payroll taxes, which creates a widespread sense of entitlement. At the same time, public support for the elderly does not present the problems of work incentives which both weaken the claims of other constituencies to public income transfers and may mobilize opposition from organized groups such as employers.

These constituency characteristics clearly matter, and have helped make pension systems relatively resistent to reform. The truly distinctive characteristic of pension systems is, however, their pronounced *temporal quality*. By this I mean the ways in which pension systems link public commitments and expectations, and structures of interdependence between generations, across long periods of time. Only by appreciating the significance of this peculiar feature of pension programs can we understand the character of pension politics.

Of course, all policies have a temporal dimension. In few areas, however, is that dimension as prominent as it is for pensions, or its repercussions of such profound importance for the evolution of policy. In pension systems, the implications of current decisions will be felt decades down the road. Politicians make choices whose repercussions will be felt half a century later. At the micro-level, millions of individuals are compelled to make major (and hard to reverse) decisions about savings and consumption based on expectations of public policy many years in the future. Public pension systems are inherently a kind of intergenerational chain letter, in which decisions taken today shape the options available decades hence, just as both voters and politicians today must live with the legacies of choices made long ago.

These temporal implications of public pension systems channel policy reform, defining the most likely reform strategies and dimensions of adjustment. In most respects, I will argue, the temporal character of pension politics acts to constrain reform and steer policymakers towards incremental adjustments of existing pension systems. Before considering why, it is necessary to note the one way in which the long time frames associated with pension systems may aid efforts to pursue retrenchment. The fact that decisions today can have implications far into the future may open up certain possibilities for reform, especially by making it possible to defer some of the pain associated with policy change.

## The Advantages of Lagged or Incremental Cutbacks

Not all consequences of policy change are equally apparent. Some reforms will have consequences that attract massive attention; others will not. This is the one major respect in which the distinctive temporal character of pension policies will generally facilitate efforts at reform. Because the impact of decisions made now may only be experienced with considerable time lags, policymakers may be in a strong position to obscure the visibility of reforms. Indeed, most of the successful efforts to trim public sector pension obligations have taken the form of long-term revisions that phase in very gradually, often in ways that affect only future retirees. The magic of compounding means that incremental reforms which impose relatively small changes in benefits, indexation, or retirement rules can generate very substantial savings over time. When carefully crafted and designed in ways that do not inflict heavy immediate losses on retirees, these reforms have often been introduced with relatively little opposition.

Features of specific pension systems may also facilitate efforts to lower the visibility of reforms. The fact that Britain already had a history of maintaining private, "contracted-out" alternatives to the state earnings-related pension system meant that changes in rules that actually tilted pension policy much more heavily toward the private sector could be presented as relatively incremental adjustments to the status quo. Another option in many systems is to make cutbacks "automatic" (Weaver 1986). Changes in indexation, for example, can lead to annual reductions without requiring repeated, visible actions on the part of policymakers. Canada's OAS and Britain's Basic Pension are both instances where restrictive indexation methods have been used to generate considerable savings over time with limited public opposition. Benefit formulas can be made dependent upon economic performance, levels of taxation, or other variables, making adjustment an apolitical response that does not require politicians to openly enact painful reforms. Again, this is a popular technique for restraining growth in pension outlays.

Germany, for instance, now links benefit formulas to post-tax rather than pre-tax earnings, forcing retirees to share the burdens of rising tax rates.

These examples of reform suggest an important conclusion. Because the costs of reform can sometimes be imposed gradually, with much of the pain deferred, pension systems need not be rigidly fixed. Substantial modifications in the financial burdens associated with public pensions are possible, especially over the long term. Yet if the temporal quality of pensions creates possibilities for incremental adjustment, it also has other effects. Indeed, the dominant impact of this feature of pensions is to diminish the prospects for radical changes in program design. Focusing on the temporal aspect of pensions allows us to identify three important characteristics of pension politics which tend to impede efforts to radically alter existing pension commitments: the fluid character of taxpayer interests, the gap between the short time horizons of politicians and the long-term implications of their decisions, and the embeddedness of mature public pension systems.

## The Fluid Character of Taxpayer Interests

The temporal features of pension policy make it difficult to mobilize the diffuse interests which might favour cutbacks. Critics of expansive public pension systems often stress that current workers will get a bad deal from pension arrangements, and should therefore favour reform (Peterson and Howe 1988; Auerbach, Gokhale and Kotlikoff 1993). I have already noted the circumstances that generally mitigate against the expression of such diffuse interests. The design of public pension systems exacerbates the problem: those paying for pensions are at the same time the children of pensioners. Furthermore, as the contributory structure of payroll taxes constantly reminds them, they are also future pension recipients. Their status as taxpayer is a transitory one.

Some observers — especially those who advocate radical steps towards privatization — suggest that young workers are ready to rebel against existing arrangements. These workers, it is argued, know that they are getting a bad deal. Indeed, opinion polls in some countries suggest that they doubt that pensions will be available to pay for their retirement when the time comes. Yet poll results that reveal such alienation should be viewed sceptically. Asking young voters about a hypothetical event three decades hence may trigger a response from a citizenry primed for cynicism. But this is little grounds for concluding that those voters would support cuts in programs for the elderly. Generational animosity is likely to be of limited salience, and in any rate would tend to be short-lived. By the time such voters are in their forties, their parents will be receiving public pensions. By the time these voters hit 50 and start to anticipate their own retirement, they will begin to appreciate that they have a very personal stake in the preservation of pension benefits. Despite repeated efforts to rally the troops, generational war remains much-discussed but rarely observed.

There is little reason to expect those paying for current pensions to reward politicians for successful cutbacks. The "us" versus "them" perspective that is supposed to fuel generational conflict is, in fact, quite uncommon (Heclo 1988). In comparision with, say, welfare benefits, where an "us" versus "them" mentality is easy to construct, pension recipients are rarely seen as "them." Those paying for pensions are both the children of pensioners and future pension recipients. The political outcry against even quite substantial intergenerational redistribution is likely to remain relatively muted.

## The Time Horizons of Policymakers

The long-term implications of pension systems interact with a central characteristic of politics: the short time horizons of politicians. Although many of the implications of political decisions only play out in the long run, political decisionmakers are frequently most interested in the short-term consequences of their actions. Long-term effects of policy are often heavily discounted. The principal reason is the logic of electoral politics. Keynes once noted that in the long run we are all dead; for politicians in democratic polities, electoral death can come much faster. Since the decisions of voters that determine political success are taken in the short run, politicians are likely to employ a high discount rate in designing public policies. They have a strong incentive to pay close attention to long-term consequences only if these become politically salient, or when they have little reason to fear short-term electoral retribution. Again, while a disjuncture between short-term thinking and long-term consequences may be present in all policymaking, it is especially relevant to pension politics because the gap between short-term and long-term policy implications is unusually vast.

The gap between the short time horizons of politicians and the long-term consequences of their policy choices has been relevant both during the formation of pension systems and in the current era of austerity. As I will discuss in detail below, during periods of program initiation and expansion politicians are drawn to pay-as-you-go (PAYGO) financing. This arrangement may, as some economists claim, entail significant long-term costs, but it offers tremendous short-term political advantages.

The time horizons of politicians are at least as relevant to the contemporary issues of reform. Policymakers heavily discount long-term implications of policy initiatives, and therefore have tremendous incentives to avoid harsh immediate cutbacks in pensions, seeking short-term, stop-gap solutions instead. A statement attributed to David Stockman, Reagan's budget director, is unusual among political decisionmakers only for its candor. Asked by an advisor to consider pension reforms to combat social security's severe long-term financing problems, he dismissed the idea out of hand, exclaiming that he had no interest in wasting "a lot of political capital on some other guy's problem in [the year] 2010...." (quoted in Greider 1982, p. 43).

## Embeddedness

A third, related temporal factor is what might be called the embedded nature of pension systems. Recent work in the "new institutionalism" has drawn the attention of political scientists to the ways in which the "rules of the game" help to structure political conflicts (North 1990; Skocpol 1992). While this discussion has often focused on formal institutions, extensive policy arrangements also become fundamental institutional frameworks, creating rules, constraints, and incentives for future political action. Where government activity is widespread, "policy feedback" is likely to be a major contributor to the dynamics of political reform (Skocpol 1992; Pierson 1993).

In part because most such systems are very extensive and have been in place for decades, the specific design of established public pension arrangements have helped determine the tenor of contemporary welfare state politics. As I will discuss later in this essay, a number of features of pension systems can significantly influence the prospects for political reform, including the existence of trust funds, indexation methods, and the nature of integration with private pension schemes. As Myles and Quadagno point out in their contribution to this volume, whether governments earlier initiated Beveridge-style or Bismarckian pension schemes may have substantial repercussions for contemporary reform efforts.

The evolution of Canada's contributory pension system offers a particularly dramatic example of embedded policy — a case where past decisions have decisively diminished the manoeuvring room for current decisionmakers. As Keith Banting has argued, the need to protect provincial interests led to the adoption of decision rules that severely restrict the options for significant policy reform of the Canada and Quebec Pension Plans (C/QPP). According to Banting, under the terms of the original intergovernmental compromise:

> Change requires the agreement of the federal government and at least seven provinces representing two-thirds of the population, making [it] more difficult to amend than most sections of the constitution of the country. The federal government has a veto over changes to the Canada Pension Plan; Ontario also has a veto by virtue of its share of the Canadian population; and several combinations of other provinces can block change. In addition, because Quebec decided to operate its own pension plan, the Canada and Quebec plans need to be coordinated, giving Quebec additional

weight in the process. Here is a joint decision process of withering complexity (Banting 1995).

Thus, past decisions about programmatic design have fundamentally altered the politics surrounding a major social program. Locked-in by the decision rules governing reform, Canadian officials — provincial and national alike — find their ability to adapt the CPP to new circumstances severely constrained.

The significance of each of these temporal characteristics of pension politics — fluid interests, disjunctions between the short time horizons of politicians and the long-term implications of pension policies, and the embeddedness of previous policy frameworks — can be illustrated through a discussion of the most politically consequential aspect of public pension systems: the evolution of financing structures. To the chagrin of many economists, almost all public pension systems operate on a pay-as-you-go basis rather than a funded one. The explanation has much to do with the short time horizons of politicians, because the former framework offers tremendous advantages in the short run for the politicians who initiate such programs. As Robert Brown puts it,

> Politically, it can be argued that a PAYGO system creates two dollars of benefits for every dollar of contributions. Actuaries know that in a PAYGO scheme, every dollar of contribution that comes in in the morning becomes a dollar of benefits that are paid out in the afternoon. So the contributions to the scheme have that dollar of value. At the same time, however, the worker who makes the dollar contribution has created the expectation that there is now a one dollar commitment that (s)he will get a dollar's worth of benefits (plus interest) when it is his (her) turn to retire (Brown 1993, p. 3).

Nor are the immediate political benefits of pay-as-you-go schemes limited to the fact that two dollars of benefits can be offered for one dollar of taxes. In their early years, pay-as-you-go systems will benefit from a favourable demographic profile. Usually only small numbers of citizens will have paid sufficient contributions to qualify for benefits, while the entire working population is available to pay taxes. Thus taxes can be kept far lower — and benefits higher — than the levels required to keep the system running at a steady state. The United States experience in the early years of Social Security help to explain why such a system became enormously popular. The "first" Social Security recipient, Ida May Fuller, received 25 years of pension benefits after her retirement in 1940. She had paid a grand total of $24.50 in payroll taxes.[3]

Pay-as-you-go is not only significant at the outset of a public pension scheme. Brown's argument can also be reversed. If in a context of expansion PAYGO systems offer two dollars of benefits for every dollar of contributions, cutbacks offer two dollars of benefit cuts (one for the current recipient, one for the current contributor) in return for one dollar of savings.

Indeed, inheriting a mature pay-as-you-go scheme has even greater implications for the politics of pension reform. This common financial arrangement creates a rolling intergenerational contract: current revenues are used to finance current pensions; the pensions of current contributors will be paid by future contributors. Once it has been sustained for an extended period of time, such a system becomes deeply embedded, providing a classic example of *path dependence*.

Research on the development of technology (David 1985; Arthur 1989), has demonstrated how certain courses of development, once initiated, are difficult to reverse. The QWERTY typewriter keyboard may be inefficient, the Macintosh superior to the IBM, but once a particular path of technology takes hold it gains tremendous advantages. The improved efficiency that comes from repeated use, the development of technology-specific skills, the need to coordinate one's actions with others, and the costs of betting on the wrong horse, all make certain technologies subject to "increasing returns." The more established they become, the harder they are to dislodge.

This analysis has recently been extended to the evolution of institutions and policies (North 1990; Pierson 1993). In many cases, organizations and individuals will adapt to particular institutional and policy arrangements, making commitments that may render the cost of change (even to some potentially more efficient alternative) far higher than the costs of continuity. Existing commitments lock in policymakers.

The evolution of pay-as-you-go pension systems represent an excellent example of such a path-dependent process (Pierson 1992). Once mature, such systems may face incremental cutbacks, but they are highly resistant to radical reform. Any proposal to shift to private, occupationally based arrangements, which must necessarily be "funded" systems, creates a "double-payment" problem. Because it is too late for retirees to create an alternative source of retirement income, current payroll taxes are "pre-committed." Privatization thus requires current workers to continue financing the previous generation's retirement while simultaneously saving for their own. It is difficult to see how the imposition of such a heavy burden could prove politically feasible. The "double-payment" problem, coming on top of already heavy pressures to lower benefits and increase taxes on the working population in other areas of government, is likely to present an insurmountable barrier to privatization or any other reform intended to transform an extensive, mature pay-as-you-go pension scheme into a funded one. Efforts to shift away from a mature pay-as-you-go system simply defy the laws of political gravity, requiring politicians to inflict tremendous short-term pain in return for diffuse, uncertain, and long-term benefits. Carrying out such a proposal is akin to putting toothpaste back into the tube.

The contrasting experiences of Thatcher and Reagan in the 1980s illustrate the powerful effects of programmatic histories (Pierson 1992). The Thatcher government inherited a relatively new earnings-related pension system, SERPS, because government turnover had prevented agreement on a policy until 1975. The Tories were well aware that the immaturity of SERPS provided a brief window of opportunity for privatization. As then-junior-minister John Major noted in the House of Commons debate over pensions reform, "the way in which SERPS works means that every year of delay leaves people clocking up expensive rights which must be honoured in the future" (United Kingdom. House of Commons 1986, col. 105).

Radically revising even a system that had been in place for less than a decade created big problems. The Thatcher government's initial gambit, to quickly shut down the immature earnings-related pension system (SERPS), was withdrawn following withering criticism from all directions. The opponents included not only the Labour Party and groups representing the elderly, but the major private insurance companies and the Confederation of British Industry. The latter groups, typically alligned with the Conservative government, were concerned that the double-payment problem would lead to higher payroll taxes, lower benefits, or both. Forced to retreat, the Thatcher government had to pursue a more gradual approach. The 1986 reforms incrementally but decisively shifted policy towards private pension alternatives to the state earnings-related scheme. The government is currently pursuing policies that will further diminish the public plan. The government's success has been possible only because of the system's immaturity, and because the government agreed to cover a significant share of the "double-payment" problem itself in order to limit the political outcry. Tax subsides for the expanded private pension system will offset much of the budgetary savings anticipated.

In the United States, by contrast, the "double-payment" problem was not a future prospect but an immediate reality. When the Reagan administration arrived in 1981, Social Security had been in place for almost five decades. The window for privatization had long since closed. The financial resources needed to build a private sector alternative were already committed, through payroll taxes, to the current generation of elderly. Those advocating steps equivalent to Britain's SERPS reform, like the CATO Institute's Peter Ferrara, remained politically marginal figures. Similarly, the attempt during the past decade to even partially fund Social Security in the United States is instructive. Creating a truly funded system, which would have required much more stringent budgetary policies, has proven an elusive goal. The "surplus" appears to be simply a set of IOUs, more than offset by continuing deficits in the rest of the federal budget.

Other cross-national evidence also suggests the impact of pay-as-you-go financing. As Myles and Quadagno note, reform has been easier where current pay-as-you-go sytems were more limited in scope (the Beveridge countries), or where Bismarckian schemes were of recent origin and therefore not yet mature. Even in these cases, reform has had to be incremental and accompanied by sizable tax concessions to offset some of the burden on the working generation, although these concessions undermined the fiscal justifications of the reform.

Thus, the interaction of the temporal aspects of pensions and characteristic features of democratic politics generate a strong bias towards creating and then sustaining public, pay-as-you-go arrangements. Most public pension systems are deeply embedded. As Brown stated, "once a society has chosen a PAYGO retirement income security system, it is almost impossible ever to turn away from that funding basis" (Brown 1993, p. 11). Although generally sceptical of such efforts in the social sciences, I am tempted to propose the following "law": the likelihood of privatization declines in direct relation to the scope and maturity of a pay-as-you-go scheme.[4]

The lasting political implications of PAYGO financing are simply the most dramatic illustration of the broader point developed here. The politics surrounding pension systems is fundamentally shaped by the processes that bind policy choices and societal outcomes across long periods of time. Recognizing this temporal dynamic provides a key to understanding both the opportunities and constraints facing those seeking cutbacks in public pension systems. Considerable incremental reform is often possible because of policymakers' ability to lag negative effects. More radical change is difficult, however, because policymakers have short time horizons, voters have fluid preferences regarding pensions, and existing arrangements are deeply embedded.

THE POLITICS OF PENSION REFORM

Having offered both a general account of retrenchment politics and an analysis of the distinctive political implications of pension systems, I wish now to point to some more specific features of particular national contexts that are likely to influence the dynamics of pension reform efforts. My intention is to link arguments about particular political environments to the claims made in the first section of this essay, which stress the distinctive nature of retrenchment politics, and the claims in the second section about the crucial features of pension systems. The goal is not parsimonious theory, but an overview of how features of national policies and polities may interact to channel reform in particular directions.

## Formal Political Institutions

One might believe that the structure of formal political institutions will facilitate or impede reform efforts. Some political systems are far more centralized than others. Because concentration of authority also concentrates accountability for unpopular decisions, however, it is unclear whether centralization makes retrenchment easier. It is probably safer to say that whether political power is concentrated or not helps to structure the choices available to retrenchment advocates (Pierson and Weaver 1993). Where authority is concentrated (as in Britain or Sweden), governments will be hard-pressed to limit the traceability of unpopular decisions, but they will have a greater capacity to develop and implement strategies that make the cutbacks themselves less discernible. Governments in more fragmented systems (e.g., the United States, Canada, or Germany) must fashion strategies that minimize the need to force multiple policy changes through institutional veto points (Immergut 1992). However, they may find it easier to duck accountability for unpopular policies.

While this stands as a general proposition about retrenchment, my sense is that in the case of pensions it needs to be modified.[5] In centralized systems, the trick is hiding the pain of policy reform, and I have stressed that the possibilities for lagged, low visibility cutbacks is relatively high in most pension systems. Thus centralized governments have the advantage of being able to implement their chosen policies, and in this case may be able to avoid public outcries if they adopt a long-term strategy. This suggestion fits with the Canadian experience. The pension policy dealt with by the central government, OAS, has been cut substantially through the politics of stealth. The C/QPP, which has a more fragmented decision-making structure, has been resilient.

## Government Popularity

It seems plausible that the presence of significant *electoral slack* will facilitate reform. That is, governments will be more ambitious when they believe that they are in a strong enough position to absorb the electoral consequences of unpopular decisions (Garrett 1993). Thus, one reason for Thatcher's *relative* (though still limited) success may have been the division among her opponents within a first-past-the-post electoral system. This may have given her more room to pursue unpopular policies that would have been beyond the reach of a government in a precarious electoral position. However, as George Bush learned when the American electorate forgot about Desert Storm, calculating electoral slack *ex ante* is a tricky business. As a result, most governments are likely to proceed cautiously. As I have indicated, even the Thatcher government generally retreated when confronted with widespread opposition. Pension cutbacks are usually so unpopular that even a government winning a landslide will probably hesitate before shouldering the blame for such an effort alone.

## *"Crisis" Moments*

Moments of budgetary crisis may open opportunities for reform. Advocates of retrenchment will try to exploit such moments to present reforms as an effort to save pension systems rather than destroy them. Framing the issue in this manner may allow governments to avoid widespread blame for program cutbacks. Here again, the specific design of pension systems can matter. Where program design (e.g., the use of trust funds) automatically "triggers" a crisis when finances become imbalanced, politicians may find it easier to avoid blame for cuts in benefits. The US experience suggests that trust fund imbalances make it possible to present cutbacks as necessary to prevent "bankruptcy." Indeed, trust fund imbalances created the only two opportunities for cuts in Social Security, in 1977 and 1983 (Pierson 1992).

Making the claim of crisis credible, however, generally requires collaboration with the political opposition. In turn, the need for consensus makes it difficult to utilize crises to promote radical restructuring. Thus, while the appearance of fiscal stress encourages downward adjustments in social programs, it is far less clear that it provides a platform for a radical overhaul of social policy.

## *Capacity to form Grand Coalitions*

The need for political "cover" in pursuing potentially unpopular strategies suggests that arrangements facilitating collective agreement among the most relevant groups will often be important. Reform is less likely to provoke an outcry when a plan for long-term initiatives can be implemented, since losses can be imposed gradually. Reform is also promoted when there are not well-organized opponents — that is, when the major organized groups all agree to spread the blame for hard times. Such an outcome usually requires that these groups be brought into decision making. As a result, reform plans will represent a compromise among competing interests, which usually implies incremental changes.

As Myles and Quadagno note, such "grand coalition" reforms will often be easier to pursue in "corporatist" systems which are distinguished by strong political parties, encompassing and centralized labour and employer organizations, and a history of collaboration and negotiated settlements on difficult issues. Such organizational arrangements and traditions facilitate collective action (Myles and Quadagno in this volume; Katzenstein 1985). They keep the number of "players" small, and encourage trust by establishing repeated interactions that make commitments credible. In such a context, adjusting pension systems can become a positive sum game among political actors in which the major groups have insider status and therefore eschew efforts to radicalize debate or inflame public passions.

In Germany, for instance, employer and labour organizations made *joint* presentations to the commission reviewing the public pension system. A number of European countries, including Finland, Germany, and Sweden, have recently used such institutional arrangements to make significant long-term adjustments to their pension system.

Carrying out such adjustments may be much more difficult in non-corporatist systems, which lack many of the arrangements that facilitate collaboration. Groups outside the corridors of power may have more incentive, and more capacity, to mobilize popular discontent. Even in highly fragmented systems, however, quasi-corporatist solutions may sometimes be found. This was the case in the 1983 Social Security Amendments in the United States, for instance (Light 1985).

## Prospects for Changing Institutions

As I have argued, the rules of the game may be of great significance for the reform of social policy. Retrenchment advocates may be able to shift the balance of political power if they can restructure the ways in which trade-offs among taxes, spending, and deficits are presented, evaluated, and decided, they may be able to shift the balance of political power. So far, these institutional shifts have been rare, but several instances may be of growing relevance. In Europe, the increasing policy significance of the EC may alter the terrain for struggles over the welfare state. If reforms can be presented as legally required or economically imperative because of the single market or moves towards monetary union, national governments may be freed from some blame for welfare state cutbacks. Indeed, it has been suggested that the main cause of the EU's growing policy role is the way in which it shelters national executives from domestic political forces. In this view, far from eroding national sovereignty, the EU actually "strengthens the state" (Moravcsik 1994).

The move towards Economic and Monetary Union (EMU), with its tough convergence criteria, has provided an impetus for significant pension cutback initiatives in some countries, including France and Italy. The criteria will require considerably tighter fiscal policies in member states that hope to participate in monetary union. In this context, member states may be able to use the EU to provide political cover for reforms in pensions that they have been afraid to pursue. This appears to be the case in Italy, for instance. As the French experience suggests, however, EMU may be a two-edged sword. Because it requires rapid adjustments in fiscal policy, it pushes governments towards precisely the short-term, painful initiatives that are most likely to provoke political trouble. France's attempt to lower the budget deficit from 5 percent of GDP to 3 percent of GDP in two years was a recipe for political disaster.

In the United States, institutional reform has also been on the agenda. The new Republican majority in Congress deferred efforts to cut programs until after a strong (but so far largely unsuccessful) push to change the rules of the game. The intent of the rule changes was to increase the salience of taxes and create a more favourable climate for attacking social spending. Should these institutional reforms — especially the balanced budget amendment — eventually succeed, they might in time allow Social Security cuts to be put "on the table" despite a healthy balance within the Social Security budget itself.

A wide range of factors — characteristics both of national pension systems and of national polities — can influence whether and how reform of pension systems occurs. Nonetheless, we lack, inevitably, a convincing simple theory of pension reform politics. A few broad conclusions stand out. First, the extent of budgetary burdens alone tells us little about the nature of pension politics. One might well suspect that much would depend on the severity of the pressures facing a particular system — a factor that can be measured with some degree of accuracy (OECD 1995). What is striking, however, is the lack of correlation cross-nationally between the economic burdens associated with present and future pension costs and national assessments of sustainability. All OECD countries have probably crossed the invisible threshold at which such pressures are large enough to create a potential issue. Beyond that threshold, the magnitude of prospective imbalances or burdens appears to tell us little about the politics of pension reform. Pension reforms are politically constructed. Countries with relatively small burdens may have large "crises" and conflictual politics; countries with much larger burdens may not. What needs more consideration, therefore, is the "translation process" through which the broad pressures appearing everywhere enter very distinctive national political environments. In particular, we need to examine what happens when these substantial fiscal constraints collide with popular, deeply institutionalized public pension programs.

Second, the character of both retrenchment politics and modern pension systems means that radical reform — a dramatically new design of retirement benefits, such as a shift towards Chilean-style mandatory private pensions — is likely to be the exception rather than the rule. Pension programs are popular, and they are profoundly embedded in contemporary economic, social, and political structures. Radical change will often require the imposition of considerable immediate pain; assembling a political coalition for such efforts will be extremely difficult. While this analysis suggests some of the possible keys to variation in policy outcomes, the most significant finding concerns not variation but commonality. Everywhere, retrenchment is a difficult undertaking. The welfare state remains the most resilient aspect of the postwar political economy, and pensions are probably the most resilient part of the welfare state.

Third and finally, it is the corporatist countries — often criticized as "sclerotic," unadaptive systems — that may fare best in facing their problems without provoking political upheaval.[6] It has taken a long time to build public pension systems, and the stakes are enormous for many citizens. Reform will be easier, and more successful, where political systems favour quiet diplomacy over soundbite politics, collaborative over winner-take-all solutions, and long-term sustainability over short-term advantage.

## NOTES

1. This section is drawn from Pierson 1994 and Pierson 1996, which offer much more detailed discussions.
2. To say that the welfare state has not been dismantled is not to deny that there have been significant cutbacks in some programs, or that income inequality has grown in many countries.
3. Before one deplores such massive intergenerational transfers, it is worth remembering that in the United States as elsewhere this first generation of public pensioners was far less affluent than the generations that followed. Pay-as-you-go pensions thus offered this generation a chance to share in the benefits of economic growth which their own sacrifices had helped to make possible.
4. The late arrival and limited scope of C/QPP thus makes Canada one of the few places where privatization of an earnings-related scheme might still be viable, though I am sceptical. CPP is significantly more mature than SERPs was when the Thatcher government began its privatization initiatives.
5. This somewhat modifies the argument presented in Pierson and Weaver (1993).
6. An important qualification: the much greater size of the future pension obligations facing these countries will at least partly offset any advantage they may have in their capacity to cope with those obligations (OECD 1995).

## REFERENCES

Arnold, R.D. (1990), *The Logic of Congressional Action,* New Haven: Yale University Press.

Arthur, W.B. (1989), "Competing Technologies, Increasing Returns, and Lock-In by Historical Events," *Economic Journal*, 99 (March):116-31.

Auerbach, A.J., J. Gokhale and L.J. Kotlikoff (1993), "Generational Accounts and Lifetime Tax Rates, 1900-1991," *Economic Review*, 29, 1.

Banting, K. (1995), "The Welfare State as Statecraft: Territorial Politics and Canadian Social Policy," in *European Social Policy: Between Fragmentation and Integration*, ed. S. Leibfried and P. Pierson, Washington, DC: The Brookings Institution.

Bloom, H.S. and H. D. Price (1975), "Voter Response to Short-Run Economic Conditions: The Asymmetric Effect of Prosperity and Recession," *American Political Science Review*, 69, 4:1240-1254.

Brown, R.L. (1993), "The Future of the Canada/Quebec Pension Plans," Research Report 93-10, Institute of Insurance and Pension Research.

David, P. (1995), "Clio and the Economics of QWERTY," *American Economic Review*, 75:332.

Day, C.L. (1990), *What Older Americans Think: Interest Groups and Aging Policy,* Princeton: Princeton University Press.

Esping-Andersen, G. (1985), *Politics against Markets: The Social Democratic Road to Power,* Princeton: Princeton University Press.

Flora, P. (1989), "From Industrial to Postindustrial Welfare State?" *Annals of the Institute of Social Science*, special issue (Institute of Social Science, University of Tokyo).

Flora, P. and A.J. Heidenheimer, eds. (1981), *The Development of Welfare States in Europe and America,* New Brunswick, NJ: Transaction.

Garrett, G. (1993), "The Politics of Structural Reform: Swedish Social Democracy and Thatcherism in Comparative Perspective," *Comparative Political Studies*, 25, 4:521-47.

Gray, G. (1990), "Social Policy by Stealth," *Policy Options*, 11 (March):17-29.

Greider, W. (1982), *The Education of David Stockman and Other Americans,* New York: E.P. Dutton.

Heclo, H. (1988), "Generational Politics," in *The Vulnerable,* ed. J.L. Palmer, T. Smeeding and B. Boyle Torrey, Washington, DC: The Urban Institute.

Immergut, E. (1992), *Health Politics: Interests and Institutions in Western Europe,* Cambridge: Cambridge University Press.

Kahneman, D. and A. Tversky (1979), "Prospect Theory: An Analysis of Decision under Risk," *Econometrica*, 47, 2:263-91.

_____ (1984), "Choices, Values and Frames," *America Psychologist*, 39.

Katzenstein, P. (1985), *Small States in World Markets: Industrial Policy in Europe*, Ithaca: Cornell University Press.

Kernell, S. (1977), "Presidential Popularity and Negative Voting: An Alternative Explanation of the Midterm Congressional Decline of the President's Party," *American Political Science Review*, 71, 1:44-66.

Lau, R.R. (1985), "Explanations for Negativity Effects in Political Behavior," *American Journal of Political Science*, 29, 1:119-38.

Light, P. (1985), *Artful Work: The Politics of Social Security Reform,* New York: Random House.

Moravcsik, A. (1994), "Why the EC Strengthens the State," unpublished manuscript, Harvard University: Center for European Studies.

North, D.C. (1990), *Institutions, Institutional Change, and Economic Performance*, Cambridge: Cambridge University Press.

Olson, M. (1965), *The Logic of Collective Action: Public Goods and the Theory of Groups,* Cambridge: Harvard University Press.

Organisation for Economic Cooperation and Development (1995), "Effects of Ageing Populations on Government Budgets," *OECD Economic Outlook*, 57 (June):33-42.

Peterson, P.G. and N. Howe (1988), *On Borrowed Time: How the Growth in Entitlement Spending Threatens America's Future,* New York: Simon and Schuster.

Pierson, P. (1992), "Policy Feedback and Political Change: Contrasting Reagan and Thatcher's Pension-Reform Initiatives," *Studies in American Political Development*, 6, 2:359-90.

_____ (1993), "When Effect Becomes Cause: Policy Feedback and Political Change," *World Politics*, 45, 4:595-628.

_____ (1994), *Dismantling the Welfare State? Reagan, Thatcher and the Politics of Retrenchment,* Cambridge: Cambridge University Press.

_____ (1996), "The New Politics of the Welfare State," *World Politics*, 48.

Pierson, P. and R.K. Weaver (1993), "Imposing Losses in Pensions Policy," in *Do Institutions Matter? Government Capabilities at Home and Abroad,* ed. R.K. Weaver and B. Rockman, Washington, DC: The Brookings Institution.

Skocpol, T. (1992), *Protecting Soldiers and Mothers: The Political Origins of Social Policy in the United States,* Cambridge: Harvard University Press.

United Kingdom. House of Commons (1986), *Hansard Parliamentary Debates*, London: HMSO.

Weaver, R.K. (1986), "The Politics of Blame Avoidance," *Journal of Public Policy*, 6 (December).

Wilson, J.Q. (1973), *Political Organizations,* New York: Basic Books.

# Comments

*Keith G. Banting*

Both these papers are premised on the political sensitivity of pension politics in modern democracies. As Paul Pierson emphasizes, the elderly represent a large component of the electorate; they are more electorally active than young voters; they are heavily dependent on public programs for their well-being; and they tend to be seen as deserving beneficiaries by the rest of society. During the expansion of the welfare state, when pension programs were being introduced and expanded, politicians reaped the political benefits, often competing to outdo each other in generosity to the elderly. In the contemporary context of demographic and fiscal pressures, politicians approach the trimming of pension commitments with considerable anxiety, searching for political cover and seeking to build as broad a consensus as possible for change.

Both these papers develop their perspectives through comparative analysis, and this comment seeks to extend their insights further into Canadian experience.

## MORAL CLAIMS AND CANADIAN PUBLIC PHILOSOPHY

John Myles and Jill Quadagno emphasize the moral basis of pension entitlement. Is the right to a pension grounded in need, citizenship or previous employment? Each of these bases of moral claim has distinctive implications for the design of pensions and for who should benefit. As a result, the scope for redesign of pension programs depends in part on the extent to which these bases of moral claim are embedded in the historical traditions, political culture, and public philosophy of the country.

In the case of Canada, it is striking that all three moral claims have a prominent part in the history of Canadian pensions. The original Old Age Pension, which was introduced in 1927, was premised on the basis of need, providing a means-tested benefit to the elderly poor; and a modernized version of a needs-based benefit was introduced in the mid-1960s in the form of the Guaranteed Income Supplement (GIS). Although the GIS was originally expected to fade away as the Canada and Quebec Pension Plans (C/QPP) matured, it gained added life as politicians enriched the supplement in real terms repeatedly in subsequent years, usually just before or after an election. The Seniors Benefit, to be introduced in the year 2001, will extend and reinforce the moral imperative of need in the Canadian political tradition.

Citizenship also played an important role in Canadian pension history. The introduction of Old Age Security in 1951 established a universal pension benefit to all Canadians who reached the age of entitlement, which was initially set at 70 but later reduced to 65. Admittedly, citizenship as the basis of eligibility was qualified by residency regulations, which required an individual to be resident in Canada for a minimum of ten years before receiving benefit.[1] With this exception, however, the moral basis of the right to Old Age Security was simply being an elderly member of the Canadian community.

Finally, the concept of a pension as an earned benefit was entrenched in the Canadian pension history with the introduction of the Canada and Quebec Pension Plans in 1965. Individuals acquire a right to support by virtue of previous employment and contributions, and benefits are related to previous earning levels. People with limited attachment to the paid labour force do not build up an entitlement to support. Proposals to extend C/QPP benefits to housewives have failed to be adopted, and those with intermittent employment records or a history of work in the grey economy face diminished or no benefits.

Canadian history has thus incorporated all three bases for claim on society. Perhaps as a result, we have never developed a clear and coherent public philosophy about the moral basis of claim to a pension. This has had several important implications for the politics of pension reform. At one level, pension politics in Canada are more malleable than in other countries where a simpler conception of entitlement has sunk more deeply into the public consciousness and expectations. Advocates of almost any line of change can point to antecedents in our collective past. At another level, however, this sheer diversity of historical roots may also make it more difficult to establish a clear consensus on reforms. Without settled understandings about the moral parameters of pensions claims, policymakers must build consensus more carefully.

Although Canadian history is complex, the future will be much simpler. As Myles and Quadagno point out, we are witnessing the "end of citizenship" as a moral basis of claim to a pension in Canada and elsewhere. Universal benefits such as Old Age Security are giving way to income-tested instruments modelled on the idea of a negative income tax. According to the emerging philosophy of pensions, there will be only two bases of claim on the wider society: pension entitlement will represent either an earned right based on previous employment, or a transfer to low-income individuals. The erosion of the citizenship model in pensions is in part a wider trend in the income security sector, as the parallel replacement of Family Allowances with the Child Benefit attests. Indeed, in the early 1960s, selective benefits represented less than 20 percent of all income security expenditures in Canada; by the mid-1990s, approximately half of all income security dollars were flowing through selective benefit programs.[2]

The end of citizenship as a basis for moral claim on society in the income security system has wider potential implications. The trend is heightening a basic schizophrenia at the heart of the Canadian welfare state. Citizenship is no longer the basis for moral claim in income security policy; but the health-care system is fundamentally premised on the citizenship model. Medicare is not an earned right based on employment; nor is it a benefit restricted to low-income or needy individuals. All Canadian citizens are eligible.

The essential question is whether schizophrenia is a stable psychological condition. Can the Canadian public philosophy accommodate sharply different moral claims in different sectors? Or are there future implications for health care implicit in the erosion of the citizenship model in our income security programs?

Finally, there is an interesting irony in the fact that we are moving away from the citizenship model at precisely the same time as we are trying to invest Canadian citizenship with greater meaning in the context of the struggle over national unity. If we drain Canadian citizenship of its social content, where will we find alternative symbols and experiences that unite us? Unity advertising campaigns cannot fill a void.

POLITICS AND CONSENSUS

Both papers emphasize the importance of mechanisms for building consensus over the restructuring of pension systems. As Pierson argues, the need for political "cover" when pursuing politically unpopular policies suggests that the capacity to form a "grand coalition" among the affected interests is often important. Both he and Myles-Quadagno suggest that countries with corporatist forms of consultation and policy making have greater consensus-building capacity and therefore enjoy an advantage in managing difficult policy transitions in ways that moderate social conflict.

Canada, however, has evolved its own form of "grand coalition." The rules governing changes in the Canada Pension Plan require an elaborate federal-provincial consensus: changes must be approved by the federal government and seven provinces representing two-thirds of the population. This is a more demanding requirement than the formula governing changes to most of the Canadian constitution. In addition, it is important to sustain parallelism between the Canadian and Quebec plans, giving Quebec an enhanced role in the process. In effect, decision rules give a formal veto to the federal government and Ontario; Quebec has an informal veto; and several combinations of smaller provinces also have a veto. In this context, changes in contributory pensions require an elaborate process of federal-provincial bargaining, and a high level of consensus before action is taken.

The Canadian politics of "grand coalitions" clearly differ from corporatism in the European model, which incorporates class-based interests into the policy process. The Canadian process governing contributory pensions, however, does incorporate the regional and linguistic forces that actually move Canadian politics. Moreover, the process normally reflects the diverse ideological strains in Canadian life. At any point in time, there are likely to be conservative, liberal, and social-democratic governments at the table. The balance in the representation of these ideological strains undoubtedly shifts over time, as various governments rise and fall. Nevertheless, the intergovernmental process does function in ways reminiscent of systems with corporatist politics or coalition governments. In particular, policy making for contributory pensions tends to be dominated by compromise and incrementalism.

A "grand coalition" established in the closed world of federal-provincial diplomacy provides political cover for nervous governments. The federal government can present the outcome to Parliament as a *fait accompli,* since any significant amendments would unravel the package as a whole. Moreover, opposition parties in the federal Parliament find their room for manoeuvre reduced by the approval given to the package by their sister parties at the provincial level. To be sure, the separation between federal and provincial parties in Canada means that this protection is not absolute; and in the current Parliament, the Reform Party is unconstrained by provincial counterparts. Nevertheless, changes to contributory pensions are premised on a wider coalition than is needed for virtually any other public program in Canada.

In the current round of negotiations, the choices are more painful than in the past, since no government likes to cut benefits or raise contribution rates dramatically. The governments at the table will undoubtedly bring conflicting objectives to the negotiations. The federal government seems to favour contribution increases with few if any benefit reductions; the Ontario government, committed as it is to an agenda of tax reduction, may well have a different view. And the approach of a separatist government in Quebec to the one area of public policy that actually manifests the idea of "sovereignty-association" will be important. The outcome of this complex process is uncertain at the time of writing. What is clear, however, is that these political processes will be critical to the future of Canadian pension policy.

NOTES

1. The residency requirement was made more complicated in 1977, when it was established that new pensioners who had been resident in Canada for more than ten but less than 40 years would receive only partial benefits, unless covered by a pension agreement between Canada and their country of origin.
2. Even this understates the extent of the change as elements of selectivity have crept into unemployment insurance benefits as well.

# Comments

## Harvey Lazar

What lessons can Canadians learn from the political experiences of other countries that have recently reformed their retirement income systems? To help us in answering this question, we rely on the two papers — one by Paul Pierson and the second by John Myles and Jill Quadagno — that describe and analyze the experience of several Western countries. Together, these papers provide valuable insight into the politics of pension reform and help us to understand the forces helping to shape the "art of the possible."

The Pierson and Myles/Quadagno papers are about *real politic* in an age of fiscal restraint. Both papers accept, as a starting point, that fiscal realities in most Western countries make retrenchment or consolidation of public pensions the only practical possibilities. There is no discussion of enlarging public pensions. Since the Canadian pension reform debate mirrors this situation, this starting point adds to the relevance of these papers for Canada.

The two papers focus on political frameworks, institutions and cultures that have helped to dictate the acceptable range of policy action in other Western countries. Assuming Canada's political leaders are influenced by the same kinds of considerations as their counterparts in other Western democracies, the experience elsewhere may provide a useful guide to the political context surrounding pension reform efforts here.

### PIERSON'S ANALYSIS

Pierson begins by noting that the politics of welfare state retrenchment are "treacherous." This is in part because the winners in the process are diffuse and slow to recognize their gains (or take them for granted), whereas the losers, that is, those on whom the costs of retrenchment are concentrated, will be quick to recognize their losses and to act politically to punish those governments or legislators that are the authors of their misfortune. Pierson explains that the welfare state has created its own clientele — a dense interest group network and large number of workers who earn their living delivering the relevant programs; he argues that the self-interest of these groups and groupings make it relatively easy for them to mobilize in opposition to change. They thus help to give social programs a life of their own that is somewhat independent of the political parties and other institutions, like labour unions, that may have been instrumental in their birth.

Pierson also draws attention to some special attributes of the public pension component of the safety net, in particular the contrast between its long time horizons and the much shorter time horizons of elected politicians; and he links this contrast to the political attractions of using pay-as-you-go financing when public plans are started and the corresponding political difficulties in making fundamental changes to a mature pay-as-you-go system. He further argues that since the current recipients of public pensions are the parents of those who are paying for those pensions, the "us" versus "them" perspective that may be found, for example, in welfare politics is relatively uncommon in pension politics.

The decision rules — and the degree of "embeddedness" of these rules — are another variable in his analysis. A unitary state, or a country in which decision-making power is concentrated, with relatively simple decision rules, will have more freedom of action, for example, than a federal state or a country in which power is more diffuse and where rule changes are subject to the approval of several players.

Given these observations, it is not surprising that Pierson finds that Western governments that are in the retrenchment business try to lower the "visibility" of their actions to avoid the "retribution" of the voters. They seek to "avoid blame" for their expenditure cuts; and the politically easiest way to do this is to implement measures that do not impose heavy immediate losses on current pensioners but instead make themselves felt (i.e., generate savings) only gradually and over an extended period of time.

Pierson's conclusions, about the processes and politics of welfare state retrenchment in other Western countries fit well with Ken Battle's characterization of social policy change under the Mulroney government. Battle argued that the structure of Canada's social safety net was being eroded not by principled legislative action following extensive public debate about values and choices, but by a large number of relatively small technical measures, most (if not all) of which were linked to the fiscal conditions of the country — a process Battle dubbed "social policy by stealth." The deficit was the engine of reform and the federal Finance Department was the engineer (see Gray 1990).

It is important to note that, in Battle's analysis, "stealth" did not mean that the government's actions were illegal, secret or unparliamentary. Instead, stealth implied incremental policy change that was frequently opaque and complex. The policy change was incremental in two senses. First, the reform measures were introduced piecemeal, over time, and not as a comprehensive redesign package. Perhaps, more importantly, the expenditure reductions entailed in individual reforms were designed to grow year after year, as the new design features gradually worked their magic. For example, program costs that were de-indexed partially from the inflation rate would fall year after year in real terms (even with low levels of inflation) and without the need to seek annual Parliamentary approval. In the remainder of this comment, the terms "stealth" and "incrementalism" will be used interchangeably to reflect the kinds of processes described by Pierson and Battle.

The question that arises from the Pierson analysis, particularly in light of Battle's work, is whether the low visibility, opaque, and incrementalist approach he describes is the only politically practical option to federal and provincial governments as they deal with pension reform.

## MYLES AND QUADAGNO

Here the paper by Myles and Quadagno is instructive. Myles and Quadagno point out that the language and imagery of the debate surrounding public pensions varies from one jurisdiction to another and reflects the differing moral and political justification that surrounds public pensions in different countries. They distinguish between Beveridge-type and Bismarckian systems. They also observe that the Beveridge model is more amenable to the language of retrenchment. Since that system has its roots in Elizabethan poor law and the taxation of the better off to help the poor, it is more vulnerable to cutbacks that are rationalized on the basis of a greater targeting of expenditures on those who are most in need. The overall direction is consistent with a negative income tax.

In contrast, having their roots in the employment contract, and an entitlement based on work history, the Bismarckian systems are less susceptible to cutbacks linked to targeting. In countries where these systems have provided relatively high benefits, they may have been restructured and at the same time made smaller. But in such cases, the rationale is linked to preserving rather than eliminating or downsizing the system, for example, by making benefit levels "more insurance-like" or fairer in relation to, say, the earnings of the working-age population (they cite recent changes in Germany) or by linking them more closely to actual lifetime earnings and actual lifetime contributions (reference is made to Sweden and Italy). A common theme in some of these countries is that the defined benefit system is starting to become more like a defined contribution plan.

One inference that might be drawn from the Myles and Quadagno paper is that the Pierson analysis is likely to have less salience in a Bismarckian system than in a Beveridge-based system (especially English-speaking Beveridge systems) because the beneficiaries in a Bismarckian system do not see themselves as the recipients of state largesse but instead as receiving earned benefits in return for their many years of contributions. In some cases there are also corporatist structures (i.e., representing employees, employers, and perhaps pensioners) operating these plans and the leaders or managers of these institutions may find it easier than elected politicians to make the accommodations required to ensure sustainability, efficiency, and fairness.

A second and related inference is that the language and imagery of reform in Bismarckian systems will need to be significantly different than it is for Beveridge-type systems. Expressions like "rolling back the frontiers of the welfare state" and the language of targeting will resonate less well than the "sustainability" or "fairness" language referred to above. If the public plans include a significant management role for the representatives of employees and employers, and perhaps pensioners, efforts to achieve reform through stealth are also less likely to succeed. These people will be well-equipped to see through technical and opaque provisions to their practical implications.

Finally, from the examples in Myles and Quadagno, it appears that retrenchment is most likely to succeed in those Bismarckian systems that are relatively large.

## LESSONS FOR CANADA

Before applying the lessons from the international experience to Canada, there are several points to note about the Canadian context. First, Canada's public retirement income system has elements of both the Beveridge (OAS/GIS) and the Bismarckian (Canada Pension Plan and Quebec Pension Plan, C/QPP) models and the two components are roughly equal in size. Second, seniors groups in Canada are well-organized lobbies that mobilize quickly and promise severe sanctions against those considering legislated reductions in their benefits. It will be recalled, for example, that a former prime minister decided to withdraw proposed reductions in Old Age Security and the Guaranteed Income Supplement (OAS/GIS) in the face of a determined senior citizen reproaching him in front of a national television audience. As for the CPP, it has the "embeddedness" that Pierson refers to in the form of highly complex federal-provincial amending formulas. Finally, as noted earlier, pension issues do have a long time horizon. Significant changes in pension benefits, therefore, typically do require long periods of advance notice so that affected individuals can have adequate time to take the action needed to cope with those changes. In that sense, good policy should be gradualist or incrementalist in nature.

Given these points, what are the lessons for Canada in the papers by Pierson and Myles/Quadagno? In the case of OAS/GIS, it is arguable that policy change has followed closely the path outlined by both papers. Fiscal necessity has been the overriding imperative. The measures have been complex and opaque. For example, the introduction of the "clawback" on OAS benefits was designed to increase gradually the returns to the fisc, and reduce gradually benefits to middle-income recipients, by the less than complete indexing of the threshold. The object of this measure, and the subsequent income testing of the age credit, was on cost-cutting while protecting those who were most needy. But these actions were also designed so that middle-income earners, at least initially, were not entirely cut out (a consideration that also sits well with Pierson's analysis of pension reform in other countries). Thus, both the redistributive and political calculus was a strong element in these changes.

Looking ahead, therefore, and recognizing the continued pressure for expenditure reduction, these papers would suggest even further efforts at OAS/GIS targeting and not so much as an outcome of a wide-ranging public debate about values but as fiscally-inspired incrementalist measures. Such a view is consistent with the principles for reform outlined in the 1995 federal budget. The fact that the finance minister did not act immediately on those principles, but left time for working on details, is also consistent with Pierson's analysis about the difficulties that envelop the politics of pension reform.

It is less obvious, however, how the analysis of these two papers applies to the CPP and QPP. The comments here will be linked mainly to CPP since amending it is a more difficult and complex task, both legally and politically, than are changes to the QPP.

Pierson is clear that converting a mature pay-as-you-go system, such as the CPP, to a funded system is very difficult to do politically. The difficulty is in the transition towards the funded system because younger cohorts will effectively be required to pay twice; they will have to pay for the pensions of the current pensioners, and those soon to become pensioners, as well as for their own pensions. Pierson believes this is politically impractical.

If we add to this difficulty the "embeddedness" of the CPP one might also expect stealth in CPP reform. But the paper by Myles and Quadagno imply that an effort to reform CPP that is done by stealth will run up against a "we paid for it" objection by many pensioners and contributors. Moreover, the C/QPP are relatively small by international standards and the Myles and Quadagno paper seems to suggest that reductions are easier in larger Bismarckian pension systems.[1]

Therefore, it is unlikely that the reform of the CPP will fit into Battle's characterization of "policy by stealth." To the contrary, one of Canada's opposition parties is calling for a phase-out of the CPP and its replacement with a super-RRSP; and both the C.D. Howe Institute and the *Globe and Mail* have lent their prestige to this position. So a serious and wide-ranging policy debate and political debate about the future of the CPP seems likely.

Nonetheless, neither of the authors would suggest that a phase-out is a likely political outcome. Pierson would say that the politics of eliminating it are too treacherous and that it is too embedded. Myles and Quadagno would remind us that it is hard to take away what people believe they have earned through their work years and paid for through earmarked contributions.

For those who wish to preserve the CPP, but with modifications to its benefit and financing structures to ensure sustainability, a low visibility incrementalist approach would perhaps work best.[2] But it has already been suggested above that the prospects of avoiding a big political debate, at least on present reckoning, are not great. If there is such a debate, there is a risk that the battle lines that will be drawn will be stark and, in a political effort to rally support for the CPP, the modifications watered down to the point where not enough is done to achieve sustainability. In that event, in five years time, there is every possibility of the sustainability issue reemerging but with much more at stake financially, socially, and politically.

CONCLUDING REMARKS

The two papers under review indicate that "incrementalism," "stealth," is a common feature of pension reform activities in Western countries, including Canada. What are we to make of this observation? Is it cause for great concern?

In the social policy area, measures to reduce social expenditures (or the rate of growth in such expenditures) were implemented by the Conservative government without attacking head-on the basic principles of the relevant program. For example, the complex growth formula for fiscal transfers to the provinces was pared back. The income tax system was partially de-indexed. The clawback was introduced into Old Age Security and Family Allowance, ending their universal nature (even while the end of universality was being denied).

The government of the day, however, probably paid a much smaller political price for its social program cuts than it did for its highly visible and explicit introduction of the GST. In some sense, "stealth worked." It worked in the sense that the fiscal circumstances of the time required expenditure reduction and the social envelope could not be exempt. That there may have been better ways — more open ways for making the changes of the 1980s — may be true in some abstract sense. But incrementalism was better than inaction and there is reason to believe that if fiscal action had been made conditional on wide-ranging prior public debate, little action would have been taken.

We have already concluded that, based on the lessons from other countries, further reform of OAS/GIS and related tax measures, is most likely to continue in a relatively low profile incrementalist fashion, with actions that are technically complex, and with careful attention to those who are most needy. Being driven by the fiscal agenda, these measures will generate increasing savings. But what about C/QPP?

For the C/QPP, there may also have been a natural desire on the part of governments to proceed in a low key incrementalist way. But for these programs, especially the CPP, this approach has significant downsides. The issue of sustainability has become too controversial and too high profile for governments to resolve in a low visibility way that defuses most of the political risk. But that very same political risk could also block, or blunt, the reform that is needed. In that event, sustainability will in all likelihood be a growing concern and the same set of choices will re-surface in five years time with the stakes having grown substantially in the interim.

Achieving fiscal objectives while preserving as much of the public pension system as possible is what pension reform is about. A principal lesson from the foreign experience is that this kind of reform is best done in a cool political climate. But federal and provincial governments will not be able to set the thermostat unilaterally; and it is entirely possible that the temperature surrounding the reform of the CPP may turn out to be hotter than is conducive to a rational and informed public debate.

Pension issues are inherently complex. Achieving a good outcome to the C/QPP debate thus requires that more light, not more heat, be shed on the key issues surrounding sustainability. Based on the analysis of our two sets of authors, shining this additional light on the issues will be a very large challenge.

## NOTES

1. The combined OAS/GIS and C/QPP are at best a modest public pension system by the standards of industrialized countries. In this regard, the paper by Estelle James, setting out the World Bank analysis of a model retirement income system (for developing countries), is relevant. Her paper calls for a three-tiered system of retirement income. The first component is the public pension system. While the World Bank's proposed system would give the public pension tier an anti-poverty objective only, the size of Canada's public system, which combines both anti-poverty and earnings-related objectives, is roughly in line with the World Bank formula. Its size thus meets the test of balance between public and private income sources that the World Bank proposes. It follows also that scaling back a relatively small system, like Canada's, is

politically tougher, and in other respects more questionable, than is the case in countries like Germany and Sweden, which have much larger systems.
2. In the C/QPP context, sustainability is as much or more a political notion as it is a financial one. In the current political climate, sustainability appears to imply enough action on the finances of the CPP and QPP to restore political confidence.

REFERENCES

Gray, G. (1990), "Social Policy by Stealth," *Policy Options*, II, 2:17-29. (Gratton Gray was the pseudonym used by Ken Battle, a prominent social policy analyst.)

# PART FOUR

## THE WAY AHEAD

# CHAPTER TEN

# Generation X vs. Generation XS: Reflections on the Way Ahead

*Thomas J. Courchene*

## INTRODUCTION

The papers in this volume expand our knowledge and insights with respect to the historical, political, and socio-economic forces at play in the retirement income subsystem. My role is to formulate some thoughts on "the way ahead." This allows me to pick and choose from various ideas in the papers and then to integrate them with my own views of how the retirement-income system and, in particular, the Canada and Quebec Pension Plans (C/QPP) ought to evolve.

Accordingly, in the third section I shall focus on a somewhat more general analysis of the intergenerational transfer than was presented in any of the individual papers, although not necessarily more general than that in the collective papers. Essentially, this is a rough and ready exercise that attempts to put a few numbers on some aspects of the intergenerational transfer. Not surprisingly, perhaps, what will become clear is that the intergenerational transfer is multifaceted and that Canada is, appropriately, addressing it on a wide variety of fronts. In spite of this general approach to the retirement income subsystem, the high-profile policy issue with respect to this subsystem is clearly the C/QPP. Hence, section four directs attention to the CPP and its unfunded liability. To anticipate the conclusions, the societal focus on the C/QPP ought to be broadened to encompass the larger intergenerational tax and expenditure issues raised in section three; while the CPP is admittedly in trouble, the solutions must transcend the CPP itself. In the final part of the paper I shall direct attention to the salient features that ought to guide our way through the challenges posed by the intergenerational transfer. The overall message that emerges is one that holds more optimism than one would obtain from the various treatises (both in and out of government) attempting to "solve" the underfunding of the public pension system.

However, prior to addressing this agenda, I want to offer an alternative perspective to the dominant, if often implicit, view of this volume, namely that the elderly are a "burden" that we must somehow accommodate and minimize.

CELEBRATING SUCCESS

While not in any way intending to diminish the policy challenges of an aging population (which will occupy the remainder of the paper), it is nonetheless important to recognize the significant upsides in relation to the golden agers. Among these, I would include the following:

- Not all that long ago, the received wisdom was that we Canadians were the most insured people on earth — presumably the fear was that we would die too young. Now the focus has shifted from insurance to pensions — the concern is that we might live too long! The dramatic increase in life expectancy underlying this shift in focus from insurance to pensions is surely a matter for celebration.

- Over the past quarter century, our policies that substantially reduced poverty among the elderly are also a cause for celebration, particularly since this was accomplished in a period where the proportion of the elderly in the population doubled. This is surely one of the noteworthy achievements of Canadian postwar social policy. While we now face another doubling of the proportion of elderly, the challenge is one of *sustaining* this achievement. In other words, the starting point is an enviable one.

- The elderly and near-elderly cohorts own the vast majority of assets in the country. I shall focus on this in more detail later. For present purposes, the relevant message is that while the elderly will account for a larger fraction of societal consumption, a larger portion of tax revenues will also come from the elderly, in part because of their numbers but also because a segment of the over-65 age group will be among the wealthiest Canadians. Hence, we should not lose sight of the fact that the elderly will in effect be financing a larger proportion of the looming intergenerational transfer. Too much of the current debate focuses only on the financial transfer between generations and not *within* generations;

- Whereas in the first few postwar generations the attaining of age 65 implied (or was perceived to imply) that such individuals essentially became non-contributors to society on the economic front, this is clearly no longer the case. In part, this relates to improved health outcomes and enhanced life expectancy. However, it also relates to the changing nature of work and the substitution of brain for brawn as the generator of economic activity. What this means is that the next generation's 75-year old will be the equivalent of the postwar 65-year olds. In other words, we will have to think of the 65-75-year olds as the "young elderly." Relatedly, I suspect that we will see substantial labour force participation of these young elderly in the near future. They certainly have the ability to contribute. (Figure 1 presents one dimension of this.) Moreover, there will likely be a demand for their services since we are headed for a decline in the traditionally defined labour force when the boomers reach the societal retirement age. This adds an important degree of flexibility in terms of policy options. In particular, it suggests that we have to rethink the range of policies that tend to assume that the elderly will not be in the labour force. Perhaps a bill of rights and privileges for the elderly is going too far, but we must remove features such as age discrimination and our willingness to embed confiscatory or near-confiscatory tax-back rates in their income support programs.

FIGURE 1: Education Levels Canadians Aged 65 and Over

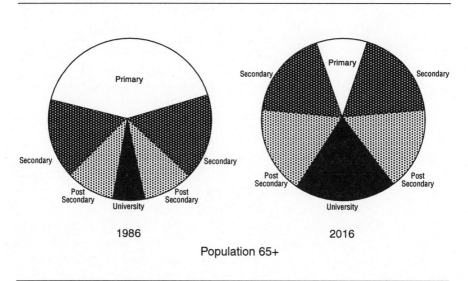

Population 65+

Source: Caledon Institute (1995, p. 7).

By way of summary, therefore, we have to balance our concern over the looming intergenerational transfer with a companion view that treats the elderly as an invaluable societal asset. One wonders if the politics of pension reform, as elaborated by Paul Pierson in this volume, might become more "doable" if they were accompanied by a set of policies designed to ensure that the elderly can continue to participate fully in Canadian economic, social, political, and cultural life.

AN OVERVIEW OF THE INTERGENERATIONAL TRANSFER CHALLENGE

Table 1 presents a reasonably comprehensive listing of the components of the intergenerational transfer, accompanied by an admittedly feeble attempt to attach some dollar figures to several of these components. As an important aside, this will not be the only occasion in what follows where numerical estimates, critical to sorting out the full implications of the intergenerational transfer, are not readily available.

For 1995-96, the cost of OAS/GIS/SPA roughly matches the cost of the C/QPP — just over $20 billion each. All these programs are unfunded. One could attempt to calculate the "unfunded liability" associated with OAS, for example. But this exercise tends to be limited to contributory schemes such as the C/QPP and workers' compensation. The recent paper, *An Information Paper for Consultations on the Canada Pension Plan*, released in February 1996 by the federal, provincial, and territorial governments (and, henceforth, referred to as the *CPP Information Paper*) suggests that the C/QPP unfunded liability is in the order of $550 billion.[1]

Item 5 of Table 1 relates to occupational pensions and RRSPs. The value of *existing* accumulated assets is estimated to be in the $600 billion range. This fact has been largely ignored in the other papers in this volume. Hence, as the system matures, the unfunded CPP liability will be "offset" by an even larger funded asset. More on this later.

Items 7 through 10 of the table focus on tax expenditures — the pension income credit for the elderly costs $.5 billion and the age credit $2.2 billion, although the latter is now being clawed back.[2] More intriguing is the net tax impact of RPPs and RRSPs. In terms of the former, the income tax "cost" of the RPP contribution deduction amounts to $8 billion, with an additional $12.2 billion in terms of the deferred interest provision relating to these funds. Partially offsetting this is the $7.3 billion of taxes on RPP benefits. This $13.6 billion net cost will surely fall over time as more Canadians with occupational pensions reach retirement age (i.e., the $7.3 billion figure will increase substantially). This is one facet of the overall case that a substantial portion of the future transfer to the elderly can be viewed as being financed *within* the elderly cohort.

TABLE 1:  An Overview of the Retirement Income Subsystem
(with some ballpark estimates)

| Category | 1995/96 Expenditures | Comments |
|---|---|---|
| A.  *Tax Transfers* | *$Billions* | |
| 1. OAS | 16.0 | Unfunded |
| 2. GIS | 4.7 | Unfunded |
| 3. SPA | 0.5 | Unfunded |
| B.  *Public Pensions* | | |
| 4. CPP | 16.7 | Unfunded liability $550 Billion |
| QPP | 5.1 | Unfunded liability $550 Billion |
| Total | 43.0 | |
| C.  *Occupational Plans* | | |
| 5. RRSPs/RPPs | | Prefunded (Assets over $600B) |
| 6. Government Pensions | | Typically unfunded (federal gov't) |
| D.  *Tax Expenditures* | | |
| 7. Elderly Credits | | |
| • pension income credit | 0.5 | |
| • age credit | 2.2 | |
| 8. Net RPPs | | |
| • deductions | 7.9 | |
| • deferred interest | 12.2 | |
| • tax on benefits | 7.3 | |
| Net | 12.8 | |
| 9. Net RRSPs | | |
| • deductions | 5.9 | |
| • deferred interest | 4.4 | |
| • taxes on benefits | 1.5 | |
| Net | 8.8 | |
| Sum (8+9) | 21.6 | |
| 10. CPP Credit | 1.5 | |
| E.  *Private Assets* | | |
| F.  *Health* | | |
| 11. Health Care | | Unfunded |
| 12. Provincial Programs | | |
| • Drugs | | Unfunded |
| G.  *Provincial Programs* | | |
| 13. Top-up (GAINS) | | Unfunded |
| 14. Workers' Compensation | | Unfunded liability |
| H.  *Shares of Tax Paid by Elderly* | | |
| 15. CPP | | Tax rate is about 28% |
| 16. Pensions (RPPs and RRSP) | | Tax rate well above 28% |
| I.  *Capital Gains and a Succession Duty/Inheritance Tax?* | | |

Source: Caledon Institute (1995, adapted from Appendix C).

RRSPs are less "mature" than RPPs, so that the value of the deduction ($5.4 billion) is well above the taxes paid on withdrawals ($1.5 billion). As with RPPs, this latter figure will soon begin to increase dramatically.

Finally, the value of the CPP credit is $1.5 billion (row 10 of the table). Note that CPP contributions are treated as a credit at the lowest tax rate whereas RPP and RRSP contributions are deductible (offset at the contributor's marginal tax rate).

Row E of the table simply draws attention to the fact that private assets of the elderly are yet another source for financing old age.

The entries under row panels F and G of Table 1 are intended to focus on aspects of provincial obligations to the elderly — health care in general, drug programs, and provincial top-ups (e.g., GAINS in Ontario). All of these are unfunded. Workers' Compensation (item 14) is especially important. While most Workers' Compensation (WC) programs are in financial trouble, (i.e., have large unfunded liabilities) it may be inappropriate to view them as an intergenerational transfer, since benefits normally cease at retirement age. However, WC is relevant in the context of the CPP challenge because a major component of CPP benefits relates to disability payments (Robson 1996). Again, this will be elaborated below.

The final components of the table relate to tax recoupments. Each dollar of CPP benefits brings in roughly 28 cents in taxes (federal and provincial). This raises an important issue. The $550 billion unfunded liability is a *gross* figure. Why not calculate it *net* of tax, which would yield a net unfunded liability of $360 billion (72 percent of 500 billion)?[3] Why should contributions be set to generate $550 rather than $360 billion? Phrased differently, the tax revenues from C/QPP benefits could be dedicated to the CPP fund. To my knowledge, no one has attempted to view the C/QPP on an after-tax basis.

As the $600 billion of existing pension (RPP and RRSP) assets mature, this will put roughly $240 billion (undiscounted, at a presumed 40 percent marginal rate) into federal and provincial tax coffers. This puts a ballpark estimate on the point raised earlier, namely that a substantial amount of the transfers to the future elderly will come from the elderly themselves. In none of the existing projections of the "burden" of the C/QPP does one find any mention of this. This speaks to one of the themes of my paper, namely that the retirement income subsystem is inherently an interrelated *system*, not a set of independent programs. And, as I shall argue later, the solutions should also be system related.

The table concludes with a query: Why not a succession duty-inheritance tax to ensure that assets and incomes do not escape untaxed? If it is good enough for the Americans ... .

While many implications can be drawn from Table 1, I shall focus on a select few:

- The intergenerational transfer is a very complex phenomenon and it relates to the entire age spectrum.

- More importantly, Canadian policymakers, both federal and provincial, are directing policy attention to almost all the entries in the table. For example:

  - The OAS/GIS/SPA is being converted into a version of a negative income tax, which will be fully clawed back for the elderly rich and, perhaps, for the elderly middle class.[4] And beginning in July 1996, the OAS will not even be paid to the upper-income elderly.

  - The age credit is now being clawed back. Can the pension credit survive for long? (It will be clawed back under the provisions of the 1996 federal budget.)

  - Look for major changes in financing health care. If Ontario follows through with its intentions, then its income tax reduction will be partly offset by a high-income "health levy," which presumably would apply to the high-income elderly as well.

  - Following Saskatchewan's lead, other provinces are moving to ensure that well-off seniors begin to pay for some portion of their drug costs.

  - Workers' Compensation is under review or reform in most jurisdictions, and so on.

- Tax expenditures merit separate attention. The paper by Jack Mintz and Tom Wilson in this volume argues strongly for an "expenditure approach" to the income tax system, which would imply that all savings be given RRSP-type treatment. However, with the shift from deductions to credits (and the removal of horizontal equity features from the tax system since these credits are clawed back), the tax system has shifted towards a vertical equity or social policy conception rather than an expenditure conception. In turn, this means that the politics of income distribution within the personal income tax are now pitted against the economic case for an expenditure tax. If, for example, we were to raise CPP contribution rates to 14 percent or even to 10 percent, the politics of the income tax would almost surely imply some comparable trimming of the RRSP/RPP tax treatment — a move to credits or a stricter limit on contributions. If the Mintzes and Wilsons of this world want to preserve the status quo on the RRSP front, then they would be well advised to direct some attention to ensuring that the overall tax system does not become more regressive.

The thrust of these comments is that Canada is actively addressing the intergenerational challenge across a wide variety of fronts. If one then takes account of the fact that (i) future revenues from the elderly will be very significant, (ii) that the elderly are relatively well-off now, and (iii) that many of the "young elderly" will likely have the desire and, hopefully, the opportunity to remain gainfully employed after age 65, then this picture is, I think, more optimistic than it is typically painted. What is needed now is some competent "number cruncher" to provide more reliable data with respect to these issues.

Finally, while the CPP may be the key "program" challenge in terms of the intergenerational transfer, I submit that it should not be viewed in isolation but, rather, in the more general context of the overview of Table 1. This is particularly the case since, in the Myles-Quadagno terminology, it is somewhere between a Beveridge and a Bismarckian scheme. Why, then, are we attempting to place the full burden of financing the unfunded CPP liability on the backs of future generations? I now turn in more detail to addressing this issue.

## A PUBLIC POLICY APPROACH TO THE CPP

### The Mechanics of the CPP

Under the assumption of retirement at 65, a contribution period of 40 years, life expectancy of 85 years and a 2 percent real rate of return, Lam, Cutt and Prince calculate in their paper that a 7 percent contribution rate would allow each individual to provide for his or her own retirement income at the same real benefit rate that currently exists. Under the existing C/QPP provisions, which allow for a full pension at much less than 40 years of contributions and which allow for disability pensions, this internal actuarial rate is closer to 10 percent. For purposes of this paper, I shall assume that an 8 percent contribution rate is the appropriate number. (This will be rationalized later, but essentially it reflects pre-funding, some tightening up of the existing scheme, some de-indexation of benefits and some integration of disability benefits across the CPP and WC programs.) This is a critical conceptual rate because it represents a "fair deal" to the contributor since it matches what, under similar assumptions, could be achieved with a World Bank or RRSP-type proposal.

However, an 8 percent contribution rate ignores completely the unfunded C/QPP liability. If future generations are also required to fund this liability then their contribution rates will have to be much higher, about 14 percent by year 2030 according to the CPP chief actuary. And in the process these future generations will be saddled with a situation where they will have every incentive to opt-out/ renege on the CPP since they will be forced to contribute at a rate nearly double that at which a "market plan" would deliver the same benefits. In a nutshell, this is the policy challenge.

## The Anatomy of Contribution Rate Increases

Prior to proceeding to the policy discussion, it is important to focus on a few background points relating to the C/QPP unfunded liability. Drawing from the *CPP Information Paper*:

> This unfunded liability is the result of two factors. First, full benefits were phased in over 10 years when CPP was created in 1966, rather than requiring people to contribute for some 35-40 years. Even persons retiring today have only paid into the plan for some 30 years, whereas those retiring in 2006 and beyond will need 40 years of contributions for a full pension. Second, no one — past or present — has paid the full cost of their CPP benefits (Canada. Minister of Finance 1996, p. 62).

In terms of the latter factor, whether one assumes that 8 percent is a "fair" rate or the 10 percent rate assumed by the *CPP Information Paper*, the key point here is that either of these rates is well above the current 5.6 percent contribution rate and way above the 3.6 percent rate which held sway for 20 years after the plan's inception in 1966.

Table 2 presents an "anatomy" of the increase in the pay-as-you-go equilibrium rates in 2030. The original estimates (made in 1966, at the plan's inception) were that rates would have to be 5.5 percent by 2030. The new estimates call for a 14.2 percent contribution rate. The key components of this increase appear in Table 2, with some explanatory detail below the chart.

The category "benefit enrichments" of Table 2 merits further attention. By way of elaboration, the *CPP Information Paper* (pp. 23-24) details the principal enrichments to the plan:

- Introduction of a *child-rearing drop-out provision* (1978). This allows working Canadians to leave a job or reduce their hours while caring for children under seven years and protect their entitlements under the plan.

- An increase in *disability benefits* (1987), and relaxation in the minimum contributory requirements.

- Widows and widowers receiving *survivor benefits* (1987) were allowed to keep this entitlement upon remarriage.

- *Full indexation* of benefits to changes in the cost of living (1975). Previously there was *a 2 percent* ceiling.

- Payment of *survivor benefits* (1975) to widowers as well as widows. Initially benefits were paid only to widowers if they were disabled and dependent.

- Dropping the *retirement and earnings tests* (1975). Originally, contributors aged 65 to 69 could only receive their retirement benefits if they passed a retirement test, and their subsequent benefit up to age 70 was reduced if they earned more than a set amount.

As noted in Table 2, these benefit enrichments have increased the forecast contribution rates in 2030 by 2.4 percentage points. These initiatives are especially intriguing in light of the Myles-Quadagno distinction between Beveridge (tax-transfer) and Bismarck (earnings related) programs for the elderly. Essentially, these arbitrary increases in benefits *loosen the link between contributions and benefits in the CPP* and move it away from a Bismarck conception and towards a Beveridge model. This distinction will play a key role in my approach to resolving the CPP challenge, since, to anticipate the analysis, I shall not attempt to solve the CPP underfunding by focusing only on the CPP parameters. However, this is not the way that the various reform proposals view the CPP challenge. Enter the "mathematics of annuities."

TABLE 2:   The Anatomy of Rising CPP Contribution Rates

|  | Costs as a Percentage of Contributory Earnings |
| --- | --- |
| Costs in 2030 as projected when CPP started (1966) | 5.5 |
| Changed demographics | 2.6 |
| Changed economics | 2.2 |
| Enrichment of benefits | 2.4 |
| Disability | 1.5 |
| Costs in 2030 as now projected | 14.2 |

Explanatory Notes:

- *Changed demographics*
  Improved health as a result of lifestyle changes and medical advances means that Canadians are living considerably longer than when the CPP was introduced in 1966.
- *Changed economics*
  Slower growth in output per worker has added a further 2.2 percentage points.
- *Benefit enrichments*
  Enrichments have boosted costs by 2.4 percentage points.
- *Disability*
  The increased numbers of Canadians claiming disability benefits for longer periods of time has added another 1.5 percentage points.

Source: Canada (1996, pp. 19-20).

## *The Mathematics of Annuities Approach to CPP Reform*

The Lam, Cutt and Prince paper is one of several (Robson 1996; Slater 1995; and Canada 1996) which essentially utilize the mathematics of annuities to alter the parameters of the CPP to ensure that future generations are not saddled with the full 14 percent contribution rate in order to keep the CPP afloat. The mathematics are straightforward. To get the steady state contribution rate down one can:

- raise contribution rates *now* in order to build up a fund. This is generally referred to as pre-funding. An alternative way to raise contributions is to expand the insurable earings base. Thus, Lam, Cutt and Prince recommend that the YBE (Year's Basic Exemption, which is 10 percent of YMPE, the Year's Maximum Pensionable Earnings) be eliminated;

- assuming pre-funding, one could invest the funds in a diversified market portfolio in order to increase fund earnings (as an intriguing aside, the existing fund — roughly $40 billion — is actually earning a very *high* rate of return, in the range of 11 percent nominal and 9 percent real, even though the fund is invested only in provincial bonds. This is a result of the fact that the fund was built up during periods of high interest rates and that the provincial obligations have a 20-year maturity. As these bonds roll over, the return on the fund will decrease);

- raise the retirement age. This is a powerful instrument because it simultaneously increases the contribution years and decreases the benefit years;

- decrease benefits, either by de-indexing or by discretionary action (Robson 1996).

Using a combination of all of these parameters, one can create a virtually limitless number of CPP reform alternatives. One especially valuable feature of the Lam, Cutt and Prince paper is that it presents the implications of manipulating some of these parameters. Likewise, Table 3, reproduced from the *CPP Information Paper* presents a catalogue of impacts of potential CPP changes and their impact on "equilibrium" contribution rates, although it ignores the impact of pre-funding.

Nonetheless, the essential feature of *all* of these approaches is that they require future generations to pay for both their own pensions *and* much of the existing unfunded liability. For example, Robson's (1996) proposal keeps contribution rates to the 8 percent range but increases the retirement age to 70 and reduces the real CPP benefits to 60 percent of today's level. Clever as this may be, it is still a "bad deal" for future generations because individuals (i) contribute more and for longer, (ii) collect for a shorter period, and (iii) receive 60 percent of real benefits of existing recipients. This does not remove the incentive to renege, but it *is* a better deal than saddling future generations with 14 percent contribution rates. At least under the Robson proposal, *some* of the unfunded liability is pushed on to those currently in the system, as it were.

TABLE 3:  Financial Impacts of Possible CPP Measures

| | Savings in 2030 | |
| --- | --- | --- |
| | As Percent of CPP Expenditures | As Reduction in Pay-As-You-Go Rate |
| *Retirement Benefits* | % | % |
| Reduce income replacement rate to 22.5 per cent (from 25%) | 8.8 | 1.25 |
| Reduce drop out to 10 percent over 5 years[2] | 2.2 | 0.31 |
| Raise age of entitlement to 67 | 4.2 | 0.63 |
| Index benefits in pay by CPI minus 1 percent | 9.0 | 1.28 |
| *Disability Benefits* | | |
| Tighten administration | 1.5 | 0.22 |
| Lower benefit by 25 percent of Workers Compensation[3] | 0.6 | 0.08 |
| Stronger labour force link[4] | 1.2 | 0.17 |
| Convert pension at age 65 to actuarially reduced pension | 2.7 | 0.39 |
| Base retirement pensions on YMPE at time of disablement[5] | 1.1 | 0.15 |
| *Survivor Benefits* | | |
| New rule for combined benefits | 1.2 | 0.17 |
| Eliminate death benefit | 1.5 | 0.21 |
| *CPP Earnings Base*[1] | | |
| Cut YBE to 5 percent and index | -0.1 | 1.10 |
| Freeze YBE at 1997 level | -0.2 | 1.63 |

Notes:
1. Savings as a percent of CPP costs are negative because more people would be brought into the system, thus increasing expenditures.  However, the pay-as-you-go rate would decline because the earnings base on which contributions are paid would expand.
2. Current provisions allow contributors to drop from their earnings record 15 percent of their non-working or low-income years to a maximum of seven years.
3. In several provinces, disabled persons can receive both CPP and Workers' Compensation.  This proposal would "stack" the two to a limited degree — it would subtract 25 percent of WC benefits from CPP benefits.
4. Currently, to get disability payments, a worker needs to have contributed in two of the last three years or five of the last ten.  This provision would require contributions in four of the last six years.
5. Rather than on YMPE (Year's Maximum Pensionable Earnings) at time of retirement eligibility.

Source: Canada (1996).

However, this mathematics-of-annuities approach is, I submit, considerably off-base. Given the several Beveridge-type characteristics of the CPP alluded to earlier as well as the fact that the unfunded liability is a societal "sunk cost," there is no economic or public policy rationale for dumping the unfunded liability on future generations. The public policy solution is, in my view, to integrate aspects of this mathematics-of-annuities approach with the general intergenerational transfer approach implicit in Table 1, and, then, to filter all of this through a set of policy goals or objectives. What these public policy goals might be is the subject of the following section.

## Alternative Policy Goals Relating to CPP Reform

As Lam, Cutt and Prince emphasize (and as Robson, both in his comments in this volume and in 1996, touches upon as well), there is a major "credibility" problem associated with the CPP — the young generation does not think that the CPP will be there for them when they retire. This is actually a much more difficult policy issue than at first it might appear. One way to convince the young and future generations that the CPP will be there for them would be to build up a fund, that is, to pre-fund. But as we have seen, if this is accomplished solely through a mathematics-of-annuities approach, the young generation will quickly and correctly perceive that this is an actuarially unsound deal, probably involving negative returns. Thus, the incentive to renege increases or at least remains. Hence the "Bismarckian" approach to the CPP — that is, to solve the CPP problem solely *within* the CPP — is a dangerous intergenerational policy gamble. Addressing the credibility issue constitutes an important CPP reform objective.

A second goal of CPP reform must be to place it in the context of the overall deficit (debt) reduction challenge. Even though the CPP is not "on budget," the unfunded liability does not play well with the "kids in red suspenders" (the international money markets). Here, the solution is straightforward — reduce the unfunded liability by any and all of increasing premiums. pre-funding, increasing the age of retirement and reducing benefits (e.g., de-indexing or partial de-indexing). This may create problems down the road (as alluded to earlier), but from the deficit-debt perspective reducing the unfunded liability is the name of the game. That the various goals/objectives of reform may be in conflict is certainly not limited to CPP reform.

The third policy perspective relates to the intergenerational transfer. My perspective here (perhaps not widely shared) is that the approach to the CPP should, in part at least, be driven by the Beveridge (tax-transfer) conception rather than the Bismarckian conception. This follows because the CPP benefits have been arbitrarily enhanced (as noted earlier) and because the implicit contract nature of the CPP implies that the unfunded liability is *predetermined* and, therefore, a "sunk" cost. Hence, it should be addressed in the context of the overall intergenerational transfer presented in Table 1. Phrased differently, this is a *societal* liability, not a liability that should rest solely or largely on the future generations. Details will be outlined later, but this perspective would lead to approaches like transferring any increase in tax revenues from CPP benefits into a dedicated CPP fund. This will increase pre-funding and release the pressure on premium increases. It also leads to another approach, namely that part of the unfunded liability attaches to persons currently in the labour force whose contributions, until recently, were fixed at 3.6 percent (shared equally with employers). Intergenerational equity considerations would dictate that these workers should not be able to retire without bearing a greater proportion of the cost of their CPP benefits. This would call for an *age-related* premium structure (on employees, not employers). Slater (1995) suggests this in passing. While this may be a politically difficult policy to implement, any consideration of intergenerational equity would dictate that the boomers not be able to slide into retirement without bearing a larger funding share of their future CPP benefits.

The final two policy perspectives relate to the younger generations. The first of these focuses on the lifetime income prospects of young, unskilled Canadians whose numbers are, unfortunately, far too numerous. Their employment-income prospects are not all that rosy. They face sharp increases in CPP premiums and in Workers' Compensation premiums. The proposed reforms of UI do not give them any premium relief. As part of the overall deficit reduction exercise, all provinces are in the process of substantially increasing tuition fees. And all of this is on top of the fact that they are facing a much larger debt-servicing burden than that faced by earlier generations. This might be acceptable if sharply increased CPP contributions guaranteed enhanced future income. However, my calculations (Courchene 1994, ch. 3) indicate that the value to an Ontario retiree with a CPP benefit equal to half the maximum level will *not add one penny* to his/her retirement income. This is because the Ontario's GAINS is stacked upon the federal GIS (each with a 50 percent clawback), so that the entire one-half CPP is clawed back. One could argue that this is an unfair comparison, since the OAS/GIS is the last resort guarantee for those who have not been able to generate substantial pension (or private) savings. But the lower-income classes of the young cohort recognize that CPP contributions are *equivalent to taxes, not to deferred savings*. Their key problem is *current* (not *future*) income and hikes in employment taxes lower both their employment and income prospects (since employer CPP contributions will in all likelihood be passed on to workers).

The second aspect relates to the growing inequality *within* cohorts. Globalization and the knowledge-information revolution are polarizing market incomes.

The generous RPP and RRSP arrangements will ensure that this polarization of income will be *magnified* in retirement. This does not auger well for social cohesion, either in terms of intergenerational or within-cohort equity.

This, then, is my downloading of some of the public policy imperatives that ought to be brought to bear on the resolution of the CPP challenge. How these imperatives might relate to the range of policy options is the subject of the following section.

## Policy Options

Bringing all of these perspectives to bear on CPP reform (with special emphasis on the last two, namely the intergenerational equity and income distribution implications within each cohort) leads me to reject both the "no-problem" scenario as outlined by Monica Townson (1995)[5] as well as the Lam, Cutt and Prince (this volume), Robson (1996) and to a lesser extent the Slater (1995) models which attempt to solve the CPP underfunding entirely within the confines of the CPP. From my perspective, none of these is either equitable or appropriate.

The outlines of my preferred approach would be as follows. First, raise contribution rates rather quickly to the level where these contributions will, on an actuarially appropriate basis, generate a pension in line with market returns. Assume that this is 8 percent, allocated equally between employers and employees. At this point some elaboration is warranted. As part of the mid-1980s reform of the personal income tax, employee contributions to the CPP (but not to RPPs or RRSPs) were shifted from a deduction to a credit at the lowest marginal tax rate. The result was a substantial tax grab by both levels of government from CPP contributors (or an after-tax increase in premiums for those in the middle- and upper-income-tax brackets, depending on one's perspective). Returning the CPP contributions to a deduction can offset the impact of the rise in premiums, at least for upper-income Canadians. Relatedly, if one is concerned, as I am, about the level of these "employment taxes," then the existence of the roughly $4 billion surplus in the UI system that is currently being pocketed by Ottawa can be transformed into UI premium reductions and the resulting tax room can then be "assigned" to the CPP. In other words, there is the possibility of transferring tax room from UI to the CPP, without much in the way of an increase in the overall "employment tax."

Second, this will result in considerable pre-funding and this fund should pursue market returns (more on this later, since this is a major departure for the CPP, though not for the QPP).

Third, age-related premiums are appropriate to ensure that the boomers contribute a fairer share to their prospective benefits. If the appropriate rate for the young generation is 8 percent (4 percent for employers and 4 percent for employees), the employee contribution for 45-55-year olds might be 4.5 percent and for 55-65-year olds 5 percent, with no change in the 4 percent employer contribution rate. Alternatively, the overall 8 percent rate could be applied immediately to the older cohorts and phased in for the younger cohorts. To be sure, this proposal may never see the light of legislative day, but it is important that it be highlighted in the CPP debate because it brings home in the starkest possible way that the soon-to-be-retired are enjoying a free (subsidized) CPP ride.

Fourth, there is room for some "housekeeping" reforms in the CPP. Robson (1996) is certainly right when he flags the "disability" disaster in the CPP. We have nearly two full-blown disability programs (actually three if we count aspects of UI). We need to rationalize all of this. Intriguingly, the QPP and WC overlap in Quebec in terms of persons accessing both types of disability pensions is much less than it is for the CPP and the WC programs in the other nine provinces, presumably because Quebec has full control of both. Hence, part of the overlap is a jurisdictional issue. In terms of other "housekeeping issues," the Lam, Cutt, Prince recommendation that the Year's Basic Exemption (YBE) be subject to contribution also makes sense. I would add that, for those persons who have limited employment earnings, the contribution on income up to the YBE be refunded via the tax system. This conversion of the YBE exemption to low-earnings refundable credit is also a recommendation of the *CPP Information Paper* (1996, p. 31). This would remove employer discrimination in terms of favouring short-turn (CPP exempt) workers, it would lower overall contribution rates, *ceteris paribus,* and it would effectively maintain the YBE for the lowest-earning cohort. Finally, it seems appropriate to subject CPP benefit rates to partial indexation, that is, to de-indexing. To be sure, this is eroding benefits by "stealth" but it is becoming an increasingly typical aspect of Canada's approach to transfers. More to the point, it will reduce the *growth* in (not the level of) CPP benefits for that group that has benefited or will soon benefit from dramatic underfunding. This measure may also be appropriate in analytical terms as well since the evidence is that the CPI *overestimates* the true inflation rate because of inadequate consideration of substitution, quality changes, new products, and the like.[6]

In tandem, these changes to the CPP would serve to ensure that an 8 percent contribution rate alluded to earlier is probably close to a "market" rate.

Now comes the really tough part. Recommendation five is that the full responsibility for funding the CPP's unfunded liability *cannot* rest on future generations. There is absolutely no policy rationale for this approach and there is ample evidence that this would be a wholly inappropriate decision, intergenerational-wise and income-distribution-wise. My approach to the unfunded liability is that it is inherently a societal tax-transfer issue, not a CPP issue. This suggests that we ought to supplement the CPP from sources beyond premiums. In principle, this could come from any source, for example, a surtax on income taxes that would be directed either to CPP benefits or to the dedicated CPP fund. However, certain tax sources are more obvious.

The first of these would be the tax receipts arising from CPP benefits themselves. Why not direct a substantial proportion of any *increase* in taxes on CPP benefits into the CPP fund? What this would do would be to ensure that contribution rates relate to the *net* (after-tax) cost of the unfunded liability, not the *gross* (before-tax) cost. Surely, this is appropriate — the tax revenues will only arise because we are honouring the unfunded liability.[7] As noted earlier, given the assumed 30 percent tax on C/QPP benefits, this represents a huge source of potential CPP funding.

A second potential source of supplementary income that could be directed to the CPP arises from the ability of persons to tax-defer accumulations in RRP and RRSP accounts between age 65-71. There is little rationale for allowing continuing contributions and the tax-deferral beyond the societal retirement age. To the extent that there is a rationale for the status quo, it would be along the following lines. Some individuals (particularly women who entered the labour force later in life) may not have had the opportunity to accumulate sufficient tax-assisted savings. The way to handle this is to set some *minimum* level of tax-assisted savings that apply to all citizens. If these minimum limits have not been achieved by age 65, then extending the privilege to 71 can be maintained. However, the major beneficiaries of this 65-71 extension are persons with very substantial tax-assisted asset accumulations. The proposal here is to ensure that these pensions must begin to be drawn down and taxed at age 65 and the proceeds transferred into the CPP fund.[8] Beyond this, I would also suggest that Canada follow the Americans and levy a succession of duty/inheritance taxes, also to be dedicated to the CPP fund. Most of these tax revenues will have arisen from tax concessions for those who have also benefited from the underfunding of the CPP. On both intergenerational and equity grounds, this would seem to make sense. The politics may be quite different, as I shall detail later.

In terms of the four earlier-enumerated policy goals, what this approach to the CPP accomplishes is:

• It addresses the trade-off between credibility and opting-out. The credibility aspect would be solved because of the dedicated fund. Future generations will be more confident of their CPP pensions if a substantial CPP fund exists. And the opting-out or reneging problem is minimized because a substantial portion of the unfunded liabilities are accommodated from general tax revenues and not just from future premiums. In other words, contribution rates will not be far off from what a market plan could deliver.

• The fiscal issue is probably a saw-off. International capital markets will be assuaged by virtue of the fact that unfunded liability will be reduced substantially (indeed, why not express the existing unfunded liability in *net-of-tax* terms rather than in *gross-of-tax* terms). This will provide the international capital markets with more comfort. On the other hand, selected revenues that could otherwise be devoted to deficit reduction will now be directed to the CPP fund. My impression, and it is only an impression, is that revenue projections have not taken adequate account of the fact that there will be very substantial taxes coming from the elderly. What I am suggesting is that a portion of these future revenues be directed to the CPP fund in order to help finance the intergenerational unfunded liability. At the very least, it is incumbent on the federal authorities to present a full intergenerational transfer picture in the millennium. To the best of my knowledge, these projections do not exist. This is nothing short of incredible, particularly since their absence tends to overestimate the magnitude of the intergenerational transfer, that is, it understates the degree to which the shift in resources to the elderly will also be financed by tax revenues from the elderly.

The principal argument in favour of the above approach to the CPP is that it accords well with the intergenerational and income distribution issues. Others may (and hopefully will) present alternative approaches along these lines, since focusing on the intergenerational inequities and the principle of ability to pay would appear to be solid and equitable foundations on which to tackle the CPP challenge.

Were Canada to adopt the above approach to the CPP, some additional problems would also be ameliorated. With higher premium rates, the CPP will begin to run up against (i.e., "crowd out") occupational plans and RRSPs. Pressures will build for the conversion of the CPP into an employer-employee RRSP-type plan with full deduction of premiums, that is, in the direction of the Estelle James-World Bank analysis in this volume. Were this to occur, the implicit-intergenerational-transfer aspect to this tier of the pension system will begin to fade away. This problem, namely the potential for the CPP to crowd out occupational-RRSP plans, would be dramatically magnified if the "all-is-well" approach holds sway, since contribution rates will rise to 14 percent.

## The Politics of Pensions

The above analysis of CPP options ignores the politics of pension reform, including the fact that agreement on any change in the parameters has to get the approval of Ottawa and of seven of the provinces with two-thirds of the population.

On the surface, this would appear to bolster the Paul Pierson view that pension reform is difficult to engineer because the costs typically occur in the near future with the benefits arising beyond the typical politicians' electoral horizons. This is the "in the long run we are all dead" dictum of Keynes. Thus, if the actual crisis in the contribution rates occurs only in 15 years time or so, why are Canadians and, particularly, Canadian politicians focusing on the CPP now. Part of the answer is, I think, that the concept of unfunded liabilities effectively brings the future to the present. And when combined with Canada's overall debt problem, the CPP underfunding cannot be avoided if we wish to set our overall fiscal house in order. Hence, the more appropriate perspective is that *Keynes is dead, but we live in the long run.*

Quebec acts as an effective catalyst in all of this. Quebecers can do whatever they wish with the QPP. However, they also have a vote on any changes in the CPP. But I find it difficult to conceive that they would exercise their CPP vote to thwart the desires of the majority of provinces. There is no political gain for them in such a position. The more relevant Quebec influence relates to the overall un-certainty that the national unity crisis lends to Canada's longer term prospects. Specifically, we have had to take *more aggressive* action both on the fiscal and CPP fronts in order to offset this national unity influence in capital markets. And the fact that Quebec MPs are concentrated in the Bloc Québécois helps in all of this. Given that they have been uniformly against the social policy changes in the last budget, could the federal government have accomplished this degree of social policy reform if these 50-plus Bloc members were part of the Liberal Caucus? I think not.

Nonetheless, political problems will surely arise in light of the above option. The most obvious relates to any pre-funding of the CPP. Will the provinces agree to a privately managed or, at least, an arms-length fund? To this point, the CPP fund, which now stands at roughly $40 billion, has been invested in provincial bonds at interest rates equivalent to that on long-term federal government debt. (As already noted, because much of this fund was accumulated in the 1970s and 1980s, the current rate of return on this fund is rather high.) A compromise may be possible. Any fund portfolio would carry some bonds. If this bond share took the form of a weighted average of provincial bonds (with the weights being the share of premium income by province) the provinces might come on side, espe-cially if the fund becomes sizeable.

But a sizeable fund runs into a concern raised by Robson in his comments. Specifically, how do we guarantee that the fund will not be used, politically, to increase benefits? As Table 2 indicates, this is exactly what has happened in the past. One only has to look at the recent UI proposals to see that the federal depart-ment of Human Resources Development views premiums as an appropriate income source to fund job creation and income support initiatives. Sheltering any dedicated CPP fund from political goals will probably have to involve some federal-provincial version of a Crown corporation run, say, by employees and employers. Presumably this is why some analysts prefer private sector plans and management.

A final political stumbling block is that the C/QPP is "off-budget." What this means is that earmarking selected future tax receipts either for CPP benefits or for investment in the CPP fund will *worsen* the fiscal position. The compensating improvement in the CPP underfunding does not appear "on budget," as it were. In a deficit-reduction-strategy era, this may not be an appealing trade-off for our political masters.

To conclude this section on the politics of CPP reform, one has to recognize that Banting and Lazar (in their comments) may be right — the politics of CPP reform may be too daunting to accomplish anything other than tinkering (e.g., increasing contribution rates and a bit of "tightening" of the system). This will mean that the CPP will limp along towards its ultimate demise. The credibility issue will become exacerbated and, with it, the increased potential for reneging and opting-out. Note that this reneging on the part of future generations will also involve reneging on the "implicit contract" to the retirees. The CPP would then probably have to be folded into some enhanced version of a negative income tax for the elderly. Although coming at this from a different perspective, Robson (1996) anticipates as much as he recommends the gradual phasing out of the CPP and its likely replacement with a compulsory, private, savings plan along World Bank or RRSP-type lines. This clearly *is* an option, one that I have not focused on in my analysis. But I have two comments on this alternative. First, if this is where we are headed, let us prepare for it *now* and not run headlong into this wall early in the next century, with its accompanying dramatic rupture of the implicit societal intergenerational contract. My second comment is that I prefer to maintain the CPP as some combination of a Beveridge-Bismarck program rather than replace it with an individual, market-driven, compulsory savings program. Others may differ.

## CONCLUSION: THE WAY AHEAD

Short of the potential break-up of the country, the reform of the retirement income system is probably the most daunting policy challenge on the horizon. Its dimensions are staggering: it is essentially a cradle-to-grave issue; it embodies implicit societal contracts; it is a jurisdictional quagmire and it is underpinned by every conceivable type of equity issue. There are no right answers in this area. And any so-called "preferred" approach (such as that proffered above) will depend on the weighting given to the various equity issues.

In this context, my approach is based on two key assumptions. The first is that one has to view the intergenerational transfer in its entirety. It is, at base, a full-blown "system" and ultimately what matters to individuals is how the overall system affects them, not the impact of one particular program (which could be offset by other programs in the system). In Table 1, I attempted to illustrate, with no intention of being exhaustive, some key elements of the retirement income system.

As an operational approach, my clear preference is for a fully diversified approach — to act on all fronts simultaneously and to attempt to address any particular program in terms of its larger system implications. And on this score, I think that Ottawa and the provinces deserve high marks: there is policy concern, if not action, in terms of virtually all the entries in Table 1. But the time has now come to also view the C/QPP within this more general context.

My second assumption derives from David Thomson's book, *Selfish Generations?* which argues that the welfare state in his country (New Zealand) has largely been hijacked by a single cohort — the soon-to-be elderly. This also has reasonable resonance with the Canadian situation. It is not just that this is the first generation where the elderly are better off than the young. It is that we seem to feel no compunction about saddling the young with "obviously rational" initiatives like sharply rising tuition fees and mounting payroll taxes in the very time frame when their income prospects are quite bleak and the incomes in their cohort appear to be polarizing. Should we dare tell them that allowing a federal civil servant to access Ottawa's early retirement package at age 50 is probably roughly equivalent to putting a million dollars in his/her pension fund? And many of these retirees will reenter the labour force, often as consultants to governments. Can we in good faith tell the next generation that beyond servicing the debt that we ran up, they are responsible for funding the entire intergenerational unfunded CPP liability, in addition to providing their own retirement savings?

Surely, we soon-to-be-retired risk becoming a selfish generation — generation XS as the title of this paper suggests.

Thus, my approach to the CPP is driven by intergenerational and income distribution considerations. Simply put, my generation must contribute more to addressing this underfunding — hence the variety of recommendations for tax initiatives that would be directed into the CPP fund. I think that this is eminently doable. Subject to being corrected by someone who has "done" the numbers, I believe that we are underestimating the potential tax revenues that will come from the future elderly. And some version of an inheritance tax would not be inappropriate if tax-assisted savings are finding their way back (untaxed) to the next generation.

To conclude, I want to return to the rather optimistic overview in my introduction. We must balance our concerns about the intergenerational transfer with a set of policies that integrates or reintegrates the elderly into Canadian society. I recognize that, as a group, the golden agers will begin to play a more prominent role in the political system by dint of sheer numbers. But they too are caught up in an important implicit intergenerational contract of their own. Beyond their sincere commitment to the future of the country they have a more direct bridge to the younger generation — they are their grandchildren.

In the final analysis, I put great emphasis on maintaining a viable intergenerational transfer system, one that can go both ways. In turn, this is why I would prefer a CPP to a series of RRSP-like private savings vehicles. The former is more consistent with societal bonding between the young and the old. If we erode the willingness to share across generations (and in *both* directions, as I have been arguing), it will not be long before our willingness to share *within* generations will also erode. How we sort out this issue will have a lot to say about whether we will remain Canadians or whether we will simply become northern Americans.

NOTES

1.  As Robson (1996) notes, the C/QPP unfunded liability represents the difference between (a) the investment fund that would be needed, after allowing for future contributions at the "full cost" rate (the rate at which participants entering the plan would cover the cost of their own benefits) to meet all currently accrued benefits of plan participants and (b) the funds actually held in the plan accounts. In terms of the latter, the "fund" is now about $40 billion, roughly two year's worth of benefits.

2.  The 1996 federal budget has folded these credits and the OAS/GIS into a super-GIS, not unlike the proposal in the paper by Battle in this volume.

3.  This is probably a more complicated calculation than is implied here. Moreover, one might want to focus on *net* taxes, that is, tax receipts less the value of the C/QPP contribution credit.

4.  Ken Battle's paper in this volume is an important contribution to the evolution of a generalized GIS approach to the OAS-GIS-SPA system. Consistent with my earlier-noted concern that we should not impose near-confiscatory taxes on the "young elderly," why not have an "all-in" tax-back rate of, say, 40-45 percent, on this generalized GIS? By "all-in" I mean that the combination of the tax-back and the regular income tax rates should not exceed this 45 percent rate until the initial guaranteed income is clawed back, at which time the regular tax schedule would become operative. This means that provinces, like Ontario, that provide top-ups that are stacked on GIS (and, therefore, generate 100 percent, or confiscatory) tax-back rates must be integrated within this all-in federal-provincial 45 percent rate. Presumably, the clawback age and pension credits (in the following bullet in the text) can also be "buried" in this "all-in" marginal tax rate. While this rate may appear high, it is less than the current GIS tax-back rate and seniors will not be contributing to UI, CPP or

WC, etc., so that the rate is not as high as it might appear at first blush. Since I have not fleshed out this approach in full, it may well be the case that there will be a "notch" problem in terms of marginal tax rates as the clawbacks end and the individual becomes subject to the regular marginal tax rate. However, while the details may need work, the concept ought to be clear.

Since the conference, the 1996 federal budget proposes a Battle-type negative income tax for the elderly to begin in 2001. The maximum benefit is $11,420 ($18,440 for a couple), $120 more than the projected maximum value of OAS/GIS in 2001. The benefit is reduced by 50 cents for each dollar of income until it reaches $5,160 per senior (which equals the projected value of the OAS in 2001). From this income level (roughly $12,500) the tax-back rate is zero until an income level of $25,961, after which benefits are reduced by 20 cents for each additional dollar of income. Hence, the overall marginal rate (tax-back plus regular tax system) will be well over 70 percent for higher-income seniors. These tax notches could or at least might be avoided if an "all-in" approach was adopted, as outlined in the previous paragraph.

5.  This approach asserts that 14 percent premium rates are just fine, among other reasons because they would still be lower than some of the social security payroll taxes now in place in Europe.

6.  To be consistent here, for similar reasons I would also argue against the proposed full indexation of the new seniors benefits in the 1996 federal budget. One way to do this would be to maintain full indexation of the benefit, but partially de-index the "break-even" level (i.e., gradually reduce the zero-tax-back-rate portion of the new GIS. See note 4). The larger point in this context is that Ottawa has maintained its *own* programs (e.g., OAS/GIS) virtually intact while it will reduce cash transfers to the provinces from $18 billion this year to $11 billion early in the millennium. This will serve to exacerbate the existing intergenerational transfer.

7.  One of the thrusts of the analysis is that the solution to the CPP should transcend the CPP program itself. One might argue that these tax receipts on CPP benefits are really part of the CPP. The key point, however, is that, to date at least, CPP tax receipts have not been considered as part of the reform proposals. Part of the reason why the net cost of the GIS is less than one-third that of OAS (in spite of the fact that the potential GIS payment is larger than the OAS) is that the CPP provides a 50 percent tax offset to the GIS.

8.  The 1996 federal budget eliminated tax sheltering for the 69-71 age period. The notion that these revenues might be directed to support the CPP, in part because these persons have "underpaid" their CPP, would never cross Ottawa's mind because (a) it is fixated on the deficit and (b) its own approach to the CPP, as reflected in the *CPP Information Paper*, is that the solution to the CPP has to be found within the CPP itself.

## REFERENCES

Caledon Institute (1995), *Roundtable on Canada's Aging Society and Retirement Income System,* Ottawa: Caledon Institute of Social Policy.

Canada. Minister of Finance (1996), *An Information Paper for Consultation on the Canada Pension Plan,* Ottawa: Ministry of Finance.

Courchene, T.J. (1994), *Social Canada in the Millennium: Reform Imperatives and Restructuring Principles,* Toronto: C.D. Howe Institute.

Robson, W.B. (1996), *Putting Some Gold in the Golden Years: Fixing the Canada Pension Plan,* Commentary No. 76, Toronto: C.D. Howe Institute.

Slater, D. (1995), "Reforming Canada's Retirement Income System," *Canadian Business Economics* (fall):47-58.

Thomson, D. (1991), *Selfish Generations?: The Aging of New Zealand's Welfare State,* Wellington: Bridget Williams Books.

Townson, M. (1995), "Expose Myths Behind CPP Reform Proposals," *Policy Options/ Options politique,* (September):13-17.

# CHAPTER ELEVEN

# The Way Ahead

*Monica Townson*

What lies ahead for Canada as it tries to cope with population aging? What path should we be taking? The task I have been given is to build on the analysis in the papers in this volume, pull the threads of the debate together and point the way ahead.

I certainly am not going to point in the same direction as some of the other contributors. Nevertheless we have already made a number of decisions that have put us on a particular path. As I see it, Canada is already marching firmly down the road to much more individual responsibility in the provision of retirement incomes and much less collective responsibility or state involvement. That is a path that has its dangers, in my view.

When many of the pension analysts contributing to this volume met in 1981 at the National Pensions Conference in Ottawa, we were asking exactly the same questions as we are today. "How can our retirement income system cope with an aging population?" But in the "Great Pensions Debate" that took place in the early 1980s, our overriding concern was how to provide an adequate pensions income for the elderly as they form an increasing percentage of our population. This time around, this no longer seems to be the objective. Our primary focus now seems to be "How can we extricate ourselves from past commitments to the elderly (and the future elderly) and force them to fend for themselves?" That is a reflection of the political climate in Canada, at both federal and provincial levels and regardless of which political party is in power. Market forces have become the new religion. As Andrew Dilnot expressed it: "The sense of shared objective is no longer there."

Let us look at what we have done so far and where we seem to be going with it. The federal government has already spelled out what it intends to do with the first tier of the retirement income system — the OAS and GIS. As Ken Battle's paper suggests, we are — in effect — going to have one income-tested benefit for seniors. Cost control is the objective, as Ken Battle points out. But another of Paul Martin's so-called five principles for reform of this part of the system was that there would be no reduction in protection for low-income seniors, especially those now getting GIS. I take that to mean that the level of benefits currently provided by OAS and GIS combined will not be reduced. But given that the maximum for these two programs combined is below the low-income cutoff for both individuals and couples, that is not much of a guarantee. Of course, you could argue that the low-income cutoff is not an "appropriate" measure of poverty. And we could certainly define away poverty, as Christopher Sarlo has done for the Fraser Institute.

Why does this matter? The level of the basic guarantee for future seniors will be crucial, given what we seem to be contemplating for the CPP. But before we get to that, what about the third tier of the retirement income system — private occupational pension plans and RRSPs? This is where our emphasis on individuals taking on the risk and responsibility of providing for their retirement is seen very clearly. We have had significant increases in tax assistance to private retirement savings over the past decade. This part of the system is designed to give tax assistance to individuals to allow them to accumulate a pension equivalent to 70 percent of earnings up to two and a half times the average wage.

But occupational pension plans have been declining in importance in this third tier of the retirement income system, and I think that trend will continue. Only about 45 percent of those in paid employment are now covered by occupational pension plans. Coverage of public sector workers is about 100 percent and that pushes up the overall average. As government cutbacks and privatization proceed apace, public sector employment will decline still further and so will the overall coverage of occupational pension plans. The growing trend to non-standard employment will be another nail in the coffin of the traditional occupational pension plan.

Another factor, of course, is the growing regulation of these plans. It is ironic that as pension regulators have attempted to improve this part of the system for beneficiaries, plan sponsors complain that they are overregulated, so they are converting their defined benefits plan to defined contribution plans or group RRSPs.

Ironically, another improvement introduced as part of the regulatory reform of private pensions — the portability provisions — may eventually weaken these plans. Workers with vested benefits can now transfer those out when they change jobs, into a locked-in retirement account (LIRA). So many people who start out with defined benefit plans may end up with a defined contribution plan in the shape of a private savings plan.

And that is a key issue in the debate over pension reform. Private savings accounts, RRSPs, may become the main component of the third tier of the retirement income system. Those who want to get rid of the CPP are also suggesting this as the vehicle to replace the second tier of the system. This road could lead us to a retirement income system where the only pension most Canadians will have would have to be generated from a private savings fund or RRSP. In other words, we would have shifted the entire risk and responsibility of providing for retirement onto the individual.

What are the implications of that? The federal Task Force on Retirement Income Policy, which reported to the federal government in 1979, expressed it very well. The task force noted that individuals and private institutions appear to be ill-placed to offer insurance against certain economy-wide developments. "A person who saves and insures himself adequately," the task force said — and this was in the days before we used non-sexist language — "can find that unanticipated inflation, depression, or a poor investment climate seriously erodes the values of private savings and insurance."

I think the disadvantages of defined contribution pension plans are well-known to policy specialists. Yet we are in danger of having a system where a defined contribution plan is the only kind of retirement income most Canadians will have. As John Myles and Jill Quadagno put it in this volume, we are changing from a deferred wage model to a savings model.

Our current system gives very generous tax breaks to those who contribute to RRSPs. We justify those on the grounds that we are encouraging people to save for retirement. But we have absolutely no requirement that they use the funds to provide retirement income. Recent reports from Statistics Canada show that more and more people have cashed in their RRSPs before retirement because they have lost their jobs and need the cash. Jack Mintz and Tom Wilson do not have a problem with that. It is all savings, they claim, and savers should have "flexibility." I know all about the theory of lifetime income and consumption taxes. But let me suggest that there is another way of looking at this. These plans are supposed to be part of Canada's retirement income system. There is a case to be made for judging them on the same basis as any other social program — do they achieve the policy objective? Will they provide retirement income for Canadians? In the real world, this is how this kind of policy is viewed.

Can you imagine a future where the "super-RRSP" is the only form of retirement savings people have, but non-standard employment has continued to expand? As more and more people are in temporary, contract, and unstable jobs, or involuntary part-time employment, the use of RRSPs as a form of income support prior to retirement may increase. The result may be that many more people will have to fall back on the basic income-tested seniors benefit when they reach retirement.

I believe we must preserve the CPP as a defined benefit plan — whether we call it a pension or a benefit. There is no doubt in my mind that public confidence in the plan has been seriously undermined by mythology and misinformation — some of which has been deliberately fostered by people who have a vested interest in the outcome. If partial funding would help address this problem, then maybe we have to consider it. But do not throw out the baby with the bathwater.

Why are we not looking at other options? Here is a suggestion that may have some shock value. What about raising the contribution ceiling to two and a half times the average wage — the same standard that is used for tax assistance to the private retirement savings tier — but retain the same level of benefits at 25 percent of the average wage? But tax assistance to private retirement savings is paid for by all taxpayers, including those at the lower end of the income scale who do not benefit from the system. Abolishing the Year's Basic Exemption (YBE), which Newman Lam and his colleagues (this volume) suggest, would also be a transfer from lower-income workers to those with higher incomes. The Canadian Institute of Actuaries estimated that for a worker earning $10,000 abolition of the YBE would represent a 50 percent increase in CPP contribution rates. But it is only an 11 percent increase for someone earning the average wage or more. In the United States, I believe, the contribution ceiling is US$62,000 and the Social Security contribution rate is more than double what it is in Canada.

The so-called Chilean model, which seems to be the darling of the right and the gospel of the free marketeers, would be disastrous for Canada, if we have any commitment at all to maintaining at least a semblance of collective responsibility for and to seniors. This is a system where individuals carry all the risks — including (as the ILO lists them) the risk of personal misfortune, sickness, invalidity, and unemployment; risks arising from mismanagement or bankruptcy of the pension fund managing workers' savings; risks associated with economic development, in particular slower economic growth or periods of low or negative real interest rates associated with rapid inflation; uncertainties concerning the longevity of the contributor and his or her surviving dependants; and, for low-income workers, the risk that retirement income may fall below the poverty level.

Incidentally, the Chilean model is designed for a male worker. The 10 percent mandatory contribution rate (with no matching employer contribution) making certain assumptions about rates of return and so on, is structured to provide a pension of 70 percent of average earnings for workers who have uninterrupted workforce participation of 45 years from the age of 20. But women may leave the paid workforce briefly to bear and raise children. They generally retire earlier than men and they live longer. The ILO calculates that for women to achieve the projected replacement rate, they would have to contribute 15-20 percent of their earnings instead of the required 10 percent. Given that their earnings are generally lower, that is obviously impossible.

We need to look at the differential impact of their proposals on women. Currently, 53 percent of unattached elderly women have incomes below the LICO. Proposals to increase the age of eligibility for CPP pensions, to limit indexing, to get rid of the drop-out provisions in the CPP, to switch to defined contribution plans, or to downscale surviving spouse benefits, all have an adverse impact on women. So does Ken Battle's proposal (this volume) to correct what he calls the "inequality" in the OAS program between one-earner and two-earner couples by shifting to a family-income-based income test. But I should not blame Ken for that, because the Department of Finance has already announced its intention to do this. The "inequity" is corrected, of course, by taking OAS benefits away from married women, whose entitlement to OAS will now be based on their husband's income. That is a huge political problem which Finance is already wrestling with.

That brings me to my final point. This volume contains some very interesting and stimulating papers. They cover tax theory, the impact of savings on the economy, public finance analysis, how economists view pensions, and so on. But the way ahead for Canada will not be determined by economics or public finance theories. It will be a political choice. The papers by John Myles and Jill Quadagno and by Paul Pierson make that very clear. And Keith Banting's comments on this issue are very important. Finance may want to double the CPP contribution rate over a five-year period, but Ontario, because of the size of its population, effectively has a veto on CPP changes. Will Mike Harris, the "tax fighter" agree to that? What will be the quid pro quo to get him on side? Would it be further loans from a bigger CPP fund, which might then limit the ability to invest in a more diversified portfolio? What role will Quebec play in all this? If Quebec refuses to go along with any CPP changes, will we see an increasing divergence between the provisions of the QPP and the CPP? What are the implications of that? We can only wait and see.

# Contributors

*Bob Baldwin* is Director of the Social, Economic and Policy Department, Canadian Labour Congress.

*Keith G. Banting* is the Stauffer-Dunning Professor of Policy Studies and Director of the School of Policy Studies, Queen's University.

*Ken Battle* is President of the Caledon Institute of Social Policy.

*Gordon Betcherman* is Executive Director of the Human Resource Group at Ekos Research in Ottawa, and a Visiting Fellow in the School of Policy Studies, Queen's University.

*Robin Boadway* is the Sir Edward Peacock Professor of Economic Theory, and Associate Director of the John Deutsch Institute for the Study of Economic Policy, Queen's University.

*Thomas J. Courchene* is the Jarislowsky-Deutsch Professor of Economic and Financial Policy, and is Director of the John Deutsch Institute for the Study of Economic Policy, Queen's University.

*James Cutt* is Professor in the School of Public Administration, University of Victoria.

*James Davies* is Professor in the Department of Economics, University of Western Ontario.

*Andrew Dilnot* is Director of the Institute for Fiscal Studies, London, England.

*Estelle James* is Lead Economist in the Policy Research Department, World Bank.

*Newman Lam* is a Visiting Assistant Professor in the School of Public Administration, University of Victoria.

*Harvey Lazar* is Resident Fellow at Statistics Canada, and a Faculty Member, Canadian Centre for Management Development.

*Jack M. Mintz* is the Arthur Andersen Professor of Taxation, and Associate Dean (Research and Academic Resources) of the Faculty of Management, University of Toronto.

*Brian Murphy* is a Senior Research Analyst, Statistics Canada.

*John Myles* is Professor of Sociology, Florida State University.

*Paul Pierson* is Professor of Government, Harvard University.

*Michael Prince* is the Lansdowne Professor, University of Victoria.

*Jill Quadagno* holds the Mildred and Claude Pepper Eminent Scholar's Chair in Social Gerontology at Florida State University.

*William B.P. Robson* is a Senior Policy Analyst at the C.D. Howe Institute, Toronto.

*Monica Townson* is an independent economic consultant, a member of the Canada Pension Plan Advisory Board, and Vice-Chair of the Pension Commission of Ontario.

*Thomas A. Wilson* is Professor of Economics and Director of the Policy and Economic Analysis Program at the University of Toronto.

*Michael Wolfson* is Director, General Institutions and Social Statistics Branch, Statistics Canada.

OTHER SOCIAL POLICY TITLES

from the

SCHOOL OF POLICY STUDIES


*The Government as Robin Hood: Exploring the Myth,*
by G.C. Ruggeri, D. Van Wart and R. Howard
(xii, 156pp) ISBN 0-88911-711-X
(1996)


*Labour Market Polarization and Social Policy Reform,*
edited by Keith G. Banting and Charles M. Beach
(xiv, 258pp) ISBN 0-88911-667-9
(1995)


*Redefining Social Security,* by Patrick Grady, Robert Howse and
Judith Maxwell (viii, 162 pp) ISBN: 0-88911-714-4
(1995)


*A New Social Vision for Canada? Perspectives on the Federal Discussion Paper
on Social Security Reform,* edited by Keith Banting and Ken Battle
(x, 149pp) ISBN: 0-88911-687-3
(1994)


*The Future of Fiscal Federalism,* edited by Keith G. Banting,
Douglas M. Brown and Thomas J. Courchene
(x, 368pp) ISBN: 0-88911-657-1
(1994)


*Social Policy in the Global Economy,* edited by Terrance M. Hunsley
(xvi, 184pp) ISBN: 0-88911-637-7
(1992)